The FAITH OF AMERICA'S PRESIDENTS

The Faith

OF AMERICA'S

PRESIDENTS

LIVING
INK
BOOKS™
Writing Worth Reading™

DANIEL J. MOUNT

The Faith of America's Presidents

Copyright © 2007 by Daniel J. Mount

Published by Living Ink Books/AMG Publishers

6815 Shallowford Road

Chattanooga, Tennessee 37421

Unless otherwise indicated, all Scripture quotations are taken from the Holy Bible, King James Version.

Scripture quotations marked (NKJV) are from The Holy Bible, New King James Version, copyright © 1979, 1980, 1982, 1988 by Thomas Nelson, Inc. Used by permission. All rights reserved.

ISBN 978-089957108-9

First printing—March 2007

Cover designed by Bright Boy Design, Chattanooga, Tennessee

Interior design and typesetting by Reider Publishing Services, West Hollywood, California

Edited and Proofread by Agnes Lawless, Dan Penwell, Rich Cairnes, and Rick Steele

Printed in Canada

13 12 11 10 09 08 07 – T – 7 6 5 4 3 2 1

Library of Congress Cataloging-in-Publication Data

Mount, Daniel J., 1986-
  The faith of America's presidents / Daniel J. Mount.
    p. cm.
  Summary: "The Faith of America's Presidents summarizes the religious beliefs of each President of the United States and examines how those beliefs affected their lives and their presidencies"—Provided by publisher.
  Includes bibliographical references.
  ISBN 978-0-89957-108-9 (hardcover : alk. paper)
  1. Presidents—United States—Religion. I. Title.
  BR516.M68 2007
  973.09'9—dc22
                            2007001964

⭐ Contents

★ PREFACE

THE FAITH of America's presidents matters to us because the presidents' religious beliefs often influenced their courses in life, their decisions to seek the presidency, and their actions while president. Some actions of the presidents cannot be understood until we know the underlying beliefs that led them to particular decisions.

Although this book is not the first in its field, I have sought to make it the most comprehensive to date. While previous books have focused on selected aspects of a president's religion, I have attempted to provide a more complete overview of their conversion experiences, religious practices, and doctrinal beliefs. I have also looked at how their religious practices affected their presidencies.

Also included are two appendices. The first appendix discusses the presidents' personal characters. There have been presidents of integrity, reprobate presidents, and those who fall in between. As Jesus said, "A tree is known by its fruit" (Matt. 12:33, NKJV). The second appendix discusses the relevance of Masonic membership for some presidents.

Some presidents seem to be devout, born-again Christians, but it's possible they are putting on a devout appearance for political purposes. I cannot guarantee that their words have not been misleading. Yet I trust that their words express their hearts except when their actions cannot be ignored.

I am a born-again Christian historian, and because I am a historian, I want to write an accurate history. I believe that an evangelical approach to serious history is no less scholarly than the customary cynical approach. I have not made a decision as to whether a president appears to be a born-again Christian and then selectively presented the evidence to prove my point. I let the evidence determine the verdict. I tried not to portray any president as more holy or more base than his writings or the writings of his biographers lead me to believe.

A few of the conclusions I have reached differ from the heretofore accepted views. Yet I am not a revisionist historian. My goal has been to reach the most accurate conclusions possible, whether or not they are novel. While a book this extensive can never be perfectly accurate, I have done the best I could with all the information I have. Please send comments or corrections to me care of AMG Publishers.

I hope that Christians will receive a better appreciation of history and that historians will receive a better appreciation of Christianity from reading this book.

Daniel J. Mount
Mansfield, Ohio

Editorial note: As much as was possible, I preserved the original spelling of our presidents' written documents, even when it would be incorrect by today's standards. In many cases, such as in British spellings, which have since been Americanized, I did not place a [sic] after the words. The spelling was correct then; the language has changed since.

★ ACKNOWLEDGMENTS

THANK YOU to the staff at AMG Publishers for helping this project come to fruition, especially Dan Penwell, who oversaw the project from beginning to end, always with a word of encouragement. His wife, Gloria, was very helpful, also, with a variety of marketing suggestions.

A special thank you to Agnes Lawless, a professional who spent untold hours editing the book, and to Rich Cairnes, another professional who worked tirelessly proofreading the book. Also, I want to thank family and friends who helped by proofreading the book: Mason, Mary, Deborah, and Bethany Mount, Tammy Puff, and Janis Garcia.

A special word of appreciation to the staff at the Mansfield/Richland County Public Library and the staff of the Ashland University Library who helped locate books for this project.

Thank you to Doug Wead, Stewart Varnado, and Jane Cook, who were gracious enough to write endorsements for the book.

A special thanks to the following organizations and individuals who helped by answering questions and sharing useful information: Ranger Tom Martino from Lindenwald in Kinderhook, New York, E. Gordon Van Buren, Priscilla Frisbee, and Paul Clause. Each of you provided useful information on Martin Van Buren.

A special thanks to members of the staff at Wheatland, including Historic Site Manager Sue Small, who read the chapter on James Buchanan's religious beliefs and provided useful suggestions; and to Dr. Don Walters, who also read the chapter and made useful suggestions.

Thank you to Mark Corey, superintendent of the Andrew Johnson National Historic Site, who read the chapter on Andrew Johnson.

Thank you to Thomas Culbertson, executive director of the Rutherford B. Hayes Presidential Center at Speigel Grove, who read the chapter on Rutherford B. Hayes.

Thank you to Jennifer Capps, curator of the President Benjamin Harrison Home, who read the chapter on Benjamin Harrison.

Thank you to Dr. Melinda Gilpin, director of the Harding Home State Memorial, who read the chapter on Warren Harding.

Thank you to Dale Mayer, who read the chapter on Herbert Hoover and provided numerous useful suggestions, and to Matthew Schaefer, archivist at the Herbert Hoover Presidential Library, who put me in contact with Mr. Mayer.

Thank you to the Calvin Coolidge Foundation, which shared useful information on Coolidge's beliefs, and to Jim Cooke, who read the chapter on Coolidge and provided numerous useful suggestions.

And thank you to all of these, and to any whom I may have neglected to mention, I express my gratitude.

⭑ INTRODUCTION
A DEFINITION OF TERMS

MANY AUTHORS who have written about the religious beliefs of the presidents of the United States have used certain terms carelessly. They will say that "Washington was a theist" or that "Lincoln was a deist" without ever explaining what they mean by those terms.

A glossary, often found in the back of a book, usually is ignored. But if the reader does not understand what an author means by a word, the reader cannot understand the thought that the writer wants to communicate. So I put the definitions of the essential terms at the beginning of the book rather than at the end.

Agnostic: A person who believes it is impossible to know whether there is a God or life after death. An agnostic believes only in material phenomena.
Atheist: A person who believes there is no God.
Born Again: One who is born again has accepted Jesus Christ as Savior and Lord and has accepted the basic doctrines of Christianity.
Christian: One who has accepted Jesus Christ as his or her Savior and Lord. This person tries to live according to the truths of the Bible. The Christian believes:

- Jesus is God in the flesh,
- that he was born of a virgin,
- atoned for our sins by his sacrificial death on the cross,
- rose from the dead, ascended to sit on the right hand of the Father, and will return again, and

- that the Bible is the inspired Word of God and that the only way to God is through Jesus.

In popular usage, many use the term "Christian" to refer to those who live moral lives and possibly believe some of the basic Christian principles. In deference to this usage, when my research shows that a president denies basic doctrines of Christianity, I conclude that they were not "orthodox" Christians.

Conversion: A change from one belief to another. In this book, it is generally used in the context of a change from unbelief to belief in Christianity.

Deist: A deist believes that a Supreme Being created the world but has maintained no contact with it since. Deists also believe that:

- By reason alone, the existence of a Supreme Being can be proved, and no revelation is required.
- No Supreme Being has maintained contact with creation, and thus there is no Divine revelation.
- Because no Supreme Being is in contact with this earth, there is no way to supersede the laws of nature, and thus no miracle is possible.
- The world has always existed in its current state and has not fallen from an original state.
- All history was determined at the creation of the world, and humans are merely part of the universe's clockwork.

Theist: A theist believes that God created and rules the universe and is known through revelation. All Christians are theists, though not all theists are Christians.

CHAPTER 1

GEORGE WALKER BUSH

GEORGE W. BUSH was born on July 6, 1946. That summer, his parents had him baptized in an Episcopal ceremony.[1] He grew up attending the Episcopal Church with his parents. In his autobiography, *A Charge to Keep*, he said that he "even taught Sunday School and served as an altar boy."[2] Yet he became the prodigal son, the family rebel. But like the prodigal son, he too returned. Several important encounters and decisions mark his path back home.

The part of Bush's autobiography that deals with his conversion focuses on Billy Graham's role. In the summer of 1985, Graham visited the Bush family summer home in Kennebunkport, Maine. When Graham asked him if he was "right with God," Bush answered, "No, but I want to be."[3]

That weekend, Bush said, Graham planted the seeds of his decision to follow Christ. Graham's influence was not so much through his words, he recalled, but through his "gentle and loving demeanor." Bush said the meeting "was the beginning of a change in my life . . . where I would recommit my heart to Jesus Christ."[4]

His choice of the word "recommit" is interesting. He may have used the word because the story of his conversion starts before his weekend with Billy Graham. Bush had another important encounter the year before, with traveling evangelist Arthur Blessitt.

Bush and Blessitt met on April 3, 1984. According to an account Blessitt wrote of the meeting, Bush started the meeting by telling him,

"I want to talk to you about how to know Jesus Christ and how to follow Him."

"What is your relationship with Jesus?" Blessitt asked him.

When Bush responded, "I'm not sure," Blessitt then inquired if he had the assurance that he would go to heaven if he were to die.

"No," Bush answered.

Blessitt then explained the plan of salvation and answered questions that Bush asked him. He then led Bush in a sinner's prayer. To the best of Blessitt's memory (a memory corroborated by Jim Sale, the man who arranged and attended the meeting), the prayer went like this:

> "Dear God, I believe in you, and I need you in my life. Have mercy on me a sinner. Lord Jesus, as best as I know how, I want to follow you. Cleanse me from my sins, and come into my life as Savior and Lord. I believe you lived without sin, died on the cross for my sins and arose again on the third day and have now ascended unto the Father. I love you, Lord; take control of my life. I believe you hear my prayer. I welcome the Holy Spirit of God to lead me in your way. I forgive everyone, and I ask you to fill me with your Holy Spirit and give me love for all people. Lead me to care for the needs of others. Make my home in Heaven, and write my name in your book in heaven. I accept the Lord Jesus Christ as my Savior and desire to be a true believer in and follower of Jesus. Thank you, God, for hearing my prayer. In Jesus' name I pray."[5]

Bush does not mention this encounter in his autobiography. This may be because Blessitt, who has spent several decades carrying a cross around the world, has become somewhat controversial for his evangelism methods. While there is every reason to believe that both encounters actually happened, Bush's campaign autobiography likely dwells on the encounter with Billy Graham because Graham is a widely respected public figure.

In 1985, Bush joined a local Community Bible Study in Midland, Texas. The Community Bible Studies were started by Lee Campbell in 1975 to help Christians grow in their faith through systematic Bible study.[6]

Bush established and still maintains a practice of reading through a one-year Bible (a Bible split into 365 sections) every other year. During alternate years, he studies various chapters at different times.[7]

While they were in Midland, Texas, George W. and Laura Bush attended the First Methodist Church of Midland.[8] During 1987 and 1988, when the Bushes lived in Washington, D. C. while helping with George H. W. Bush's presidential campaign, they attended St. John's Church Lafayette Square, an Episcopal church.[9] During George H. W. Bush's presidency, they have attended the Highland Park United Methodist Church.[10]

During these years, Bush was still learning about the basic beliefs of born-again Christians. In the 1988 campaign, Doug Wead showed Bush statistics that showed how many Americans identified themselves as born-again Christians. Bush's reaction was one of incredulity: "These numbers can't be right. They're too high. How do they define born-again Christian?"

Wead replied, "Personal faith in Christ, Bible as the Word of God, accepting Christ as Savior being a turning point in their life."

"Well, then by that definition I'm born again," Bush responded.[11]

As governor of Texas, George W. Bush had to struggle with the issues of abortion and capital punishment. Bush has held throughout his public career that abortion should not be permitted in most circumstances; however, he has also stated his belief that (in the words of one biographer) "abortion laws were not going to change until there was first a change in culture."[12]

During his terms as governor of Texas, Bush drew criticism for his support of capital punishment. Though more than 150 convicts sentenced to death were executed during his terms, the execution that drew the most public attention was that of Karla Fay Tucker. On June 13, 1983, Tucker murdered Deborah Thornton. During her trial, she admitted the crime and said that she enjoyed committing it.[13] She was sentenced to death.

While awaiting execution, she became a Christian. Since her life had changed, she believed she should not be executed. However, the appeals board decided unanimously to uphold the conviction and the execution date.

Bush had no authority to commute her death sentence. However, some Christian leaders, including Pat Robertson and Pope John Paul II, argued that he should delay her execution by thirty days.

Bush decided not to overturn the decision of the appeals board. "Like many touched by this case, I have sought guidance through prayer," he said. "I have concluded judgments about the heart and soul of an individual on death row are best left to a higher authority. Karla Faye Tucker has acknowledged she is guilty of a horrible crime. She was convicted and sentenced by a jury of her peers. The role of the state is to enforce our laws and to make sure all individuals are treated fairly under those laws."[14]

Although Bush drew widespread criticism for permitting the execution of a fellow Christian, his decision had been influenced by an important consideration. If he granted a reprieve to someone who converted to his religion, should he also grant a reprieve to a convicted criminal who converted to another religion? If he granted thirty-day stays of execution in both cases, criminals could legitimately convert to anything and obtain stays of execution. If he granted it only in the case of a conversion to Christianity, he would be showing favoritism improper in a republic.

Some opponents of capital punishment criticized Bush as inconsistent for opposing abortion while supporting the death penalty. He discussed his positions on the two topics in his campaign autobiography. He said:

> In a perfect world, life is given from God and only taken by God. I hope some day our society will respect life, the full spectrum of life, from the unborn to the elderly. I hope someday unborn children will be protected by law and welcomed in life. I support the death penalty because I believe, if administered swiftly and justly, capital punishment is a deterrent against future violence and will save other innocent lives. Some advocates of life will challenge why I oppose abortion yet support the death penalty. To me it's the difference between innocence and guilt.[15]

In about 1999, George W. Bush decided to run for president of the United States. He told James Robison that he believed it was God's calling. He said: "I feel like God wants me to run for president. I can't explain it, but I sense my country is going to need me. Something is going to happen, and, at that time, my country is going to need me. I know it won't be easy, on me or my family, but God wants me to do it.

"In fact, I really don't want to run. My father was president. My whole family has been affected by it. I know the price. I know what it will mean. I would be perfectly happy to have people point at me someday when I'm buying my fishing lures at Wal-Mart and say, 'That was our governor.' That's all I want. And if I run for president, that kind of life will be over. My life will never be the same. But I feel God wants me to do this, and I must do it."[16]

In 1999, Bush cowrote his campaign autobiography, *A Charge to Keep*, with his advisor Karen Hughes. He chose these words to summarize his religious beliefs: "God sent His Son to die for a sinner like me. I was comforted to know that through the Son, I could find God's amazing grace, a grace that crosses every border, every barrier, and is open to everyone. Through the love of Christ's life, I could understand the life-changing powers of faith."[17]

He was elected as the forty-third president of the United States in 2000 and took office in 2001. He has frequently used religious imagery in his presidential speeches. In his inaugural address on January 20, he said:

> We are not this story's Author, Who fills time and eternity with His purpose. Yet His purpose is achieved in our duty; and duty is fulfilled in service to one another.
>
> Never tiring, never yielding, never finishing, we renew that purpose today, to make our country more just and generous; to affirm the dignity of our lives and every life.
>
> This work continues. This story goes on. And an angel still rides in the whirlwind and directs this storm.[18]

He also said that "we are guided by a power larger than ourselves, Who creates us equal in His image. And we are confident in principles that unite and lead us onward."[19]

On September 11, 2001, Bush heard the news of the attack on the World Trade Center and the Pentagon while he was at an elementary school in Sarasota, Florida. He quickly left the school and went to Air Force One while his staff attempted to figure out the next step. He called his wife to let her know he was on his way home. Referring to the possibility that a plane was headed for the White House, he told her, "If I'm in the White House, and there's a plane coming my way, all I can say is I hope I read my Bible that day."[20]

That night, safely back in the White House, Bush comforted the nation with the words of Psalm 23. He said: "Tonight I ask for your prayers for all those who grieve, for the children whose worlds have been shattered, for all whose sense of safety and security has been threatened. And I pray they will be comforted by a power greater than any of us spoken through the ages in Psalm 23: 'Even though I walk through the valley of the shadow of death, I fear no evil, for you are with me.' "

He proclaimed a National Day of Prayer and Remembrance, which took place on September 14, 2001. In a speech that day at the National Cathedral in Washington, DC, he said: "This world He [God] created is of moral design. Grief and tragedy and hatred are only for a time. Goodness, remembrance, and love have no end. And the Lord of life holds all who die and all who mourn."

He used similar language after the space shuttle *Columbia* disintegrated, comforting the nation with these words: "The same Creator who names the stars also knows the names of the seven souls we mourn today."[21]

George W. Bush has debated with his mother whether only those who personally accept Jesus Christ go to heaven; he argued the affirmative. When they asked Billy Graham for his opinion, he said, "I happen to agree with what George says about the interpretations of the New Testament, but I want to remind both of you, never play God."[22]

At one point, after receiving this advice, some voters (such as Jews) complained about his beliefs. He replied by telling reporters, "I believe God decides who goes to heaven, not George W. Bush."[23]

CONCLUSION

By his own public profession of faith, George W. Bush is a born-again Christian. His doctrinal beliefs appear to agree with the teachings of orthodox Christianity.

NOTES

1. Stephen Mansfield, *The Faith of George W. Bush* (Lake Mary, FL: Charisma House, 2003), 17–25.

2. George Walker Bush and Karen Hughes, *A Charge to Keep* (New York: Morrow, 1999), 136.

3. Mansfield, *The Faith of George W. Bush*, 68.

4. Ibid.

5. Ibid., 64–65.

6. Ibid., 69.

7. Bush and Hughes, *A Charge to Keep*, 138.

8. Ibid., 137.

9. Barbara Bush, *Reflections: Life After the White House* (New York: Scribner, 2003), 383.

10. Bill Minutaglio, *First Son: George W. Bush and the Bush Family Dynasty* (New York: Random House/Times Books, 1999), 255.

11. Peter Schweizer and Rochelle Schweizer, *The Bushes: Portrait of a Dynasty* (New York: Doubleday, 2004), 334.

12. Mansfield, *The Faith of George W. Bush*, 112.

13. Ibid., 96.

14. Ibid., 98.

15. Bush, *Reflections: Life After the White House*, 340.

16. Mansfield, *The Faith of George W. Bush*, 109.

17. Bush and Hughes, *A Charge to Keep*, 136.

18. Bush, First inaugural address, January 20, 2001.

19. Ibid.

20. Ari Fleischer, *Taking Heat: the President, the Press, and My Years in the White House* (New York: Morrow, 2005), 148.

21. Peter Singer, *The President of Good and Evil: Questioning the Ethics of George W. Bush* (New York: Dutton, 2004), 91.

22. Minutaglio, *First Son*, 289.

23. Ibid.

CHAPTER 2

WILLIAM JEFFERSON CLINTON

WILLIAM JEFFERSON BLYTHE IV was born on August 19, 1946, in Hope, Arkansas. When his mother married Roger Clinton, Blythe started using the surname "Clinton." He officially changed his name in 1962.[1]

Clinton attended St. John's Catholic School for his second and third grades. Though he was fascinated by the rituals of the church, he later described praying the rosary as "often too much for a rambunctious boy whose only church experience before then had been in the Sunday school and the summer vacation Bible school of the First Baptist Church in Hope."[2]

After his family moved to Hot Springs, Arkansas, Clinton attended the Park Place Baptist Church. He attended Sunday school and church services weekly and was converted in this church in 1955. He described it in these words: "I had absorbed enough of my church's teachings to know that I was a sinner and to want Jesus to save me. So I came down the aisle at the end of [a] Sunday service, professed my faith in Christ, and asked to be baptized."[3] He was baptized shortly thereafter.

In an English honors class in school, Clinton wrote an autobiographical essay. He described himself as "deeply religious, yet not as convinced of my exact beliefs as I ought to be."[4]

In 1964, Clinton left home to attend the Georgetown University School of Foreign Service. From this point until he became governor of Arkansas, Clinton did not attend church regularly.[5]

He married Hillary Rodham on October 11, 1975.

In 1975, Clinton witnessed a voodoo ceremony in which spirits entered people who believed in voodoo and caused them to do supernatural things. He described the ceremony in his memoirs; he said that he included the account because he had "always been fascinated by the way different cultures try to make sense of life, nature, and the virtually universal belief that there is a nonphysical spirit force at work in the world that existed before humanity and will be here when we are all long gone."

He continued, "Haitians' understanding of how God is manifest in our lives is very different from that of most Christians, Jews, or Muslims, but their documented experiences certainly prove the old adage that the Lord works in mysterious ways." He believed that the voodoo possessions were the work of the Lord. He restated this conviction later in his memoirs.

When he was describing a Pentecostal service, he said the things he saw reminded him of the voodoo service in Haiti, "except that these people believed they had been moved by Jesus."[6]

Clinton was elected governor of Arkansas in 1978. In 1980, he joined Immanuel Baptist Church and attended church regularly for the first time in sixteen years.[7] The church's pastor, W. O. Vaught, had a strong influence on his religious beliefs, at times affirming Clinton's liberal views in areas such as abortion.

Clinton was fully aware of the biblical case made by conservative theologians against abortion. He once talked with Vaught about Bible verses relating to the issue. Clinton biographer David Marriss stated: "He [Clinton] had ambivalent feelings about it personally, though he agreed with the pro-choice argument intellectually and was surrounded by strong pro-choice women, including Hillary and Betsey Wright. Yet he was struggling with the notion of the definition of a human life, and he wondered whether Vaught could provide some insight from his readings of the Old and New Testaments."[8] Vaught told him that he (Vaught) "was almost always opposed to abortion, but had seen 'some extremely difficult cases' in his life as a pastor and did not believe that the Bible forbade it in all circumstances."[9]

Vaught also told him that the Bible did not condemn abortion and said that according to the Bible, life began not at conception but "when life has been 'breathed into' a baby, when it is slapped on the behind after being taken out of the mother's body."[10] When Clinton asked him "about the biblical statement that God knows us even when in our mother's womb," Vaught reassured him that the verse dealt solely with God's omniscience.[11] Marriss said that "in all of his discussions about abortion thereafter, Clinton relied on his minister's interpretation to bolster his pro-choice position."[12]

In his memoirs, Clinton stated: "Everyone knows life begins biologically at conception. No one knows when biology turns into humanity or, for the religious, when the soul enters the body."[13]

While conceding that life had begun, Clinton utilized the fact that some deny that the life is human as an excuse for supporting legislation that ends the lives of the unborn. He stated in 1993 that he believed "that the Government of this country should not make criminal activities over which even theologians are in serious disagreement."[14]

Clinton was elected president in 1992. He concluded his first inaugural address on January 20, 1993, by quoting Galatians 6:9 : "The Scripture says, 'And let us not be weary in well doing: for in due season we shall reap, if we faint not.' From this joyful mountaintop of celebration, we hear a call to service in the valley. We have heard the trumpets. We have changed the guard. And now, each in our own way and with God's help, we must answer the call."[15]

Among Clinton's first acts as president were executive orders permitting federal aid to international agencies providing abortions, fetal-tissue research, and federally funded family clinics to counsel mothers to abort their babies.[16] Clinton appointed two pro-choice justices to the Supreme Court.[17]

Another of Clinton's early initiatives was permitting sodomite activity in the military. When unsuccessfully trying to convert Senator Robert Byrd to his cause, Clinton said: "When the Lord delivered the Ten Commandments, Senator Byrd, he did not include a prohibition on homosexuality. As a matter of conscience, the very fact of homosexuality should not prevent you from serving if you must."[18] This statement implies a belief that activities not prohibited in the Ten Commandments are permitted, even if the Bible expressly prohibits them elsewhere.

During his presidency, Clinton made references to religion on appropriate occasions. In a February 4, 1993, appearance at the National Prayer Breakfast, he spoke about faith:

> We need faith as a source of strength. "The assurance of things hoped for, the conviction of things unseen," the Scripture says.

What it means to me is that here, if we have enough faith, in spite of all the pressures to the contrary, we can define ourselves from the inside out, in a town where everybody tries to define you from the outside in.

We need our faith as a source of hope because it teaches us that each of us is capable of redemption and, therefore, that progress is possible—not perfection, for all the reasons Reverend Graham said, but progress. We need our faith as a source of challenge because if we read the Scriptures carefully, it teaches us that all of us must try to live by what we believe or, in more conventional terms, to live out the admonition of President Kennedy that here on earth God's work must truly be our own. [Clinton liked that quote, using it at least four times in his 1993 speeches and proclamations alone.]

But perhaps most important of all for me, we need our faith, each of us, President, Vice President, Senator, Congressman, General, Justice, as a source of humility, to remember that, as Bishop Sheen said, we are all sinners. St. Paul once said in an incredibly moving Scripture in the Bible, "The very thing which I would not do, that I do, and that which I would, that I do not." And even more, not only because we do wrong but because we don't always know what is right.[19]

In a December 25, 1993, Christmas radio address, Clinton said: "This holiday season is a time to remember what we value and what gives our lives meaning. Today Christians celebrate God's love for humanity made real in the birth of Christ in a manger almost 2,000 years ago. The humble circumstances of His birth, the example of His life, the power of His teachings inspire us to love and to care for our fellow men and women."[20]

Clinton's friend and political adviser Dick Morris described Clinton's religion in these words: "Not really devoted to formal religion, Clinton works hard at encoding in his memory religious insights he uses as a daily guide to his behavior."[21]

An incident Morris related in his book *Behind the Oval Office,* showed that Clinton's religious beliefs were less conservative than those of his vice president. Morris, Clinton, and Gore were planning a media event designed to portray Clinton and Gore as concerned about the environment. They were to release a bald eagle. The conversation turned to a current controversy over the snail darter, an animal threatened by commercial development. In a statement Morris described as intentional "overblown rhetoric," he quoted himself as saying: "You'll be like Noah on the ark, saving these species." The following conversation ensued:

> Clinton turned to Gore, who was sitting on his right, and said, "You know, Al, there were no snail darters on the ark."
>
> Gore's face turned rigid and stern. He moved his head ostentatiously to the left to face the president, keeping his body facing forward to exaggerate the neck motion. "Mr. President," he began with mock formality, "there were."
>
> "Really," the president said, looking quizzical. "How can you tell?"
>
> "They're *here*," the vice president said with the emphasis of a Baptist fundamentalist, his face right out of Grant Wood's *American Gothic*.
>
> "Oh," said the president, comically deflated.
>
> Gore turned forward again and emphatically nodded his head, once.[22]

Clinton was president from 1993 to 2001.

CONCLUSION

Clinton was converted to Christianity as a child. Though his commitment to the outward forms of religion, such as church attendance, varied over the years, he has described himself as a "born-again" Christian. His beliefs in the central doctrines of Christianity appear to be relatively orthodox, but he denies the Bible's teaching in other areas, such as the sanctity of human life and the accuracy of Genesis.

NOTES

1. William Jefferson Clinton, *My Life* (New York: Random House, 2004), 52.

2. Ibid., 23.

3. Ibid., 30. Clinton explained that the Baptists "require an informed profession of faith for baptism," as opposed to "the Methodists' infant-sprinkling ritual that took Hillary and her brothers out of hell's way."

4. Ibid., 58.

5. Ibid., 294.

6. Ibid., 250.

7. Ibid., 294.

8. David Marriss, *First in His Class: A Biography of Bill Clinton* (New York: Simon & Schuster, 1995; Touchstone ed., 1996), 435.

9. Ibid.

10. Clinton, *My Life*, 353.

11. Ibid.

12. Marriss, *First in His Class*, 435.

13. Clinton, *My Life*, 229. The awkward phrasing could be taken to imply that souls only enter the bodies of the religious.

14. Clinton, *Public Papers of William J. Clinton, 1993*, February 19, 1993, Remarks and a Question-and-Answer Session on the Economic Program in Chillicothe, Ohio.

15. Clinton, First inaugural address, January 20, 1993.

16. Clinton, *My Life*, 480–481.

17. This demonstrates the power of a pastor's advice. If Vaught had advised Clinton differently, and if Clinton had become pro-life and appointed pro-life judges, *Roe v. Wade* would probably have been overturned by now.

18. George Stephanopoulos, *All Too Human: A Political Education* (New York: Little, Brown, 1999), 127–28.

19. Clinton, *Public Papers of the Presidents of the United States: William Jefferson Clinton, 1993*. Washington, DC: Government Printing Office. Remarks at the National Prayer Breakfast, February 4, 1993.

20. Ibid., TV address, December 25, 1993.

21. Richard Morris, *Behind the Oval Office: Winning the Presidency in the Nineties* (New York: Random House, 1997), 102.

22. Ibid., 117.

CHAPTER 3

GEORGE HERBERT WALKER BUSH

GEORGE HERBERT WALKER BUSH was born on June 12, 1924, in Milton, Massachusetts. His family was Episcopalian and held regular family devotions. In these, Prescott Bush would lead his family in prayer and the family would read from the Bible and from John Bailey's *A Diary of Private Prayers*.[1] On Sundays, the Bush family attended Christ Church in Greenwich, Connecticut.

George Bush married Barbara Pierce on January 6, 1945. While they lived in Midland, Texas, the Bushes attended the First Presbyterian Church. Both George and Barbara Bush taught Sunday School.[2] George Bush became a deacon and later an elder in the church.[3]

In 1946, at the dedication of their young son George W. Bush, the minister asked the Bushes: "Do ye solemnly believe all the Articles of the Christian Faith, as contained in the Apostles' Creed; and do ye acknowledge the obligation, as far as in you lies, to provide that this child be brought up in the nurture and admonition of the Lord, that he be diligently instructed in the Holy Scriptures, and he be taught the Creed, the Lord's Prayer, the Ten Commandments, and all other things which a Christian ought to know and believe to his soul's health?"

They responded, "We do."[4]

In 1953, George and Barbara Bush's daughter Robin lost her battle with leukemia. During Robin's illness, George went to the church every morning to pray for her recovery. He later said: "Actually, the pain of that experience taught us just how dependent on God we really are, and how important our faith is. In a moment like that, all you have is God."[5]

When they lived in Houston, Texas, the Bushes were members of St. Martin's Episcopal Church.[6] Since settling in Kennebunkport, Maine, Bush has attended and become a vestryman at St. Anne's Episcopal Church.[7]

From October 1974 through December 1975, Bush served as the United States' liaison to China. (He was an unofficial ambassador, as the United States had not recognized mainland China's Communist government.) The Bushes attended a small interdenominational chapel meeting at a Bible institute. Because the congregation of twelve to twenty people was composed of different nationalities, with the Bushes being the only American members, services were conducted in Chinese by Anglican, Methodist, or Presbyterian ministers. Attendees sang hymns in several languages and read church creeds, but no sermon was preached.[8]

In 1980, Bush sought the Republican nomination to the presidency. He lost the nomination to Ronald Reagan. During the Republican National Convention, Ronald Reagan called Bush and told him: "I'd like to go over to the convention and announce that you're my choice for vice president . . . if that's all right with you." Bush responded, "I'd be honored, Governor."[9]

Reagan said that before he could announce his decision, he needed Bush's support on several key issues; he specifically named the proposed tax cut and abortion.[10] Bush agreed to accept Reagan's positions on these issues. At this point, his public position on abortion changed from a pro-choice to a pro-life stance.

In his 1970 campaign for the U. S. Senate, Bush had made his first stand on the issue of abortion. He said: "I realize this is a politically sensitive area. But I believe in a woman's right to choose. It should be an individual matter. I think ultimately it will be a constitutional question. I don't favor a federal abortion law as such."[11] (This was several years before *Roe* v. *Wade*.) At the time, Barbara shared his view; though his view changed a decade later, hers did not.

Although Bush changed his public stance in 1980, his personal convictions had apparently already been changing. In *The Bushes: Portrait of a Dynasty*, Peter and Rochelle Schweizer describe Bush's gradual change in these words:

He had been, prior to joining the Reagan administration, "personally opposed to abortion" but not in favor of legally restricting it. But his attitude had changed somewhat as his religious convictions evolved. The most profound change came when Marvin adopted his first child. The child could have been aborted rather than adopted. "When I have real doubts, and I do, I look at Marshall," he wrote his brother Buck.[12]

Marvin and Margaret Bush's son, Marshall, was born and adopted in 1986. Due perhaps to this influence, Bush's public statements on abortion would often refer to adoption as the preferred alternative to abortion. One such example was a 1990 speech to the annual Convention of National Religious Broadcasters in which he said: "We come next to an issue on which many Americans disagree, but for my part let me be very clear: I support the sanctity of life. We need policies that encourage adoption, not abortion. And that comes right from the heart."[13]

During the presidential campaign culminating in his 1988 election, Bush made several attempts to reach out to conservative Christians. In a video made for Christians, Bush talked about what he described as "life-changing experiences,"[14] and what Bill Minutaglio described as "his versions of a Christian conversion experience." The video was shown to members of the Christian Booksellers Association.[15]

George W. Bush was given the role of enlisting conservative Christians in his father's campaign. His assistant, Doug Wead, wrote the book, *George Bush: Man of Integrity*, highlighting the moral and religious characteristics of George H. W. Bush. The book consisted of interviews that Wead conducted with Bush.

Wead asked Bush about his position on salvation. He responded that if asked whether he was born again, he would ask for a definition of terms. He said:

If by "born again" one is asking, "Do you accept Jesus Christ as your personal Savior?" then, I could answer a clear-cut "Yes." No hesitancy, no awkwardness.

But, if one is asking, "Has there been one single moment, above any others, in which your life has been instantly changed?" –well, I can't say that that has happened. There have been many moments.

I'm not a great Biblical expert or theologian. I am a believer. I do believe strongly in the Lord and the hereafter, life after death.[16]

Bush also expressed his positions on abortion in the book: "I am opposed to abortion except when the life of the mother is threatened or when there is rape or incest."[17]

He added, "I support a Constitutional amendment that would reverse the Supreme Court's *Roe v. Wade* decision on abortion made in 1973. I also support a human-life amendment with an exception for the life of the mother, rape, or incest. In addition, I oppose the use of federal funds to pay for abortion except when the life of the mother is actually threatened."[18]

Bush also expressed his support for voluntary school prayer: "I favor a voluntary prayer in school as an extension of our commitment to teaching values. I believe that students should have the right, if they wish, for a momentary reflection, meditation, or prayer."[19]

Bush was elected president of the United States in 1988 and served from 1989 to 1993. Like Eisenhower, Bush composed an inauguration day prayer. In his inaugural address, he said:

And my first act as President is a prayer. I ask you to bow your heads:

Heavenly Father, we bow our heads and thank You for Your love. Accept our thanks for the peace that yields this day and the shared faith that makes its continuance likely. Make us strong to do Your work, willing to heed and hear Your will, and write on our hearts these words: "Use power to help people." For we are given power not to advance our own purposes, nor to make a great show in the world, nor a name. There is but one just use of power, and it is to serve people. Help us to remember it, Lord. Amen.[20]

Bush, like Eisenhower, encouraged and supported public acknowledgment of belief in God and of America's Christian heritage. In 1990, Bush said: "I believe with all my heart that one cannot be America's President without a belief in God, without the strength that your faith gives to you. Another president, Dwight Eisenhower—beloved Ike— once said: 'Free government is the political expression of a deeply felt religious faith.' Let each of us use his faith to express the noblest values of America so that together we can then serve the inalienable rights of man."[21]

Bush concluded his January 31, 1990, State of the Union address with a stirring call for for America to remember its heritage:

> And so, tonight I'm going to ask something of every one of you. Now, let me start with my generation, with the grandparents out there. You are our living link to the past. Tell your grandchildren the story of struggles waged at home and abroad, of sacrifices freely made for freedom's sake. And tell them your own story as well, because every American has a story to tell.
>
> And, parents, your children look to you for direction and guidance. Tell them of faith and family. Tell them we are one nation under God. Teach them that of all the many gifts they can receive liberty is their most precious legacy, and of all the gifts they can give the greatest is helping others.[22]

In a 1991 speech at the National Prayer Breakfast, Bush reaffirmed his commitment to the concept and heritage of America being a nation under God:

> You know, America is a nation founded under God. And from our very beginnings we have relied upon His strength and guidance in war and in peace. And this is something we must never forget. . . . I have learned what I suppose every President has learned, and that is that one cannot be President of our country without faith in God and without knowing with certainty that we are one nation under God.[23]

In a speech to the annual Convention of National Religious Broadcasters, made just a few days before his prayer breakfast speech, he also referred to his own trust in God:

> I have been honored to serve as President of this great nation for two years now and believe more than ever that one cannot be America's President without trust in God. I cannot imagine a world, a life, without the presence of the One through whom all things are possible.

During the darkest days of the Civil War, a man we revere not merely for what he did but what he was, was asked whether he thought the Lord was on his side. And said Abraham Lincoln: "My concern is not whether God is on our side, but whether we are on God's side." My fellow Americans, I firmly believe in my heart of hearts that times will soon be on the side of peace because the world is overwhelmingly on the side of God.[24]

He expressed similar sentiments in a 1989 annual National Prayer Breakfast speech. "All of us should not attempt to fulfill the responsibilities we now have without prayer and a strong faith in God," he said. He continued: "Abraham Lincoln said: 'I've been driven many times to my knees by the overwhelming conviction that I have nowhere else to go.' Surely he was not the first President, certainly not the last, to realize that."[25]

On December 11, 1991, Bush issued a statement on the observance of Christmas, in which he called the nation to follow Christ's example of selfless giving:

At Christmas, we celebrate the promise of salvation that God gave to mankind almost 2,000 years ago. The birth of Christ changed the course of history, and His life changed the soul of man. Christ taught that giving is the greatest of all aspirations and that the redemptive power of love and sacrifice is stronger than any force of arms. It is testimony to the wisdom and the truth of these teachings that they have not only endured but also flourished over two millennia. . . .

By His words and by His example, Christ has called us to share our many blessings with others. As individuals and as a Nation, in our homes and in our communities, there are countless ways that we can extend to others the same love and mercy that God showed humankind when He gave us His only Son. During this holy season and throughout the year, let us look to the selfless spirit of giving that Jesus embodied as inspiration in our own lives—giving thanks for what God has done for us and abiding by Christ's teaching to do for others as we would do for ourselves.[26]

In an attempt to reach out to religious conservatives, the 1992 Bush-Quayle reelection campaign convinced the Republican National

Convention's platform committee to word an acknowledgment of God into the party platform. President Bush got mileage out of the campaign's success, telling a Religious Roundtable meeting that he was "struck by the fact that the other party took thousands of words to make up its platform and left out three simple letters, G-O-D."[27]

His most recent published religious statement is found in *Heartbeat: George Bush in His Own Words*, a book compiled by his post-presidential spokesman and speechwriter Jim McGrath. In 1996, during a lecture at Texas A&M University entitled "Rhetoric and the Presidency," a student asked him about his religion. Bush said:

> Regarding my own religion, I am a Christian. I do believe in Jesus Christ. And I felt uncomfortable, very honestly, talking about the depth of my religion when I was President. I'm an Episcopalian. I'm kind of an inward kind of guy when it comes to religion. I felt it strongly. I think Lincoln was right: you can't be President without spending some time on your knees professing your faith and asking God for strength, and to save our nation. But I believe strongly in the separation of church and state. I don't believe a President should be advocating a particular denomination, or particular religion. And yet, I can tell you in direct response to your inquiry that we, in our family, say our prayers every night—Barbara and I do, we say the blessing. And it's more than rote.[28]

CONCLUSION

George H. W. Bush is not a publicly demonstrative man. Yet, he has publicly stated that he has accepted Jesus Christ as his personal Savior. While he does not point to any specific day or hour as the time when his life changed, he has publicly affirmed his belief in the doctrines of orthodox Christianity.

NOTES

1. Herbert Parmet, *George Bush: The Life of a Lone Star Yankee* (Piscataway, NJ: Transaction Publishers, 2000), 31.

2. Peter Schweizer and Rochelle Schweizer, *The Bushes: Portrait of a Dynasty* (New York: Doubleday, 2004), 105; Parmet, *George Bush*, 79.

3. Bill Minutaglio, *First Son: George W. Bush and the Family Dynasty* (New York: Random House/Times Books, 1999), 39.

4. Stephen Mansfield, *The Faith of George W. Bush* (Lake Mary, FL: Charisma House, 2003), 24.

5. David Aikman, *A Man of Faith: The Spiritual Journey of George W. Bush* (Nashville: Thomas Nelson/Word Publishing, 2004), 32.

6. Parmet, *George Bush*, 87.

7. George Walker Bush with Doug Wead, *George Bush: Man of Integrity* (Eugene, OR: Harvest House, 1988), 42.

8. Parmet, *George Bush*, 177.

9. Schweizer and Schweizer, *The Bushes*, 287.

10. Ibid.

11. Ibid., 202.

12. Ibid., 290.

13. Bush, *Public Papers of the Presidents of the United States: George Herbert Walker Bush, 1989-1993.* Washington, DC: Government Printing Office. January 29, 1990.

14. Minutaglio, *First Son*, 211.

15. Ibid.

16. Bush with Wead, *George Bush*, 34.

17. Ibid., Issues section, "Abortion."

18. Ibid., 33.

19. Ibid., Issues section, "School prayer."

20. Bush, Inaugural address, January 20, 1989.

21. Bush, *Public Papers of George H. W. Bush,* Remarks at the annual Convention of National Religious Broadcasters, January 29, 1990.

22. Ibid. Address before a joint session of Congress on the State of the Union, January 31, 1990.

23. Ibid. Remarks at the National Prayer Breakfast, January 31, 1991.

24. Ibid. Remarks at the annual Convention of National Religious Broadcasters, January 28, 1991.

25. Ibid. Remarks at the National Prayer Breakfast, February 2, 1989.

26. Ibid. Message on the observance of Christmas, December 11, 1991.

27. Ralph E. Reed, *Politically Incorrect: The Emerging Faith Factor in American Politics* (Dallas: Word Publishing, 1996), 72.

28. George Herbert Walker Bush and Barbara Bush, *Heartbeat: George Bush in His Own Words,* compiled by Jim McGrath (New York: Scribner, 2003), 286.

CHAPTER 4

RONALD WILSON REAGAN

RONALD WILSON REAGAN was born on February 6, 1911, in Tampico, Illinois. His father, John Edward Reagan, was Catholic, and his mother, Nelle Clyde Wilson, was Protestant. Since John left religious upbringing to his wife, Ronald Reagan was raised a Protestant. He was converted in 1922 and was baptized in the First Christian Church in Dixon, Illinois, on June 21 of that year.[1]

Though Reagan would later refer to this turning point when asked if he was born again, he did not become acquainted with the term "born again" until 1976. Yet even before he learned the term, he unequivocally affirmed that he was a Christian. In a 1967 letter, he said: "I was raised in the Christian Church which as you know believes in baptism when the individual has made his own decision to accept Jesus. My decision was made in my early teens."[2]

In 1984, he wrote that Harold Bell Wright's book, *That Printer of Udell's*, brought him to the decision. It "had an impact I shall always remember," he said. "After reading it and thinking about it for a few days I went to my mother and told her I wanted to declare my faith and be baptized."[3]

Reagan remained active in his church throughout his teenage years, acting in skits and plays that his mother prepared and helping clean the church.[4] He also taught Sunday school for several years.[5]

In Billy Graham's autobiography, Graham stated that he understood Reagan had done "some preaching himself in his late teens."[6] Graham could have heard about the times Reagan taught Sunday school; he may also have heard about when Reagan led his church's Easter Sunday sunrise service in 1926.[7]

One biographer stated that while Reagan attended Eureka College, "The Bible was a daily and vital part of his life."[8]

When in Hollywood, California, to begin his movie career, Reagan attended the Hollywood Beverly Christian Church. His parents also moved to Hollywood and Nelle Reagan joined the church. Ronald Reagan began tithing to the church but did not become a member at that time.[9]

He married Jane Wyman (the stage name for Sarah June Fulks) on January 24, 1940. The Reagan children attended Sunday school and Wyman taught a Sunday school class. Though Reagan eventually attended another church, he remained on the membership rolls and contributed monthly to the Christian Church for the rest of his life.[10] Wyman and Reagan divorced in 1948.

Reagan entered Hollywood as a populist Democrat and left it as a populist Republican. His conflict with the Communists helped play a role in this political conversion. As head of the Screen Actors Guild, he did everything in his power to keep Communists from controlling Hollywood. Sterling Hayden, a Communist who was part of the attempt to change Hollywood, later left the Communist party. When testifying before Congress under oath, he was asked why the Communists did not succeed in taking Hollywood. He said, "We ran into a one-man battalion named Ronnie Reagan."[11]

On March 4, 1952, Reagan married Nancy Davis. They began attending Bel Air Presbyterian Church in Los Angeles in 1963. Ronald Reagan referred to Reverend Dr. Donn D. Moomaw, the church's pastor, as "my pastor."[12]

The Reagans once asked how they could become members of the church and were told they had to attend a ten-week membership class. The church made no exceptions, and Reagan's schedule as governor of California did not permit him to go to the classes. Reverend Moomaw remembered that the Reagans said, "We will keep Bel Air as our church home, and perhaps some time it will be possible for us to become members like everyone else."[13]

From 1975 through 1979, Reagan gave a daily three-minute syndicated radio commentary heard on two hundred radio stations across the nation. While most of his talks were on political or human-interest topics, he occasionally wrote and delivered a religious commentary. One such occasion on January 9, 1978, when he discussed Christ's divinity. He said he was disturbed to read that in many seminaries "there is an increasing tendency to minimize his divinity, to reject the miracle of his birth and regard him as human."

He said he could not help wondering how anyone could explain away "the greatest miracle of all":

> A young man whose father is a carpenter grows up working in his father's shop. He has no formal education. He owns no property of any kind. One day he *PUTS DOWN HIS TOOLS* and walks out of his fathers shop. He starts preaching on street corners and in the *NEARBY* country side. Walking from place to place *preaching all the while even though he is in no way an ordained minister* he never gets farther than an area perhaps 100 miles wide at the most.
>
> He does this for 3 yrs. Then [he] is arrested, tried & convicted. There is no court of appeal so he is executed at age 33 along with two common thieves. Those in charge of his execution roll dice to see who gets his clothing—the only possessions he has. His family cannot afford a burial place so he is interred in a borrowed tomb.
>
> End of story? No this uneducated, propertyless young man who preached on street corners for only 3 yrs. *WHO LEFT NO WRITTEN WORD* has for 2000 yrs. had a greater effect on the entire world than all the Rulers, Kings & Emperors, all the conquerors, the generals & admirals, all the scholars, scientists, and philosophers who ever lived—all put together.
>
> How do we explain that?—Unless he really was what he said he was.[14]

Reverend Thomas H. Griffith wrote a letter to Reagan criticizing his statement about Christ's divinity in the above commentary. On March 1, 1978, Reagan wrote a letter to Griffith, defending Christ's divinity. He said:

> Is there really any ambiguity in his words: "I am the way, the truth and the life: no man cometh unto the Father but by me?" Then he said, "In my Father's house are many mansions. If it were not so, I would have told you. I go to prepare a place for you." In John 10 he says, "I am in the Father and the Father in me." And

he makes reference to being with God, "before the world was," and sitting on the "right hand of God."

I realize, of course, that you are familiar with these words of Jesus. These and other statements he made about himself, fore-close in my opinion, any question as to his divinity. It doesn't seem to me that he gave us any choice; either he was what he said he was or he was the world's greatest liar. It is impossible for me to believe a liar or charlatan could have had the effect on mankind that he has had for 2000 years. We could ask, would even the greatest of liars carry his lie through the crucifixion, when a sim-ple confession would have saved him?

I could refer to the scores and scores of prophecies in the Old Testament made several hundred years before his birth (all of which were realized in his life). You, of course, could answer that, as a Jew he was aware of these prophecies. But, then again, wouldn't we be describing the act of a faker? Did he allow us the choice you say that you and others have made, to believe in his teachings but reject his statements about his own identity?[15]

Reagan also discussed Christ's divinity on other occasions. In a 1985 Christmas message, he said: "When we speak of Jesus and of His life, we speak of a man revered as a prophet and teacher by people of all religions, and Christians speak of someone greater—a man who was and is divine."[16]

Reagan also believed in the Incarnation. On December 25, 1975, he wrote his wife: "The star in the East was a miracle as was the Virgin Birth. I have no trouble believing in these miracles because a miracle happened to me and it's still happening." He then wrote of his love for his wife.[17]

He also believed that the Bible was divinely inspired. In a letter written about 1967, he said: "I believe the Bible is the result of Divine inspiration and is *not* just a history. I believe in it."[18]

In a letter written during the 1980 presidential campaign, Reagan said: "I believe our nation hungers for a spiritual revival."[19]

During the campaign, he spoke to the Religious Roundtable's "National Affairs Briefing," attended primarily by evangelical and fun-damentalist Christian pastors. He said: "I know that you can't endorse me, but I want you to know that I endorse you and what you are doing."[20]

Once, in a meeting with the executive director of the Christian Booksellers Association, Reagan cited John 3:16 as his favorite Bible verse. When asked why, he explained: "It means that having accepted Jesus Christ as my Savior, I have God's promise of eternal life in Heaven, as well as the abundant life here on earth that He promises to each of us in John 10:10."[21]

While on the campaign trail, Reagan surprised many professional evolutionists when he "expressed doubts about evolution" and suggested that creationism should also be taught in public schools.[22] During his presidency, Reagan expressed his views in more detail during a speech to the Student Congress on Evangelism. He said: "You know, I know in our land of freedom everyone—if they want to choose atheism instead of a belief in God, that's their right to do so. But I have always felt that I would like someday to entertain an atheist at dinner and serve the most gourmet, perfect dinner that has ever been served and then, at the end of the meal, ask that atheist if he believes there's a cook."[23]

Reagan was elected president and served from 1981 to 1989. In his first inaugural address, he said: "I am told that tens of thousands of prayer meetings are being held on this day, and for that I am deeply grateful. We are a nation under God, and I believe God intended for us to be free. It would be fitting and good, I think, if on each Inauguration Day in future years it should be declared a day of prayer."[24]

To a degree that few other presidents have done, Reagan used his position as president to call the nation to the Lord. In a 1982 letter to Greg Brezina, head of Christian Families Today, he said: "Let me assure you that 2 Chronicles 7:14 is ever present in my mind. My daily prayer is that God will help me to use this position so as to serve Him. Teddy Roosevelt once called the presidency a bully pulpit. I intend to use it to the best of my ability to serve the Lord."[25]

On March 30, 1981, Reagan was shot and nearly killed in an assassination attempt. About a year later, a reporter from the *Los Angeles Times* asked if the attempt had changed the way he looked at life. Reagan responded: "Well, I think you're more aware, and I'm also very aware that the Lord certainly was watching out for me on that day. And I guess—from now on my time is His time."[26]

Reverend Donn Moomaw, visiting him in the hospital, asked him if he would have been ready to meet God had he died. Reagan answered in the affirmative. When asked why, he said, "I'm ready to meet God because I have a Savior."[27]

Over time, he came to see that God had a purpose for everything, even the assassination attempt. John Barletta, a Secret Service agent who was assigned to guard Reagan during and after his presidency, recalled him saying: "God thought— Well, God doesn't think, God knew that I needed a nudge. God wanted that assassination attempt to happen. He gave me a wake-up call. Everything I do from now on, I owe to God."[28]

After the attempted assassination, Reagan did not attend church outside the White House for some time. He made this decision due to the threats being made on his life. (Cynics who assert that threats on the three presidents since Reagan have not curtailed their churchgoing fail to note that none of the three presidents since have nearly died from an assassination attempt.) Reagan said, "When the President comes in, the attention is on him rather than on the sermon or the service. I'm not sure I feel comfortable with that."[29] He wrote in a letter to Jerry Mueller that he and his wife had "always been churchgoers and would be now if it were not for the terrorist threats."[30]

In spite of these concerns, Reagan did not completely abandon going to church. He had communion at the White House and attended church when he was not in Washington. When a special area in the National Presbyterian Church in Washington was set aside so the Reagans could worship without disrupting the service or distracting the parishioners, they resumed church attendance.[31] He continued throughout his presidency to attend church intermittently while in Washington, so that he would not set a pattern for terrorists.

In 1982, Ronald Reagan submitted a constitutional amendment to Congress that would have permitted voluntary school prayer. He explained his position in an accompanying message, in which he said: "The public expression through prayer of our faith in God is a fundamental part of our American heritage and a privilege which should not be excluded by law from any American school, public or private."

Because the amendment did not pass in 1982, Reagan tried again in 1983. In a 1984 speech to the nation making the case for the passage of the amendment, he said:

> Our amendment would ensure that no child be forced to recite a
> prayer. Indeed, it explicitly states this. Nor would the state be

allowed to compose the words of any prayer. But the courts could not forbid our children from voluntary vocal prayer in their schools. And by reasserting their liberty of free religious expression, we will be helping our children understand the diversity of America's religious beliefs and practices.

If ever there was a time for you, the good people of this country, to make your voices heard, to make the mighty power of your will the decisive force in the halls of Congress, that time is now.[32]

Ronald Reagan cared so deeply about the issue of abortion that he named it as one of the two most important issues on which George Bush needed to change his position before Reagan could name him as his vice-presidential nominee.[33]

He believed that abortion was morally and constitutionally wrong. "We cannot proclaim the noble ideal that human life is sacred," he said, "and then turn our backs on the taking of some 4,000 unborn children's lives every day. This must stop. Our Constitution guarantees 'life, liberty, and the pursuit of happiness,' but an abortion is the taking of a human life."[34]

Throughout his presidency, Reagan continued to take a pro-life position. In a 1983 speech to the annual Convention of National Religious Broadcasters, he said: "We once believed that the heart didn't start beating until the fifth month. But as medical instrumentation has improved, we've learned the heart was beating long before that. Doesn't the constitutional protection of life, liberty, and the pursuit of happiness extend to the unborn unless it can be proven beyond a shadow of a doubt that life does not exist in the unborn? And I believe the burden of proof is on those who would make that point."[35]

In a speech the following year to the same group, he said: "I believe no challenge is more important to the character of America than restoring the right to life to all human beings. Without that right, no other rights have meaning."[36]

In a 1988 proclamation declaring January 17, 1988, "Sanctity of Human Life Day," Reagan said:

Our Nation cannot continue down the path of abortion, so radically at odds with our history, our heritage, and our concepts of justice. This sacred legacy, and the wellbeing and the future of our country, demand that protection of the innocents must be guaranteed and that the personhood of the unborn be declared and defended throughout our land. In legislation introduced at my request in the First Session of the 100th Congress, I have asked the Legislative branch to declare the "humanity of the unborn child and the compelling interest of the several states to protect the life of each person before birth." This duty to declare on so fundamental a matter falls to the Executive as well. By this Proclamation I hereby do so.

Now, Therefore, I, Ronald Reagan, President of the United States of America, by virtue of the authority vested in me by the Constitution and laws of the United States, do hereby proclaim and declare the unalienable personhood of every American, from the moment of conception until natural death, and I do proclaim, ordain, and declare that I will take care that the Constitution and laws of the United States are faithfully executed for the protection of America's unborn children. Upon this act, sincerely believed to be an act of justice, warranted by the Constitution, I invoke the considerate judgment of mankind and the gracious favor of Almighty God. I also proclaim Sunday, January 17, 1988, as National Sanctity of Human Life Day. I call upon the citizens of this blessed land to gather on that day in their homes and places of worship to give thanks for the gift of life they enjoy and to reaffirm their commitment to the dignity of every human being and the sanctity of every human life.[37]

Reagan acknowledged God in numerous speeches and proclamations. On March 19, 1981, he issued a proclamation calling for a National Day of Prayer. The proclamation read:

Our Nation's motto "In God We Trust"—was not chosen lightly. It reflects a basic recognition that there is a divine authority in the universe to which this Nation owes homage.

Throughout our history Americans have put their faith in God and no one can doubt that we have been blessed for it. The earliest settlers of this land came in search of religious freedom. Landing on a desolate shoreline, they established a spiritual foundation that has served us ever since.

It was the hard work of our people, the freedom they enjoyed and their faith in God that built this country and made it the envy of the world. In all of our great cities and towns evidence of the faith of our people is found: houses of worship of every denomination are among the oldest structures.

While never willing to bow to a tyrant, our forefathers were always willing to get to their knees before God. When catastrophe threatened, they turned to God for deliverance. When the harvest was bountiful the first thought was thanksgiving to God.

Prayer is today as powerful a force in our Nation as it has ever been. We as a Nation should never forget this source of strength. And while recognizing that the freedom to choose a Godly path is the essence of liberty, as a Nation we cannot but hope that more of our citizens would, through prayer, come into a closer relationship with their Maker.

Recognizing our great heritage, the Congress, by Joint Resolution approved April 17, 1952 (36 U.S.C. 169h; 66 Stat. 64), has called upon the President to set aside a suitable day each year as a National Day of Prayer.

Now, Therefore, I, Ronald Reagan, President of the United States of America, do hereby proclaim Thursday, May 7, 1981, National Day of Prayer. On that day I ask all who believe to join with me in giving thanks to Almighty God for the blessings He has bestowed on this land and the protection He affords us as a people. Let us as a Nation join together before God, fully aware of the trials that lie ahead and the need, yes, the necessity, for divine guidance. With unshakable faith in God and the liberty which is heritage, we as a free Nation will surely survive and prosper.[38]

On February 23, 1983, Reagan awarded the Reverend Billy Graham the Presidential Medal of Freedom. He said: "Reverend William 'Billy' Graham's untiring evangelism has spread the word of God to every corner of the globe, and made him one of the most inspirational spiritual leaders of the Twentieth Century. As a deeply committed Christian, his challenge to accept Jesus Christ has lifted the hearts, assuaged the sorrows and renewed the hopes of millions. Billy Graham is an American who lives first and always for his fellow citizens. In honoring him, we give thanks for God's greatest spiritual gifts—faith, hope, and love."[39] Reagan had first met Reverend Graham in the 1950s.[40]

Reagan proclaimed 1983 the "Year of the Bible," encouraging all Americans to "examine and rediscover its priceless and timeless message."[41]

Reagan was reelected in 1984. In his second inaugural address, he said that we "stand as one today: One people under God determined that our future shall be worthy of our past."[42] He concluded his speech with these words: "For all our problems, our differences, we are together as of old, as we raise our voices to the God who is the Author of this most tender music. And may He continue to hold us close as we fill the world with our sound—sound in unity, affection, and love—one people under God, dedicated to the dream of freedom that He has placed in the human heart, called upon now to pass that dream on to a waiting and hopeful world. God bless you and may God bless America."[43]

In a 1988 speech to the Student Congress on Evangelism, Reagan discussed his views on God's role in our nation's history. He said:

Whenever I consider the history of this nation, I'm struck by how deeply imbued with faith the American people were, even from the very first. Many of the first settlers came for the express purpose of worshiping in freedom. Historian Samuel Morison wrote of one such group: "Doubting nothing and fearing no man, they undertook all to set all crooked ways straight and create a new Heaven and a new Earth. If they were not permitted to do that in England, they would find some other place to establish their city of God." Well, that place was this broad and open land we call America.

The debates over independence and the records of the Constitutional Convention make it clear that the Founding Fathers were sustained by their faith in God. In the Declaration of Independence itself, Thomas Jefferson wrote all men are "endowed by their Creator with certain unalienable Rights." And it was George Washington who said, "Of all the dispositions and habits which lead to political prosperity, religion and morality are indispensable supports." Well, later, the statesmen gathered in Philadelphia to write what would become our Constitution. They often found themselves at odds, their purpose lost in acrimony and self-interest, until Benjamin Franklin stood one day and said, "I have been driven many times"—oh, no, I'm sorry—"I have lived a long time, and the longer I live, the more convincing proofs I see of this truth: that God governs in the affairs of men. And if a sparrow cannot fall to the ground without His notice, is it probable that an empire can rise without His aid?" And then he called that Constitutional Convention to open each day with prayer, which it did.

For decades, America remained a deeply religious country, thanking God in peacetime and turning to him in moments of crisis. During the Civil War, perhaps our nation's darkest hour, Abraham Lincoln said, "I have been driven many times to my knees by the conviction that I have nowhere else to go." Well, believe me, no one can serve in this office without understanding and believing exactly what he said.[44]

Several times, Reagan said that 2 Chronicles 7:14 was one of his favorite Bible passages. For the observance of the National Day of Prayer on May 6, 1982, he said:

One of my favorite passages in the Bible is the promise God gives us in second Chronicles: "If my people, which are called by my name, shall humble themselves and pray and seek my face and turn from their wicked ways, then will I hear from heaven and will forgive their sin and will heal their land."

That promise is the hope of America and of all our people. . . .

Together, let us take up the challenge to reawaken America's religious and moral heart, recognizing that a deep and abiding faith in God is the rock upon which this great Nation was founded.[45]

At the annual National Prayer Breakfast on February 3, 1983, he said:

I have a very special old Bible. And alongside a verse in the Second Book of Chronicles there are some words, handwritten, very faded by now. And, believe me, the person who wrote those words was an authority. Her name was Nelle Wilson Reagan. She was my mother. And she wrote about that verse, "A most wonderful verse for the healing of the nations."

Now, the verse that she'd marked reads: "If my people, which are called by my name, shall humble themselves, and pray, and seek my face, and turn from their wicked ways; then will I hear from heaven . . . and will heal their land."[46]

Ronald Reagan saw the many moral problems plaguing America and promoted solutions to those problems. But fundamentally he remained a man of hope. He put it this way to the Student Congress on Evangelism on July 28, 1988:

> All our material wealth and all our influence have been built on our faith in God and the bedrock values that follow from that faith. The great French philosopher visited our country—Alexis de Tocqueville—150 years ago. He wanted to see if he could find the secret of our greatness already, as a young country. And then he observed that "America is great because America is good. And if she ever ceases to be good, she will cease to be great."
>
> This brings me to the challenges of the present day. For we must admit that in recent years America did seem to lose some of her religious and moral bearings. We saw the signs all around us. . . .
>
> These problems are still with us. But I believe there's been a change—a change that you young people here today are part of. The Bible says: "If my people who are called by my name humble themselves and pray and seek my face and turn from their wicked ways, then I will hear from Heaven and forgive their sins and heal their land." Many, many years ago, my mother had underlined that particular passage in the Bible. And I had her Bible that I could place my hand on when I took the oath of office in 1980. And I had it opened to that passage that she had underlined. Today more and more Americans are seeking His face. And, yes, He has begun to heal our land.[47]

In his farewell address, Reagan reiterated his firm belief that America was to be a shining city on a hill:

> The past few days . . . I've thought a bit of the "shining city upon a hill." The phrase comes from John Winthrop, who wrote it to describe the America he imagined. What he imagined was important because he was an early Pilgrim, an early freedom man. He journeyed here on what today we'd call a little wooden boat; and like the other Pilgrims, he was looking for a home that would be free.

I've spoken of the shining city all my political life, but I don't know if I ever quite communicated what I saw when I said it. But in my mind it was a tall, proud city built on rocks stronger than oceans, windswept, God-blessed, and teeming with people of all kinds living in harmony and peace; a city with free ports that hummed with commerce and creativity. And if there had to be city walls, the walls had doors, and the doors were open to anyone with the will and the heart to get here. That's how I saw it, and see it still.

And how stands the city on this winter night? More prosperous, more secure, and happier than it was eight years ago. But more than that: After 200 years, two centuries, she still stands strong and true on the granite ridge, and her glow has held steady no matter what storm. And she's still a beacon, still a magnet for all who must have freedom, for all the pilgrims from all the lost places who are hurtling through the darkness, toward home.

We've done our part. And as I walk off into the city streets, a final word to the men and women of the Reagan revolution, the men and women across America who for eight years did the work that brought America back. My friends: We did it. We weren't just marking time. We made a difference. We made the city stronger, we made the city freer, and we left her in good hands. All in all, not bad, not bad at all.

And so, good-bye, God bless you, and God bless the United States of America.[48]

Reagan died on June 5, 2004, in Santa Monica, California.

In his book, *Twice Adopted*, Michael Reagan told a story about an airline flight with his father. He noticed that his father was counting on his fingers and asked what he was doing. Ronald Reagan responded, "I'm counting the months until I can go to church again. Just nine more months."

Michael responded, "What do you mean?"

Reagan said, "Ever since I was shot and they threw me in that car, I have felt I shouldn't go to church. I remember looking out the car window and seeing people lying on the ground and bleeding because of me. I didn't want that scene repeated in a church. So I haven't attended church on a regular basis since that day. I didn't want some guy with a gun coming into church and hurting other people to get me. When I finally leave Washington in January, I can start going to church again because I really want to spend that time with the Lord."[49]Michael Reagan stated that as soon as his father was out of office, "he never missed a Sunday service until the Alzheimer's disease progressed to a point where he simply could no longer attend."[50]

Michael said that Christianity was the greatest gift his parents gave him. He said: "But there is one gift that my parents have given me that outshines all the rest. Now, as my dad's ninety-year journey through life has been completed, and as my mother approaches ninety, quick as a whip but ailing due to advancing age, I'm more grateful than ever for the gift they've given me. I know where Dad is now. I know where Mom is going. And I know that I will see them again one day in eternity."[51]

CONCLUSION

Reagan publicly stated that he was a born-again Christian. In private and public statements, his expressed views on doctrinal matters agree with the teachings of orthodox Christianity. Perhaps more than any other president in recent history, Reagan's religion influenced his presidency—and the nation—in a positive way.

NOTES

1. Anne Edwards, *Early Reagan: The Rise to Power* (New York: Morrow, 1990), 58.

2. Kiron K. Skinner, Annelise Anderson, and Martin Anderson, *Reagan: A Life in Letters* (New York: Simon & Schuster/The Free Press, 2004), 276. From a letter to Mrs. Warne in 1967.

3. Ibid., 6. From a letter to Jean B. Wright. Wright was the daughter-in-law of the book's author.

4. Ibid.

5. John McCollister, *So Help Me God: The Faith of America's Presidents* (Louisville: Westminster/John Knox Press, 1991), 199.

6. Billy Graham, *Just As I Am: The Autobiography of Billy Graham* (New York: HarperSanFrancisco/Zondervan, 1997), 534.

7. Richard G. Hutcheson Jr., *God in the White House: How Religion Has Changed the Modern Presidency* (New York: Collier Macmillan, 1989), 162.

8. Edwards, *Early Reagan*, 85.

9. Ibid., 182.

10. Kengor, *God and Ronald Reagan,* 49. After Reagan came down with Alzheimer's, Nancy sent the check in both their names.

11. Ronald Reagan, with Richard G. Hubler, *Where's the Rest of Me?* (New York: Duell, Sloan, and Pearce, 1965), 123.

12. Hutcheson, *God in the White House,* 164.

13. Ibid.

14. Kiron K. Skinner, Annelise Anderson, and Martin Anderson, *Reagan's Path to Victory* (New York: Simon & Schuster/The Free Press, 2004), 247–48.

15. Skinner, Anderson, and Anderson, *Reagan: A Life in Letters,* 276-77.

16. Reagan, *Public Papers of the Presidents of the United States: Ronald Reagan, 1985.* Washington, DC: Government Printing Office. Remarks on lighting the national Christmas tree, December 12, 1985.

17. Skinner, Anderson, and Anderson, *Reagan: A Life in Letters,* 45.

18. Ibid., 276. From a letter written in about 1967 to Mrs. Warne.

19. William E. Pemberton, *Exit with Honor: The Life and Presidency of Ronald Reagan* (Armonk, NY, and London: M. E. Sharpe, 1997), 61. From a letter written to Mary E. Rogers on January 23, 1980.

20. Ibid., 61; Ralph Reed, *Active Faith: How Christians Are Changing the Soul of American Politics* (New York: Simon & Schuster/The Free Press, 1996), 111.

21. Kengor, *God and Ronald Reagan,* 106.

22. Boller, *Presidential Campaigns,* 358.

23. Reagan, *Public Papers,* July 28, 1988, Remarks to the Student Congress on Evangelism.

24. Reagan, First inaugural address, January 20, 1981.

25. Skinner, Anderson, and Anderson, *Reagan: A Life in Letters,* 654. From a October 25, 1982, letter to Greg Brezena.

26. Reagan, *Public Papers, 1982.* January 20, 1982.

27. Kengor, *God and Ronald Reagan,* 185, quoting an interview with Don Moomaw that aired in the 2002 History Channel program, "Ronald Reagan: A Legacy Remembered."

28. John R. Barletta, with Rochelle Schweizer, *Riding with Reagan: From the White House to the Ranch* (New York: Kensington Publishing/Citadel Press, 2005), 56.

29. Graham, *Just As I Am,* 535.

30. Skinner, Anderson, and Anderson, *Reagan: A Life in Letters,* 461. From a May 31, 1984, letter to Jerry Mueller.

31. Graham, *Just As I Am,* 535.

32. Reagan, *Public* Papers, February 25, 1984, Radio address to the nation on prayer in schools.

33. Schweizer and Schweizer, *The Bushes,* 287.

34. Reagan, *Public Papers,* July 28, 1988, Remarks to the Student Congress on Evangelism.

35. Ibid., January 31, 1983.

36. Ibid., January 30, 1984.

37. Reagan, *Public Papers of Ronald Reagan–1988,* Proclamation 5761–National Sanctity of Human Life Day, 1988.

38. Reagan, *Public Papers, 1981.* A proclamation for a national day of prayer, March 19, 1981.

39. Reagan, *Public Papers, 1983.* February 23, 1983, Remarks at the Presentation Ceremony for the Presidential Medal of Freedom.

40. Pemberton, *Exit with Honor,* 61.

41. Reagan, *Public Papers, 1983.* Proclamation 5018–Year of the Bible, 1983.

42. Reagan, Second inaugural address, January 20, 1985.

43. Ibid.

44. Reagan, *Public Papers,* July 28, 1988, Remarks to the Student Congress on Evangelism.

45. Ibid., May 6, 1982, Remarks at a White House Ceremony in Observance of National Day of Prayer.

46. Ibid., February 3, 1983, Remarks at the Annual National Prayer Breakfast.

47. Ibid., July 28, 1988, Remarks to the Student Congress on Evangelism.

48. Ibid., January 11, 1989, Farewell Address to the Nation.

49. Michael Reagan, with Jim Denney, *Twice Adopted* (Nashville: Broadman and Holman, 2004), 313.

50. Ibid.

51. Ibid., 306.

CHAPTER 5

JAMES EARL CARTER

JAMES EARL "JIMMY" CARTER was born on October 1, 1924, in Plains, Georgia. He grew up in a Baptist family and attended Plains Baptist Church. His father, James Carter, taught Sunday school. However, President Carter wrote later in life, "Although my father was at ease teaching the lessons in church, I think he would have been embarrassed to bring up Christian subjects with me while we were at work in the fields or sitting together at the dinner table. In a way, I saw a different father in Sunday School."[1]

During a revival service held at his church in 1935 when he was eleven years old, Carter accepted Christ as his Savior. He was baptized the following Sunday by his pastor, Reverend Royall Conway.

However, he said that "being born again didn't happen to me when I was eleven. For me, it has been an evolutionary thing. Rather than a sudden flash of light or a sudden vision of God speaking, it involved a series of steps that have brought me steadily closer to Christ. My conversion at eleven was just one of those steps."[2]

His mother recalled that when Carter was young, he took his role in the church seriously. However, she remembered, he was not religious.[3]

When Carter went to the U.S. Naval Academy in Annapolis, Maryland, he started wondering why he was created, what his purpose in life was, and who God was.[4]

When he graduated from the naval academy, he married Rosalynn Smith on July 7, 1946. Rosalynn Carter was a Methodist before her marriage, but decided to join her husband and become a Baptist.

Carter and his wife eventually established a regular practice of reading a page or a chapter of the Bible together every evening, eventually reading in Spanish with an English translation nearby to practice their language skills.[5]

Carter's father's death in 1953 marked a turning point in Carter's life, both in his career and in his commitment to religion. He decided to leave the Navy and return to the family farm in Plains. He also began dealing with the question of how God could let his father die at the relatively young age of fifty-eight. "It seemed to me a harsh act," he said, "one I could only attribute to what I thought of as the God of the Old Testament, a stern, judgmental figure, very different from the loving, forgiving Jesus I knew from the Gospels."[6] This question led him to study the writings of Christian theologians.

After his move to Plains, he again became involved in Plains Baptist Church. He took over his father's Sunday school class of boys aged nine to twelve, and his wife taught the girls of the same age. Carter became head of the junior department and a deacon in the church.

He eventually decided to enter politics and embarked on a course that took him to the White House. However, he suffered one particularly frustrating defeat in 1966, when he ran for governor of Georgia. He was defeated by Lester Maddox, a segregationist. After that election, his sister Ruth urged him to seek a "fresh, intimate, personal, loving, caring relationship with Jesus Christ."[7] He started reading the Bible more.

Soon after, his pastor, Reverend Robert Harris, asked in a sermon, "If you were arrested for being a Christian . . . would there be enough evidence to convict you?" When Carter decided there would not, he recommitted his life to Christ.[8]

During the 1976 presidential election, the first after *Roe v. Wade*, Carter was pressed to take a public stance on the issue of abortion.

As governor of Georgia, he had "strongly supported family planning programs including abortion."[9] He even wrote a foreword to *Women in Need*, a book that advocated abortion, though he did not actually advocate abortion in his preface. He also supported the plaintiffs in the *Doe v. Bolton* lawsuit, which (along with *Roe v. Wade*) helped legalize abortion in 1973.

However, when running for president, he moved closer toward the pro-life stance of one of his target audiences, religious conservatives.

Before the 1975 Iowa caucuses, he was quoted in a Catholic newspaper saying that he would support a "national statute" to prohibit abortion.[10] This statement, distributed in Catholic churches the Sunday morning before the caucuses, helped him win the Catholic vote; some observers believe it was the most crucial key to winning the state.

Once the caucuses were won, criticism led him to back down. He said that a group of priests had asked the question, "Are there any circumstances under which you might support a national statute against abortion?"

He responded, "Yes. I suppose it is possible, although I cannot think of any."[11]

In a statement clarifying his position, he said: "I have consistently stated that I oppose constitutional amendments to overturn the Supreme Court's decision on abortion. However, I personally disapprove of abortions and do not think government should do anything to encourage abortions.

"The Supreme Court left many decisions unresolved. As president, I would be guided and bound by the courts' decisions on these and other questions pertaining to abortion services."[12] This satisfied the women's rights groups.

He opposed federal funding for abortions (except in cases of rape, incest, and life of the mother),[13] preferring to use federal funds to pay for birth control.[14]

Carter's most interesting statement on abortion came when he was once asked if he ever had to compromise his faith to carry out his duties as president. He said:

> Yes. I can only think of one issue where I had to modify my own Christian beliefs to carry out the duties of president, and that was on the subject of abortion, and this is a highly personal thing. You ask me as a human being. It is impossible for me to imagine Jesus Christ approving abortion, and my duties as a president required me to carry out the laws of our nation as interpreted by the Supreme Court, which authorized abortion, as you know, in the first three months of pregnancy if the woman and her doctor decide [to do so]. I disagreed with this, although I never failed to carry out my duty as a president.[15]

Carter's religious faith may well have helped him win the presidency. When he was asked in the campaign if he was "born again," he made headlines by responding "yes."

His private reaction to the publicity was interesting; he said, "It was headlines all over the nation. And I began to be concerned about it. I did not want to mix in religion and my duties as president."[16]

Despite his concern about the statement's impact on liberals, the statement did gain him support from conservative Christians who normally voted Republican but wanted to support a fellow born-again Christian. In a 1978 Annual National Prayer Breakfast speech, Carter explained just what he meant by being "born again":

> To me, God is real. To me, the relationship with God is a very personal thing. God is ever-present in my life—sustains me when I am weak, gives me guidance when I turn to him, and provides for me as a Christian through the life of Christ, a perfect example to emulate in my experiences with other human beings.
>
> My wife and I worship together every night, and often during the day I turn to God in a quiet and personal way.
>
> A few months back, the words "born again" were vividly impressed on the consciousness of many Americans who were not familiar with their meaning. They've been used in many headlines and on the front covers of many magazines.
>
> But for those of us who share the Christian faith, the words "born again" have a very simple meaning—that through a personal experience, we recommit our lives as humble children of God, which makes us in the realest possible sense brothers and sisters of one another. Families are bound by the closest possible ties.[17]

Carter's religious faith influenced his course as president, and the events of his presidency influenced Carter's religious faith. "I prayed more during those four years than at any other time in my life," he said, "just asking for God's guidance in making the right decisions on behalf of the American people."[18]

When he was asked in 1980 if the pressures of his job had made a negative impact on his spiritual life, he responded:

> No. I believe very deeply as a Baptist and a Christian that there ought to be a proper separation of the church and the state, and I've never let my beliefs interfere in my administration of the duties as President. But I've never found any incompatibility. I pray more than I did when I was not President, because the burdens on my

shoulders are much greater than they were when I was a Governor or when I didn't hold public office.

This Nation is one that's been acknowledged by our Founding Fathers since the first days of the idea to be founded under God. "In God We Trust" is on our coins. It's not a bad thing for Americans to believe deeply in God, but the fact is that the Constitution gives us a right to worship God or to worship as we choose. And the Congress cannot pass any law respecting the establishment of religion.

But my own personal faith and my personal belief is stronger now than it's ever been before. I pray more than I did, and I don't find any incompatibility between being a Christian, on the one hand, and being President of this country, on the other.[19]

As many presidents have before him, Carter chose to use a Bible verse in his inaugural address, 2 Chronicles 7:14: "If my people, which are called by my name, shall humble themselves, and pray, and seek my face, and turn from their wicked ways, then will I hear from heaven, will forgive their sin, and will heal their land." However, his speechwriters disagreed, arguing that the reference was too pious. So he decided to quote another verse, Micah 6:8.[20] The final draft of that section of the speech read:

Here before me is the Bible used in the inauguration of our first President, in 1789, and I have just taken the oath of office on the Bible my mother gave me a few years ago, opened to a timeless admonition from the ancient prophet Micah:

"He hath showed thee, O man, what is good; and what doth the Lord require of thee, but to do justly, and to love mercy, and to walk humbly with thy God" (Micah 6:8).[21]

Incidentally, Micah 6:8 had already been quoted in another inaugural address fifty-six years before—in the inauguration speech of Warren Gamaliel Harding.

Carter told the story of the verse-selection process in his remarks at the National Prayer Breakfast on January 27, 1977:

The first draft of my Inaugural speech did not include the reference to Micah's admonition about justice and mercy and humility. But I had chosen instead First [Second] Chronicles, 7:14, which Congressman Wright quoted this morning: "If my people who are called by my name shall humble themselves and pray and seek my face and turn from their wicked ways, then will I hear from Heaven and forgive their sins and heal their land."

When my staff members read the first draft of my speech they rose up in opposition to that verse. The second time I wrote my Inaugural draft I had the same verse in it. And they came to me en masse and said, "The people will not understand that verse. It's as though you, being elected President, are condemning the other people of our country, putting yourself in the position of Solomon and saying that all Americans are wicked."

So, correctly or wrongly, I changed it to Micah. And I think this episode, which is true, is illustrative of the problem that we face. Sometimes we take for granted that an acknowledgment of sin, an acknowledgment of the need for humility permeates the consciousness of our people. But it doesn't.[22]

In a 1978 question-and-answer session in Nashua, New Hampshire, Carter was asked if he felt that he was in a position to call the American people to repentance for their immoral acts and deeds, and if he would do it. He answered:

Well, my own religious faith is one that's much more personal. I feel that we have a direct access to God through prayer and that repentance is a personal thing. I don't believe that it's my responsibility to repent before God for what our Nation has done in the past or may do even while I'm in the White House. I think that's something that has to be initiated and carried out by individual Americans.

Obviously, if I see a sinful act or an improper or heartless act being carried out by our Nation in the past or present or future, it's my responsibility as President to stop that action and to condone through action, for inequities or suffering that has been caused by it.

So, I don't know any better way to describe the question than that. I don't consider myself to be the spiritual leader of this country. I'm the political leader. I have a right, I think, and a duty to be frank with the American people about my own belief. And I'm not a priest nor a bishop nor someone who, you know, fills a religious pulpit and is authorized nor asked to repent for the whole country.

I've answered your question in a fumbling way. But that's the way I feel about it. And I recognize my own personal shortcomings and sinfulness. I do ask God to forgive me. I try to do better. And I think that the American people, whether they are religious or not, have the same strong inclination to correct deficiencies, to repair wrongs, to turn ourselves in a much closer way, personally and collectively, to exemplify the highest possible moral principles on which our Nation has been so great.[23]

Carter chose not to invite preachers to preach at the White House. "We had observed that my predecessors had invited Billy Graham and other famous preachers to conduct well-publicized worship services in the White House," he wrote. "We respected their right to do so, but we felt that for us to do the same would violate our concept of church and state being kept separate."[24]

However, he did transfer his membership to the First Baptist Church while in Washington—a church that former presidents Martin Van Buren, Franklin Pierce, Harry S Truman, and Lyndon Baines Johnson had all attended. He taught Sunday school at that church several times a year during his presidency.[25]

In the 1980 presidential campaign, religion again became an issue. Carter stated that some questioned the sincerity of his religious beliefs. He responded with these words:

My religious beliefs are very precious to me, and I've never tried to criticize those who worshiped differently from me. But until this year, I have never had anybody question the sincerity of my belief in God and my commitment of my life as a Christian believing in Jesus Christ as my Savior.

Lately I have heard about—I have not seen them—some very vicious television advertisements questioning my religious beliefs, insinuating all kinds of damaging things to me within the religion that I love so much. I'm not going to dignify these attacks by answering them specifically.

But I feel sure about my own relationship to God. . . .

I'm not in favor of a religious definition of an acceptable politician, and I'm not in favor of a political definition for Christian fellowship or for religious fellowship.[26]

In his presidential memoirs, Carter discussed the role of prayer in his presidency. He said:

I prayed a lot—more than ever before in my life—asking God to give me a clear mind, sound judgment, and wisdom in dealing with affairs that could affect the lives of so many people in our own country and around the world. Although I cannot claim that my decisions were always the best ones, prayer was a great help to me. At least, it removed any possibility of timidity or despair as I faced my daily responsibilities.[27]

One specific instance when Carter's religious faith influenced his actions as president was in his diplomatic negotiations with China's Deng Xiaoping. During negotiations about whether relations between mainland China and the United States should be normalized, Carter urged Xiaoping to increase religious freedom in China. "I hope your people will be permitted to have Bibles and that freedom of religion can be guaranteed for them again," Carter said. "And also," he added, "there are a lot of missionaries who would like to return to China to work in education, health care, agriculture, or wherever you would prefer."[28] Xaioping said he would consider the first two requests but would "never again permit foreign religious workers to come to China."[29]

Carter was renowned as a peace negotiator. On January 20, 1977, he spoke with reporters outside First Baptist Church during Egyptian President Sadat's trip to Israel. He said: "My prayer was one that recognized this whole world wants peace; that Christ, our Savior, is the Prince of Peace; that the Middle East has been particularly afflicted by war, which no one there wanted, constantly—almost day by day—conflict, and four major wars in the last 30 years; that yesterday Prime Minister Begin, who is a very deeply religious man, worshipped God in a Jewish temple; this morning President Sadat worshipped the same God in a Moslem mosque and later worshipped the same God in a Christian holy place where Christ was buried; and that all over the world today people are praying for peace."[30]

After Reagan won the election, the Carter family was devastated. In the Carters' book *Everything to Gain*, Rosalynn Carter described conversations with her husband during the weeks following the election:

> "I don't understand it. I just don't understand why God wanted us to lose the election," I would say. Jimmy was always more mature in his Christian attitude than I was. He would say, "Do you think people are robots that God controls from heaven?"—or "You don't really think God orders things like this, do you? It's hard for us to accept the fact that our priorities are not the same as God's. We attach too much importance to things like popularity, wealth, and political success. To Him problems that seem most important to us at the time are really not very significant. But God trusts us to make the best use of the time we have, to try to live like Jesus and to make our lives meaningful and beneficial to others no matter where we are." I did finally learn to live with the results of the 1980 election, but I would never pretend that it came easily.[31]

Carter retired to his home in Plains, Georgia. He teaches the adult Sunday school class at his home church, Maranatha Baptist Church.[32]

In his retirement years, he has written more extensively than any other president about his religious beliefs. His books *Living Faith* and *Sources of Strength* are the only two books written by a president that are completely devoted to a discussion of his religious beliefs. What are some of the doctrinal beliefs he discusses in these books?

In *Living Faith*, Carter explained what his decision "to accept Christ" meant to him. He said: "What does it mean when I say that I 'decided to accept Christ'? Jesus was the Messiah, the long-awaited savior, who came both to reveal God to us and to heal the division between God and humankind. As Jesus told his disciples, 'If you have seen me, you have seen God' (John 14:9). Furthermore, the Gospels recount how Jesus, having lived a perfect and blameless life, accepted a death of horrible suffering on the cross on our behalf, as an atonement for the sins we have committed. Accepting Christ as my savior means believing all these things and entering into a relationship with God through him, so that my past and future sins no longer alienate me from my Creator.

"Putting our total faith in these concepts is what it means by being 'born again.' "[33]

He wrote that during his youth, he worried about whether there would be a literal resurrection. Throughout his teenage and early adult years, he added the request, "God, please help me believe in the resurrection" to the end of his prayers.[34] He eventually became more assured of the literal resurrection.

He stated that he does not believe in the absolute inerrancy of the Bible.[35] As his biographer Peter Bourne said, "He saw the Bible as the ultimate authoritative guide to be studied and followed in leading a truly Christian life, but not, as fundamentalists considered it, the literal word of God."[36]

However, Carter wrote that "the total wisdom of the Bible does apply to us today."[37] He explains his position in his book *Sources of Strength*:

> If we begin eliminating verses that we consider outdated, we may find just those verses that happen to suit our own temperaments, habits, or foibles. The Bible should help correct our personal tastes, not just reinforce them.
>
> At the same time, it's true that the Bible, though inspired by God, was written by fallible human beings who shared the knowledge and beliefs of their times. The science and astronomy of the Bible are inaccurate by modern standards (speaking of the earth's "four corners," for example), and biblical writers in New Testament times still wrote as if slavery were a legitimate social institution that should not be questioned. So it is appropriate to consider the times in which the Bible was written when interpreting the meaning of Scripture and its message for us today.[38]

In practice, how does he apply this tension between shaping his beliefs to fit the Bible's doctrines versus shaping the Bible to fit his beliefs?

One example concerns the ordination of female ministers. In his book *Living Faith*, he cited Galatians 3:28, "There is neither . . . male nor female, for you are all one in Christ Jesus." Carter said, "Paul included gender as one of the distinctions no longer to be recognized by believers."[39]

He then extrapolated this verse to the issue of ordination as dealt with in such passages as 1 Timothy 2, a passage that deals with church order and states that women should "learn in silence with all submission," and not "have authority over a man."

Because he interprets Galatians 3:28 to mean that women can be ordained ministers, he refers to 1 Timothy 2 in these words: "Paul's admonition to women to 'submit' is an anomaly among the attitudes of Jesus and other New Testament texts, including other more definitive writings of Paul."[40]

When the first step is taken of denying the Bible's absolute inerrancy, it becomes easier to dismiss passages that contradict your opinions as "less definitive."

Another example of how he applied the principle of the Bible being the Word of God but not being absolutely inerrant is in the issue of creation versus evolution. Carter believes in evolution. He explains how he reconciles this with his religious opinions:

> As a believer, I have no problem with discoveries in astronomy, geology, and paleontology: that the universe is enormous and expanding, the earth is ancient, and human beings have evolved from primitive ancestors. It is not difficult for me to accept the "big bang" theory of the origin of the universe, at least until it is refuted by further exploration of the heavens and a new explanation is evolved to explain what God has done. Nor does it shake my religious faith to realize that the early authors of the Scriptures thought that the earth was flat, that stars were little things like Christmas tree ornaments that could fall on us, that the entire process of creation occurred during six earthly days, and that the first woman came from the rib of the first man, both Adam and Eve created in modern human form. The gap between their understanding and ours just indicates that knowledge was revealed later to Galileo, Newton, Darwin, Einstein, and Hubble–and to most of us.[41]

This might appear to be a logical statement—if you decide that the Bible is fallible and that scientific opinion "until it is refuted" is of higher authority.

Incidentally, the only argument that can be made for the Bible saying that the earth is flat is inherently flawed. The Bible refers to the "face of the earth" twenty-seven times (of which one is in the New Testament). Faces are round, not flat. If medieval authors misinterpreted the passage, it was their fault and not the fault of the original writers.

Also, no Bible reference supports the statement of stars being "little things like Christmas tree ornaments," but the Bible does refer to stars falling. Revelation 8:10–11 says, "And the third angel sounded, and there fell a great star from heaven, burning as it were a lamp, and it fell upon the third part of the rivers, and upon the fountains of waters; And the name of the star is called Wormwood: and the third part of the waters became wormwood; and many men died of the waters, because they were made bitter." Note two things: It was a "great" star and had a severe impact.

Carter's views brought him into conflict with the conservative members of the Southern Baptist Convention (SBC), who had come into leadership and were turning the SBC in a more conservative direction.

Sadly, this dispute between conservative and liberal Baptists became heated. Adrian Rogers, president of the Southern Baptist Convention, said in a meeting with Carter: "I hope you will give up your secular humanism and return to Christianity."[42]

Carter responded to conservative Baptists in public. At a news conference in Albania, Carter stated, "Religious fundamentalism is always a threat to human rights, and to democracy and freedom." He also said, "I feel a threat in my own church from Baptist fundamentalists."[43] (The reference to the "threat" referred to the SBC becoming more conservative under Rogers' leadership.)

In response to the SBC's turn toward conservative Christianity, a group of five thousand moderate and liberal Baptists met in 1993 to form the Cooperative Baptist Fellowship (CBF). Carter left the SBC and joined the CBF at this time.

CONCLUSION

Carter, by his own description, is a born-again Christian. More than any other president, he has attempted to explain his religious beliefs. His description of his religious beliefs reveals that he adheres to most of the central doctrines of orthodox Christianity. However, he does deny that the Bible is inerrant.

NOTES

1. Jimmy Carter, *The Personal Beliefs of Jimmy Carter: Winner of the 2002 Nobel Peace Prize, Living Faith* (New York: Random House/Three Rivers Press, 2002), 17.

2. Ibid., 21–22.

3. Peter G. Bourne, *Jimmy Carter: A Comprehensive Biography from Plains to Postpresidency* (New York: Scribner, 1997), 31.

4. Carter, *Personal Beliefs*, 22.

5. Ibid., 77.

6. Ibid., 24.

7. Bourne, *Jimmy Carter*, 168.

8. Ibid., 169.

9. Ibid., 279.

10. Ibid.

11. Ibid., 280.

12. Ibid.

13. Carter, *Public Papers of the Presidents of the United States: Jimmy Carter, 1978.* Washington, DC: Government Printing Office, February 2, 1978. Remarks at the annual National Prayer Breakfast.

14. Carter, *Public Papers*, May 17, 1977. Question-and-answer session with Los Angeles area residents.

15. Richard G. Hutcheson Jr., *God in the White House: How Religion Has Changed the Modern Presidency* (New York: Macmillan, 1988), 133.

16. Bourne, *Jimmy Carter*, 305.

17. Carter, *Public Papers*, February 2, 1978. Remarks at the 26th Annual National Prayer Breakfast.

18. Carter, *Personal Beliefs*, 97.

19. Carter, *Public Papers*, September 2, 1980. Remarks at a question-and-answer session at a townhall meeting, Independence, Missouri.

20. Bourne, *Jimmy Carter*, 365.

21. Carter, Inaugural address, January 20, 1977.

22. Carter, *Public Papers,* January 27, 1977. Remarks at the annual National Prayer Breakfast. In his memoirs (*Keeping Faith: Memoirs of a President* [New York: Bantam Books, 1982], 19), Carter did not tell the whole story. He stated that he intended to use 2 Chronicles 7:14 "at first, . . . but after some second thoughts about how those who did not share my beliefs might misunderstand and react to the words 'wicked' and 'sin,' I chose Micah 6:8." In his memoirs, he accepted full responsibility for the change and did not discuss the role of his advisers.

23. Ibid., February 18, 1978. Remarks at a question-and-answer session at a town meeting with New Hampshire high-school students.

24. Carter, *Personal Beliefs*, 130.

25. Bourne, *Jimmy Carter*, 377.

26. Carter, *Public Papers,* October 31, 1980. Remarks at a question-and-answer session at a town meeting, Memphis, Tennessee.

27. Carter, *Keeping Faith*, 62.

28. Jimmy Carter and Rosalynn Carter, *Everything to Gain: Making the Most of the Rest of Your Life* (New York: Random House, 1987), 169.

29. Ibid.

30. Carter, *Public Papers*, November 20, 1977. Informal exchange with reporters on departure from the First Baptist Church.

31. Carter and Carter, *Everything to Gain*, 23.

32. Bourne, *Jimmy Carter*, 476.

33. Carter, *Personal Beliefs*, 20.

34. Ibid., 17.

35. Ibid., 197: "There are 'inerrantists,' who think that every word in the Bible, preferably the King James Version, is literally true. To argue about matters of this kind [he had also referred to intrachurch lawsuits] is divisive and counter-productive, but they are still burning issues within the fundamentalist Christian community." See also Bourne, *Jimmy Carter*, 467.

36. Bourne, *Jimmy Carter*, 467.

37. Carter, *Sources of Strength*, 128.

38. Ibid.

39. Ibid., *Living Faith*, 190.

40. Ibid., 192. Many conservative Christians interpret the verse to mean that the issue of women remaining silent in church services is not based on any equality or inequality before God, but rather is an issue of headship. (1 Tim. 2:11 ff.)

41. Ibid., 29.

42. Bourne, *Jimmy Carter*, 467.

43. Ibid., 497.

CHAPTER 6

GERALD FORD

LESLIE LYNCH KING JR. was born on July 14, 1913, in Omaha, Nebraska. After his mother and father divorced, his mother married Gerald Rudolff Ford. Though Ford never officially adopted his wife's son, young King began to be called Gerald Rudolph Ford and retained that name throughout his life.[1]

Gerald Ford married Elizabeth "Betty" Bloomer on October 15, 1948.

He was appointed to fill the office of vice president after Spiro Agnew's resignation and was sworn in on December 6, 1973.[2]

On August 1, 1974,[3] Ford realized that he could be president within a few days. He prayed this prayer with his wife:

God, give us strength, give us wisdom, give us guidance as the possibility of a new life confronts us. We promise to do our very best, whatever may take place. You have sustained us in the past. We have faith in Your guiding hand in the difficult and challenging days ahead. In Jesus' name we pray.

At the end of the prayer Ford quoted Proverbs 3:5–6, "Trust in the LORD with all thine heart; and lean not unto thine own understanding. In all thy ways acknowledge him, and he shall direct thy paths."[4]

During several years of his service in the U. S. House of Representatives, Ford attended a weekly prayer meeting with his colleagues John

Rhodes, Al Quie, and Mel Laird. He continued these meetings as vice president, last meeting with them on August 7, 1974, shortly before he became president.[5]

During Ford's years in Washington, DC, he attended Emmanuel Church on the Hill in Alexandria, Virginia. Ford said that his wife "taught Sunday School there," and that he "periodically spoke, at the request of the minister, to the congregation." He added, "I was not a vestryman, but I participated in various men's functions, dinners, etc., at Emmanuel. All of our children were born in Washington, and were baptized . . . at Emmanuel."[6]

Ford was sworn in as president on August 9, 1974. During his presidency, he attended St. John's Episcopal Church on Lafayette Square.[7]

When he made a speech explaining his controversial decision to grant a pardon to Richard Nixon, he said: "As we are a nation under God, so I am sworn to uphold our laws with the help of God. And I have sought such guidance and searched my own conscience with special diligence to determine the right thing for me to do with respect to my predecessor in this place, Richard Nixon, and his loyal wife and family." He added: "I do believe, with all my heart and mind and spirit, that I, not as President but as a humble servant of God, will receive justice without mercy if I fail to show mercy."[8]

Several months after Ford took office, his wife Betty was diagnosed with cancer. Several years later, Ford looked back at the impact this had on their spiritual walks:

> If the experience of the presidency itself led me to a greater reliance upon God, a greater appreciation of my religion, so did some of the critical events of those two and a half years in the White House. I remember particularly well when in September of 1974, just a few weeks after I had taken office, Betty had her bout with cancer. It was during that time that we came to a much deeper understanding of our personal relationship with Jesus Christ. At a time when human weakness and human frailty was such a real part of our lives, we were able to see clearly for the first time what the Apostle Paul meant when he wrote that Christ's strength is made perfect in our weakness. Having been through that experience, we found that we were better able to give comfort and hope to others in their time of pain.[9]

On December 17, 1974, Ford lit the national community Christmas tree. He talked about energy conservation in the lights on the tree but said: "The glow of Christmas, however, should come from a power source which we will never run short of, our abiding faith and our love of God."[10]

On January 30, 1975, Ford spoke at the National Prayer Breakfast. He said:

> On the day that I suddenly became President of the United States, after all the guests had gone, I walked through some of the empty rooms on the first floor of the White House and stopped by that marble mantle in the dining room to read the words carved in it— words that were a prayer of the first President who ever occupied the White House: "I pray to heaven to bestow the best of blessings on this house, and all that shall hereafter inhabit it," John Adams wrote. "May none but honest and wise men ever rule under this roof."
>
> I am grateful to President Adams for leaving that message and to all who have said amen to it for nearly two centuries.
>
> My own prayer is for God's continued blessing and God's continued guidance for our country and all its people whose servants we in government strive to be.[11]

In his 1975 Thanksgiving Day remarks, Ford said: "We recognize anew our national motto which proclaims 'In God We Trust.' We continue to trust. Our faith has been vindicated as we approach a bicentennial of national thanksgiving."[12]

As Ford met citizens around the country, he fielded questions about his religion. The first was in a March 13, 1976, press conference in Wilkesboro, North Carolina. A Baptist minister asked: "Mr. President, I am a Baptist minister and my question is this, sir: Why is it that we haven't had a President in the White House since Herbert Hoover that has mentioned Jesus Christ's name publicly?"

President Ford responded: "Mrs. Ford and—my oldest son, Mike, is studying the ministry up at Gordon Conwell Seminary in Massachusetts. He has taken a commitment and so have I, and I am proud of him, and I am proud of our commitment."[13]

When he was asked a similar question about a month later, on April 28 in Tyler, Texas, his response was more coherent. He was asked the following question: "Mr. President, my question is twofold. Do you believe the Bible is the inspired word of God and is truth when it says that Jesus Christ is King of Kings and Lord of Lords? Are you personally committed to Jesus Christ as King of your life? And as a political leader, will you commit your life to make Christ's principles the standard for all your decisions, whether judicial, legislative, executive, or personal?"

Ford responded: "The answer, without getting into the details, is yes. I have been, as a part of my own parents' family and as a part of our family, I think, been deeply committed. I have especially committed myself, and I think the decisions that I make every day have to be related to a higher authority than just what we as humans do. And in my opinion, this is the way that all of us can get the kind of help that's needed and necessary in the future."[14]

Ford served as president until 1977.

In his book *Presidential Campaigns*, Paul Boller Jr. commented on Carter's reputation to be an evangelical Christian and added that Ford "was something of an evangelical himself, having renewed his faith under the ministrations of the Reverend James Zeoli in the early 1960s."[15] Ford said of Zeoli: "He was a very active religious leader in the Grand Rapids area—attractive, dedicated, a very fine religious leader. He was especially close to my family, my wife and my children. And so when I became vice president and president, we continued that relationship."[16]

Billy Graham said of Ford, "I knew him to be a professing Christian, and we had several times of prayer together."[17]

Ford died on December 27, 2006 in Rancho Mirage, California.

CONCLUSION

Gerald Ford actively participated in his church throughout his lifetime. We will know little of his doctrinal beliefs until more of his correspondence and other personal papers have been released to the public.

NOTES

1. James Cannon, *Time and Chance: Gerald Ford's Appointment with History* (New York: HarperCollins, 1994), 9. Because he was never adopted, there is a possibility that Ford's name remained Leslie Lynch King Jr. to his death.

2. Ibid., 258.

3. Actually, the early morning of the next day; Ford stayed awake *late* into the evening.

4. Cannon, *Time and Chance*, 299–300.

5. Ibid., 326. Ford described the meetings in these words: "The pattern was always the same. One of us started out with a simple prayer. Then we went around the room in no predetermined sequence. When the last person had finished, we said the Lord's Prayer in unison."

6. Richard G. Hutcheson Jr., *God in the White House: How Religion Has Changed the Modern Presidency* (New York: Macmillan, 1988), 92.

7. Ibid., 94.

8. Ford, *Public Papers of the Presidents of the United States: Gerald Ford, 1974.* Washington, DC: Government Printing Office. September 8, 1974. Remarks on signing a proclamation granting pardon to Richard Nixon.

9. Ford, "Commencement Address to Gordon-Conwell Theological Seminary Graduates," May 28, 1977.

10. Ibid., December 17, 1974. Remarks at the Lighting of the National Community Christmas Tree.

11. Ibid.,, January 30, 1975. Remarks at the National Prayer Breakfast.

12. Ibid., November 25, 1975. Remarks for Thanksgiving Day.

13. Ibid., March 13, 1976. Question-and-answer session in Wilkesboro, North Carolina.

14. Ibid., April 28, 1976. Question-and-answer session at Tyler Junior College in Tyler, Texas.

15. Paul F. Boller Jr., *Presidential Campaigns* (New York and Oxford: Oxford University Press, 1984), 342–43.

16. Hutcheson, *God in the White House*, 94–95.

17. Billy Graham, *Just As I Am: The Autobiography of Billy Graham* (New York: HarperSanFrancisco/Zondervan, 1997), 466.

CHAPTER 7

RICHARD MILHOUS NIXON

RICHARD MILHOUS NIXON was born on January 9, 1913, in Yorba Linda, California.

He grew up in a religious family. His mother, Hannah Milhous, was a devout observant Quaker. In 1900, at the age of fifteen, she had a "spiritual awakening," and urged her younger sister, Jane Milhous, to "go forward and accept the Lord." In describing the scene, Jane Milhous remembered: "She said that I would feel so much stronger and feel such wonderful release from any feeling, guilty conscience, or anything like that."[1] Hannah literally interpreted Jesus' admonition to pray in a closet and did so daily for the rest of her life.

Nixon's father, Francis Nixon, grew up a Methodist. When he met Hannah Milhous in 1908 and wanted to marry her, he became a Quaker to answer any religious objections her family could have made. (The Quakers were so strict on the issue that, a century before, they had banished Dolley Madison from the Quaker faith for marrying James Madison, a non-Quaker.)

Two Quaker meetinghouses were in Richard Nixon's hometown, East Whittier, California. One was a relatively traditional Quaker meetinghouse, but the Nixon family attended the other, the East Whittier Friends. Francis Nixon taught Sunday school at this church, described as an evangelical Quaker fellowship with "music, singing, and passionate sermons."[2]

In contrast to the evangelical emphasis of their church, the Nixons observed a more traditional Quaker way of life at home. Silent prayer was encouraged and preceded each meal.

When Richard Nixon's younger brother Arthur died in August 1925, Francis Nixon turned to God for comfort and became more interested in religion. On Sundays, the Nixon family attended Sunday school, a worship service, and "a young people's meeting called Christian Endeavor" in the mornings, and another worship service in the evening.[3] While in junior high school, Richard Nixon played piano for some church services.[4]

During the 1920s, Francis Nixon took his family to Los Angeles for several revival meetings held by Aimee Semple McPherson at the Angelus Temple and Bob Schuler at the Trinity Methodist Church.[5]

In September 1926, when Richard Nixon was thirteen, Francis Nixon took his sons to hear evangelist Paul Rader speak. At the altar call, Richard Nixon went forward and, in his own words, "joined hundreds of others that night in making our personal commitments to Christ and Christian service."[6]

Nixon became known for holding to orthodox doctrines. His friend Raymond Burbank, who later became a Quaker minister, said: "Dick would be the one who could stand up for the position of the church, and know why. He could set them straight."[7]

In his own words, Nixon stated that during his youth, he "accepted as facts" the "infallibility and literal correctness of the Bible, the miracles, even the whale story."[8]

While Nixon attended Whittier College, he maintained the same pace of church attendance he had kept as a child, still attending East Whittier Friends. He also led the church's gospel team: In the words of biographer Roger Morris, Nixon could be found "preaching and debating before youth groups and other congregations with his own revivalist zeal."[9]

Before he went to college, his parents warned him "not to be misled by college professors who might be a little too liberal in their views" (Richard Nixon's words).[10] However, this is precisely what happened.

His faith was "shattered"[11] by the death of his brother Harold on March 7, 1933.[12] After this, his doctrines moved toward a liberal viewpoint.

In 1933, he attended a series of lectures on "The Philosophy of Christian Reconstruction" by Dr. J. Herschel Coffin.[13] A series of papers Nixon prepared for this course, entitled "What Can I Believe?", marked a major turning point in his religious beliefs. His views, which had reflected an evangelical, orthodox Christian worldview, became less orthodox during this course—though his beliefs always retained some orthodoxy. In his essays, he wrote:

> My parents, "fundamental Quakers," had ground into me, with the aid of the church, all the fundamental ideas in their strictest interpretation. The infallibility and literal correctness of the Bible, the miracles, even the whale story, all these I accepted as facts when I entered college four years ago. Even then I could not forget the admonition not to be misled by college professors who might be a little too liberal in their views! Many of these childhood ideas have been destroyed but there are some which I cannot bring myself to drop. To me, the greatness of the universe is too much for me to explain. I still believe that God is the creator, the first cause of all that exists. I still believe that He lives today, in some form, directing the destinies of the cosmos. How can I reconcile this idea with my scientific method? It is of course an unanswerable question. However, for the time being I shall accept the solution offered by Kant, that man can only go so far in his research and explanations; from that point on we must accept God. What is unknown to man, God knows.[14]

He also wrote:

> I am no longer a 'seven day-er'! In declaring that God created the world, I am only acknowledging that my own mind is not capable of explaining it any other way. . . . My education has taught me that the Bible, like all other books, is a work of man and consequently has man-made mistakes. Now I desire to find a suitable explanation of man's and the universe's creation, an explanation that will fit not only with my idea of God but also with what my mind tells me is right. I want to know why I am here in order that I may better find my place in life."[15]

In light of these statements, it is interesting to note the way he phrased a statement in his second inaugural address. He said: "Let us go forward from here confident in hope, strong in our faith in one another, sustained by our faith in God who created us, and striving always to serve His purpose."[16]

About Jesus, he wrote:

> I even go so far as to say Jesus and God are one, because Jesus set the great example which is forever pulling men upward to the ideal life. His life was so perfect that he "mingled" his soul with God's. . . .
>
> It is not necessary to show that Jesus rose from the dead on the third day and then lived on earth for forty days with his disciples before ascending into heaven. The important fact is that Jesus lived and taught a life so perfect that he continued to live and grow after his death—in the hearts of men. It may be true that the resurrection story is a myth, but symbolically it teaches the great lesson that men who achieve the highest values in their lives may gain immortality.[17]

In another essay in his series, he wrote: "My beliefs are shattered, but in their place a new philosophy has been built. Some of the fragments of my own religion have proved useful in building this new philosophy."[18]

He concluded his series with these words:

> I have as my ideal the life of Jesus. I know that the social system which he suggested would be a great boon to the world. I believe that his system of values is unsurpassed. It shall be my purpose in life, therefore, to follow the religion of Jesus as well as I can. I feel that I must apply his principles to whatever profession I may find myself attached. What Do I Believe? My answer to this question could have been better called, "What shall I do with the religion of Jesus?" For to me this intellectual log has proved to be a gradual evolution towards an understanding of the religion of Jesus. My greatest desire is that I may now apply this understanding to my life.[19]

In this essay series, he noted a change of beliefs on doctrines such as Christ's divinity, His literal resurrection, the inspiration of the Bible, and a literal seven-day creation.

In spite of his inner turmoil, he taught the college-age Sunday school class at East Whittier Friends during his college years.[20]

Later in life, in a conversation with Billy Graham, Nixon said he had been converted when young, and added: "Pray for me. I'm a backslider."[21] In Graham's autobiography *Just as I Am*, he told of another conversation with Nixon:

> Before his mother's funeral service, he [Nixon] talked with me for a few minutes about her faith.
> "Dick, do you have that kind of faith?" I asked.
> "I believe I do," he said quietly.
> "That's the only way you can be guided in life, and it's the only way you can get to Heaven," I said, and then I prayed for him. He later told me that it was one of the great moments of his life, and I believe he meant it.[22]

Nixon married Thelma Catherine ("Patricia") Ryan on June 21, 1940. He was elected president in 1968 and served from 1969 through 1974.

Investigative reporter Anthony Summers said that Nixon admired Catholicism and considered converting to that religion before the 1972 presidential election.[23] John Erlichman said that Nixon told him at times that the Quaker faith was "more authentic" and at other times would say, "You know, if I were ever to embrace a religion, it would be Catholicism, because they're so well disciplined in their dogma, so well defined."[24]

While Nixon was president, he regularly attended Key Biscayne Presbyterian Church when he was in Key Biscayne. His friend Bebe Rebozo regularly attended the church and introduced him to the church's pastor, Reverend John Huffman.[25]

On April 29, 1973, when Nixon asked H. R. Haldeman, his chief of staff, to resign, he told Haldeman (in Haldeman's words):

> We got inside and he went through a discourse, saying that while nobody knows it, and he's not a publicly religious man, that it's a fact that he has prayed on his knees every night that he has been in the Presidential office. He's prayed hard over this decision, and it's the toughest decision he's ever made. He made the points on why he had to do it, but he's come to the conclusion that he has to have our resignations.[26]

Nixon made numerous religious statements while president. In a 1969 statement about National Bible Week, Nixon quoted something that Benjamin Franklin had said. "I am especially reminded," Nixon said, "of Benjamin Franklin's immortal thought when he remarked that if no sparrow can fall to the ground without His [God's] notice, no nation can rise from the ground without His help."[27]

In a speech at the 1972 National Prayer Breakfast, Nixon said:

In the great agony of the War Between the States, which Abraham Lincoln so eloquently expressed in his Second Inaugural, he pointed out that devout men on both sides prayed to the same God. And in pointing it out, he, of course, expressed what all of us need to understand here today: that because of our faith we are not perfect, because of our faith we are not superior. Only the way we live, what we do, will deserve the plaudits of the world or of this Nation or even of our own self-satisfaction.

In that same period, as the war was drawing to an end, a man came to Lincoln and said, "Is God on our side?" And Lincoln's answer, you will all remember, was, "I am more concerned not whether God is on our side, but whether we are on God's side."

Virtually everyone this morning who has prayed, has prayed for the President of the United States, and for that, as a person, I am deeply grateful. But as you pray in the future, as these journeys take place, will you pray primarily that this Nation, under God, in the person of its President, will, to the best of our ability, be on God's side.[28]

On January 31, 1974, Nixon again spoke at the National Prayer Breakfast. In his remarks he said:

My father, who was a Methodist, believed very strongly in spoken prayer, and my mother, who was a Quaker, believed in silent prayer, and both agreed that there was a place for both.

When I was 8 or 9 years old, I asked my grandmother—a very saintly woman, a little Quaker lady who had nine children—I asked her why it was that the Quakers believed in silent prayer. When we sat down to table we always had silent grace, and often at church, while we sometimes would have a minister or somebody got up when the spirit moved him, we often just went there and sat and we prayed.

Her answer was very interesting, and perhaps it relates to why Lincoln prayed in silence. My grandmother spoke to me on this occasion, as she always did to her grandchildren and children, with the plain speech. She said, "What thee must understand, Richard, is that the purpose of prayer is to listen to God, not to talk to God. The purpose of prayer is not to tell God what thee wants but to find out from God what He wants from thee."

Later in the speech, he returned to the topic of prayer:

So, my friends, may I thank you all for the prayers that I know you have offered for our national leaders; may I urge you all, whatever your faiths may be, to pray in the future at times, perhaps, in silence. Why? Because too often I think we are a little too arrogant. We try to talk to God and tell Him what we want, and what all of us need to do and what this Nation needs to do is to pray in silence and listen to God and find out what He wants for us, and then we will all do the right thing.[29]

He also discussed the role of America in the world and expressed his belief that our destiny is not "to conquer any other country" nor "to start [a] war against any other country" but "to defend" freedom. He said that we must "recognize the right of people in the world to be different from what we are," even though "some may have different religions. Even some, we must accept, may not have a religious belief, as we understand a religious belief, to believe." He added:

But on the other hand, while I know this goes counter to the ideas of many of my good friends in this audience who believe as my mother and father deeply believed in the missionary work of our church, I think that America today must understand that it is in its role as a world leader that we can only have peace in the world if we respect the rights, the views of our neighbors, our friends, and of the people of all the nations of the world.[30]

H. R. Haldeman, Nixon's chief of staff, stated in his diaries that although Nixon attended and spoke at the prayer breakfasts, he did not like them. In a diary entry for February 2, 1972, Haldeman said: "Day started with Prayer Breakfast, which he regards as total torture at best. This one went pretty well except that the Chief Justice, who was supposed to be the main speaker and go on for only twenty minutes, took twenty-five minutes to explain word-for-word over and over the true meaning of the 23rd Psalm."[31]

During and after his presidency, Nixon adopted liberal stands on issues such as abortion and homosexuality. He once expressed his position on abortion in these words: "I don't want to hear about abortion. That's people's own business. Tolerance in this party is far too low."[32]

In the same statement, he also said: "So many people are gay—or go both ways. I don't care. I don't want to hear about it. . . . We've got to reach out—and mean it."[33]

However, he did not believe that homosexuals should be permitted to serve in the military. He said: "I have nothing against gays. We had plenty of them in my administration. I don't care what people do behind closed doors; that's their own business. But life in the military is not life behind closed doors; it's life without doors, literally. As a practical matter, gays do not belong in the trenches. It is not about their ability to fight; it is about living in close quarters without having to worry about the tension."[34]

In 1990, Nixon wrote *In the Arena*, a book of his recollections and views. He included a chapter on his religion, in which he quoted this passage from his college essays on religion:

> I still believe that God is the creator, the first cause of all that exists. . . . How can I reconcile this idea with my scientific method? . . . For the time being I shall accept the solution offered by Kant, that man can only go so far in his research and explanations; from that point on we must accept God. What is unknown to man, God knows. The resurrection symbolically teaches the great lesson that men who achieve the highest values in their lives may gain immortality. Orthodox teachers have always insisted that the physical resurrection of Jesus is the most important cornerstone in the Christian religion. I believe that the modern world will find a real resurrection in the life and teachings of Jesus.[35]

He added that he "adhere[d] to those same beliefs to this day."[36]

Throughout his life, he maintained a high respect for the Bible and read it regularly.[37] He wrote biographer Jonathan Aitken: "I did not read it every day which was my custom in my earlier years, but I probably read it more often than many of those who wear their religion on their sleeves." He also stated: "Incidentally, I always read the King James version. I am really turned off by all of these modern translations."[38]

However, he maintained the view of the Bible's fallibility into his old age. In his book *In the Arena*, he included a chapter on his wife, Pat. He said: "The Bible is a wellspring of truths, but it contains one falsehood—that women are the weaker sex. Statistics tell us that women live longer than men. Experience tells me that women are stronger, too, physically, mentally, and emotionally. Whether it was confronting the Fund crisis, facing a killer mob in Caracas, standing up to anti-war demonstrators, or going through the ordeal of resignation, Pat was always stronger. Without her, I could not have done what I did."[39] If the Bible said one thing and statistics said another, Nixon would have chosen to believe the statistics, placing statistics on a higher level of authority.

By one account, however, his views on the issue of the Bible's inspiration may have moved back toward his childhood views. In Billy Graham's autobiography, Graham stated: "I had some misgivings about Nixon's religious understanding, based on what glimpses I got, but then he was a layman in such matters, not a biblical scholar. I've never doubted the sincerity of his spiritual concern, though, or the sincerity of his identification with the evangelical position toward the authority of the Bible and the person of Christ. He told me, 'I believe the Bible from cover to cover.' "[40]

Patricia Nixon died on June 22, 1993. Richard Nixon died less than a year later on April 22, 1994. At Nixon's funeral, Billy Graham said:

"For the believer who has been to the Cross, death is no frightful leap into the dark, but is an entrance into a glorious new life. . . .

"For the believer, the brutal fact of death has been conquered by the resurrection of Jesus Christ.

"For the person who has turned from sin and has received Christ as Lord and Savior, death is not the end.

"For the believer there is *hope* beyond the grave. . . .

"Richard Nixon had that hope, and today that can be our hope as well."[41]

CONCLUSION

Nixon made a personal commitment to Christ at age thirteen. He became quite involved in his church and remained so through the rest of his youth.

When he went to college, his mother warned him to not be misled by liberal professors. But his college essays reveal a young man unable to defend his biblical beliefs from arguments made against them. Rather than seeking evidence to defend his beliefs, he modified them to a more liberal stance. As his life progressed, his views on some doctrines moved closer to his original orthodox position, but his views on other doctrines remained unchanged.

Once, when Nixon was talking with Billy Graham about Hannah Milhous Nixon's deeply held religious faith, Graham asked him if he had that kind of faith. Nixon quietly responded: "I believe I do."

NOTES

1. Roger Morris, *Richard Milhous Nixon: The Rise of an American Politician* (New York: Henry Holt, 1990), 31.

2. Anthony Summers, *The Arrogance of Power* (London: Weidenfeld & Nicholson, 2001), 11.

3. Ibid.

4. Morris, *Richard Milhous Nixon*, 86.

5. Ibid., 87.

6. Ibid.

7. Ibid.

8. Morris, *Richard Milhous Nixon*, 128. In Nixon's words found in his series of papers, "What Can I Believe?"

9. Ibid., 127.

10. Ibid., 128; Jonathan Aitken, *Nixon: A Life* (Washington, DC: Regnery, 1993), 43.

11. Nixon's word. Aitken, *Nixon*, 56.

12. Summers, *The Arrogance of Power*, 11–12.

13. Aitken, *Nixon*, 55.

14. Morris, *Richard Milhous Nixon*, 128.

15. Aitken, *Nixon*, 55.

16. Nixon, Second inaugural address, January 20, 1973.

17. Morris, *Richard Milhous Nixon*, 128–29. Aitken, *Nixon*, 57.

18. Aitken, *Nixon*, 56.

19. Ibid., 57.

20. Morris, *Richard Milhous Nixon*, 220.

21. Summers, *The Arrogance of Power*, 12.

22. Billy Graham, *Just As I Am: The Autobiography of Billy Graham* (New York: HarperSanFrancisco/Zondervan, 1997), 461.

23. Summers, *The Arrogance of Power*, 12.

24. Ibid., 12.

25. Hutcheson, *God in the White House*, 83.

26. Harry R. Haldeman, *The Haldeman Diaries: Inside the Nixon White House* (New York: G. P. Putnam's Sons, 1994), 672.

27. Nixon, *Public Papers of the Presidents of the United States: Richard Milhous Nixon, 1969*. Washington, DC: Government Printing Office. October 22, 1969. Statement about the National Bible Week.

28. Ibid., February 1, 1972. Remarks at the National Prayer Breakfast.

29. Ibid., January 31, 1974. Remarks at the National Prayer Breakfast.

30. Ibid.

31. Haldeman, *The Haldeman Diaries*, 241.

32. Monica Crowley, *Nixon Off the Record: His Candid Commentary on People and Politics* (New York: Random House, 1996), 109.

33. Ibid.

34. Ibid., 135.

35. Richard Nixon, *In the Arena: A Memoir of Victory, Defeat, and Renewal* (New York: Simon & Schuster, 1990), 88–89.

36. Ibid.

37. Ibid., 88.

38. Aitken, *Nixon*, 338.

39. Nixon, *In the Arena*, 235.

40. Graham, *Just As I Am*, 459.

41. Ibid., 465.

★

CHAPTER 8

LYNDON BAINES JOHNSON

L YNDON BAINES JOHNSON was born on August 27, 1908, near
Stonewall, Texas. His family had been Baptist for generations; his
great-grandfather, George Washington Baines Sr., became a Baptist
minister at age 25.[1] Baines began preaching in Alabama and planted
churches in Arkansas and Louisiana before ending up in Texas, where
he became the second president of Baylor University. In a 1964 speech
to members of the Southern Baptist Convention Leadership Seminar,
Johnson explained the religious heritage passed down in his family,
specifically mentioning Baines but added: "It is not good to dwell on
the past, for faith is a personal power by which we live today and not a
monument for the dead. The faith of our fathers, the faith of men like
George Baines, may become the folly of their children if individually
we fail to see God face to face. No man knows that better than I do."[2]

In a March 26, 1968, speech to the Christian Citizenship Seminar
of Southern Baptist Leaders, Johnson emphasized that he grew up in a
family full of Baptists. He said: "I am not fortunate enough to be a
Baptist. I am a member of the Disciples of Christ, but I have always felt
very close to your denomination. Everybody else in my household that
I grew up in was Baptist. My part of the country is Baptist. My mother
was a Baptist. My grandfather and great-grandfather were Baptists.
George Washington Baines was an early Baptist preacher who became
the second President of Baylor University during the Civil War.

"He came to Texas in a buckboard to be a circuit-riding preacher.
He came the way that most of the Baptists came to the frontier: very

early, by the cheapest form of transportation. He was determined to do one thing—and that was save souls."[3]

Why did Lyndon Baines Johnson become a member of the Disciples of Christ? In his autobiography, *Just as I Am*, Billy Graham said that Johnson joined the Christian Church "at some point because it was nearest to his home."[4] The Disciples of Christ church in Johnson City was a member of the International Convention of Christian Churches.[5]

Johnson married Claudia Alta "Lady Bird" Taylor on November 17, 1934. Since she was an Episcopalian, the Johnsons raised their daughters in the Episcopal Church, though their daughter Luci later converted to Catholicism.

Johnson became president after Kennedy's assassination on November 22, 1963. In Parkland Memorial Hospital in Dallas when he heard that Kennedy was dead, he told Congressman Homer Thornberry, "This is a time for prayer if there ever was one, Homer."[6]

Plans had to be improvised quickly. It was arranged that Johnson would take the oath of office on board *Air Force One*. Just before he took the oath, a book thought to be a Bible was produced for him to place his hand on. However, several writers believe that the book was not Kennedy's Bible but rather was his Catholic missal. Interestingly enough, Johnson himself eventually concluded that he had been sworn in on a Catholic missal. In his memoirs, he said: "Larry O'Brien went to look for a Bible, and he returned with a Catholic missal, unopened in its original box."[7]

Lyndon Baines Johnson made a brief statement shortly after his sudden accession to the presidency. He said:

> This is a sad time for all people. We have suffered a loss that cannot be weighed. For me, it is a deep personal tragedy. I know that the world shares the sorrow that Mrs. Kennedy and her family bear. I will do my best. That is all I can do. I ask for your help—and God's.[8]

One of Johnson's highest priorities in office was to turn America into a welfare state. On April 17, 1964, Lyndon Johnson spoke to members of the American Society of Newspaper Editors. He believed that part of our nation's duty as a "Christian society" was to "visit the widow and the fatherless" and to provide "the foundation for a better life for all humanity." He believed that this was not only the duty of individuals, but also the duty of the government of a Christian society. He said:

> The world is no longer the world that your fathers and mine once knew. Once it was dominated by the balance of power. Today, it is diffused and emergent. But though most of the world struggles fitfully to assert its own initiative, the people of the world look to this land for inspiration. Two-thirds of the teeming masses of humanity, most of them in their tender years under 40, are decreeing that they are not going to take it without food to sustain their body and a roof over their head.
>
> And from our science and our technology, from our compassion and from our tolerance, from our unity and from our heritage, we stand uniquely on the threshold of a high adventure of leadership by example and by precept. "Not by might, nor by power, but by my spirit, saith the Lord." From our Jewish and Christian heritage, we draw the image of the God of all mankind, who will judge his children not by their prayers and by their pretensions, but by their mercy to the poor and their understanding of the weak.
>
> We cannot cancel that strain and then claim to speak as a Christian society. To visit the widow and the fatherless in their affliction is still pure religion and undefiled. I tremble for this Nation. I tremble for our people if at the time of our greatest prosperity we turn our back on the moral obligations of our deepest faith. If the face we turn to this aspiring, laboring world is a face of indifference and contempt, it will rightly rise up and strike us down.
>
> Believe me, God is not mocked. We reap as we sow. Our God is still a jealous God, jealous of his righteousness, jealous of his mercy, jealous for the last of the little ones who went unfed while the rich sat down to eat and rose up to play. And unless my administration profits the present and provides the foundation for a better life for all humanity, not just now but for generations to come, I shall have failed.[9]

Eventually, the pressures of the Vietnam War shifted Johnson's primary focus away from his welfare-state programs. Mounting casualties forced Johnson to do some soul-searching about his responsibilities in the conflict. In a conversation with investigative journalist Jack Anderson, Johnson stated that the pressures of "sending young men on missions knowing some of them aren't going to return" were weighing heavily on his shoulders. He said, "I believe that I'm doing right. I believe their sacrifice will save many lives. But I'm just not sure. I pray about it. But it's hard to know what God wants you to do."[10]

Though Johnson was a member of the Disciples of Christ Church and frequently attended the National City Christian Church in Washington, DC, and the First Christian Church in Johnson City, Texas, he visited many different churches. One of the churches he visited most frequently with his wife was St. Mark's Episcopal Church, where he sometimes received communion. When a clergyman rebuked him for doing so, the church's rector and the bishop of Washington welcomed him as a communicant. Johnson also visited Roman Catholic churches frequently during his presidency, going to mass in Washington, DC, and in Texas fourteen times in 1967 alone.[11]

Johnson became friends with Billy Graham. In Graham's autobiography, he recounted several conversations the two men had shared on religious matters. One took place on Johnson's Texas ranch. Graham asked:

"Mr. President, have you ever personally, definitely received Jesus Christ as your Savior?"

He gazed out across the landscape. "Well, Billy, I think I have."

I waited quietly for more.

"I did as a boy at a revival meeting." He paused. "I did reading one of the sermons in my great-grandfather's book of evangelistic sermons." Another pause. "I guess I've done it *several* times."

"When someone says that, Mr. President," I said carefully, "I don't feel too sure of it."

He looked at me with a puzzled expression.

"It's a once-for-all transaction," I said. "You receive Christ and He saves you. His Spirit bears witness with your spirit that you're a child of God."

He nodded. I did not feel that this was the time to say more, but I knew he would be thinking about what I had said.[12]

Graham summarized Johnson's Christianity in these words:

I tried to be a spiritual counselor to Lyndon Johnson, but I was not his confessor. He said to me that he had done a lot of things of which he was ashamed, though he refused to go into detail. He was, however, able to express his belief: "I believe I am saved and that I will spend eternity in Heaven." Nothing I knew personally about him contradicted that. Christ came to save sinners, not the righteous, as He Himself said (*see* Luke 5:32).[13]

Johnson served as president until 1969. He died on January 22, 1973, in San Antonio, Texas. Johnson had asked Billy Graham to preach his burial sermon. He said: "Billy, one day you're going to preach at my funeral. . . . You'll read the Bible, of course, and preach the Gospel. I want you to. But I hope you'll also tell folks some of the things I tried to do."[14] Graham did, indeed, preach at Johnson's burial.

CONCLUSION

Johnson was a member of the Disciples of Christ Church, a communicant in the Episcopalian Church, and a visitor to churches of other denominations. When speaking with Billy Graham, Johnson said: "I believe I am saved and that I will spend eternity in Heaven." While we know little about what he believed on specific doctrines by which orthodoxy is customarily measured, we know nothing that would contradict this belief.

NOTES

1. Robert Dallek, *Lyndon Johnson and His Times.* Vol. 1, *Lone Star Rising, 1908–1960* (New York and Oxford: Oxford University Press, 1991, 1998), 26.
2. Johnson, *Public Papers of the President of the United States: Lyndon B. Johnson, 1964.* Washington, DC: Government Printing Office. March 25, 1964. Remarks to members of the Southern Baptist Christian Leadership Seminar.
3. Ibid., March 26, 1968. Remarks to the Christian Citizenship Seminar of Southern Baptist Leaders.
4. Billy Graham, *Just As I Am: The Autobiography of Billy Graham* (New York: HarperSanFrancisco/Zondervan, 1997), 405.
5. Edmund Fuller and David E. Green, *God in the White House: The Faiths of American Presidents* (New York: Crown Publishers, 1968), 224.

6. William Manchester, *The Death of a President* (New York: Harper & Row, 1967), 232.

7. Lyndon B. Johnson, *The Vantage Point: Perspectives of the Presidency, 1963–1969* (New York: Holt, Rinehart & Winston, 1971), 15.

8. Sol Barzman, *Madmen and Geniuses: The Vice Presidents of the United States* (Chicago: Follett, 1974), 270.

9. Johnson, *Public Papers*, April 17, 1964. Remarks to the American Society of Newspaper Editors.

10. Jack Anderson, *Peace, War, and Politics* (New York: Tom Doherty Associates, 1999), 134.

11. Joseph A. Califano Jr., *The Triumph and Tragedy of Lyndon Johnson: The White House Years* (New York: Simon & Schuster, 1991), 334–35

12. Graham, *Just As I Am*, 412.

13. Ibid., 414.

14. Ibid., 403.

CHAPTER 9

JOHN FITZGERALD KENNEDY

John F. Kennedy was born on May 29, 1917, in Brookline, Massachusetts. His parents were Roman Catholics; his mother, Rose, was even eventually named a papal countess by the Vatican.[1] In her memoirs, *Times to Remember,* Rose Kennedy said: "Religion was never oppressive nor even conspicuous in our household, but it was always there, part of our lives, and the church's teachings and customs were observed."[2]

As a young man, John F. Kennedy expressed doubts about his Roman Catholicism. These would almost not be worth mentioning except for two facts. First, in his youth he talked more about his religion than he did when he was older. Second, thus far I have found no record of his opinions changing. (Other historians have flatly stated that these are his only recorded religious opinions.[3] I will not yet make such a definitive statement.)

As a young man, he wrote his mother: "We're not a completely ritualistic, formalistic, hierarchical structure in which the Word, the truth, must only come down from the very top–a structure that allows for no individual interpretation–or are we?"[4]

In 1939, Kennedy toured Europe. After his return, he asked a Catholic priest, "I saw the rock where our Lord ascended into Heaven in a cloud, and [in] the same area, I saw the place where Muhammad was carried up to Heaven on a white horse, and Muhammad has a big following and Christ has a big following, and why do you think we should believe Christ any more than Muhammad?"

The priest feared Jack would turn into an "atheist if he didn't get some of his problems straightened out."[5]

One of his friends at Harvard University observed him attending mass on a holy day and asked him why. He seemed to get an "odd, hard" look on his face, and responded, "This is one of the things I do for my father. The rest I do for myself."[6] However, he would only go so far for his father. According to historian Doug Wead, Kennedy threatened to join a Protestant Bible class in 1942 after his parents had him end a relationship with a girlfriend.[7]

After his young adulthood, Kennedy made few statements about his religion. However, he faithfully adhered to the external forms of Roman Catholicism and regularly attended Sunday mass. As president, he continued the practice, noting that the attendance of reporters and photographers had "surely done them no harm."[8] His friend Dave Powers stated that Kennedy prayed every night on his knees at his bedside.[9] He also took his Bible with him when he traveled on *Air Force One*: According to William Manchester, Kennedy would "read it evenings before snapping off the night light."[10] His initials were embroidered on the back cover.

However, his speechwriter and friend Theodore Sorensen said:

> While he was both a Catholic and a scholar, he could not be called a Catholic scholar. He cared not a whit for theology, sprinkled quotations from the Protestant version of the Bible in his speeches, and once startled and amused his wife by reading his favorite passage from Ecclesiastes (". . . a time to weep and a time to laugh, a time to mourn and a time to dance . . .) with his own irreverent addition from the political world: "a time to fish and a time to cut bait."[11]

Sorensen said that he "never heard him pray aloud in the presence of others." He also stated that "not once in eleven years—despite all our discussions of church-state affairs—did he ever disclose his personal views on man's relation to God."[12]

Sorensen also said: "He did not believe that all virtue resided in the Catholic Church, nor did he believe that all non-Catholics would (or should) go to hell. He felt neither self-conscious nor superior about his religion but simply accepted it as part of his life."[13]

Kennedy married Jacqueline Bouvier on September 12, 1953.

During the 1960 presidential campaign, the issue of Kennedy's Catholicism came up. He emphatically stated that he was not "the Catholic candidate for President" but was the "Democratic Party's candidate for President who happens also to be a Catholic." He even said that if his conscience did not permit him to take a necessary action, he would resign his office rather than violate the national interest.

Some Protestants feared that a Roman Catholic mass might be held in the White House. Theodore Sorensen called this "the least explicable religious objection" encountered during the campaign. "To those who expressed this worry," Sorenson said, "I can give assurance that it happened only once—on November 23, 1963."[14] Incidentally, as this was after Kennedy's death, this sole Roman Catholic mass was actually held during the presidency of a member of a Protestant church.

Kennedy concluded his inaugural address with a request for God's blessing and help. He said: "With a good conscience our only sure reward, with history the final judge of our deeds, let us go forth to lead the land we love, asking His blessing and His help, but knowing that here on earth God's work must truly be our own."[15]

In the speech, he also included part of Isaiah 58:6: "Let both sides unite to heed in all corners of the earth the command of Isaiah—to 'undo the heavy burdens, to let the oppressed go free.' "[16]

Perhaps as a way to reassure concerned Protestants, Kennedy made numerous religious statements as president. On February 9, 1961, he spoke to the dedication breakfast of International Christian Leadership Inc. about the faith of the presidents of the United States:

> No man who enters upon the office to which I have succeeded can fail to recognize how every President of the United States has placed special reliance upon his faith in God. Every President has taken comfort and courage when told, as we are told today, that the Lord "will be with thee. He will not fail thee nor forsake thee. Fear not—neither be thou dismayed."
>
> While they came from a wide variety of religious backgrounds and held a wide variety of religious beliefs, each of our Presidents in his own way has placed a special trust in God. Those who were strongest intellectually were also strongest spiritually.[17]

In remarks at the eleventh annual Presidential Prayer Breakfast (1961), he said:

We cannot depend solely on our material wealth, on our military might, or on our intellectual skill or physical courage to see us safely through the seas that we must sail in the months and years to come.

Along with all of these we need faith. We need the faith with which our first settlers crossed the sea to carve out a state in the wilderness, a mission they said in the Pilgrims' Compact, the Mayflower Compact, undertaken for the glory of God. We need the faith with which our Founding Fathers proudly proclaimed the independence of this country to what seemed at that time an almost hopeless struggle, pledging their lives, their fortunes, and their sacred honor with a firm reliance on the protection of divine providence. We need the faith which has sustained and guided this Nation for 175 long and short years. We are all builders of the future, and whether we build as public servants or private citizens, whether we build at the national or the local level, whether we build in foreign or domestic affairs, we know the truth of the ancient Psalm, "Except the Lord build the house, they labour in vain that build it."[18]

In some of his public statements, Kennedy discussed moral law and its religious foundation. In a 1961 speech to the officers of the National Conference of Christians and Jews, he said: "It has always seemed to me that when we all—regardless of our particular religious convictions—draw our guidance and inspiration, and really in a sense moral direction from the same general area, the Bible, the Old and the New Testaments, we have every reason to believe that our various religious denominations should live together in the closest harmony.

"We have a great advantage, really, in so much of the world, in having such common roots, and therefore though our convictions may take us in different directions in our faith, nevertheless the basic presumption of the moral law, the existence of God, man's relation to Him—there is generally consensus on those questions."[19]

Yet Kennedy could also be offended by moral law questions. Theodore Sorensen related this incident: "A priest, angered by his answer at a Catholic girls' school that 'recognition of Red China was not a moral issue,' asked him, 'Senator Kennedy, do you not believe that all law comes from God?' The Senator snapped back, 'I'm a Catholic, so of course I believe it—but that has nothing to do with international law.' "[20]

In his first Thanksgiving proclamation issued on October 28, 1961, he said:

> "It is a good thing to give thanks unto the Lord."
> More than three centuries ago, the Pilgrims, after a year of hardship and peril, humbly and reverently set aside a special day upon which to give thanks to God for their preservation and for the good harvest from the virgin soil upon which they had labored. Grave and unknown dangers remained. Yet by their faith and by their toil they had survived the rigors of the harsh New England winter. Hence they paused in their labors to give thanks for the blessings that had been bestowed upon them by Divine Providence.[21]

Kennedy then listed America's blessings of freedom and material benefits. He urged Americans to spend the day in contemplation, reverence, and prayer, and said: "I ask the head of each family to recount to his children the story of the first New England Thanksgiving, thus to impress upon future generations the heritage of this nation born in toil, in danger, in purpose, and in the conviction that right and justice and freedom can through man's efforts persevere and come to fruition with the blessing of God."[22]

In his annual Message to Congress on the State of the Union, delivered on January 14, 1963, he concluded by saying: "Today we still welcome those winds of change—and we have every reason to believe that our tide is running strong. With thanks to Almighty God for seeing us through a perilous passage, we ask His help anew in guiding the 'Good Ship Union.' "[23]

Kennedy observed at the one hundredth anniversary of Lincoln's Emancipation Proclamation in January 1963 that "righteousness does exalt a nation." He also cited other things that he believed exalted a nation, including "services instead of support, rehabilitation instead of relief, and training for useful work instead of prolonged dependency," improvements in government health care, creating the National Institutes of Health, and mass immunization programs.[24]

In Kennedy's third Thanksgiving proclamation, issued on November 5, 1963, he said: "Let us therefore proclaim our gratitude to Providence for manifold blessings—let us be humbly thankful for inherited ideals—and let us resolve to share those blessings and those ideals with our fellow human beings throughout the world." He then named

Thursday, November 28, 1963, as "a day of national thanksgiving." "On that day," he said, "let us gather in sanctuaries dedicated to worship and in homes blessed by family affection to express our gratitude for the glorious gifts of God; and let us earnestly and humbly pray that He will continue to guide and sustain us in the great unfinished tasks of achieving peace, justice, and understanding among all men and nations and of ending misery and suffering wherever they exist."[25]

In public, then, Kennedy upheld America's civil religion—a belief in a God who guides the destinies of nations and the decisions of their leaders. What do those who knew Kennedy personally say about his religion?

Arthur Krock, a friend of the Kennedys, reported a comment that Jacqueline made on her husband's devotion to his faith. In the 1960 presidential campaign, Kennedy was receiving some harsh treatment in the press due to his Roman Catholicism. Jackie responded to this by telling Arthur Krock: "I think it is so unfair for Jack to be opposed because he is a Catholic. After all, he's such a poor Catholic. Now if it were Bobby; he never misses mass and prays all the time."[26]

Kennedy's sister, Eunice Kennedy Shriver, said the same thing but more bluntly. When a person suggested that a book should be written on Kennedy and his Catholicism, she responded: "It will be an awfully slim volume."[27]

Of all the statements about his religion, these two are by the people who knew him best. Some friends have described him as more religious. Perhaps the truth lies somewhere between his friends' rosy portrait and his family's blunt statements. Kennedy's public image may not have conveyed his private thoughts.

Kennedy did not express a hope of life after death. "I feel that death is the end of a lot of things," he said. "I just hope the Lord gives me the time to get all these things done."[28]

Billy Graham saw another side of Kennedy's views—perhaps a lack of hope but an interest in eventually knowing more. In his autobiography, *Just as I Am*, Graham described a conversation with Kennedy while the latter was president-elect:

> On the way back to the Kennedy house, the President-elect stopped the car and turned to me. "Do you believe in the Second Coming of Jesus Christ?" he asked unexpectedly.
>
> "I most certainly do."
>
> "Well, does *my* church believe it?"

"They have it in their creeds."

"They don't preach it," he said. "They don't tell us much about it. I'd like to know what you think."

I explained what the Bible said about Christ coming the first time, dying on the cross, rising from the dead, and then promising that He would come back again. "Only then," I said, "are we going to have permanent world peace."

"Very interesting," he said, looking away. "We'll have to talk more about that someday."[29]

In his autobiography, Graham also said: "One couldn't help but like Kennedy personally. As far as his own spiritual commitment was concerned, I really had no idea."[30]

CONCLUSION

Kennedy accepted the outward ritual of Catholicism as part of his heritage. Yet I have to agree with his sister Eunice that a book about Kennedy's religion must remain an "awfully slim volume." It appears that religion was simply not a priority in his life. When he considered it, he probably thought he had decades left to turn to God.

NOTES

1. Carl Sferazza Anthony, *The Kennedy White House: Family Life and Pictures, 1961–1963* (London: Touchstone, 2001), 93.

2. Rose Fitzgerald Kennedy, *Times to Remember* (Garden City, NY: Doubleday, 1974), 161.

3. Anthony, *The Kennedy White House*, 92.

4. Ibid. Anthony stated: "There are no further recorded statements about what direction Kennedy's Catholicism took." However, Anthony's statements are hardly infallible; he misidentified a famous quote Kennedy copied. The quote was "I know there is a God–and I see a storm coming. If He has a place for me, I believe that I am ready." Anthony identified it as an "original composition in his [Kennedy's] own handwriting." Abraham Lincoln wrote the quote originally and other sources correctly state that Kennedy copied the quote.

5. Robert Dallek, *John F. Kennedy: An Unfinished Life, 1917–1963* (New York: Little Brown, 2003), 59.

6. Ibid. Dallek's source was Peter Horowitz and David Collier, *The Kennedys: An American Drama* (Orangeville, ON: Summit Books, 1984), 102.

7. Doug Wead, *All the Presidents' Children* (New York: Atria Books, 2003), 226. Wead cited Doris Kearns Goodwin, *The Fitzgeralds and the Kennedys* (New York: Simon & Schuster, 1987), 635.

8. Dallek, *John F. Kennedy*, 375.

9. Anthony, *The Kennedy White House*, 92.

10. William Manchester, *The Death of a President* (New York: Harper & Row, 1967), 324.

11. Theodore C. Sorensen, *Kennedy* (New York: Bantam Books, 1966), 19–20.

12. Ibid.

13. Ibid.

14. Ibid., 364–65.

15. Kennedy, *Public Papers of the Presidents of the United States: John Fitzgerald Kennedy, 1961.* January 20, 1961. Inaugural address.

16. Ibid.

17. Ibid., February 9, 1961. Remarks at the dedication breakfast of the International Christian Leadership.

18. Ibid., February 7, 1963. Remarks at the annual Presidential Prayer Breakfast. The prayer breakfast of International Christian Leadership, Inc., a nondenominational group of laymen, was held at the Mayflower Hotel in Washington, DC. Dr. Abraham Vereide was secretary general of the International Council for Christian Leaders.

19. Ibid., November 21, 1961. Remarks to the officers of the National Conference of Christians and Jews.

20. Sorensen, *Kennedy*, 19–20.

21. Kennedy, *Public Papers*, October 28, 1961. Thanksgiving Day proclamation.

22. Ibid.

23. Ibid., January 14, 1963. Annual Message to Congress on the State of the Union.

24. Dallek, *John F. Kennedy*, 490.

25. Kennedy, *Public Papers*, November 5, 1963. Thanksgiving Day proclamation.

26. Carl Sferazza Anthony, *As We Remember Her: Jacqueline Kennedy Onassis in the Words of Her Friends and Family* (New York: HarperCollins, 1997), 116.

27. Anthony, *The Kennedy White House*, 92.

28. Ibid., 91.

29. Graham, *Just As I Am*, 395.

30. Ibid., 390.

★

CHAPTER 10

DWIGHT DAVID EISENHOWER

DWIGHT EISENHOWER was born on October 14, 1890, in Denison, Texas.

His family's religious roots were Mennonite. His first ancestor to emigrate to the United States, Hans Jacob Eisenhauer, was a Mennonite.[1] Eisenhauer may have left Switzerland for the United States because of religious persecution.

By the early 1800s, the Eisenhower family joined the Mennonite body named Brethren in Christ. Because they performed baptisms in rivers, they were called River Brethren.[2]

Dwight Eisenhower's grandfather, Jacob Eisenhower, was a River Brethren minister of the Lykens Valley River Brethren in Pennyslvania.[3] Dwight Eisenhower's father and mother, David Eisenhower and Ida Stover, both attended Lane University, a River Brethren school in Lecompton, Kansas.[4]

Dwight Eisenhower once said: "It was part of the privilege into which I was born that my home was a religious home."[5] Eisenhower told Billy Graham that Eisenhower's parents "read the New Testament in the original Greek and had taught their sons to memorize Scripture."[6] According to family tradition, Ida Stover Eisenhower once won a prize for memorizing 1,325 Bible verses.[7]

When dedicating his presidential museum, Eisenhower recalled his boyhood days. He said that his parents "believed the admonition 'the fear of God is the beginning of all wisdom.' Their Bibles were a live and lusty influence in their lives."[8] Twice a day, in the morning and in the evening, the Eisenhower family prayed. Dwight Eisenhower's father read the Bible both before and after meals.[9] However, Dwight Eisenhower's brother Milton recalled that though the Bible readings were "a good way to get us to read the Bible mechanically," they were possibly not "a good way to help us understand it." Eisenhower biographer Stephen Ambrose wrote: "They never discussed what they had read, never asked 'Why?,' never explored the deep subtlety or rich symbolism of the Bible. It was the word of God, sufficient unto itself. The duty of mortals was not to explore it, investigate it, question it, think about it, but rather to accept it."[10]

When Eisenhower was fourteen, he scraped his knee. He thought nothing more of the accident until infection set in. The infection eventually spread so much that the doctors seriously considered amputating his leg. Eisenhower said they must not do that, and after several weeks, his leg healed. Though the healing was considered a miracle, members of the Eisenhower family "insisted that they prayed no more, and no less, than at other times."[11] (Their statements were in response to accounts that their family prayed around the clock until Eisenhower recovered. According to Stephen Ambrose, the Eisenhower boys "hated" the implication "that their parents believed in faith healing."[12])

Eisenhower's grandfather Jacob did not fight in the Civil War because of his Mennonite/River Brethren pacifist doctrines.[13] Eisenhower's parents belonged to the same denomination; however, in a 1954 press conference, he recalled that his father "had all the temper of a Pennsylvania Dutchman, and there was nothing pacifist about him."[14] Though his mother was a "passionate pacifist," Eisenhower said, "she never said one single word to me."[15] Eisenhower remained in friendly contact with his parents through his years in the military.

He married Mamie Geneva Doud on July 1, 1916. From her youth, she had been a member of the Presbyterian Church.[16] She maintained her membership for decades before her husband joined her.

In a 1985 speech at the annual National Prayer Breakfast, Ronald Reagan talked about a conversation Eisenhower had with Senator Frank Carlson during Eisenhower's 1952 presidential campaign. He said: "Eisenhower confided to Senator Carlson that during the war, when he was commanding the Allied forces in Europe, he had had a spiritual experience. He had felt the hand of God guiding him and felt the presence of God. And he spoke of how his friends had provided real spiritual strength in the days before D-Day."[17]

In 1952, Eisenhower decided to run for president of the United States. He opened his campaign with a speech in his hometown, Abilene, Kansas. (A conservative congressman, B. Carroll Reece of Tennessee, criticized his speech, saying: "It looks like he's pretty much for home, mother, and heaven."[18])

During the campaign, Eisenhower met with Billy Graham. Graham asked him, "General, do you still respect the religious teaching of your father and mother?"

Eisenhower responded, "Yes, but I've gotten a long way from it." Graham encouraged him to join a church, saying: "Frankly, I don't think the American people would be happy with a President who didn't belong to any church or even attend one."

Eisenhower told Graham that he would join a church "as soon as the election is over" because he didn't "want to use the church politically."[19]

Eisenhower was elected president in 1952; he served from 1953 to 1961. On Inauguration Day, he broke precedents by praying a prayer of his own composition before delivering his inaugural address. His prayer was:

My friends, before I begin the expression of those thoughts that I deem appropriate to this moment, would you permit me the privilege of uttering a little private prayer of my own. And I ask that you bow your heads:

Almighty God, as we stand here at this moment, my future associates in the executive branch of government join me in beseeching that Thou will make full and complete our dedication to the service of the people in this throng, and their fellow citizens everywhere.

Give us, we pray, the power to discern clearly right from wrong, and allow all our words and actions to be governed thereby, and by the laws of this land. Especially we pray that our concern shall be for all the people regardless of station, race, or calling.

May cooperation be permitted and be the mutual aim of those who, under the concepts of our Constitution, hold to differing political faiths; so that all may work for the good of our beloved country and Thy glory. Amen.[20]

In his autobiography, *Mandate for Change*, Eisenhower explained his reasons for doing this. He said: "Religion was one of the thoughts that I had been mulling over for several weeks. I did not want my Inaugural Address to be a sermon, by any means; I was not a man of the cloth. But there was embedded in me from boyhood, just as it was in my brothers, a deep faith in the beneficence of the Almighty. I wanted, then, to make this faith clear without creating the impression that I intended, as the political leader of the United States, to avoid my own responsibilities in an effort to pass them on to the Deity. I was seeking a way to point out that we were getting too secular."[21]

Eisenhower believed that "America makes no sense without a deeply held faith in God—and I don't care what it is."[22] This probably indicated that he was indifferent as to which *denomination*, not which *God*.

Eisenhower also started his cabinet meetings with prayer. The prayer was silent prayer only if no cabinet member at that meeting desired to make a vocal prayer.[23]

Once he had taken office, he joined the National Presbyterian Church in Washington, DC, with his wife. In a "private meeting with the Church Session and according to Presbyterian standards," Eisenhower and his wife were received into full communicant membership. On the same Sunday morning that they were received into the church's membership, they took communion with the rest of the church.[24]

"That church affiliation was no perfunctory ritual," Billy Graham recalled. "When the President made his intentions known, Pastor Ed [Edward L. R.] Elson told him they must first spend an hour a day together for five days for religious instruction. Eisenhower complied humbly and became grounded in what it means to be a Christian and a Presbyterian before he was baptized into church membership."[25]

Eisenhower's diary entry for the day notes his membership but focuses on his displeasure over the fact that Dr. Elson publicized the event despite his promise that he would not. On February 1, 1953, Eisenhower wrote: "Mamie and I joined a Presbyterian church. We were scarcely home before the fact was publicized, by the pastor, to the hilt. I had been promised, by him, that there was to be no publicity. I feel like changing at once to another church of the same denomination. I shall if he breaks out again."[26]

Eisenhower was instrumental in placing our national motto, "In God We Trust," on a series of stamps called "the Liberty issue." At a dedication ceremony on April 8, 1954, for the first stamp bearing this motto, he said:

> The reason that I was particularly honored to come here today, aside from the opportunity of meeting with friends, was to be a part of the ceremony which now gives to every single citizen of the United States, as I see it, the chance to send a message to another. Regardless of any eloquence of the words that may be inside the letter, on the outside he places a message: "Here is the land of liberty and the land that lives in respect for the Almighty's mercy to us." And to him that receives that message, the sender can feel that he has done something definite and constructive for that individual.
>
> I think that each of us, hereafter, fastening such a stamp on a letter, cannot fail to feel something of the inspiration that we do whenever we look at the Statue of Liberty, or read "In God We Trust."[27]

He also led the push to add the words "under God" to the Pledge of Allegiance. On Flag Day, June 14, 1954, he signed a bill making the additional words law. He said:

> FROM THIS DAY FORWARD, the millions of our school children will daily proclaim in every city and town, every village and rural school house, the dedication of our nation and our people to the Almighty. To anyone who truly loves America, nothing could be more inspiring than to contemplate this rededication of our youth, on each school morning, to our country's true meaning.
>
> Especially is this meaningful as we regard today's world. Over the globe, mankind has been cruelly torn by violence and brutality and, by the millions, deadened in mind and soul by a materialistic philosophy of life. Man everywhere is appalled by the prospect of atomic war. In this somber setting, this law and its effects today have profound meaning. In this way we are reaffirming the transcendence of religious faith in America's heritage and future; in this way we shall constantly strengthen those spiritual weapons

which forever will be our country's most powerful resource, in peace or in war.[28]

He was reelected in 1956. In his second inaugural address, he said: "Before all else, we seek, upon our common labor as a nation, the blessings of Almighty God. And the hopes in our hearts fashion the deepest prayers of our whole people."[29]

These religious statements and actions were part of Eisenhower's stated plan to remind the United States that it was a Christian nation. He once told Billy Graham, "I think one of the reasons I was elected was to help lead this country spiritually. We *need* a spiritual renewal."[30] He believed that the United States was a Christian nation, and that Americans wanted a chief executive who shared their faith. His vice president, Richard Nixon, recalled Eisenhower gave him the following advice: "Before the 1960 campaign, President Eisenhower suggested that it would be very effective if I were to refer to God more in my speeches. After all, he pointed out, America is a Christian nation, so voters will relate to someone who quotes the Bible and shows in other ways that he shares their faith."[31]

"I ask you this one question," Eisenhower once said. "If each of us in his own mind would dwell more upon those simple virtues— integrity, courage, self-confidence and unshakeable belief in the Bible— would not some of these problems [the nation was facing] tend to simply solve themselves?"[32]

On November 18, 1953, he spoke to the National Council of Churches. He said:

Now I feel a very definite reason for being here. I happen to be the Chief Executive of a nation of which the Government is merely a translation in the political field of a deeply felt religious faith. The Magna Charta, our Declaration of Independence, and the French Declaration of the Rights of Man were certainly nothing else than the attempt on the part of men to state that in their government there would be recognized the principle of the equality of man, the dignity of man. That is a completely false premise unless we recognize the Supreme Being, in front of whom we are all equal.

So the fact that our Government rests and is founded on a deeply felt religious faith gives to my appearance, even before such a body, a certain validity—say, a certain fitness.[33]

On November 9, 1954, Eisenhower spoke to the First National Conference on the Spiritual Foundations of American Democracy. Eisenhower was introduced as a man who believed in a "God in Heaven and an Almighty power." To this, he said: "Well, I don't think anyone needs a great deal of credit for believing what seems to me to be obvious." He added:

> Now it seems to me that this relationship between a spiritual faith, a religious faith, and our form of government is so clearly defined and so obvious that we should really not need to identify a man as unusual because he recognizes it.[34]

He said that the reason given in the Declaration of Independence for our decision to establish a government was that our Creator had endowed us with inalienable rights. He added that "when you come back to it, there is just one thing: it is a concept, it is a subjective sort of thing, that a man is worthwhile because he was born in the image of his God."[35]

When President Kennedy was shot and killed on November 22, 1963, Eisenhower sent a letter to Lyndon B. Johnson. He suggested that Johnson make a speech to a joint session of Congress, and advised: "Point out first that you have come to this office unexpectedly and you accept the decision of the Almighty, who in His inscrutable wisdom has now placed you in the position of the highest responsibility of this nation."[36]

Near the end of his life, Eisenhower had a heart attack. Before the heart attack, he had a conversation with Billy Graham about salvation. Graham wrote later: "I sensed he was reassured by that most misunderstood message: Salvation is by grace through faith in Christ alone, and not by anything we can do for ourselves."[37]

Graham's final conversation with Eisenhower was in December 1968 at Walter Reed Hospital. Graham described the conversation in these words:

> As my scheduled twenty minutes with him extended to thirty, he asked the doctor and nurses to leave us. Propped up on pillows amidst intravenous tubes, he took my hand and looked into my eyes. "Billy, you've told me how to be sure my sins are forgiven and that I'm going to Heaven. Would you tell me again?"

I took out my New Testament and read to him again the familiar Gospel verses, the precious promises of God about eternal life. Then, my hand still in his, I prayed briefly.

"Thank you," he said, "I'm ready."

I knew he was.[38]

Eisenhower died on March 28, 1969. His last words were: "I have always loved my wife. I have always loved my children. I have always loved my grandchildren. I have always loved my country."[39]

CONCLUSION

Eisenhower lived much of his life as a moderately religious churchgoer. The responsibilities of the presidency drew him to God; he received instruction in the Christian faith and joined the Presbyterian Church once he had taken office as president. His words and life after that point indicate that his commitment to Christianity was sincere and heartfelt.

NOTES

1. Stephen E. Ambrose, *Eisenhower: Soldier, General of the Army, President-Elect, 1890–1952,* vol. 1 (New York: Simon & Schuster, 1983), 14.

2. Ibid.

3. Ibid. Jacob Eisenhower preached in German, because that was the predominant language of the River Brethren in the mid-1800s.

4. Ambrose, *Eisenhower,* vol. 1, 152.

5. Edmund Fuller and David E. Green, *God in the White House: The Faiths of American Presidents* (New York: Crown Publishers, 1968), 215. Quoted from a 1952 article in *Episcopal Church News.*

6. Billy Graham, *Just As I Am: The Autobiography of Billy Graham* (New York: HarperSanFrancisco/Zondervan, 1997), 190.

7. Ambrose, *Eisenhower,* vol. 1, 16.

8. Cranston Jones, *Homes of the American Presidents* (New York: Bonanza Books, 1962), 210.

9. Ambrose, *Eisenhower,* vol. 1, 20.

10. Ibid., 24.

11. Ibid., 36.

12. Ibid.

13. Ibid., 14.

14. Ibid., 41.

15. Ibid. Quoted from the July 8, 1954, *New York Times.*

16. Dwight D. Eisenhower, *The White House Years, 1953–1956: Mandate for Change* (Garden City, NY: Doubleday, 1963), 100.

17. Reagan, *Public Papers,* January 31, 1985. Remarks at the annual National Prayer Breakfast.

18. Eisenhower, *Mandate for Change,* 34.

19. Graham, *Just As I Am,* 191.

20. Eisenhower, *Public Papers of the Presidents of the United States: Dwight David Eisenhower, 1953.* Washington, DC: Government Printing Office. January 20, 1953. First inaugural address.

21. Eisenhower, *Mandate for Change,* 100.

22. Richard G. Hutcheson Jr., *God in the White House: How Religion Has Changed the Modern Presidency* (New York: Macmillan, 1988), 51.

23. Fuller and Green, *God in the White House: The Faiths of American Presidents,* 217.

24. Olga Anna Jones, *Churches of the Presidents in Washington: Visits to Fifteen National Shrines* (New York: Exposition Press, 1954), 19.

25. Graham, *Just As I Am,* 200.

26. Robert H. Ferrell, *The Eisenhower Diaries* (New York and London: Norton, 1981), 226.

27. Eisenhower, *Public Papers,* April 8, 1954. Remarks at the ceremony marking the issuance of the first stamp bearing the motto, "In God We Trust."

28. Ibid., June 14, 1954. Statement by the president upon signing the bill to include the words "under God" in the pledge to the flag. The joint resolution amending the Pledge of Allegiance to the flag is Public Law 396, 83rd Congress (68 Stat. 049).

29. Ibid., January 21, 1957. Second inaugural address.

30. Graham, *Just As I Am,* 199.

31. Richard Nixon, *In the Arena: A Memoir of Victory, Defeat, and Renewal* (New York: Simon & Schuster, 1990), 88.

32. Jones, *Homes of the American Presidents,* 210.

33. Eisenhower, *Public Papers,* November 18, 1953. Remarks to the general board of the National Council of Churches.

34. Ibid., November 9, 1954. Remarks to the First National Conference on the Spiritual Foundations of American Democracy.

35. Ibid.

36. Lyndon B. Johnson, *The Vantage Point: Perspectives of the Presidency, 1963–1969* (New York: Holt, Rinehart, and Winston, 1971), 32.

37. Graham, *Just As I Am,* 204.

38. Ibid., 205–06.

39. George H. W. Bush, *Public Papers,* March 27, 1990. Remarks at a luncheon commemorating the Dwight D. Eisenhower Centennial.

CHAPTER 11

HARRY S TRUMAN

HARRY S TRUMAN was born on May 8, 1884, in Lamar, Missouri. While he lived in Kansas City, Missouri, Truman attended the Benton Boulevard Baptist Church.

Truman began his lifelong study of Christianity at an early age; he once recalled that he "read the Bible clear through twice" before he went to school.[1] At age 18, Truman "felt a sense of salvation,"[2] was baptized by immersion,[3] and became a member of the First Baptist Church in Grandview, Missouri. He was a "life-long member" of the church.[4] Later in life, he stated that he attended the church because the preacher treated him as just another member of the congregation and not as a celebrity.[5]

Harry Truman prayed this prayer regularly from before he was eighteen until late in his life:

Oh! Almighty and Everlasting God, Creator of Heaven, Earth and the Universe:

Help me to be, to think, to act what is right, because it is right; make me truthful, honest and honorable in all things; make me intellectually honest for the sake of right and honor and without thought of reward to me. Give me the ability to be charitable, forgiving and patient with my fellowmen—help me to understand their motives and their shortcomings—even as Thou understandest mine!

Amen, amen, amen.[6]

As Truman eventually became involved in other activities, his church attendance "became infrequent." In his later years, he ignored the Baptist prohibitions against "liquor, cards, and swearing."[7]

He met Elizabeth "Bess" Wallace in a Presbyterian Sunday school. After five years of attending the same Sunday school, he eventually worked up the courage to speak to her for the first time. Before long, they began to correspond; Truman felt comfortable putting thoughts on paper that he could not express in person. During this correspondence, they touched on religion at least once. As Truman biographer David McCullough stated, Truman said he "was only a reasonably good Baptist as the term was understood in Grandview. 'I am by religion like everything else. I think there's more in acting than in talking.' "[8]

Truman married Wallace on June 28, 1919.

He ascended to the office of the presidency in 1945 upon the death of Franklin Delano Roosevelt and served until 1953. In an April 16, 1945, address before a joint session of Congress, Truman said: "At this moment, I have in my heart a prayer. As I have assumed my heavy duties, I humbly pray Almighty God, in the words of King Solomon: 'Give therefore thy servant an understanding heart to judge thy people, that I may discern between good and bad; for who is able to judge this thy so great a people?' I ask only to be a good and faithful servant of my Lord and my people."[9]

On May 8, 1945, Truman held a V-E (Victory in Europe) Day press conference. He said: "For the triumph of spirit and of arms which we have won, and for its promise to peoples everywhere who join us in the love of freedom, it is fitting that we, as a nation, give thanks to Almighty God, who has strengthened us and given us the victory.

"Now, therefore, I, Harry S. Truman, President of the United States of America, do hereby appoint Sunday, May 13, 1945, to be a day of prayer."[10]

On January 20, 1948, Truman began his first full term as president. He concluded his inaugural address with these words: "Steadfast in our faith in the Almighty, we will advance toward a world where man's freedom is secure. To that end we will devote our strength, our resources, and our firmness of resolve. With God's help, the future of mankind will be assured in a world of justice, harmony, and peace."[11]

Truman believed that America was fundamentally a Christian nation. In an address to the Washington Pilgrimage of American Churchmen, he said, "[T]his Nation was established by men who believed in God. You will see that our Founding Fathers believed that God created this Nation. And I believe it, too."[12]

He said: "If we go back to the Declaration of Independence, we notice that it was drawn up by men who believed that God the Creator had made all men equal and had given them certain rights which no man could take away from them. In beginning their great enterprise, the signers of the Declaration of Independence entrusted themselves to the protection of divine providence.

"To our forefathers it seemed something of a miracle that this Nation was able to go through the agonies of the American Revolution and emerge triumphant. They saw, in our successful struggle for independence, the working of God's hand. In his first inaugural address, George Washington said, 'No people can be bound to acknowledge and adore the invisible hand, which conducts the affairs of men, more than the people of the United States.' "[13]

"When the United States was established," he said in a 1949 radio address, "its coins bore witness to the American faith in a benevolent deity. The motto then was 'In God We Trust.' That is still our motto and we, as a people, still place our firm trust in God. . . . The basic source of our strength as a nation is spiritual. We believe in the dignity of man. We believe that he is created in the image of God, who is the Father of us all."[14]

Truman believed that "the foundation of the things for which we stand" was in the "Book of the Law, and in the Gospel according to St. Matthew, St. Mark, St. Luke, and St. John."[15]

In a 1947 letter to Pope Pius XII, Truman used these words to describe the United States:

"Your Holiness, this is a Christian Nation. More than a half century ago that declaration was written into the decrees of the highest court in this land. It is not without significance that the valiant pioneers who left Europe to establish settlements here, at the very beginning of their colonial enterprises, declared their faith in the Christian religion and made ample provision for its practice and for its support. The story of the Christian missionaries who in earliest days endured perils, hardship—even death itself in carrying the message of Jesus Christ to untutored savages is one that still moves the hearts of men.

"As a Christian Nation our earnest desire is to work with men of good will everywhere to banish war and the causes of war from the world whose Creator desired that men of every race and in every clime should live together in peace, good will and mutual trust. Freedom of conscience, ordained by the Fathers of our Constitution to all who live under the flag of the United States, has been a bulwark of national strength, a source of happiness, from the establishment of our Nation to this day.[16]

However, he believed, the fact that we were a Christian nation didn't make it easier for us than for other nations. "The people of Israel, you will remember, did not, because of their covenant with God, have an easier time than other nations. Their standards were higher than those of other nations and the judgment upon them and their shortcomings was more terrible. A religious heritage, such as ours, is not a comfortable thing to live with. It does not mean that we are more virtuous than other people. Instead, it means that we have less excuse for doing the wrong thing—because we are taught right from wrong."[17]

On November 23, 1952, he made a speech on the occasion of laying a cornerstone for Westminster Presbyterian Church in Alexandria, Virginia. He said: "Democracy is first and foremost a spiritual force. It is built upon a spiritual basis—and on a belief in God and an observance of moral principles. And in the long run only the church can provide that basis. Our founders knew this truth—and we will neglect it at our peril."[18]

He did not believe that our nation's spiritual heritage was merely a nice thing. He believed that we dare not ignore it. When the Washington Hebrew Congregation laid a cornerstone for a new temple, Truman spoke at the ceremony. In his speech he said: "We know that the deepening of religion and the growth of religion are essential to our welfare as a nation. If we ignore the spiritual foundations of our birth as a nation, we do so at our peril. It took a faith in God to win our freedoms. We will need that same faith today if we are to keep those freedoms in the face of the terrible menace of totalitarianism and war. If we do not hold to our faith in God, we cannot prevail against the dangers from abroad and the fears and distrust that those dangers create among us here at home."[19]

On December 15, 1952, Truman spoke at the dedication ceremony of a new shrine for the Declaration of Independence, the Constitution, and the Bill of Rights. In his address he said:

The motto on our Liberty Bell, "Proclaim liberty throughout all the land unto all the inhabitants thereof," is from the book of Leviticus, which is supposed to have been written nearly 1,500 years before Christ. In the 35 centuries since that date, the love of liberty has never died, but liberty itself has been lost again and again.

We find it hard to believe that liberty could ever be lost in this country. But it can be lost, and it will be, if the time ever comes when these documents are regarded not as the supreme expression of our profound belief, but merely as curiosities in glass cases.[20]

Truman believed the menace of Communism was more than a political or ideological battle but it was a moral battle:

This is the great problem we must meet. We cannot yield to Soviet communism, without betraying the ideals we live for. We cannot have another world war without jeopardizing our civilization.

In this perilous strait, our greatest source of strength, our greatest hope of victory, lies in the God we acknowledge as the ruler of us all. We turn to faith in Him to give us the strength and the wisdom to carry out His will. We ask Him to lead us out of the dangers of this present time into the paths of peace.

In this crisis of human affairs, all men who profess to believe in God should unite in asking His help and His guidance. We should lay aside our differences and come together now—for never have our differences seemed so petty and so insignificant as they do in the face of the peril we confront today.

It is not just this church or that church which is in danger. It is not just this creed or that creed that is threatened. All churches, all creeds, are menaced. The very future of the Word of God—the teaching that has come down to us from the days of the prophets and the life of Jesus—is at stake.[21]

Truman served as president until 1953, when he retired to Independence, Missouri.

Truman told Thomas Murray: "I am not a religious man. Mrs. Truman takes care of that."[22] This attitude was reflected in a 1950 conversation with Reverend Billy Graham. Graham asked Truman to tell him about his "religious background and beliefs."

"Well, I try to live by the Sermon on the Mount and the Golden Rule," Truman answered.

"It takes more than that, Mr. President," Graham responded. "It's faith in Christ and His death on the Cross that you need."[23]

Truman's response to the statement was to stand up and end the interview. After a prayer, Graham and his colleagues left.

Truman believed that Billy Graham was a fake. He said: "But now we've just got this one evangelist, this Billy Graham, and he's gone off of the beam. He's . . . well, I hadn't ought to say this, but he's one of those counterfeits I was telling you about. He claims he's a friend of all the Presidents, but he was never a friend of mine when I was President. I just don't go for people like that. All he's interested in is getting his name in the paper."[24]

On September 26, 1952, the Standard Bible Committee gave him the first copy of the Revised Standard Version. He told Dr. Luther Weigle, dean emeritus of the Yale Divinity School and chairman of the committee, that he appreciated the gift. He said:

> My mother owned a big deckle-edged Bible published in 1881, which contained the first revised version of the New Testament parallel to the King James version. I was raised on that book, and I want to say to you that my fondness for the King James version will never leave me.
>
> I shall read this with great interest, and try to use it for a better understanding of the Bible on which I was brought up.
>
> The only thing that James I of England and James VI of Scotland are remembered for is the fact that they had a number of scholars–such as you had in this undertaking–make a direct translation of the Old Testament and the New Testament from what they thought were the original documents on which they were first set up.
>
> Now you have gone further, and have, I am sure, investigated other documents that clarify the meaning of the words in the King James version. And I am certainly most happy to have it.
>
> I think, as you said, that if people understood the contents of this book from cover to cover, and we could get a complete understanding of it behind the Iron Curtain, there would be but one thing in this world: peace for all mankind.[25]

However, Truman's private comments about modern translations were not as positive. Truman thought the King James Version could not be superseded. He said, "I always read the King James Version." He added: "The King James Version of the Bible is the best there is or ever has been or will be, and you get a bunch of college professors spending *years* working on it, and all they do is take the poetry out of it."[26]

This had, apparently, been his view for some time. His friend Judge Albert A. Ridge recalled: "I remember he said even back then that the King James Version was the best and that he doubted it could be improved on. I believe he still thinks that."[27]

In several speeches and statements, he referred to his respect for the Golden Rule. On one occasion, he said:

We are going to have difficulties. You can't do anything worthwhile without difficulties. No man who ever accomplishes anything can expect to do it without making mistakes. The man who never does anything never makes any mistakes. We may make mistakes. We may have difficulties, but I am asking you to exercise that admonition which you will find in the Gospels, and which Christ told us was the way to get along in the world: Do by your neighbor as you would be done by. . . .

We can't stand another global war. We can't ever have another war, unless it is total war, and that means the end of our civilization as we know it. We are not going to do that. We are going to accept that Golden Rule, and we are going forward to meet our destiny which I think Almighty God intended us to have.

And we are going to be the leaders.[28]

In an address at the lighting of the national Christmas tree, he said:

Selfishness and greed, individual or national, cause most of our troubles. He whose birth we celebrate tonight was the world's greatest teacher. He said:

"Therefore all things whatsoever ye would that men should do to you, do ye even so to them; for this is the law and the prophets."

Through all the centuries since He spoke, history has vindicated His teaching.[29]

Truman called the Sermon on the Mount the "greatest of all things in the Bible, a way of life, and maybe someday men will get to understand it as the real way of life."[30] In a conference of the Federal Council of Churches, he said:

> If men and nations would but live by the precepts of the ancient prophets and the teachings of the Sermon on the Mount, problems which now seem so difficult would soon disappear.
>
> That is the great task for you teachers of religious faith. This is a supreme opportunity for the Church to continue to fulfill its mission on earth. The Protestant Church, the Catholic Church, and the Jewish Synagogue—bound together in the American unity of brotherhood—must provide the shock forces to accomplish this moral and spiritual awakening. No other agency can do it. Unless it is done, we are headed for the disaster we would deserve.[31]

At a luncheon for the press in Kansas City on December 22, 1950, he said:

> Our growth and our laws are founded on those originating with Hammurabi in the Mesopotamian Valley, propounded by Moses, and elaborated on by Jesus Christ, whose Sermon on the Mount is the best ethical program by which to live.[32]

He mistakenly believed that Hammurabi originated the laws that God gave Moses, but he again praised Christ's Sermon on the Mount.

To representatives of the National Council of Churches on September 26, 1952, Truman said:

> The people who believe in the teachings of the 20th Chapter of Exodus, and the 5th, 6th, and 7th Chapters of the Gospel according to St. Matthew can't hold any malice against his neighbor or his friend if he does what is right.[33]

> It is this faith that inspires us to work for a world in which life will be more worthwhile—a world of tolerance, unselfishness, and brotherhood—a world that lives according to the precepts of the Sermon on the Mount.

I believe that every problem in the world today could be solved if men would only live by the principles of the ancient prophets and the Sermon on the Mount.[34]

Truman frequently quoted from the Bible to illustrate one of his speeches. Below are a few examples:

Let us not forget that the coming of the Saviour brought a time of long peace to the Roman World. It is, therefore, fitting for us to remember that the spirit of Christmas is the spirit of peace, of love, of charity to all men. From the manger of Bethlehem came a new appeal to the minds and hearts of men: "A new commandment I give unto you, that ye love one another."[35]

At this point in the world's history, the words of St. Paul have greater significance than ever before. He said:
   "And now abideth faith, hope, charity, these three; but the greatest of these is charity."
   We believe this. We accept it as a basic principle of our lives.[36]

As we light this National Christmas tree tonight, here on the White House lawn—as all of us light our own Christmas trees in our own homes—we remember another night long ago. Then a Child was born in a stable. A star hovered over, drawing wise men from afar. Shepherds, in a field, heard angels singing: "Glory to God in the highest, and on earth peace, good will toward men." That was the first Christmas and it was God's great gift to us.
   This is a wonderful story. Year after year it brings peace and tranquility to troubled hearts in a troubled world. And tonight the earth seems hushed, as we turn to the old, old story of how "God so loved the world, that He gave His only begotten Son, that whosoever believeth in Him should not perish, but have everlasting life." . . .
   Through Jesus Christ the world will yet be a better and a fairer place.[37]

We must work for morality in public life and in private life. You can't make an honest man by law. He has to be raised by the rules of the 20th chapter of Exodus, and the Sermon on the Mount, if he has the right moral fiber to become an ethical public or private citizen.[38]

Truman's private comments on religion, however, could be quite iconoclastic. A classic example was Truman's June 1, 1952, diary entry. He was commenting on a news report that several golden crowns had been stolen from images of Jesus and Mary at a Roman Catholic shrine. He said:

> I've an idea if Jesus were here his sympathies would be with the thieves and not with the Pharisees who crowned him with gold and jewels.
>
> The only crown he ever wore was one of thorns placed there by the emissaries of the Roman Emperor and the Jewish Priesthood. He came to help the lowly and down trodden. . . .
>
> If Jesus Christ were to return he'd be on the side of the persecuted all around the world. He would not be wearing a golden crown and fine raiment, he'd most likely be wearing a ready made sack suit and be standing on a street corner preaching tolerance, brother love and truth. He'd be stoned and persecuted by the most liberal of our modern day followers of the man with the golden crown. He'd probably be placed in a sanitarium in the free countries. He'd be shot, hanged, or sent to a slave labor camp behind the iron curtain.
>
> He'd no more recognize his teachings in St. Peter's or Canterbury Cathedrals than he would in Riverside or Trinity Churches in New York or the First Baptist or Foundry Methodist Churches in Washington. He was a reformer and a protestant against organized, priesthood-controlled religion.
>
> He taught that every man is the creation of a merciful God, that men are sinners and that he had come into the world to teach sinners how to approach His Father—and the way was not through Caiaphas [sic] the High Priest or Augustus the Roman Emperor. The way is direct and straight. Any man can tell the Almighty and Most Merciful God his troubles and directly ask for guidance. *He will get it.*[39]

In a diary entry on June 1, 1945, Truman wrote: "The Jews claim God Almighty picked 'em out for special privilege. Well, I'm sure He had better judgment. Fact is I never thought God picked any favorites. It is my studied opinion that any race, creed or color can be God's favorites if they act the part—and very few of 'em do that."[40]

By the phrase "any . . . creed," Truman could have either meant any creed of the Christian faith or any creed of any faith. His precise meaning is unclear.

In an August 8, 1951, letter to Nellie Noland, Truman wrote:

> Bill Hassett [his correspondence secretary] and myself have decided to start a new religious sect when we are done saving the country in this job. . . .
>
> About that new religious racket that Bill and I are working on—we haven't decided whether we'll sell medicine, ideas, or another New Testament or Book of Mormon.[41]

In his February 26, 1952, diary entry, Truman wrote: "[I]f I could succeed in getting the world of morals associated against the world of no morals, we'd have world peace for ages to come. Confucius, Buddha, Moses, our own Jesus Christ, Mahomet, all preached: 'Do as you'd be done by.' Treat others as you'd be treated. So did all the other great teachers and philosophers.

"But along comes Marx, Lenin, Trotsky, Stalin to upset morals and intellectual honesty and a lot of 'crackpots' want to follow them.

"The Great Creator of the Universe won't allow it! I am sure of that."[42]

CONCLUSION

At age eighteen, Truman accepted the basic tenets of the Christian faith and was baptized. Over time, he apparently turned away from aspects of the religion of his youth. He understood Christianity well but believed some parts of it and rejected others.

NOTES

1. David McCullough, *Truman* (New York: Simon & Schuster, 1992), 44.

2. Alonzo L. Hamby, *Man of the People: A Life of Harry S Truman* (New York and Oxford: Oxford University Press, 1995), 21.

3. Bliss Isley, *The Presidents: Men of Faith* (Boston: W. A. Wilde, 1953), 255.

4. William G. Clotworthy, *Presidential Sites: A Discovery of Places Associated with Presidents of the United States* (Blacksburg, VA: McDonald and Woodward, 1998), 231.

5. Edmund Fuller and David E. Green, *God in the White House: The Faiths of American Presidents* (New York: Crown Publishers, 1968), 209.

6. Harry S Truman, *Off the Record: The Private Papers of Harry S Truman*, ed. Robert H. Ferrell (New York: Harper & Row, 1980), 188.

7. Hamby, *Man of the People*, 21.

8. McCullough, *Truman*, 83.

9. Truman, *Public Papers of the Presidents of the United States: Harry S Truman, 1945.* Washington, DC: Government Printing Office. April 16, 1945. Address before a joint session of Congress.

10. Ibid., May 8, 1945. Press conference on Victory in Europe (V-E) Day.

11. Ibid., January 20, 1949. Inaugural address.

12. Ibid., September 28, 1951. Address to the Washington Pilgrimage of American Churchmen.

13. Ibid.

14. Ibid., November 1949. Radio address as part of the program, *Religion in American Life*. The president spoke at 11:25 p.m. from the projection room at the White House, following an introduction by Charles E. Wilson, president of General Electric, who served as chairman of the nationwide, interfaith campaign. The campaign ran from November 1–24, 1949.

15. Ibid., June 13, 1948. Remarks in San Francisco at a luncheon of the Northern California Democratic Presidential Delegation.

16. Ibid., August 6, 1947. Exchange of messages with Pope Pius XII.

17. Ibid., September 28, 1951. Address to the Washington Pilgrimage of American Churchmen.

18. Ibid., November 23, 1952. Remarks at the cornerstone laying of Westminster Presbyterian Church in Alexandria, Virginia.

19. Ibid., November 16, 1952. Remarks on laying the cornerstone of a new temple of the Washington Hebrew Congregation.

20. Ibid., December 15, 1952. Address at the National Archives dedicating a new shrine for the Declaration of Independence, the Constitution, and the Bill of Rights.

21. Ibid., September 28, 1951. Address to the Washington Pilgrimage of American Churchmen.

22. Hamby, *Man of the People*, 474.

23. Billy Graham, *Just As I Am: The Autobiography of Billy Graham* (New York: HarperSanFrancisco/Zondervan, 1997), xx.

24. Merle Miller, *Plain Speaking: An Oral Biography of Harry S Truman* (New York: Berkeley Publishing/G. P. Putnam's Sons, 1973, 1974), 363.

25. Truman, *Public Papers,* September 26, 1952. Remarks to representatives of the National Council of Churches.

26. Miller, *Plain Speaking,* 214–15.

27. Ibid., 111.

28. Truman, *Public Papers,* October 7, 1945. Remarks at the Pemiscot County Fair, Caruthersville, Missouri.

29. Ibid., December 24, 1946. Address at the lighting of the national community Christmas tree on the White House grounds.

30. Fuller and Green, *God in the White House,* 209.

31. Truman, *Public Papers,* March 6, 1946. Address in Columbus, Ohio, at a conference of the Federal Council of Churches.

32. Ibid., December 22, 1950. Remarks in Kansas City at a luncheon for the press.

33. Ibid., September 22, 1952. Remarks to representatives of the National Council of Churches.

34. Ibid., November 1949. Radio address as part of the program, "Religion in American Life."

35. Ibid., December 24, 1945. Address at the Lighting of the National Community Christmas Tree on the White House Grounds.

36. Ibid., December 24, 1947. Address at the lighting of the national community Christmas tree on the White House grounds.

37. Ibid., December 24, 1952. Remarks Upon Lighting the National Community Christmas Tree.

38. Ibid., September 28, 1951. Address to the Washington Pilgrimage of American Churchmen.

39. Truman, *Off the Record,* 41.

40. Ibid.

41. Ibid., 214–15.

42. Ibid., 242.

CHAPTER 12

FRANKLIN DELANO ROOSEVELT

FRANKLIN DELANO ROOSEVELT was born on January 30, 1882, at Hyde Park, New York. On March 20, 1883, he was christened in St. James Episcopal Church in Hyde Park. He was a lifelong communicant in that church.[1]

During his high school years, he attended Groton School. The headmaster at the time was Reverend Endicott Peabody, an Episcopalian who was rector of the parish in which the school was located.[2] The school's prospectus said: "Every endeavor will be made to cultivate manly, Christian character, having regard to moral and physical as well as intellectual development."[3] An 1896 letter to his parents written during his time at Groton thanks them for sending him a Bible and a prayer book.[4]

When his grandfather, Warren Delano II, died in 1898, Franklin's letter to his mother reflected an orthodox view of heaven. He said: "You can never imagine how deeply grieved I was to hear that my darling Grandfather had passed away. I know you are heartbroken, but we must remember that he has gone to a better place than this earth, and will be far happier there."[5]

In a December 4, 1898, letter to his parents, he told them that he had been elected to the missionary society. "We had my first meeting tonight, and a splendid talk by a Mr. Blatt, the chaplain of the Mass. reformatory at Concord. It was very interesting all about the fine things they do for the prisoners."[6]

Roosevelt did missionary work for several months during his Groton years. In a March 23, 1899, letter to his parents, he wrote:

"You will be surprised to hear that I am to be a new missionary. There was a lack of organ-players for the various mission houses in the neighborhood, so I volunteered and tonight I am to drive over with two other boys and Mr. Higley to hold a service at Rockey Hill in a little school-house, which is about six miles from here. I have almost forgotten how to play the piano, but have been practising on the small organ in the school-room and can play four hymns fairly decently. We leave at 6.30 tonight and expect to return about 10, when we go into Faculty supper!"[7]

That particular service did not go very well; in a March 26 letter to his parents, he described the service. "You know I wrote you on Thursday that I had become an organ-player. Well, on Thursday night in the midst of a blinding snow-storm four of us left in a two seated wagon. We picked up Mr. Higley who was to deliver the address, & then drove six miles out into the country to a little bit of a school-house called Rocky Hill. When we got there we found a congregation composed of the stove-lighter (who had to be there) and a little boy. It was then 8.30 and as it was sleeting and nobody was there we locked up the house & drove home again so I did not have a chance to perform."[8]

The March 30 meeting went better. He described it in a March 31 letter to his parents: "We had a congregation of 17, quite respectable, as it is composed only of scattered farmer's families round the school-house. We had a pleasant drive, and I drove coming back in the dark. I drummed the organ for all it was worth & drowned out the singers, but I got on fairly well for the first time and only got off the time once in the four hymns. It was hard as I had to pump, play and use the swells all at the same time. I only played the soprano and alto parts right through with an occasional bass chord. It was the last service, as they are only held there during Lent."[9]

That October, he helped with organ in at least one Sunday school service. In an October 15 letter to his parents, he wrote: "This a.m. before church I helped Mr. Griswold with his Sunday school in the old building. We had 10 children & I played two hymns."[10]

He married Eleanor Roosevelt on March 17, 1905. Shortly after their marriage, he was elected a vestryman in the church.[11] He eventually became a senior warden, following in the footsteps of his father. Although his father, James Roosevelt, grew up in the Dutch Reformed Church, James decided to become an Episcopalian and became a warden and vestryman in St. James Episcopal Church in Hyde Park.[12]

During the years when Franklin and Eleanor Roosevelt were raising their children, Eleanor once asked her husband whether their children should be raised in the Christian religion and attending church, or whether they should receive no religious instruction and choose their religion when they were mature. Kenneth Davis described the conversation:

> He replied that he thought the children had better attend church and receive the teachings he had received. These could do them no harm. But suppose the teachings were not true? She wanted to know. Did he himself believe all of them? He looked at her with an "amused and quizzical smile" and said, "I never really thought about it. I think it is just as well not to think about things like that too much." At that time she resented "heatedly" his manner of closing the subject—it seemed to her flippant and contemptuous— and for years afterward she continued to feel "a kind of virtuous grievance" whenever, in accordance with the wish *he* had expressed, *she* took the children to church while he played golf with friends, a fairly frequent occurrence in summer.[13]

By 1918, Roosevelt's churchgoing had become infrequent. Eleanor Roosevelt noted in her diary one day that her husband "went to church last Sunday and goes again today, which I know is a great sacrifice to please me."[14]

Early on, Eleanor was upset by her husband's infrequent attendance. She herself was so faithful a churchgoer and communicant that once, when she skipped communion, it was so noteworthy that she noted it in her diary.[15] Later in her life, she was able to joke about it. In 1918, when Franklin was assistant secretary of the Navy,[16] he was elected a vestryman in St. Thomas's Church, an Episcopal church in Washington. In a letter to his mother, Sara Delano Roosevelt, Eleanor stated that the news was a "fearful shock" to him and expressed her hope that he would not accept the position.[17] He ended up accepting it; later, while president, he was selected as an honorary warden in the church.[18]

Biographer Kenneth Davis said that Roosevelt seldom attended church services "because, as he had said, he hated to be 'stared at' while he said his prayers. Of religious fervor, religious feeling, he displayed none at all."[19] Roosevelt viewed his religion as a matter so private that he could not share his experiences with fellow believers. In a 1928 letter to Democratic presidential candidate Al Smith, Roosevelt said that he fully shared Smith's longing for "a quiet two weeks and a complete absence from crowds and worshipers."[20]

In July 1921, Roosevelt came down with infantile paralysis, also known as polio. Years later, he told Frances Perkins that he (in the words of biographer Kenneth Davis) "felt utterly abandoned by God."[21]

Roosevelt was elected president in 1932. On the day he was inaugurated, March 3, 1933, he attended a worship service at St. John's Episcopal Church conducted by Reverend Endicott Peabody.[22] His first inaugural address concluded with the words, "In this dedication of a Nation we humbly ask the blessing of God. May He protect each and every one of us. May He guide me in the days to come."[23]

In proclamations and speeches, Roosevelt frequently made references to Christianity appropriate for the occasion. On November 21, 1933, he issued a Thanksgiving Day proclamation and said: "May we on that day in our churches and in our homes give humble thanks for the blessings bestowed upon us during the year past by Almighty God."[24]

In a December 24, 1933, Christmas message, Roosevelt said: "Even more greatly, my happiness springs from the deep conviction that this year marks a greater national understanding of the significance in our modern lives of the teachings of Him whose birth we celebrate. To more and more of us the words 'Thou shalt love thy neighbor as thyself' have taken on a meaning that is showing itself and proving itself in our purposes and daily lives."[25]

In Roosevelt's 1934 Thanksgiving Day proclamation, he said: "Thus to set aside in the autumn of each year a day on which to give thanks to Almighty God for the blessings of life is a wise and reverent custom, long cherished by our people. It is fitting that we should again observe this custom."[26]

He was reelected president in 1936. He concluded his second inaugural address by stating: "In taking again the oath of office as President of the United States, I assume the solemn obligation of leading the American people forward along the road over which they have chosen to advance.

"While this duty rests upon me, I shall do my utmost to speak their purpose and to do their will, seeking Divine guidance to help us each and every one to give light to them that sit in darkness and to guide our feet into the way of peace."[27]

In his 1937 Thanksgiving Day proclamation, he urged Americans to "forego our usual occupations and, in our accustomed places of worship, each in his own way, humbly acknowledge the mercy of God from whom comes every good and perfect gift."[28]

By 1939, Roosevelt's messages increasingly dealt with the impending war. His 1939 Christmas greeting to the nation began with these words: "In these days of strife and sadness in many other lands, let us in the nations which still live at peace forbear to give thanks only for our good fortune in our peace." He urged Americans to pray to "be given strength to live for others," and to live and pray that the nations at war could understand the Sermon on the Mount. He then quoted the Sermon on the Mount in its entirety.[29]

War came on December 7, 1941 when Japan attacked Pearl Harbor. Then on December 11, Germany declared war on the United States, and the United States declared war on Japan and Germany. Less than a month later, Roosevelt delivered his annual State of the Union address. He concluded by saying:

> Our enemies are guided by brutal cynicism, by unholy contempt for the human race. We are inspired by a faith that goes back through all the years to the first chapter of the Book of Genesis: "God created man in His own image."
>
> We on our side are striving to be true to that divine heritage. We are fighting, as our fathers have fought, to uphold the doctrine that all men are equal in the sight of God. Those on the other side are striving to destroy this deep belief and to create a world in their own image—a world of tyranny and cruelty and serfdom.
>
> That is the conflict that day and night now pervades our lives.
>
> No compromise can end that conflict. There never has been—there never can be—successful compromise between good and evil. Only total victory can reward the champions of tolerance, and decency, and freedom, and faith.[30]

In a November 1942 Thanksgiving proclamation, Roosevelt reminded the country that we must "solemnly express our dependence upon Almighty God," especially in the face of the war. He quoted the entire text of Psalm 23, urging the nation to be "inspired with faith and courage by these words" and to "turn again to the work that confronts us in this time of national emergency."[31]

On February 22, 1943, Roosevelt delivered a radio address commemorating George Washington's Birthday. He compared Washington's situation with the situation then, and reminded the country that Washington's "simple, steadfast faith . . . kept him to the essential principle of first things first."

He went on to criticize those who "still believe in the age of miracles," telling them that "there is no Joshua in our midst" and that we had to rely upon our faith, hope, and love to carry us through the conflict. He quoted the entire Beatitudes and several verses from 1 Corinthians 13, concluding with these words:

> Those truths inspired Washington, and the men and women of the thirteen colonies.
>
> Today, through all the darkness that has descended upon our Nation and our world, those truths are a guiding light to all.
>
> We shall follow that light, as our forefathers did, to the fulfillment of our hopes for victory, for freedom, and for peace.[32]

On December 24, 1944, Roosevelt said this in his Christmas address to the nation:

> It is not easy to say "Merry Christmas" to you, my fellow Americans, in this time of destructive war. Nor can I say "Merry Christmas" lightly tonight to our armed forces at their battle stations all over the world—or to our allies who fight by their side.
>
> Here, at home, we will celebrate this Christmas Day in our traditional American way—because of its deep spiritual meaning to us; because the teachings of Christ are fundamental in our lives; and because we want our youngest generation to grow up knowing the significance of this tradition and the story of the coming of the immortal Prince of Peace and Good Will. But, in perhaps every home in the United States, sad and anxious thoughts will be continually with the millions of our loved ones who are suffering hardships and misery, and who are risking their very lives to preserve for us and for all mankind the fruits of His teachings and the foundations of civilization itself.[33]

Roosevelt was elected to a fourth term in 1944. He concluded his fourth inaugural address with these words:

The Almighty God has blessed our land in many ways. He has given our people stout hearts and strong arms with which to strike mighty blows for freedom and truth. He has given to our country a faith which has become the hope of all peoples in an anguished world.

So we pray to Him now for the vision to see our way clearly—to see the way that leads to a better life for ourselves and for all our fellow men—to the achievement of His will to peace on earth.[34]

Roosevelt was president until his death on April 12, 1945.

Roosevelt's religious beliefs were simple. He believed that there was a God; he also believed in the value of the Bible, especially Psalm 23, the Beatitudes, and 1 Corinthians 13. His writings abound with references to those beliefs; beyond this, he seldom ventured.

Roosevelt said, "I feel that a comprehensive study of the Bible is a liberal education for anyone. Nearly all of the great men of our country have been well versed in the teachings of the Bible."[35]

In 1935, he made a statement commemorating the four hundredth anniversary of the printing of the first English Bible. He discussed the Bible's impact on American culture:

In the formative days of the Republic the directing influence the Bible exercised upon the fathers of the Nation is conspicuously evident. To Washington it contained the sure and certain moral precepts that constituted the basis of his action. That which proceeded from it transcended all other books, however elevating their thought. To his astute mind moral and religious principles were the "indispensable supports" of political prosperity, the "essential pillars of civil society." Learned as Jefferson was in the best of the ancient philosophers, he turned to the Bible as the source of his higher thinking and reasoning. Speaking of the lofty teachings of the Master, he said: "He pushed His scrutinies into the heart of man; erected His tribunal in the region of his thoughts, and purified the waters at the fountain head." Beyond this he held that the Bible contained the noblest ethical system the world has known. His own compilation of the selected portions of this Book, in what is known as "Jefferson's Bible," bears evidence of the profound reverence in which he held it.

Entirely apart from these citations of the place the Bible has occupied in the thought and philosophy of the good and the great, it is the veneration in which it has been and is held by vast numbers of our people that gives it its supreme place in our literature. No matter what the accidents and chances of life may bring in their train, no matter what the changing habits and fashions of the world may effect, this Book continues to hold its unchallenged place as the most loved, the most quoted and the most universally read and pondered of all the volumes which our libraries contain. It has withstood assaults, it has resisted and survived the most searching microscopic examination, it has stood every test that could be applied to it and yet it continues to hold its supreme place as the Book of books. There have been periods when it has suffered stern and searching criticism, but the hottest flame has not destroyed its prevailing and persistent power. We cannot read the history of our rise and development as a Nation, without reckoning with the place the Bible has occupied in shaping the advances of the Republic. Its teaching, as has been wisely suggested, is ploughed into the very heart of the race.[36]

In a 1938 letter to Bishop Ernest Lyon Waldorf of the United Methodist Council, Roosevelt stated that "there is need for a return to religion, religion as exemplified in the Sermon on the Mount. . . . Today when we see religion challenged in wide areas of the earth we who hold to old ideals of the Fatherhood of God and the Brotherhood of Man must be steadfast and united in bearing unceasing witness to our faith in things of the spirit."[37]

Beyond these areas of certainty, Roosevelt did not wish to venture. Eleanor Roosevelt once tried to find out whether her husband was truly convinced that the Christian doctrine was true. He said, "I never really thought much about it. I think it is just as well not to think about things like that too much."[38]

In her autobiography, *This I Remember*, Eleanor painted the same picture of her husband, adding more detail:

I am quite sure that Franklin accepted the thought of death as he accepted life. He had a strong religious feeling and his religion was a very personal one. I think he actually felt he could ask God for guidance and receive it. That was why he loved the 23rd Psalm, the Beatitudes, and the 13th Chapter of First Corinthians. He never talked about his religion or his beliefs and never seemed to have any intellectual difficulties about what he believed. Once, in talking to him about some spiritualist conversations which had been sent in to me (people were always sending me their conversations with the dead), I expressed a somewhat cynical disbelief in them. He said to me very simply: "I think it is unwise to say you do not believe in anything when you can't prove that it is either true or untrue. There is so much in the world which is always new in the way of discoveries which we are simply unable now to fathom. Therefore I am interested and have respect for whatever people believe, even if I can not understand their beliefs or share their experiences."

That seemed to me a very natural attitude for him to take. He was always open-minded about anything that came to his attention, ready to look into it and study it, but his own beliefs were the beliefs of a child grown to manhood under certain simple influences. He still held to the fundamental feeling that religion was an anchor and a source of strength and guidance, so I am sure that he died looking into the future as calmly as he had looked at all the events of life.[39]

She also said:

I always felt that my husband's religion had something to do with his confidence in himself. As I have said, it was a very simple religion. He believed in God and His Guidance. He felt that human beings were given tasks to perform and with those tasks the ability and strength to put them through. He could pray for help and guidance and have faith in his own judgment as a result. The church services that he always insisted on holding on Inauguration Day, anniversaries and whenever a great crisis impended were the expression of his religious faith. I think this must not be lost sight of in judging his acceptance of responsibility and his belief in his ability to meet whatever crisis had to be met.[40]

Otis Graham and Meghan Wander described Roosevelt's religion in their book, *Franklin D. Roosevelt: His Life and Times: An Encyclopedic*

View. They said he found Anglicism satisfactory because it did not require him to speak publicly on his inner thoughts. They added that Roosevelt believed "in an all-wise, all-powerful, wholly good, and infinitely loving God the Father, and in Jesus Christ as Son of God."[41]

Roosevelt Biographer Kenneth Davis said that Roosevelt's religious beliefs were simple: "He believed in a loving God who had created and now ruled a world which must therefore be essentially or at least mostly good and in Jesus Christ as the Son of God who had preached the Word of God and whose earthly sufferings had redeemed a sinful mankind. He believed in the immortality of the soul and that a good life is rewarded by heaven."[42]

CONCLUSION

While Roosevelt sometimes attended church and publicly and privately expressed belief in a God who rules the nations and in the value of the Bible for edification and instruction, religion was not a high priority in his life.

NOTES

1. Olga Anna Jones, *Churches of the Presidents in Washington: Visits to Fifteen National Shrines* (New York: Exposition Press, 1954), 68.

2. Kenneth S. Davis, *FDR: The New York Years* (Westminster, MD: Random House, 1979), 6.

3. Franklin Roosevelt, *FDR: His Personal Letters: Early Years*, ed. Elliott Roosevelt (New York: Duell, Sloan and Pearce, 1947), 30.

4. Ibid., 50.

5. Ibid., 159.

6. Ibid., 240.

7. Ibid., 282.

8. Ibid., 284.

9. Ibid., 286.

10. Ibid., 346.

11. Joseph P. Lash, *Eleanor and Franklin: The Story of Their Relationship Based on Eleanor Roosevelt's Private Papers* (New York: Norton, 1971), 153.

12. Otis L. Graham Jr. and Meghan Robinson Wander, *Franklin D. Roosevelt: His Life and Times: An Encyclopedic View* (Boston: G. K. Hall, 1985), 355; Geoffrey C. Ward, *A First-Class Temperament: The Emergence of Franklin Roosevelt: An Intimate Portrait of the Private World, Personal Ordeal, and*

Public Triumph of the Man Who Became FDR (New York: Harper & Row, 1989), 53.

13. Kenneth S. Davis, *FDR: The Beckoning of Destiny, 1882–1928)* (New York: Putnam, 1972), 200–01.

14. Lash, *Eleanor and Franklin*, 228; Ward, *A First-Class Temperament*, 416.

15. Lash, *Eleanor and Franklin*, 244.

16. Roosevelt served as assistant secretary of the Navy from 1913–1920.

17. Lash, *Eleanor and Franklin*, 228.

18. Jones, *Churches of the Presidents in Washington*, 68.

19. Davis, *FDR: The New Deal Years, 1933–1937*, 213.

20. Roosevelt, *FDR: His Personal Letters, 1928–1945*, vol. 1, 10.

21. Davis, *FDR: Into the Storm, 1937–1940*, 143.

22. Davis, *FDR: The New York Years, 1928–1933*, 445–47.

23. Ibid., 443.

24. Roosevelt, *Public Papers of the Presidents of the United States: Franklin D. Roosevelt, 1933.* Washington, DC: Government Printing Office. November 21, 1933. A Thanksgiving Day proclamation.

25. Ibid., December 24, 1933. A Christmas greeting to the nation.

26. Ibid., November 15, 1934. A Thanksgiving Day proclamation.

27. Ibid., January 20, 1937. Second inaugural address.

28. Ibid., November 9, 1937. A Thanksgiving Day proclamation.

29. Ibid., December 24, 1939. A radio Christmas greeting to the nation.

30. Ibid., January 6, 1942. State of the Union address.

31. Ibid., November 26, 1942. A Thanksgiving Day proclamation.

32. Ibid., February 22, 1943. Radio address on Washington's birthday.

33. Ibid., December 24, 1944. Address to the nation.

34. Ibid., January 20, 1945. Fourth inaugural address.

35. Bliss Isley, *The Presidents: Men of Faith* (Boston: W. A. Wilde, 1953), 245; Edmund Fuller and David E. Green, *God in the White House: The Faiths of American Presidents* (New York: Crown Publishers, 1968), 203.

36. Roosevelt, *Public Papers,* October 6, 1935. Statement on the 400th anniversary of the printing of the English Bible.

37. Ibid., January 17, 1938. Letter of greeting to the United Methodist Council.

38. Graham and Wander, *Franklin D. Roosevelt,* 355.

39. Eleanor Roosevelt, *This I Remember* (New York: Harper & Brothers, 1949), 346–47.

40. Ibid., 69–70.

41. Graham and Wander, *Franklin D. Roosevelt,* 355.

42. Davis, *FDR: The Beckoning of Destiny,* 83.

CHAPTER 13

HERBERT CLARK HOOVER

HERBERT HOOVER was born on August 10, 1874, in West Branch, Iowa. His family had been Quakers since the early 1700s. He said of his great-great-great-grandfather Andrew Hoover, "Andrew Hoover was of the Quaker faith as were all his descendants." Hoover said that some of his ancestors were persecuted for their beliefs, and came to the United States to find religious freedom.[1]

Hoover described his Quaker upbringing in these words:

> Individual Bible-reading was a part of the Quaker concept of education—and before I left Iowa I had read the Bible in daily stints from cover to cover. Religious training among the Quakers in fact began almost from birth. Even the babies were present at the invariable family prayers and Bible readings every morning. They were taken to meeting every Sunday, since there was obviously no other place in which to park them. Their cries and hushings thereof were the only relief from the long silences of Quaker worship. The men and women sat divided by a low partition. The elders of the women who sat upon the high "facing-bench" were the only ones of that sex that I could see.[2]

Hoover described permitted reading material by saying: "Mine was a Quaker family unwilling in those days to have youth corrupted with stronger reading than the Bible, the encyclopedia, or those great novels where the hero overcomes the demon rum."[3]

In his *Memoirs*, Hoover described the Quaker faith in these words:

Those who are acquainted with the Quaker faith, and who know the primitive furnishing of the Quaker meeting-house, the solemnity of the long hours of meeting awaiting the spirit to move someone, will know the intense repression upon a ten-year-old boy who might not even count his toes. All this may not have been recreation, but it was strong training in patience.

The Quakers–more properly the "Friends"–were given that sobriquet in the early 17th century, not because they quaked but because of their founder, George Fox's repetitive demand for the authorities of his time to quake and tremble before the Lord. They were one of the many Protestant sects which sprang into being because of the repressions on religious liberty and in protest against religious formalism. Their protest against religious rote up to the recent times expressed itself in their peculiar garb of "plain clothes" and adherence to the "plain language." But as time went on, these very customs, the uniform architecture of meeting-houses, the method of conducting meetings, became a sort of formalism itself. . . .

The religious characteristics of the faith were a literal belief in the Bible, great tolerance, and a conviction that spiritual inspiration sprang from the "inward light" in each individual.[4]

Hoover was a member of the first class to attend Stanford University. The university opened formally on October 1, 1891, and Hoover attended the ceremony.

The University helped shape his thinking. He said:

I attended many lectures on biology, evolution and the reconciliation of science and religion. The impact of the University upon fundamentalist religion of the times brought spiritual conflicts to many youngsters–with much debate. The Quaker "inner light" as the basis of faith, however, suffered less than some others. I much more easily adapted fundamental natural law into my spiritual complex than those whose early training was in the more formalistic sects and of wider doctrinal base.[5]

While at Stanford, Hoover met Lou Henry. Although a branch of Henry's family had been Quakers, and the Quaker traditions had been passed to her through her father, she had been raised as an Episcopalian and was not a practicing Quaker at the time they met.[6] She had been exposed to Quaker teachings while spending three years in the Quaker settlement of Whittier, California.

The couple decided to marry. Though they wanted a Quaker wedding, there was unfortunately no Quaker meetinghouse in Monterey, California, so this could not be arranged. They arranged for a Protestant Minister, Reverend Thoburn, to perform the wedding. However, he died six weeks before the ceremony was to be performed. After a search to find another Protestant minister to perform the wedding proved unsuccessful, family friend Father Mestres, a Catholic minister, agreed at the last minute to perform the wedding.[7] He secured special dispensation from the Catholic church to marry two Protestants and performed the ceremony on February 10, 1899.[8]

Hoover became an engineer in the mining industry in 1895. Between 1903 and 1917 he led what one Hoover expert, Dale Mayer, termed a "one-man campaign to raise ethical standards in the mining industry." He strenuously objected to dishonest advertising and marketing of highly speculative stocks. He wrote numerous letters to the editor and articles exposing the dishonest tactics used in the industry, and eventually left Bewick, Moering (the firm in which he was a junior partner) after discovering that his boss, Algernon Moering, was engaging in marketing speculative stocks.[9] After leaving Bewick, Moering in 1908, he formed his own firm.

Beginning in 1899, Hoover spent several years overseeing mining operations in China. Hoover and his wife were not there long before the Boxer Rebellion erupted in 1900. When it appeared that the Boxers were going to kill everyone in Tientsin, most of the servants fled. However, the Hoover's servants were so loyal that about half stayed, despite Lou Hoover urging them to leave.[10] Hoover also successfully rescued several of his employees from execution when they were wrongfully accused and taken before an illegally constituted court that was executing innocent Chinese.[11]

During his world travels, Herbert and Lou Hoover were unable to maintain a regular membership in Quaker meetings. However, during the years 1901-28, whenever they returned to Stanford and Palo Alto, California, they attended meetings at Dr. Augustus T. Murray's home. Lou Hoover explained the situation in a 1928 letter to a Mrs. Brun:

Living as we did at Stanford most of the time while in this country and having no Meeting nearer than San Jose, and in most the communities of our mining sojourns finding no Meeting at all, I naturally did not carry a Meeting membership although my husband always maintained his in Oregon. The last few years at Stanford have been very interesting with the little Meeting in Professor Murray's house but of course this is not an established one and does not carry 'memberships.'[12]

Although Lou Hoover is not known to have ever become a formal member of a Quaker meeting, she considered herself a Quaker all her married life and regularly attended Quaker services with her husband whenever possible.

Interestingly, this statement is the only known written documentation of Herbert Hoover's status as a recorded member of the Quaker church. While there is no reason to doubt the statement, we have no other external confirmation of the fact. In all likelihood, Hoover did not transfer his recorded membership because they did not attend a formal meetinghouse in California.

Hoover was secretary of commerce under Harding and Coolidge. In his position, he oversaw early federal regulations of radio. Some of the problems that had to be corrected were radio stations that refused to take out licenses and radio stations that frequently shifted from one frequency to another.

Radio evangelist Aimee Semple McPherson owned a radio station in Chicago that not only defied regulations but also drifted from one frequency to another, interfering with the legitimate stations. Hoover, in charge of radio-station regulations, objected. McPherson sent back a vitriolic message: "Please order your minions of Satan to leave my station alone. You cannot expect the Almighty to abide by your wave length nonsense. When I offer my prayers to Him I must fit into His wave reception."[13]

In Herbert Hoover's book *The Cabinet and the Presidency*, he relates how the issue was resolved: "Finally our tactful inspector persuaded her to employ a radio manager of his own selection, who kept her upon her wave length."[14]

Religion was a major issue—perhaps the central issue—in the 1928 presidential election. It was so hotly contested that Hoover called it the "worst plague in the campaign."[15] He was the first candidate of a major party to be a Quaker. This, however, did not stir up as much controversy as the Catholic religion of the Democratic Party's presidential candidate, Al Smith. Since Hoover did not want a political fight over religious questions, he said the following in his August 11, 1928, speech accepting the Republican presidential nomination:

> In this land, dedicated to tolerance, we still find outbreaks of intolerance. I come of Quaker stock. My ancestors were persecuted for their beliefs. Here they sought and found religious freedom. By blood and conviction I stand for religious tolerance both in act and in spirit. The glory of our American ideals is the right of every man to worship God according to the dictates of his own conscience.[16]

Hoover maintained this public stance in private, as his associate director of publicity, Alfred H. Kirchoffer, later recalled. Kirchoffer stated that Hoover gave this policy: "We were not to attack or mention the religion of the opposing candidate, Gov. Smith, [and] we were to conduct a clean fight."[17] However, Governor Smith brought the issue into the open in an Oklahoma speech in which he maintained that religious faith does not disqualify a man from public office.

Both Hoover and his wife believed that Smith did this with the intent to arouse sympathy. Herbert Hoover stated in his memoirs that he believed Smith "thought he would gain by bringing it out into the open."[18] Lou Hoover wrote in a 1928 letter to a friend that Smith did it to "inflame sympathy for himself, and to distract the attention of the thoughtless from the real political issues which he finds are so difficult to meet."[19]

When a Virginia Protestant organization circulated a letter opposing Governor Smith based upon his Catholic beliefs, Hoover issued this statement:

> Whether this letter is authentic or a forgery, it does violence to every instinct that I possess. I resent and repudiate it. Such an attitude is entirely opposed to every principle of the Republican Party. I made my position clear in my acceptance speech. I meant that then and I mean it now.[20]

However, such letters continued to be circulated throughout the campaign. Hoover issued an even stronger repudiation in a September 28 speech:

I cannot fully express my indignation at any such circulars. Nor can I reiterate too strongly that religious questions have no part in this campaign. I have repeatedly stated that neither I nor the Republican Party want support on that basis.[21]

Although the religious question was hotly debated, Hoover believed that it did not have much effect on the result of the election. He said:

Had he [Smith] been a Protestant, he would certainly have lost and might even have had a smaller vote. An indication of the small importance of the religious issue in final results was the vote in New York State. Here Governor Smith, a Catholic, had been twice elected Governor, and therefore no great amount of religious bigotry could have existed. It was for other reasons than his Catholicism that his own state rejected him for President.[22]

Hoover began his inaugural address by saying:

This occasion is not alone the administration of the most sacred oath which can be assumed by an American citizen. It is a dedication and consecration under God to the highest office in service of our people. I assume this trust in the humility of knowledge that only through the guidance of Almighty Providence can I hope to discharge its ever-increasing burdens.[23]

He ended his address by saying: "I ask the help of Almighty God in this service to my country to which you have called me."[24] He also listed several ideals he believed that his election mandated. One was "the growth of religious spirit and the tolerance of all faiths."[25] He repeated similar sentiments in his 1929 State of the Union address to Congress.[26]

On August 8, 1931, Hoover made an interesting radio address to the International Convention of the Young Men's Christian Association. In it he said:

No thoughtful person can overlook the profound truth that the ideas and ideals of Christ which you uphold not only have dominated the course of civilization since His time but are the foundations of our economic and social life today.[27]

His choice of wording in the phrase "which you uphold" is rather interesting, for that wording is sometimes used by those who respect but do not hold the ideals of their audience.

As Hoover prepared for his reelection campaign, he started reconsidering his position on Prohibition. In his 1928 campaign, he expressed support for prohibition. However, under his administration, increased efforts to enforce the ban showed that even a three-fold increase in convictions caused no decline in the illegal activity. By 1930, he concluded that Prohibition could not be enforced. In 1932, he decided to propose this compromise plank to the Republican Platform Committee:

> An amendment should be promptly submitted that shall allow the states to deal with Prohibition as their citizens may determine but subject to the retained power of the Federal government to protect those states where Prohibition may exist. There should be a safeguard against the return of the saloon and its attendant abuses.

The proposed solution of essentially returning the issue to the states was not adopted by the committee; the factions of the committee eventually produced a compromise that did not satisfy any faction.[28] Hoover's compromise position angered some in the religious community. However, he felt that adopting this position was necessary due to the impossibility of actually enforcing the ban.

On June 16, 1932, he accepted the Republican presidential nomination. In an acceptance statement, he outlined his goals, and said that "with unceasing effort, with courage and faith in Almighty God, they will be attained."[29]

While in the White House, the Hoovers were instrumental in building a Quaker meetinghouse in Washington, DC. The Friends Meeting House was completed in January 1931. Respected Quaker leader Dr. Augustus Murray, in whose home the Hoovers had met while in Palo Alto, was persuaded to take a two-year leave of absence from Stanford to head the meetinghouse. The Hoovers contributed to a fund to cover his expenses during the sabbatical.[30]

In an October 22, 1932, speech Hoover gave in Detroit, Michigan, he discussed his thoughts on the cause of our nation's longevity: "Our Nation has survived thus far because it was founded in the favor of God by men and women who were more concerned with His will than they were with selfish aggrandizement and material acquisitions. The ultimate source of great constructive measures of government and of law are in the moral and spiritual impulses of our people."[31]

In a speech delivered on the one hundred fiftieth anniversary of the Battle of Kings Mountain, he touched on a similar theme. After discussing the constitutional principles of liberty, freedom, self-government, and checks and balances, he then said: "No student of American history can fail to realize that these principles and ideals grew largely out of the religious origins and spiritual aspirations of our people."[32] He added: "Our ideals are a binding spiritual heritage. We cannot abandon them without chaos. We can follow them with confidence."[33]

On December 3, 1931, and December 6, 1932, Hoover wrote Christmas messages to be sent to the nation's Christmas Tree Association. In his two messages, he said:

> Your annual Christmas service held at the foot of a living tree ante-dating the birth of Christ, is a dramatic and inspiring event of national interest. It symbolizes and vivifies our greatest Christian festival with its eternal message of unselfishness, joy and peace.[34]

> Your Christmas service held each year at the foot of a living tree which was alive at the time of the birth of Christ, has now for several years lent an inspiring note to the celebration of Christmas. It should be continued as a further symbol of the unbroken chain of life leading back to this great moment in the spiritual life of mankind.[35]

Herbert Hoover believed that Jesus' birth was a historic event, and that it was "a great moment in the spiritual life of mankind."

Hoover had a high respect for the Bible. He said:

> There is no other book so various as the Bible, nor one so full of concentrated wisdom. Whether it be of law, business, morals, or that vision which leads the imagination in the creation of constructive enterprises for the happiness of mankind, he who seeks for guidance in any of these things may look inside its covers and find illumination. The study of this Book in your Bible classes is a postgraduate course in the richest library of human experience.
>
> As a nation we are indebted to the Book of Books for our national ideals and representative institutions. Their preservation rests in adhering to its principles.[36]

He also said:

"The whole inspiration of our civilization springs from the teachings of Christ and the lessons of the prophets. To read the Bible for these fundamentals is a necessity of American life."[37]

For years after his presidency, Hoover kept in touch with world affairs. As an example, he believed that the United Nations should not include Communist countries. On April 27, 1950, he said:

What the world needs today is a definite, spiritual mobilization of the nations who believe in God against this tide of Red agnosticism. . . .

I believe that the United Nations should be reorganized without the Communist nations in it. If that is impractical, then a definite New United Front should be organized of those peoples who disavow communism, who stand for morals and religion, and who love freedom. . . .

It is a proposal for moral and spiritual cooperation of God-fearing free nations. And in rejecting an atheistic other world, I am confident that the Almighty God will be with us."[38]

Hoover died on October 20, 1964, in New York City.

His wife, Lou Hoover, once described him in these words: "He has deeply ingrained in him the Quaker feeling that nothing matters if you are 'right with God.' "[39]

CONCLUSION

Hoover was a Quaker, and Quakers rarely discuss their religious beliefs. What Hoover did say was usually in accordance with traditional Christian doctrine; however, his reticence in religious matters leaves us certain only that he cared about religion, lived an exemplary life, and was active in his church.

NOTES

1. Herbert Hoover, from a 1928 campaign message. Quoted in Eugene Lyons, *Herbert Hoover: A Biography* (Garden City, NY: Doubleday, 1964), 177.

2. Herbert Hoover, *The Memoirs of Herbert Hoover*, vol. 1, *Years of Adventure* (New York: Macmillan, 1951), 8.

3. Ibid., 2.

4. Ibid., 7–8.

5. Ibid., 21.

6. From a letter Lou Henry Hoover wrote to Mrs. Brun on September 15, 1928. It is in the "Personal Correspondence" file of the Lou Henry Hoover Papers at the Herbert Hoover Presidential Library.

7. Dale C. Mayer, *Lou Henry Hoover: A Prototype for First Ladies* (New York: Nova History Publications, 2004), 46–47. In 1930, after becoming frustrated by inaccurate newspaper accounts concerning the wedding prompted by Father Mestres' August 1930 death, Lou Hoover prepared a memorandum on the topic. This memorandum can be found in the "Family History and Genealogy: Information Compiled by Secretaries: Wedding" folder in the Lou Henry Hoover Papers at the Herbert Hoover Presidential Library.

8. Hoover, *Memoirs*, vol. 1, 36.

9. From pp. 13–14 of a Hoover "Information for Biographers, 1916" memorandum in the Pre-Commerce Subject File of the Herbert Hoover Papers in the Herbert Hoover Presidential Library.

10. Mayer, *Lou Henry Hoover*, 75–76.

11. Ibid., 88–91.

12. From a letter Lou Henry Hoover wrote to Mrs. Brun on September 15, 1928. It is in the "Personal Correspondence" file of the Lou Henry Hoover Papers at the Herbert Hoover Presidential Library.

13. Robert H. Ferrell, *The Presidency of Calvin Coolidge* (Lawrence: University Press of Kansas, 1998), 33.

14. Hoover, *The Memoirs of Herbert Hoover*, vol. 2, *The Cabinet and the Presidency*, 143.

15. Ibid., 207.

16. Ibid.

17. From a September 4, 1962, oral history recording made by Albert H. Kirchoffer for the Herbert Hoover Oral History Program at the Herbert Hoover Presidential Library.

18. Hoover, *Memoirs*, vol. 2, 208.

19. From a letter written to Ludmilla Sayre on October 11, 1928, in the "Campaign of 1928: Publicity" subject file of the Lou Henry Hoover Papers in the Herbert Hoover Presidential Library. For an in-depth discussion of the issue, see Mayer, *Lou Henry Hoover: A Prototype for First Ladies*, 232–37.

20. Hoover, *Memoirs*, vol. 2, 208.

21. Ibid.

22. Ibid.

23. Hoover, *Public Papers of the Presidents of the United States: Herbert Hoover, 1929.* Washington, DC: Government Printing Office. March 2, 1929. Inaugural address.

24. Ibid.

25. Ibid.

26. Ibid., December 3, 1929. Annual message to Congress on the State of the Union. The exact quote here was a reference to "the test of the rightfulness of our decisions" being, in part, "the growth of religious spirit [and] the tolerance of all faiths."

27. Ibid., August 8, 1931. Radio address to the world's conference of the Young Men's Christian Association (YMCA).

28. Mayer, *Lou Henry Hoover,* 296-300.

29. Hoover, *Public Papers,* June 16, 1932. Message accepting the Republican presidential nomination.

30. Mayer, *Lou Henry Hoover: A Prototype for First Ladies,* pp. 255-56.

31. Ibid., October 22, 1932. Address in Detroit, Michigan.

32. Ibid., October 7, 1930. Address on the 150th Anniversary of the Battle of Kings Mountain.

33. Ibid.

34. Ibid., December 25, 1931. Message to the Nation's Christmas Tree Association. A note in the *Public Papers of the Presidents* reads: "The message was read at the annual ceremony around the General Grant tree in Grant National Park, Calif. The tree, believed to be the world's oldest living thing, had been designated in 1925 as the Nation's Christmas tree."

35. Ibid., December 25, 1932. Message to the Nation's Christmas Tree Association.

36. William J. Federer, ed. *America's God and Country: Encyclopedia of Quotations* (Coppel, TX: Fame Publishing, 1994), 297.

37. Ibid.

38. Ibid., 296–97.

39. Cranston Jones, *Homes of the American Presidents* (New York: Bonanza Books, 1962), 195.

★

CHAPTER 14

CALVIN COOLIDGE

JOHN CALVIN COOLIDGE (known as Calvin Coolidge) was born on July 4, 1872, in Plymouth, Vermont.

Coolidge's hometown of Plymouth Notch was too small to support a full-time preacher. However, itinerant preachers often visited and delivered sermons. Most preachers were Congregationalists, though Baptists or Methodists sometimes came.[1] Coolidge described the religious attitude of his community in these words: "They kept up no church organization, and as there was little regular preaching, the outward manifestation of religion through public profession had little opportunity, but they were without exception a people of faith and charity and good works. They cherished the teachings of the Bible and sought to live in accordance with its precepts."[2]

Author William Allen White wrote in his Coolidge biography *A Puritan in Babylon*:

> Indeed formal religion did not seem to influence the childhood and youth of Calvin Coolidge. No tradition of the revival nor of any emotional phase of religion survives in the Coolidge story. Doctrinal controversy had no place in Plymouth and particularly in the Notch where the Coolidge store was the core of the social crystal. John Calvin Coolidge and Victoria Josephine did not rear their children like heathen. Children who learn their letters from blocks and begin to read out of the Bible generally pursue their pious way, and when they are old they do not depart from it.[3]

Coolidge attended Sunday school weekly in his childhood and his youth. In his autobiography, Coolidge said: "For most of the time during my boyhood regular Sunday School classes were held in the church which my grandmother Coolidge superintended until in her advanced years she was superseded by my father. She was a constant reader of the Bible and a devoted member of the church, who daily sought for divine guidance in prayer."[4] Coolidge's grandmother also read a chapter of the Bible to him daily.[5]

When Calvin Coolidge's grandfather, Calvin Galusha Coolidge, was dying, he asked his grandson to read him John 1, which he did. At the time, Calvin Coolidge was six years old.[6]

Coolidge attended Amherst College. He described it in these words:

> The places of general assembly were for religious worship, which consisted of the chapel exercises at the first morning period each week day, and church service in the morning, with vespers [evening services] in the late afternoon, on Sundays. Regular attendance at all of these was required. Of course we did not like to go and talked learnedly about the right of freedom of worship, and the bad mental and moral reactions from which we were likely to suffer as a result of being forced to hear scriptural readings, psalm singings, prayers and sermons. We were told that our choice of a college was optional, but that Amherst had been founded by pious men with the chief object of training students to overcome the unbelief which was then thought to be prevalent, that religious instruction was a part of the prescribed course, and that those who chose to remain would have to take it. If attendance on these religious services ever harmed any of the men of my time, I have never been informed of it. The good it did I believe was infinite. Not the least of it was the discipline that resulted from having constantly to give some thought to things that young men would often prefer not to consider. If we did not have the privilege of doing what we wanted to do, we had the much greater benefit of doing what we ought to do. It broke down our selfishness, it conquered our resistance, it supplanted impulse, and finally it enthroned reason.[7]

In college, Professor Charles E. Garman strongly influenced Coolidge's thinking. Coolidge said of Garman:

We looked upon Garman as a man who walked with God. His course was a demonstration of the existence of a personal God, of our power to know Him, of the Divine immanence, and of the complete dependence upon Him as Creator and Father "in whom we live and move and have our being." Every reaction in the universe is a manifestation of His presence. Man was revealed as His son, and nature as the hem of His garment, while through a common Fatherhood we are all embraced in a common brotherhood. The spiritual appeal of music, sculpture, and all other art lies in the revelation it affords of the Divine beauty.

The conclusions which followed from this position were logical and inescapable. It sets man off in a separate kingdom from all the other creatures in the universe, and makes him a true son of God and a partaker of the Divine nature.[8]

If he was not in accord with some of the current teachings about religion, he gave to his class a foundation for the firmest religious convictions. He presented no mysteries or dogmas and never asked us to take a theory on faith, but supported every position by facts and logic. He believed in the Bible and constantly quoted it to illustrate his position. He divested religion and science of any conflict with each other, and showed that each rested on the common basis of our ability to know truth.

To Garman was given a power which took his class up into a high mountain of spiritual life and left them alone with God.

In him was no pride of opinion, no atom of selfishness. He was a follower of the truth, a disciple of the Cross, who bore the infirmities of us all.[9]

After graduation from college, Coolidge studied in a law office. He "fully expected to become the kind of country lawyer" he saw all about him. He planned to spend his life practicing law and perhaps end up a judge. "But it was decreed to be otherwise," he later said. "Some Power that I little suspected in my student days took me in charge and carried me on from the obscure neighborhood at Plymouth Notch to the occupancy of the White House."[10]

He married Grace Anna Goodhue on October 4, 1905.

During both his days as a Massachusetts politician[11] and his days as president,[12] he faithfully attended a Congregational church every Sunday.

He had a pew in the Edwards Congregational Church in Northampton, Massachusetts.[13] He even kept a Bible next to his bed.[14]

When Warren Harding died on August 2, 1923, it was the middle of the night in New England, where Calvin Coolidge was on vacation at his father's house. The attempt to notify Coolidge of Harding's sudden death was complicated by the fact that his father's house had no telephone. So a telegraph brought the news as close as possible, and runners carried it the rest of the way.

Coolidge was awakened in the middle of the night. "Before leaving the room," he said, "I knelt down and, with the same prayer with which I have since approached the altar of the church, asked God to bless the American people and give me power to serve them."[15] His father, a public notary, found the oath that a president is supposed to swear when taking office. He administered the oath to his son—after which the entire family went back to sleep.

Coolidge returned to Washington, DC. The first Sunday after his return, he attended services at Washington's First Congregational Church. "Although I had been rather constant in my attendance," he said in his autobiography, "I had never joined the church." He wrote an account of the service and the subsequent events:

> While there had been religious services, there was no organized church society near my boyhood home. Among other things, I had some fear as to my ability to set that example which I felt always ought to denote the life of a church member. I am inclined to think now that this was a counsel of darkness.
>
> This first service happened to come on Communion day. Our pastor, Dr. Pierce, occupied the pulpit, and, as he can under the practice of the Congregational Church, and always does, because of his own very tolerant attitude, he invited all those who believed in the Christian faith, whether church members or not, to join in the partaking of the communion.
>
> For the first time I accepted this invitation, which I later learned he had observed, and in a few days without any intimation to me that it was to be done, considering this to be a sufficient public profession of my faith, the church voted me into its membership.
>
> This declaration of belief in me was a great satisfaction.
>
> Had I been approached in the usual way to join the church after I became President, I should have appeared that such action

might appear to be a pose, and should have hesitated to accept. From what might have been a misguided conception I was thus saved by some influence which I had not anticipated.

But if I had not voluntarily gone to church and partaken of communion, this blessing would not have come to me.

Fate bestows its rewards on those who put themselves in the proper attitude to receive them.[16]

Grace Coolidge was already a member of a Congregational church in Northampton. She became an associate member in the First Congregational Church of Washington, while Calvin Coolidge became a member.[17]

Though Coolidge may not have engaged in active evangelism, he did recommend his church to one friend, Gilbert H. Grosvenor. He told Grosvenor that Reverend Pierce's sermons were (in the words of Claude Fuess) "the best in Washington."[18]

Customarily, Reverend Dr. Jason Noble Pierce would escort Coolidge out of the church at the end of each service before any of the other attendees left. Once, a visiting minister conducted services. After the sermon, he escorted Coolidge outside. Coolidge, who as usual was quite laconic, did not say a word until the pastor and Coolidge were out of the church. The pastor's hopes of a compliment were crushed when Coolidge's only comment was about the weather: "Rotten day!"[19]

Another story that circulated in Washington during Coolidge's term has not been officially confirmed. People in Washington said that one day Grace Coolidge was unable to attend church. After President Coolidge returned from the service, she asked him what the topic of the minister's sermon was.

President Coolidge responded, "Sin."

"What did he say about it?" Grace Coolidge wondered.

"He didn't like it," Coolidge said.[20]

Grace Coolidge later denied the story.[21]

In his biography, *Calvin Coolidge: The Man from Vermont*, Claude Fuess related this anecdote: "When he was presiding over a meeting of the American Antiquarian Society, a member told him of the magnificent Gutenberg Bible recently purchased by Congress for a fabulous sum. 'I should think,' he commented, 'that an ordinary copy of the King James version would have been good enough for those Congressmen.' "[22]

Coolidge was crushed when his son and namesake Calvin died on July 7, 1924, at age 16. But he resigned himself to God's will. "The ways of Providence are often beyond our understanding," he said. Yet he still wished that God's will had decreed that Calvin would live: "It seemed to me that the world had need of the work that it was probable he could do."[23]

In 1925, Coolidge was sworn in for his second term. The Bible upon which he took the oath was the same Bible from which he had read to his grandfather decades before; at the inauguration, as before, it was open to John 1. Though some 1925 accounts stated that John 1 was Coolidge's favorite passage, if it was, his wife was unaware of it. She wrote: "It always seemed to me that Mr. Coolidge always refrained from expressing a preference for those things that appealed to him most strongly. If he had a favorite passage from the Scriptures, and I feel sure he did, they meant too much to him to permit his talking about them."[24]

Coolidge's inaugural address concluded with these words:

America seeks no earthly empire built on blood and force. No ambition, no temptation, lures her to thought of foreign dominions. The legions which she sends forth are armed, not with the sword, but with the cross. The higher State to which she seeks the allegiance of all mankind is not of human, but of divine origin. She cherishes no purpose save to merit the favor of Almighty God.[25]

In his autobiography, Coolidge said: "The President gets the best advice he can find, uses the best judgment at his command, and leaves the event in the hands of Providence."[26] He also said: "Any man who has been placed in the White House can not feel that it is the result of his own exertions or his own merit. Some power outside and beyond him becomes manifest through him. As he contemplates the workings of his office, he comes to realize with an increasing sense of humility that he is but an instrument in the hands of God."[27]

During his presidency, Coolidge spoke to a national council of Congregational churches, which met in Washington, DC. He said:

I do not know of any source of more power other than that which comes from religion.

I do not know of any adequate support for our form of government except that which comes from religion.

If there are any general failures in the enforcement of the law, it is because there have first been failures in the disposition to observe the law. I can conceive of no adequate remedy for the evils which beset society except through the influences of religion.

There is no form of education that will not fail, there is no form of government that will not fail, there is no form of reward that will not fail.

Redemption must come through sacrifice, and sacrifice is the essence of religion.

It will be of untold benefit if there is a broader comprehension of this principle by the public and a continued preaching of this made by the clergy.

Without that faith all that we have of an enlightened civilization cannot endure.[28]

Calvin Coolidge preferred that clergymen teach Christianity and not the social gospel. In 1932, he granted an interview to a student from Boston Theological Seminary and said:

I wouldn't for a minute be critical of the church and its work, but I think most of the clergy today are preaching socialism. . . .

I think that the church must preach a new birth, a change of heart, and a change of living. I feel that too often this is not done.

I remember a sentence by an old writer to the effect that Jesus Christ never sat in the lobby of the Caesars. In other words, He did not depend for legislation for the advancement of His principles and His kingdom.[29]

In his book, *So Help Me God*, John McCollister stated:

He felt that preaching should be limited to the standard themes: "salvation by grace," "a change of heart," or "the power of prayer." He became highly suspicious of the clergymen who spoke in support of the budding "Social Gospel."[30]

In a September 23, 1926, interview with Bruce Barton, Coolidge explained his religion:

I have always attended church regularly when I could, but there being no organized church in our town when I was a boy, I did not join a church. After I became President the First Congregational Church of Washington, without consulting me, voted to make me a member. I was pleased that they took such action and of course accepted the election to membership which they offered me. . . . It would be difficult for me to conceive of anyone being able to administer the duties of a great office like the Presidency without a belief in the guidance of a divine providence. Unless the President is sustained by an abiding faith in a divine power which is working for the good of humanity, I cannot understand how he would have the courage to attempt to meet the various problems that constantly pour in upon him from all parts of the earth.[31]

After Coolidge's term ended, he returned to Northampton, Massachusetts. He regularly attended Edwards Congregational Church with his wife.[32]

He died on January 3, 1933, in Northampton, and his funeral was held in Edwards Congregational Church.[33]

Conclusion

Though Coolidge's lifetime practice of restraint in public and private kept him from making many religious statements, it appears that the beliefs he did express were in accordance with the basic tenets of Christianity. As with numerous other presidents, he was married to a woman who was a longtime church member. He eventually joined the church himself, gratefully accepting church membership when he was chosen for the honor.

Notes

1. William Allen White, *A Puritan in Babylon: The Story of Calvin Coolidge* (New York: Macmillan, 1938), 14.

2. Calvin Coolidge, *Autobiography of Calvin Coolidge* (New York: Cosmopolitan Book Corporation, 1929), 17–18.

3. White, *A Puritan in Babylon*, 14.

4. Coolidge, *Autobiography*, 17–18.

5. Ibid., 30.

6. White, *A Puritan in Babylon*, 13. Galusha had read it to his grandfather when he was young.

7. Coolidge, *Autobiography*, 54–55.

8. Ibid., 65–66. Partially quoted in White, *A Puritan in Babylon*, 38–39.

9. Coolidge, *Autobiography*, 68–69.

10. Ibid., 79.

11. White, *A Puritan in Babylon*, 83.

12. Ibid., 347. Coolidge would, however, sometimes ride a boat called the *Mayflower* down the Potomac on Sunday afternoons.

13. Ibid., 441.

14. Robert H. Ferrell, *The Presidency of Calvin Coolidge* (Lawrence: University Press of Kansas, 1998), 5.

15. Coolidge, *Autobiography*, 175.

16. Ibid., 178–80.

17. Olga Anna Jones, *Churches of the Presidents in Washington: Visits to Fifteen National Shrines* (New York: Exposition Press, 1954), 74.

18. Claude M. Fuess, *Calvin Coolidge: The Man from Vermont* (New York: Little, Brown, 1939), 315.

19. Jones, *Churches of the Presidents*, 75.

20. Ibid.

21. Fuess, *Calvin Coolidge*, 478.

22. Ibid., 483–84. These incidents are just a few examples of Coolidge's remarkable abilities in laconic wit. Another favorite (though nonreligious) example is when a lady at a dinner in Washington, DC, once told him that she had made a bet with a friend that she could get more than two words out of him during the entire meal. He said "You lose" and passed the rest of the meal in silence.

23. Coolidge, *Autobiography*, 190.

24. Bliss Isley, *The Presidents: Men of Faith* (Boston: W. A. Wilde, 1953), 230.

25. Coolidge, March 4, 1925. Inaugural address.

26. Coolidge, *Autobiography*, 215.

27. Ibid., 234–35.

28. Isley, *The Presidents*, 231. Quoted from February 4, 1933, *Literary Digest*.

29. Ibid., 231–32. Quoted from a publication named *Zion's Herald*.

30. John McCollister, *So Help Me God: The Faith of America's Presidents* (Louisville: Westminster/John Knox Press, 1991), 144.

31. Fuess, *Calvin Coolidge*, 27.

32. Donald R. McCoy, *Calvin Coolidge: The Quiet President* (New York: Macmillan, 1967), 396.

33. White, *A Puritan in Babylon*, 441.

CHAPTER 15

WARREN GAMALIEL BANCROFT WINNIPEG HARDING

WARREN HARDING was born on November 2, 1865, in Corsica, Ohio. His father, George Tryon Harding, was a Baptist. His mother, Phoebe Elizabeth Dickerson Harding, was a Methodist. She became a Seventh-Day Adventist during the last years of her life.[1]

Phoebe Harding gave her son a religious education and taught him how to read: Some of his first lessons were from the Bible. She gave him the middle name "Gamaliel" with hopes that he would become a "teacher of God's people," that is, a preacher.[2]

In 1932, E. Stacy Matheny, former chaplain of the Ohio Senate, published a small volume called *American Patriotic Devotions*. He included a section on the faith of America's presidents. In his chapter on Harding, he said: "At fourteen years of age he was converted in a Methodist revival in Caledonia, Ohio, conducted by the pastor, Reverend G. L. Hahnawalt. Moving to Marion, Warren joined the Baptist church. He never ceased to take an active interest in the church, and for years he was a trustee."[3]

I have found no other book that mentions this otherwise unsubstantiated account. We do know that Harding chose to become a Baptist, although one biographer, Andrew Sinclair, stated that he first flirted with atheism.[4]

Harding married Florence Kling on July 8, 1891. He joined Trinity Baptist Church in Marion, Ohio, and became a trustee of the church. He also joined the Masons, the Elks, and the Moose.

He edited the *Marion Daily Star* and the *Marion Weekly Star*. In a December 19, 1911, editorial, he said:

> The force of moral law has been ignored by seeking cure-alls in statutory laws enacted by men. There has been more concentration on civic correction than moral redemption. . . . The latter must come first and must have its beginning in the individual heart.
>
> The American people are not drifting from the influence of the church, but the pulpit has too often failed to convince and carry the needed conviction. The great truth has never failed, the failure is in its utterance. Not enough preaching has stirred the individual conscience.[5]

He was elected president in 1920. When he heard the news of his election, he said: "It is not the time for exultation but for prayer to God to make me capable of playing my part."[6] He concluded his inaugural address with these words:

> I accept my part with single-mindedness of purpose and humility of spirit, and implore the favor and guidance of God in His Heaven. With these I am unafraid, and confidently face the future.
>
> I have taken the solemn oath of office on that passage of Holy Writ wherein it is asked: "What doth the Lord require of thee but to do justly, and to love mercy, and to walk humbly with thy God?" This I plight to God and country.[7]

In a speech to the American people in Colorado Springs, Colorado, he said:

> I tell you, my countrymen, the world needs more of the Christ, the world needs the spirit of the Man of Nazareth, and if we could bring into the relationships of humanity among ourselves and among nations of the world the brotherhood that was taught by the Christ, we would have a restored world; we would have little or none of war and we would have a new hope for humanity throughout the earth.[8]

In what may have been Harding's last public statement, he said:

> We need less of sectarianism, less of denominationalism, less of fanatical zeal and its exactions, and more of the Christ spirit, more

of the Christ practice, and a new and abiding consecration and reverence for God. I am a confirmed optimist as to the growth of the spirit of brotherhood. . . . We do rise to heights at times when we look for the good rather than the evil in others, and give consideration to the views of all. The inherent love of fellowship is banding men together, and when envy and suspicion are vanquished, fraternity records a triumph and brotherhood brings new blessings to men and to peoples. . . . Christ was the Prince of Peace, and we who seek to render His name glorious must move in the ways of peace and brotherhood and loving service.[9]

While president, Harding attended the Calvary Baptist Church in Washington, DC. The church's minister at the time, Reverend William S. Abernethy, said that Harding often talked with him at the door after the service. Olga Jones, in her book *Churches of the Presidents in Washington*, states that Harding "knew the Bible well." Though Harding participated in many church activities, he felt unworthy to partake in Communion and did not do so.[10]

Harding died on August 2, 1923, on a train near San Francisco, California.

Harding once said: "It is my conviction that the fundamental trouble with the people of the United States is that they have gotten too far away from Almighty God."[11]

CONCLUSION

Harding attended church regularly. We know little of his beliefs on the essential doctrines of Christianity; we do know that he had a high respect for parts of Christianity, declining to take Communion because he believed himself unworthy of the honor. E. Stacy Matheny's account of Harding's conversion at age 14, if accurate, would reveal a hitherto unknown (or, more precisely, forgotten) aspect to his religious character in his youth. It also might supply part of the reason that he chose to remain a Methodist when the rest of his family became Seventh-Day Adventists.

NOTES

1. Robert K. Murray, *The Harding Era: Warren G. Harding and His Administration* (Minneapolis: University of Minnesota Press, 1969), 6.

2. Ibid.

3. E. Stacy Matheny, *American Patriotic Devotions* (New York: Associated Press, 1932), 255.

4. Andrew Sinclair, *The Available Man: The Life Behind the Masks of Warren Gamaliel Harding* (New York: Morrow, 1965), 4.

5. Ralph Chandler Downes, *The Rise of Warren Gamaliel Harding, 1865–1920* (Columbus: Ohio State University Press, 1970), 42.

6. Matheny, *American Patriotic Devotions*, 255.

7. Harding, *Public Papers of the Presidents of the United States: Warren G. Harding, 1921.* Washington, DC: Government Printing Office. March 4, 1921. Inaugural address.

8. Matheny, *American Patriotic Devotions*, 255–56.

9. Herbert Hoover quoted this statement when he dedicated the Harding Memorial in Marion, Ohio, on June 16, 1931. (Hoover, *Public Papers,* June 16, 1931. Address at the dedication of the Harding Memorial in Marion, Ohio.)

10. Olga Anna Jones, *Churches of the Presidents in Washington: Visits to Fifteen National Shrines* (New York: Exposition Press, 1954), 95.

11. John McCollister, *So Help Me God: The Faith of America's Presidents* (Louisville: Westminster/John Knox Press, 1991), 140.

CHAPTER 16

WOODROW WILSON

THOMAS WOODROW WILSON was born on December 29, 1856, in Staunton, Virginia. His parents, Joseph and Jeanie Wilson, were both Presbyterians of Scottish descent. Joseph Wilson was a Presbyterian minister and professor of theology. He was one of the leading pastors in the Southern Presbyterian Church; in fact, the first general assembly of the Southern Presbyterian Church was held in 1861 in his church. He was also the stated clerk of the church's general assembly from 1865 through 1898,[1] and was elected moderator of the general assembly in 1879.[2]

Reverend Wilson taught his son the Bible and the Shorter Catechism:[3] In the words of a granddaughter, Reverend Wilson believed that if parents "couldn't give their own children religious instruction at home, Sunday School wouldn't help much."[4] This belief was passed down to Woodrow Wilson, for he did not send his three daughters to Sunday school, either. Ellen Wilson taught them at home before church services.[5]

Mrs. E. F. Verdery, a church pianist in the church Wilson attended as a child, told Wilson biographer Ray Stannard Baker "that the minister's boy [Woodrow Wilson], whom she thought shy and reserved, was peculiarly affected by music, and that when certain doleful selections were played, such as the hymn, 'Twas on that dark and doleful day,' sung often at communion services, the little boy would sit crying."[6]

During the winter of 1872–73, Wilson attended a series of services hosted by Frank J. Brooke, a student at Columbia Theological

Seminary. At one of these services, Wilson responded to Brooke's invitation for all who accepted Christ to come to the front.[7] Wilson regarded that day as when he became converted to Christianity.

On July 5, 1873, Woodrow Wilson made a confession of faith and applied for a membership in the First Presbyterian Church in Columbia, South Carolina. Church records state that Wilson, along with two other applicants "out of the Sunday school and well known to us all," applied for membership. The church record stated: "After a free confession, during which they severally exhibited evidences of a work of grace begun in their hearts, [they] were unanimously admitted into the membership of this church."[8]

In 1874, a year after his confession of faith and joining the Presbyterian church, Wilson brought "philosophical doubts" to his father. Reverend Wilson answered by saying: "My son, don't you worry about doctrinal problems. Ask yourself this question: Do I love and want to serve the Lord Jesus Christ? If you can answer that in the affirmative, you need not worry."[9]

On May 3 of that year, he discussed his religious beliefs in a journal entry. He said:

> "For in that he himself hath suffered, being tempted, he is able to succor them that are tempted." Heb. 2.18.
>
> I am now in my seventeenth year and it is sad, when looking over my past life to see how few of those seventeen years I have spent in the fear of God, and how much time I have spent in the service of the Devil. Although having professed Christ's name some time ago, I have increased very little in grace and have done almost nothing for the Savior's Cause here below. O, how hard it is to do that which ought to be my greatest delight! *If God will give me the grace I will try to serve him from this time on, and will endeavour to attain nearer and nearer to perfection.*[10]

He then quoted from Dr. Cabot's letter in "Stepping Heavenward." Dr. Cabot said that as gratitude for the infinite favor of redemption granted by the Savior, we must consecrate ourselves entirely to him. Dr. Cabot urged his readers to study their Bible daily, to choose devout and holy associates, and to spend time in prayer.

Wilson attended Davidson College in North Carolina. As part of his studies, he took courses on the Bible in every term. In his freshman year, he studied "Old Testament History, Chronology, and Geography." In his sophomore year, he studied "New Testament in Greek, Harmony of the Gospels." In his junior and senior years, he studied "New Testament in Greek, Epistles." In his junior year, he also studied "Evidences of Christianity."[11]

In an April 2, 1880, debate on whether the "Roman Catholic element in the United States" was "a menace to American Institutions," Wilson argued in the negative. He held that the Roman Catholic Church's claim of supreme authority did not threaten our nation because "the danger was proclaimed and we forearmed" and "because of the unassailable defences of *self-government*." The *Virginia University Magazine* printed a report of the debate. Wilson made this conclusion to his argument: "Our liberties are safe until the memories and experiences of the past are blotted out and the Mayflower with its band of pilgrims forgotten; until our public-school system has fallen into decay and the nation into ignorance; until legislators have resigned their functions to ecclesiastical powers and their prerogatives to priests."[12]

During Wilson's college years, a debate between fundamentalism and modernism split the Presbyterian Church. Biographer Ray Stannard Baker states that Wilson's "scientific" uncle, James Woodrow, "was one of the pioneer leaders of modernism in America and among the first to suffer the discipline of embattled orthodoxy."[13]

The specific point of contention that disturbed conservative Presbyterians was James Woodrow's advocacy of Darwin's evolution theory. As early as 1873, Woodrow had attacked the Reverend Robert Lewis Dabney for "alleged ignorance of modern science."[14] In 1884, James Woodrow notified the board of directors of his university, the Columbia Theological Seminary, that he had accepted Darwin's theory.[15] The seminary leadership asked for James Woodrow's resignation.

In a letter to his future wife, Ellen Louise Axson, Woodrow Wilson clearly aligned himself on the side of modernism and evolution. He said:

> There is something almost amusing in the request that uncle James should confess himself unchristian by resigning before any action has been taken by anybody but Dr. M[ack]! If Dr. M[ack] would but wait and read uncle James's views when they appear, as they will, in print, he would find Dr. Woodrow quite as good a Christian as he—only more conversant with the indisputable[16] facts of science. If uncle J. is to be read out of the Seminary, Dr. McCosh

ought to be driven out of the church, and all private members like myself ought to withdraw without waiting for the expulsion which should follow belief in evolution. If the brethren of the Mississippi Valley have so precarious a hold upon their faith in God that they are afraid to have their sons hear aught of modern scientific belief, by all means let them drive Dr. Woodrow to the wall[.][17]

By January 1885, James Woodrow resigned his seat as the Perkins Professor at Columbia Theological Seminary. Dr. Joseph Mack, the conservative creationist professor who led the fight against evolution in the seminary, was selected to fill his place. Woodrow Wilson was infuriated on hearing the decision; he expressed his opinions in these words:

You will be disgusted and bitterly disappointed to learn that *Dr. Mack* has been elected to fill uncle James's place! I hope that the Seminary *will* die, and die soon, if such pestiferous fellows as he are to be put into its hitherto honoured chairs. *He* in the chair of Science and Religion! He knows about as much of the facts of the one as about the true spirit of the other! What *is* to become of our dear church! She has indeed fallen upon evil times of ignorance and folly![18]

Wilson's modern unorthodox beliefs were not limited to his belief in Darwin's embattled theory of evolution. Wilson biographer Arthur Walworth said of him that he "often joked about 'orthodoxy,' for nothing so much irked this spiritual practitioner of religion as the cant of fundamentalists. To him and to Ellen, hell was only a state of mind."[19]

Wilson's daughter Eleanor confirmed Arthur Walworth's statement. In Eleanor Wilson McAdoo's book, *The Woodrow Wilsons*, she described a scene from her childhood:

[Margaret Wilson] ran into the nursery where Jessie and I were playing on the floor. "I know something," she cried, "something father and mother don't believe in!"

I gazed up at her enquiringly, but Jessie merely said calmly, "I guess it's only Santa Claus."

Margaret's eyes were shining as she answered, "Oh, no! It isn't Santa Claus—it's something important!" Then suddenly she looked a little frightened and ran away as fast as she had come.

Years afterward I remembered that day and asked her to tell me at last what father and mother didn't believe in. "It was Hell," she said. "I heard them say that it was only a state of mind."[20]

On December 28, 1889, Wilson discussed his approach to religious belief in his journal. He said: "I used to wonder vaguely that I did not have the same deep-reaching spiritual difficulties that I read of other young men having. I *saw* the intellectual difficulties, but I was not *troubled* by them: they seemed to have no connection with my faith in the essentials of the religion I had been taught. Unorthodox in my reading of the standards of the faith, I am nevertheless orthodox in my faith. I am capable, it would seem, of being satisfied spiritually without being satisfied intellectually."[21]

He once said, "There are people who *believe* only so far as they can *understand*—that seems to me presumptuous and sets their understanding as the standard of the universe."[22] While he thought the understanding of evolutionary scientists was a standard higher than the Bible, he believed that other parts of the Bible were more authoritative than man's opinions.

Throughout his life, Wilson prayed and read one chapter of the Bible daily.[23] (He wore out several Bibles in his lifetime.) Every Sunday, he attended church services; his observance of the Sabbath was so strict that he even hesitated to read newspapers on Sundays.[24]

By 1884, Wilson was courting Ellen Louise Axson. During their engagement, they maintained a steady correspondence; this often touched on religious subjects. In February 1884, they discussed her father's health. She introduced the topic into their correspondence with these words:

> The Bible, when it tells us to "rejoice evermore," surely means what it says,—means that there shall be evermore something in which to rejoice, and that we should seek and find it.
>
> But oh, it is hard to remember all that when I think of my dear father's "future"! What future is there for one who, at best, *has been* the inmate of an insane asylum? Ah, yes, he has a future,— a glorious future! I *can* "rejoice," even now, and when thinking of *him*;—but it is only by looking steadily away from the present, across the dark, the *hopeless*, but, thank God, the narrow tract which lies between, to that wonderful beyond;—remembering that

"the sufferings of this present time are not worthy to be compared with the glory which shall be revealed." I *am sure* that the God, whose love is as infinite as His wisdom, has ordered it all for His own great and good purposes; and I want to be not merely *submissive* to his will, but gladly acquiescent.[25]

Woodrow Wilson responded:

You are a dear, brave little girl to take your great trouble as you do, with faith and patience and courage. The bright, trustful tone of your letters fills me with a very sweet joy. It does give me such unspeakable comfort, as my thoughts turn, during these quiet Sabbaths, these grave pauses before a new week's work, to the greatest subjects of life, diligence and duty and Christian love and faith, to think that you and I love and confide in and seek to serve the same Saviour, that we are one in these greatest things, as in all things else, and in that wedded life of ours, to which I look forward so eagerly and for which I long so fervently, we shall have that highest joy and strength added to the joy and strength of our love for each other. How can man and woman be happy, I wonder, without that most sure and sacred bond of union?[26]

When Axson's father died, Wilson comforted her with these words: "Your dear father, however sad or tragic his death may have been, is happy now. His Saviour, we may be sure, did not desert his servant at the supreme moment; and it is a joy to think that he is now reunited to the sweet, noble mother who went before him."[27]

Not all of Wilson's letters were this elevated in tone. On March 23, 1884, Wilson informed Axson that he had begun attending the First Presbyterian Church of Baltimore, where the Reverend Dr. James T. Leftwich was the pastor. He described the church in the following words:

I recently made a great "find," namely, a Presbyterian church where there is first rate preaching—first rate by the Baltimore standard, which is not very high or exacting—and plenty of pretty girls. I am now a regular attendant upon its services. One don't [sic] often find attractive orthodoxy in the pulpit and beauty in the pews, so that I am specially gratified because of this discovery. See the advantage of a strict training in doctrine! No amount of beauty in the damsels of an Episcopalian or Methodist or Baptist church could have led me off; but beauty in one's own church may be admitted weekly with a conscience void of offense. By-the-way my orthodoxy has stood still another test. I was invited a short time since to join the finest choir in town; but it was a Methodist choir, and I declined. True, I did not care to join *any* choir; but of course the controlling motive in this case was connected with the question of doctrine. Should I be asked to sing in a Presbyterian choir, I could easily find some other, equally creditable, reason for saying "nay": for Presbyterian choirs should be of the best.[28]

Interestingly enough, Wilson had no such theological compunction about singing in a Unitarian church. On January 11, 1885, he told his future wife that she would be "amused to learn that, at the request of a friend to whom the Glee Club owes return of many favours, I have consented to sing for a few Sundays in a Unitarian church choir. I sang this morning there—and heard a *fine* sermon—a sort of echo from strong New England days."[29]

In an interesting exchange in May 1884, Wilson and Axson discussed predestination. The discussion began with a reference Ellen Axson made to her attempts to find a job as a teacher. She said: "I am sure that, however it turns out, it will be *right*."[30]

Wilson responded: "That's rather an odd philosophy of yours, Miss, that, whatever comes of this will be '*right*': it is almost too near to saying that 'whatever is is right,' wh[ich] is very far from being true. I have full faith in the right ordering of Providence; but we cannot be too careful in seeing to it that we do our duty, not only, but that we do it *in the wisest way*. A false step on our part would not be right because it belonged to the general fore-ordained order of events."[31]

To this, Axson replied: "There is nothing so dreadful in teaching; indeed, it is excellent discipline—'twill do me good. And I *am* sure that all will be well in the end. Beware, Sir, how you try to persuade me to the contrary; for if I once lose faith in all things working together for good, I will, that very hour, lie down and die!"[32]

Wilson reassured her with these words: "Do you really think, my precious mature little sweetheart, that I was trying to persuade you that all things do *not* work together for good? I would as soon try to persuade you that there is no God. I meant only that your little piece of philosophy, as you put it in one of your letters, would justify one in letting things drift, in the assurance that they would drift to a happy result. I was simply expressing, too awkwardly, no doubt, my idea of *how* all things work together for good—through the careful performance of our duty."[33]

In this correspondence, Wilson once wrote to Axson: "I believe in your faith in me as I believe in nothing else except the existence of God and the way of salvation."[34]

Wilson and Axson married on June 24, 1885.

While Wilson was a professor (1888–90) at Wesleyan University in Middletown, Connecticut, Dwight Moody visited the town. Wilson and Moody met at a barber shop; Wilson recalled the incident in the following words:

> I was in a very plebeian place. I was in a barber's shop, sitting in a chair, when I became aware that a personality had entered the room. A man had come quietly in upon the same errand as myself and sat in the chair next to me. Every word that he uttered, though it was not in the least didactic, showed a personal and vital interest in the man who was serving him; and before I got through with what was being done to me, I was aware that I had attended an evangelistic service, because Mr. Moody was in the next chair. I purposely lingered in the room after he left and noted the singular effect his visit had upon the barbers in that shop. They talked in undertones. They did not know his name, but they knew that something had elevated their thought. And I felt that I left that place as I should have left a place of worship.[35]

In 1890, Wilson became a professor at Princeton University. Two Presbyterian churches were in the town and the Wilson family regularly attended the Second Presbyterian Church.[36] Biographer Arthur Link stated that the Wilsons joined the church on June 2, 1897.[37] The May 22 *Princeton Press* stated that Woodrow Wilson was elected a ruling member of the church on May 19, 1897.[38] If both dates are true, Wilson was elected a ruling member of the church a few weeks before he joined the church, an improbable but not impossible situation.

After an attempt he made to reconcile and combine the two Presbyterian churches failed, Wilson and a group of other members left the Second Presbyterian Church and joined the First Presbyterian Church.[39]

Wilson was a member of the Presbytery of New Brunswick; on April 12, 1902, he was appointed a member of that body's Committee on the Historical Society.[40]

In 1900, the Philadelphian Society held a series of meetings at Princeton University on the topic of "Why Thinking Men Should be Christians." On March 1, 1900, Wilson spoke in this series, titling his talk "Some Reasons Why a Man Should Be a Christian." He said that godliness is "profitable in both lives," because it "not only results in salvation of the soul, but enables a man to pursue a confident course in this worldly life, like a straight course in the direction of a visible goal." He said that godliness even "has benefited men who do not believe in Christianity, men who imitate the ways of the righteous, because it has brought to the world through the Bible, humanity, justice, higher civilization and love."

He added: "The only way to carry salvation from this world into the next is by accepting Jesus Christ, by giving him the highest form of love; the love of allegiance."[41]

While it is interesting to note what Wilson said, it is also revealing to note what is *not* said. Wilson reduced salvation to loving Jesus with "the love of allegiance." Even if he would have conceded, if specifically asked, that forgiveness from sins and acceptance in Jesus' substitutionary death was a part of salvation, it evidently did not occur to him to state this in his speech.[42]

In 1902, Wilson was selected as the president of Princeton University. While holding the position, he once spoke to the campus religious society. Biographer Arthur Walworth sums up the speech in these words:

> Standing halfway up the aisle, he confided in the earnest young disciples, told them how his own father had helped him, in his youth, to understand things that his mind could not then grasp. Speaking of the Bible as "the book that best sums up the human spirit," he proclaimed the way of Christ the hardest of paths, and as proof of the vitality of Christianity he cited "the great amount of modern preaching it survives."[43]

During his years as a professor at and as the president of Princeton University, Wilson conducted many chapel services. Though he was the first president of the university who was not an ordained minister, his religious background and knowledge helped him fill this responsibility well. His notes for some of his talks have survived and are reproduced in *The Papers of Woodrow Wilson*. Some talks were theological in tone. In a Sunday afternoon chapel talk on January 13, 1895, his notes state: "*For the Christian, to fear* = to heed with reverence. *What will that lead us to? The plan of salvation*, which comes by belief, acceptance, and saves, not by conduct, but by *regeneration*, by becoming of the blood of Christ. *To know Christ, that is wisdom; and to accept him, understanding.*"[44]

Other talks were more practical; in one of these, he challenged the students with these words: "We have prayed for an intellectual awakening in Princeton that she may be a University indeed: we ought to pray for a spiritual awakening that she may be a power indeed."[45]

In a February 9, 1903, address to the Trenton Young Men's Christian Association, Wilson said: "The culmination of the whole matter is to love somebody higher and nobler than yourself. A man ought not love the Lord Jesus just to be saved. That is selfish. It should not be love for salvation's sake, but service for love's sake. Jesus Christ presents the only perfect example of service for love's sake."[46]

In a 1904 talk on Christian education, Wilson spoke at length on how to teach religion. Fortunately, this speech was transcribed. Wilson said:

> Religion is communicable, I verily believe, aside from the sacred operations of the Holy Spirit, only by example. . . . no amount of didactic teaching in a home whose life is not Christian will ever get into the consciousness and life of the children. If you wish your children to be Christians, you must really take the trouble to be Christians yourselves. Those are the only terms upon which the home will work the gracious miracle.
>
> And you cannot shift this thing by sending your children to Sunday-school. You may remedy many things, but you cannot shift this responsibility. If the children do not get this into their blood atmospherically, they are not going to get it into their blood at all until, it may be, they come to a period of life where the influences of Christian lives outside of the home may profoundly affect them and govern their consciences. We must realize that the first and most intimate and most important organization for the indoctrinating of the next generation is the home, is the family. This is the key to the whole situation. This is the reason that you must get hold of the whole family when you get hold of the children in your

Sunday-school work; that your work will not be half done when you merely get the children there, and it may be, their mothers. You must include the fathers, and get your grip upon the home organization in such wise that the children will have the atmospheric pressure of Christianity the week through.[47]

He added that he believed too much effort was made "to get people to believe for fear of the consequences of unbelief." He believed that nobody was ever drawn into a "personal relationship between man and his maker" for "fear he would go to hell."[48]

While president of Princeton, Wilson maintained orthodoxy in his religious statements. However, he initiated and implemented a major restructuring of the university that directed it away from orthodoxy. Biographer August Heckscher, describing Wilson's policies as a "modernization," stated that Wilson put "Princeton's fundamentalist past behind" and "helped liberate the board from domination by conservative Presbyterians."[49] Wilson appointed the first Roman Catholic and the first Jewish faculty members and "began a major enlargement of the science program." During Wilson's tenure, Princeton's board adopted a resolution in 1906 that made the college a nonsectarian institution.[50]

Wilson believed that ministers should focus not on preaching the social gospel but on the "effectual preaching of the word." He believed that churches should be spiritual institutions, not "philanthropic societies." However, he believed that Christianity was a force through which the whole world must be changed if individuals were to be changed. He said: "Christianity came into the world to save the world as well as to save individual men, and individual men can afford in conscience to be saved only as part of the process by which the world itself is regenerated."[51] While he referred to the role of the church in society, his statement appears to conflict with the orthodox Christian doctrine of individual salvation by faith.

In 1911, Wilson, who had by that time been elected governor of New Jersey, traveled the nation on a speaking tour in anticipation of a possible presidential nomination. On May 7, he spoke to a group of Protestant Christians in Denver on the topic of "The Bible and Progress." He described the Bible in these words: "We know that there is a standard set for us in the heavens, a standard revealed to us in this book which is the fixed and eternal standard by which we judge ourselves."[52]

He concluded this speech with these words: "And the man whose faith is rooted in the Bible knows that reform cannot be stayed, that the finger of God that moves upon the face of the nations is against every man that plots the nation's downfall or the people's deceit; that these men are simply groping and staggering in their ignorance to a fearful day of judgment and that whether one generation witnesses it or not, the glad day of revelation and freedom will come in which men will sing by the host of the coming of the Lord in His Glory."[53]

Wilson was elected president in 1912 and served two terms beginning in 1913. Just before his first inauguration, he gave a speech at Trenton, New Jersey, and said:

> The opinion of the Bible bred in me, not only by the teaching of my home when I was a boy, but also every turn and experience of my life and every step of study, is that it is the one supreme source of revelation, the revelation of the meaning of life, the nature of God and the spiritual nature and need of men. It is the only guide of life which really leads the spirit in the way of peace and salvation. If men could but be made to know it intimately, and for what it really is, we should have secured both individual and social regeneration.[54]

On August 6, 1914, Ellen Wilson died. Shortly afterwards, he typed a brief card to Mrs. Mary Hulbert: "Of course you know what has happened to me; but I wanted you to know direct from me. God has stricken me almost beyond what I can bear."[55]

In January 1915, Nancy Toy visited the Wilsons. In her diary, she recounted a discussion with Wilson concerning religion. This is a rare account describing how Wilson maintained his religious beliefs in conversation. Toy wrote:

> This morning the President went to church accompanied by Margaret and myself. I suggested walking home but the President hates walking and asked if I should enjoy it always followed by four secret service men. In the afternoon Helen and I went with him for a 2? hours motor ride. He talked much about Mrs. Wilson, about my mother and about religion. This began with a question from Helen—did I not enjoy Mr. Fitch's sermons very much? I said I had heard him only once and then he aroused my opposi-

tion by declaring that in this breakdown of civilization, these hugenesses of suffering, life would not be worth living did we not believe that God was behind everything and working out His own plan. I do not believe that and I still think life is worth living, I added. The President took up my challenge. His views are those of Dr. Fitch's.

"*My* life would not be worth living," he declared, "if it were not for the driving power of religion, for *faith*, pure and simple. I have seen all my life the arguments against it without ever having been moved by them."

"Did you never have a religious *Sturm und Drang* period?" I asked.

"No, never for a moment have I had one doubt about my religious beliefs. There are people who *believe* only so far as they *understand*—that seems to me presumptuous and sets their understanding as the standard of the Universe."[56]

Woodrow Wilson married Edith Bolling on December 18, 1915.

While president, Wilson regularly attended Central Presbyterian Church in Washington, DC, and was a member from April 23, 1913, until his death on February 3, 1924.[57] He occasionally attended an Episcopalian church.[58]

In his second inaugural address, Wilson said: "I know now what the task means. I realize to the full the responsibility which it involves. I pray God I may be given the wisdom and the prudence to do my duty in the true spirit of this great people. I am their servant and can succeed only as they sustain and guide me by their confidence and their counsel. The thing I shall count upon, the thing without which neither counsel nor action will avail, is the unity of America—an America united in feeling, in purpose and in its vision of duty, of opportunity and of service."[59]

When he visited Raleigh, North Carolina, in February 1919, he made an address before presenting a portrait of "Stonewall" Jackson to the Capital Club. In this speech he said: "I do not understand how any man can approach the discharge of the duties of life without faith in the Lord Jesus Christ."[60]

He believed in personal belief; he also believed in national belief, once saying that "our country cannot survive materially unless it be redeemed spiritually."[61]

When his League of Nations failed to pass the Senate, he was crushed. He asked his doctor to read him 2 Corinthians 4:8–9: "We are troubled on every side, yet not distressed; we are perplexed, but not in despair; persecuted, but not forsaken; cast down, but not destroyed." During the debate, he said, "If I were not a Christian I think I should go mad."[62] Though he never gave up hope of success, the United States never entered the League.

He died on February 3, 1924, in Washington, DC.

CONCLUSION

Woodrow Wilson was perhaps our most theological president. Throughout his life, and especially during his tenure as president of Princeton University, he expressed his thoughts on numerous and diverse doctrines. Most were orthodox; some were not.

Wilson regularly attended church and maintained membership in the Presbyterian Church after his public profession of faith in 1873.

NOTES

1. John M. Mulder, *Woodrow Wilson: The Years of Preparation* (Princeton, NJ: Princeton University Press, 1978), 3.

2. Ibid., 20.

3. Arthur Walworth, *Woodrow Wilson* (Boston: Houghton Mifflin, 1965), 10.

4. Eleanor Wilson McAdoo, in collaboration with Margaret Y. Gaffey, *The Woodrow Wilsons* (New York: Macmillan, 1937), 42.

5. Mulder, *Woodrow Wilson*, 113.

6. Ray Stannard Baker, *Woodrow Wilson: Life and Letters*, vol. 1, *Youth, 1856–1890* (Garden City, NY: Doubleday, Page, 1927), 47.

7. Mulder, *Woodrow Wilson*, 38.

8. Baker, *Woodrow Wilson*, vol. 1, 67.

9. Walworth, *Woodrow Wilson*, 16.

10. Woodrow Wilson, *The Papers of Woodrow Wilson*, ed. Arthur Stanley Link, vol. 9 (Princeton, NJ: Princeton University Press, 1970), 693–94.

11. Ibid., vol. 1, 26–27.

12. Ibid., 645–46. Quoted from the *Virginia University Magazine*, xix (April 1880), 445–50. I have quoted from the Virginia University Magazine's article, as no exact transcript of Wilson's words survives.

13. Baker, *Woodrow Wilson*, vol. 1, 209.

14. Wilson, *The Papers of Woodrow Wilson*, vol. 3, 219.

15. Ibid.

16. Today the supposed "facts" of evolution are disputed. Among the most prominent defenses of biblical creationism are *The Genesis Flood* by Henry Morris and John Whitcomb; *The Genesis Record* by Henry Morris; *Evolution: The Fossils Still Say No!* by Duane Gish; *Evolution: The Lie* by Ken Ham; and *Refuting Evolution and Refuting Compromise* by Jonathan Sarfati.

17. Wilson, *The Papers of Woodrow Wilson*, vol. 3, 598. From a January 11, 1885, letter to Ellen Louise Axson.

18. Ibid., vol. 3, 218–19.

19. Walworth, *Woodrow Wilson*, 40–41.

20. McAdoo, *The Woodrow Wilsons*, 42.

21. Wilson, *The Papers of Woodrow Wilson*, vol. 6, 462.

22. August Heckscher, *Woodrow Wilson: A Biography* (New York: Scribner, 1991), 23; Wilson, *The Papers of Woodrow Wilson*, vol. 32, 8–9.

23. Baker, *Woodrow Wilson*, vol. 1, 68. See also Walworth, *Woodrow Wilson*, 13; Edmund Fuller and David E. Green, *God in the White House: The Faiths of American Presidents* (New York: Crown Publishers, 1968), 176; Ishbel Ross, *Power with Grace: The Life Story of Mrs. Woodrow Wilson* (New York: G. P. Putnam's Sons, 1975), 66, 123.

24. Wilson, *The Papers of Woodrow Wilson*, vol. 3, 396.

25. Ibid., 7.

26. Ibid., 13.

27. Baker, *Woodrow Wilson*, vol. 1, 208.

28. Wilson, *The Papers of Woodrow Wilson*, vol. 3, 96.

29. Ibid., 598.

30. Ibid., 171.

31. Ibid., 177.

32. Ibid., 187.

33. Ibid., 191–92.

34. Ibid., vol. 6, 126.

35. Baker, *Woodrow Wilson*, vol. 1, 317. Later, when Wilson was asked if this story was a legend, he responded, "No, this is not a legend; it is a fact, and I am perfectly willing that you should publish it. My admiration and esteem for Mr. Moody was very deep indeed." The account and Wilson's comment were published in the November 12, 1914, *Congregationalist*.

36. Wilson, *The Papers of Woodrow Wilson*, vol. 10, 201, 210–11. On March 20, 1897, Wilson wrote the pastor of the First Congregational Church in Middletown, CT, where he had held membership, to ask him to send a letter to his Princeton church so the Wilson family's membership could be changed. He wrote: "It has been a solace to us to feel that we were still members of your church, even if we could not see or hear you—and the churches here have for

long been in such a condition of would-be change that we have had no very ill conscience on the matter. But now we have settled conditions at last, and a clear duty in the matter:—we *must* ask for a letter to the Second Presbyterian Church of Princeton. Indeed we have waited already too long, reluctant to break the last actual tie to Middletown!" (Wilson, *The Papers of Woodrow Wilson*, vol. 10, 201.) The affection that the pastor, Azel Washburn Hazen, felt for the Wilson family is evident from the tone of his return letter, dated April 1, 1897. He said, "Now, my dear friend, I cannot let you sever this formal tie which has for nine years bound you to our church without telling you once more of my esteem and my love for Mrs. Wilson and yourself. You were *ideal* parishioners while here and your expressions ever since have been most friendly. I can never forget your reverent, worshipful bearing in our services, nor your *patient* attention to my too barren words, while your many utterances of regard for myself will long be cherished as a comfort and an inspiration" (Wilson, *The Papers of Woodrow Wilson*, vol. 10, 210–11).

37. Baker, *Woodrow Wilson*, vol. 2, 49.

38. Wilson, *The Papers of Woodrow Wilson*, vol. 10, 242.

39. Baker, *Woodrow Wilson*, vol. 2, 49. This took place on November 29, 1905, while Wilson was president of Princeton University.

40. Wilson, *The Papers of Woodrow Wilson*, vol. 12, 328.

41. Ibid., 453. From the *Daily Princetonian*, March 1, 1900.

42. Wilson commented on speech preparations in a March 1, 1900, letter to his wife: "I was agonizing over an address appointed for the evening in the chapel. I had to speak at a meeting of the Philadelphian Society—one of a ten days' series of meetings arranged, not as a revival in the usual sense of that word, but as a means of rousing the men to a sense of their responsibility for making or not making a choice in respect of Christ. I felt the difficulty and weight of the task in an unusual degree, and my darling's letter brought me the sweet private tonic I needed."

43. Walworth, *Woodrow Wilson*, 95. Interestingly, Wilson had been a proponent of some of that modern preaching—evolutionism—in his own college years.

44. Wilson, *The Papers of Woodrow Wilson*, vol. 10, 121.

45. Ibid., 42, November 8, 1896.

46. Ibid., vol. 14, 354–55.

47. Ibid., vol. 15, 514–15. Printed in Woodrow Wilson, *The Young People and the Church* (Philadelphia: Sunday School Times Co., 1905).

48. Wilson, *The Papers of Woodrow Wilson*, vol. 15, 518–19. Printed in Woodrow Wilson, *The Young People and the Church* (Philadelphia: Sunday School Times Co., 1905).

49. Heckscher, *Woodrow Wilson*, 138.

50. Ibid.

51. Mulder, *Woodrow Wilson*, 41–42.

52. Arthur Stanley Link, *The Life of Wilson*, vol. 1, *The Road to the White House* (Princeton, NJ: Princeton University Press, 1947), 321.

53. Ibid.

54. Josephus Daniels, *The Life of Woodrow Wilson, 1856–1924* (Philadelphia: Winston, 1924), 359.

55. Baker, *Woodrow Wilson*, vol. 4, 479–80.

56. Ibid., vol. 6, 144; Wilson, *Life of Woodrow Wilson*, vol. 2, 64–65.

57. Olga Anna Jones, *Churches of the Presidents in Washington: Visits to Fifteen National Shrines* (New York: Exposition Press, 1954), 37.

58. Ross, *Power with Grace*, 69.

59. Wilson, March 5, 1917, Second Inaugural Address.

60. Wilson, March 5, 1917, Second inaugural address.

61. Daniels, *Life of Woodrow Wilson*, 358.

62. Ross, *Power with Grace*, 212–13.

★

CHAPTER 17

WILLIAM HOWARD TAFT

WILLIAM HOWARD TAFT was born on September 15, 1857, in Cincinnati, Ohio. His father, Alphonso Taft, had been raised as a Baptist but rejected Baptist doctrines for those of Unitarianism. Alphonso and Louise Taft raised their son in the Western Unitarian Conference Church in Cincinnati, where William Taft attended Sunday school in his youth.[1]

Taft's authorized biographer, Henry Pringle, stated that Taft's childhood home "was not a religious one," and through Taft's life, religion "was a matter of relatively slight importance" to him.[2]

In 1878, Taft graduated from Yale University, second in his class. He married Helen Herron on June 19, 1886.

In 1899, after Taft had established his reputation as a lawyer and judge, his brother Henry forwarded him an invitation to become Yale's president. Taft declined, citing two "insuperable objections" that prevented him from accepting the position: "The first is my religious views. The second is that I am not qualified to discharge the most important duties of that office."

He stated that Yale's strongest supporters were "those who believe in the creed of the orthodox evangelical churches." While he recommended departing from "a narrowing tradition" by selecting a layman and not "an ordained minister of the gospel" as the school's next president, he believed that he was not the man.[3] He thought "it would shock the large conservative element of those who give Yale her power and influence in the country to see one chosen to the Presidency who could not subscribe to the creed of the orthodox Congregational Church of New England. If the election of such a one were possible, it would provoke a bitterness of feeling and a suspicion of his every act among those with whom he would have to cooperate in the discharge of his duties that would deprive him of all usefulness and would be seriously detrimental to the university."[4]

He then explained his religious views: "I am a Unitarian. I believe in God. I do not believe in the Divinity of Christ, and there are many other of the postulates of the orthodox creed to which I cannot subscribe. I am not, however, a scoffer at religion but on the contrary recognize, in the fullest manner, the elevating influence that it has had and always will have in the history of mankind."[5] He is never recorded as having changed his mind.

Taft was aware that his beliefs were not in line with those held by most Americans. Thus, in his 1908 campaign for the presidency, he declined to discuss religious questions, stating: "Of course I am interested in the spread of Christian civilization, but to go into a dogmatic discussion of creed I will not do whether I am defeated or not. If the American electorate is so narrow as not to elect a Unitarian, well and good. I can stand it."[6]

Yet Taft was elected president despite the concerns of numerous orthodox Christians—including the pastor of Cincinnati's Second Presbyterian Church, who urged his congregation (among whom were Charles and Annie Taft, the candidate's brother and sister-in-law) to vote for William Jennings Bryan due to Taft's unorthodox religious beliefs.[7]

As president, Taft made religious references in speeches and proclamations. He concluded his inaugural address with these words: "Having thus reviewed the questions likely to recur during my administration, and having expressed in a summary way the position which I expect to take in recommendations to Congress and in my conduct as an Executive, I invoke the considerate sympathy and support of my fellow-citizens and the aid of the Almighty God in the discharge of my responsible duties."[8]

He also referred to God in several Thanksgiving proclamations. In his 1909 proclamation, he listed ways in which God had blessed the nation and concluded: It is altogether fitting that we should humbly and gratefully acknowledge the Divine source of these blessings. Therefore, I hereby appoint Thursday, the twenty-fifth day of November, as a day of general thanksgiving, and I call upon the people on that day, laying aside their usual vocations, to repair to their churches and unite in appropriate services of praise and thanks to Almighty God."9

He expressed similar thoughts in his 1910 Thanksgiving proclamation. After reviewing the blessings of the year, he said: "They are the blessings and bounty of God." He urged the people to "meet in their churches for the praise of Almighty God and to return heartfelt thanks to Him for all His goodness and loving-kindness."10

Theodore Roosevelt, who had handpicked Taft as his successor, disliked the way Taft ran the nation. Roosevelt's decision to run as the candidate of the Bull Moose party split the Republican vote in the 1912 election and resulted in Woodrow Wilson's election.

President Harding appointed Taft chief justice of the Supreme Court. Taft served the remainder of his life in that position, dying on March 8, 1930, in Washington, DC.

CONCLUSION

William Howard Taft believed in God the Father. In official proclamations, he acknowledged that blessings come from God and that we should return thanks to Him for them. He was also tolerant of other religions. He was a religious man, but he privately admitted that he did not believe that Jesus was divine, thereby denying one of the essential elements of Christian doctrine. Thus, if his words expressed his beliefs, and those beliefs did not change before his death, he apparently was not an orthodox Christian.

NOTES

1. Henry Fowles Pringle, *The Life and Times of William Howard Taft: A Biography*, 2 vols. (New York: Holt, Rinehart, and Winston, 1939), 25.

2. Ibid.

3. Ibid., 45.

4. Ibid.

5. Edmund Fuller and David E. Green, *God in the White House: The Faiths of American Presidents* (New York: Crown Publishers, 1968), 170.

6. Pringle, *Life and Times of William Howard Taft*, 374; Fuller and Green, *God in the White House*, 171–72.

7. Pringle, *Life and Times of William Howard Taft*, 374. William's brother Charles Taft was a trustee of the church; Annie was a member.

8. Taft, March 4, 1909, Inaugural address.

9. Taft, *Public Papers of the Presidents of the United States: William Howard Taft, 1909*. Washington, DC: Government Printing Office. November 15, 1909. A Thanksgiving proclamation.

10. Ibid., November 5, 1910. A Thanksgiving proclamation.

CHAPTER 18

THEODORE ROOSEVELT

THEODORE ROOSEVELT was born on October 27, 1858, in New York City. For some time, his family attended Madison Square Presbyterian Church in New York City because no Reformed church was in their area.

At age 16 or 17, Theodore Roosevelt joined St. Nicholas Dutch Reformed Church in New York. He asked his pastor, "When a man believes a thing, is it not his duty to say so? If I joined the church, wouldn't that be the best way for me to say to the world that I believed in God?"[1]

During his years at Harvard University, he taught a Sunday school class for three and a half years at Christ Episcopal Church. When the rector of the church discovered that he was not Episcopalian, he offered Roosevelt an opportunity to become a member. Roosevelt later wrote, "This I refused to do, and so I had to leave. . . . I told the clergyman I thought him rather narrow minded."[2]

The death of his father in 1878 prompted the most religious statements he made in his life. In diary entries, he said: "It is lovely to think of our meeting in heaven," and "Nothing but my faith in the Lord Jesus Christ could have carried me through this, my terrible time of trouble and sorrow."[3] The first of the two diary entries refers to a belief in life after death—a belief Roosevelt did not carry into older age.

He married Alice Hathaway Lee on October 27, 1880. After she died, he married Edith Kermit Carow on December 2, 1886.

Lyman Abbott edited a "liberal religious journal" called *The Outlook*, and in 1909, Roosevelt became a contributing editor. Abbott said of Roosevelt's religion:

> He was very slow to give expression to any religious experience. . . . But there is no doubt in my own mind of his faith in God. But he would not define the term "God" . . . . I do not know Mr. Roosevelt's doctrine of Christ. I can simply say that he demanded the concrete as I do and certainly personified God. He did not endeavor to explain the Godward side of Jesus but was attracted to and imitated the manward side of service.[4]

Theodore Roosevelt said:

> I am mighty weak on the Lutheran and Calvinistic doctrines of salvation by faith, myself, and though I have no patience with much of the Roman Catholic theory of church government, including the infallibility of the Pope, the confessional, and a celibate clergy, I do believe in the gospel of works as put down by the Epistle of James.[5]

He expressed his views in the title and content of his book *Fear God and Take Your Own Part*. He stated the theme of the book in these words: "Fear God; and take your own part! Fear God, in the true sense of the word, means love God, respect God, honor God; and all of this can only be done by loving our neighbor, treating him justly and mercifully, and in all ways endeavoring to protect him from injustice and cruelty; thus obeying, as far as our human frailty will permit, the great and immutable law of righteousness."[6]

He said that fearing God meant acting justly toward "the men within our own borders," the weak and the strong. It also meant treating those outside our borders "as we would wish to be treated in return."[7] He added: "Unless we are thorough-going Americans and unless our patriotism is part of the very fiber of our being, we can neither serve God nor take our own part."[8] Interestingly enough, Roosevelt equated patriotism with religion. For him, perhaps, the two were inextricably connected.

Several of Roosevelt's statements indicate that he had no certainty of life after death. He said: "We have got but one life here, and what comes after it we cannot with certainty tell." As a result of this view, he said: "Death is always and under all circumstances a tragedy, for if it is not, then it means that life itself has become one."[9] He also said: "It is idle to complain or rail at the inevitable; serene and high of heart we must face our fate and go down into the darkness."[10]

In the 1912 presidential campaign when he attempted to win a third term, he told Felix Frankfurter, in the words of biographer William Harbaugh, " 'I've got no glory to get out of being President again. I have no particular religious beliefs' and no sense of assurance that there is a hereafter."[11]

Yet despite Roosevelt's disagreement with orthodox beliefs on doctrines such as eternal life and salvation by faith, he respected the Bible's moral guidelines. H. W. Brands described Roosevelt's religion in these words: "Once when asked to summarize his thoughts on the subject, he cited the Book of Micah: 'To do justly, to show mercy, and to walk humbly before the Lord thy God.' That, he said, was the whole of religion." Brands pithily observed that of the three commands, Roosevelt was "strongest on justice, weaker on mercy, and often conspicuously deficient in humility."[12]

Another time, Roosevelt wrote, "I know not how philosophers may ultimately define religion, but from Micah to James it has been defined as service to one's fellowmen rendered by following the great rule of justice and mercy, of wisdom and righteousness."[13]

Roosevelt also adhered to the outward practices of religion and believed in regular church attendance. He said: "I know all the excuses for not going to church. I know that one can worship the Creator and dedicate oneself to good living in a grove of trees, or by a running brook, or in one's own house, just as well as in a church. But I also know that as a matter of cold fact the average man does not thus worship or dedicate himself."[14] Biographer Edmund Morris observed that "though Sabbath observance meant little to him personally, it meant a lot to many Americans, and he felt an obligation, as President, to respect such common beliefs."[15]

Roosevelt's favorite hymns were "How Firm a Foundation," "Holy, Holy, Holy," "Jerusalem the Golden," and "The Son of God Goes Forth to War."[16]

Roosevelt became president in 1901 after William McKinley was assassinated. He issued a proclamation paying tribute to McKinley, who had lived "a life of largest love for his fellow men" and died "a death of Christian fortitude." He set aside September 19, 1901, the date on which

McKinley would be buried, as a date for the American people to "assemble on that day in their respective places of divine worship, there to bow down in submission to the will of Almighty God, and to pay out of full hearts the homage of love and reverence to the memory of the great and good President, whose death has so sorely smitten the nation."[17]

A few months later, on November 2, 1901, Roosevelt issued his first Thanksgiving proclamation. The nation was still mourning President McKinley's death. However, "in spite of this great disaster," Roosevelt said, "it is nevertheless true that no people on earth have such abundant cause for thanksgiving as we have." After listing some of the blessings God had given he concluded: "We can best prove our thankfulness to the Almighty by the way in which on this earth and at this time each of us does his duty to his fellow men."[18]

Roosevelt's second Thanksgiving proclamation, issued on October 29, 1902, continued the same theme introduced in the first. Roosevelt said that we "seek to praise" the "Giver of Good, . . . not by words only but by deeds, by the way in which we do our duty to ourselves and to our fellow men."[19]

He issued his third Thanksgiving proclamation on Reformation Day (October 31), 1903. In it, he said: "During the last year the Lord has dealt bountifully with us, giving us peace at home and abroad and the chance for our citizens to work for their welfare unhindered by war, famine or plague. It behooves us not only to rejoice greatly because of what has been given us, but to accept it with a solemn sense of responsibility, realizing that under Heaven it rests with us ourselves to show that we are worthy to use aright what has thus been entrusted to our care."[20]

On November 1, 1904, he issued a Thanksgiving proclamation and began by saying: "It has pleased Almighty God to bring the American people in safety and honor through another year, and, in accordance with the long unbroken custom handed down to us by our forefathers, the time has come when a special day shall be set apart in which to thank Him who holds all nations in the hollow of His hand for the mercies thus vouchsafed to us." He then recounted the many blessings given America in 1904 and urged Americans to "cease from their ordinary occupations and gather in their several places of worship or in their homes, devoutly to give thanks unto Almighty God for the benefits he has conferred upon us as individuals and as a nation, and to beseech Him that in the future His Divine favor may be continued to us."[21]

In 1907, President Roosevelt ordered the motto "In God We Trust" to be taken off coins. The silver one-dollar coin had only fifty cents of silver in it, thus, one irreverent person said, "In God we trust—for the other fifty cents." So many protests, however, arose at this move that Congress put the motto back on within a year.[22]

On Reformation Day 1908, Roosevelt issued his last Thanksgiving proclamation. He talked about the nation's material well-being, and said:

> For the very reason that in material well-being we have thus abounded, we owe it to the Almighty to show equal progress in moral and spiritual things. With a nation, as with the individuals who make up a nation, material well-being is an indispensable foundation. But the foundation avails nothing by itself. That life is wasted, and worse than wasted, which is spent in piling, heap upon heap, those things which minister merely to the pleasure of the body and to the power that rests only on wealth. Upon material well-being as a foundation must be raised the structure of the lofty life of the spirit, if this Nation is properly to fulfil its great mission and to accomplish all that we so ardently hope and desire. The things of the body are good; the things of the intellect better; the best of all are the things of the soul; for, in the nation as in the individual, in the long run it is character that counts. Let us, therefore, as a people set our faces resolutely against evil, and with broad charity, with kindliness and good-will toward all men, but with unflinching determination to smite down wrong, strive with all the strength that is given us for righteousness in public and in private life.
>
> Now, therefore, I, Theodore Roosevelt, President of the United States, do set apart Thursday, the 26th day of November, next, as a day of general thanksgiving and prayer, and on that day I recommend that the people shall cease from their daily work, and, in their homes or in their churches, meet devoutly to thank the Almighty for the many and great blessings they have received in the past, and to pray that they may be given the strength so to order their lives as to deserve a continuation of these blessings in the future.[23]

While president, he attended Grace Reformed Church, in Washington, DC.[24]

Roosevelt died on January 6, 1919, in Oyster Bay, New York.

Conclusion

Roosevelt exuded self-confidence throughout his life. One Roosevelt scholar, Gamaliel Bradford, tied his self-confidence to his religious beliefs in an interesting way. Bradford stated: "I cannot find God insistent or palpable anywhere in the writings or the life of Theodore Roosevelt. He had no need of him and no longing, because he really had no need of anything but his own immensely sufficient self. And the abundant, crowding, magnificent presence of this world left no room for another."[25]

We have no evidence that Roosevelt ever accepted the doctrine of salvation by faith. He believed in works, and of works he had plenty, but works do not bring salvation. Unless he did turn to God, his statement that "death is always and under all circumstances a tragedy" was true in his case, as he undoubtedly faced his fate and, as he said he would, went "down into the darkness."

Notes

1. William Henry Harbaugh, *Power and Responsibility: The Life and Times of Theodore Roosevelt* (New York: Farrar, Straus, 1961), 221.

2. Henry Fowles Pringle, *Theodore Roosevelt: A Biography* (New York: Harcourt, Brace, 1931, 1958), 39; Edmund Fuller and David E. Green, *God in the White House: The Faiths of American Presidents* (New York: Crown Publishers, 1968), 163.

3. Harbaugh, *Power and Responsibility*, 222.

4. Fuller and Green, *God in the White House*, 163–64.

5. Ibid., 163.

6. Theodore Roosevelt, *Fear God and Take Your Own Part* (New York: George H. Doran, 1914, 1915, 1916), 15.

7. Ibid., 15–16.

8. Ibid., 18.

9. Fuller and Green, *God in the White House*, 167.

10. Harbaugh, *Power and Responsibility*, 222. Edmund Morris, *Theodore Rex* (New York: Random House, 2001), 8. Quoted in regard to an assassination attempt.

11. Harbaugh, *Power and Responsibility*, 409.

12. H. W. Brands, *TR: The Last Romantic* (New York: Perseus Books/Basic Books, 1997), 716.

13. Harbaugh, *Power and Responsibility*, 222.

14. Fuller and Green, *God in the White House*, 163.

15. Morris, *Theodore Rex*, 533.

16. Ibid.

17. Roosevelt, *Public Papers of the Presidents of the United States: Theodore Roosevelt, 1901*. Washington, DC: Government Printing Office. September 14, 1901.

18. Ibid., November 2, 1901. A Thanksgiving proclamation.

19. Ibid., October 29, 1902. A Thanksgiving proclamation on Reformation Day.

20. Ibid., October 31, 1903. A Thanksgiving proclamation.

21. Ibid., November 1, 1904. A Thanksgiving proclamation.

22. E. Stacy Matheny, *American Patriotic Devotions* (New York: Associated Press, 1932), 117.

23. Roosevelt, *Public Papers*, October 31, 1908. A Thanksgiving proclamation.

24. Olga Anna Jones, *Churches of the Presidents in Washington: Visits to Fifteen National Shrines* (New York: Exposition Press, 1954), 78; Harbaugh, *Power and Responsibility*, 154.

25. Harbaugh, *Power and Responsibility*, 222.

CHAPTER 19

WILLIAM MCKINLEY

WILLIAM MCKINLEY was born on January 29, 1843, in Niles, Ohio.

At age ten, he was saved during a camp-meeting revival. He became a probationary member of the Methodist Church and became a full member six years later after reaffirming his commitment to the faith.

He married Ida Saxton on January 25, 1871. The McKinleys joined the First Methodist Episcopal Church in Canton, Ohio. He became superintendent of the Sunday school, and remained a member of the Methodist Episcopal Church throughout his life.[1]

McKinley was also active in the Canton Young Men's Christian Association (YMCA), participating in its literary club and eventually becoming president of the Canton branch.[2]

McKinley biographer Margaret Leech said of McKinley's religion: "His devout Methodism did not lead him to concern himself with dogma or denominational differences. The loving-kindness of God was McKinley's religion, and the source of his inner serenity. His favorite hymns—'Nearer, My God, to Thee,' 'Lead, Kindly Light,' 'Jesus, Lover of My Soul,' 'There's a Wideness in God's Mercy'—were expressions of a sustaining spiritual communion." She added: "In a day of sharp sectarian prejudice, McKinley was devoid of bigotry, possessing as a grace of his nature the tolerance that is unconscious of its own virtue."[3]

In 1892, McKinley ran for the office of governor of Ohio. In a speech delivered on September 6, he said:

The men who established this government had faith in God and sublimely trusted in Him. They besought His counsel and advice in every step of their progress. And so it has been ever since; American history abounds in instances of this trait of piety, this sincere reliance on a Higher Power in all great trials of our national affairs. Our rulers may not always be observers of the outward forms of religion, but we have never had a president, from Washington to Harrison, who publicly avowed infidelity, or scoffed at the faith of the masses of our people.[4]

Four years later, in 1896, he was elected president of the United States. He began his first inaugural address with these words:

In obedience to the will of the people, and in their presence, by the authority vested in me by this oath, I assume the arduous and responsible duties of President of the United States, relying upon the support of my countrymen and invoking the guidance of Almighty God. Our faith teaches that there is no safer reliance than upon the God of our fathers, who has so singularly favored the American people in every national trial, and who will not forsake us so long as we obey His commandments and walk humbly in His footsteps.[5]

He concluded the speech by again repeating the words of the oath of office. He said, "This is the obligation I have reverently taken before the Lord Most High. To keep it will be my single purpose, my constant prayer; and I shall confidently rely upon the forbearance and assistance of all the people in the discharge of my solemn responsibilities."[6]

He was reelected in 1900. In his second inaugural address, he said:

Entrusted by the people for a second time with the office of President, I enter upon its administration appreciating the great responsibilities which attach to this renewed honor and commission, promising unreserved devotion on my part to their faithful discharge and reverently invoking for my guidance the direction and favor of Almighty God.[7]

While president, he attended the Metropolitan Methodist Church in Washington, DC.[8] He also hosted hymn sings at the White House.

Discussing his daily schedule, biographer Lewis Gould stated, "His evenings were spent with Mrs. McKinley and friends, often reading the Bible aloud, until ten."[9]

McKinley said, "We need God as individuals and we need Him as a people." On May 26, 1899, he wrote in his letter-book: "My belief embraces the Divinity of Christ and a recognition of Christianity as the mightiest factor in the world's civilization."[10]

McKinley issued four Thanksgiving proclamations during his presidency. His first, issued on October 29, 1897, said: "In remembrance of God's goodness to us during the past year, which has been so abundant, let us offer unto Him our thanksgiving and pay our vows unto the Most High." He then recounted the blessings given under God's "watchful providence" and "His mighty hand." He continued:

> For these great benefits it is our duty to praise the Lord in a spirit of humility and gratitude and to offer up to Him our most earnest supplications That we may acknowledge our obligation as a people to Him who has so graciously granted us the blessings of free government and material prosperity, I, William McKinley, President of the United States, do hereby designate and set apart Thursday, the twenty-fifth day of November, for national thanksgiving and prayer, which all of the people are invited to observe with appropriate religious services in their respective places of worship. On this day of rejoicing and domestic reunion, let our prayers ascend to the Giver of every good and perfect gift for the continuance of His love and favor to us, that our hearts may be filled with charity and good will, and we may be ever worthy of His beneficent concern.[11]

On July 6, 1898, the president made an "Address to the People for Thanksgiving and Prayer." The address dealt with the news of military successes in Cuba and in the Philippines. However, McKinley urged his countrymen to withhold their natural feelings of exultation to give praise to God and to pray for the continued success and safety of the American military forces. He said that in the exultation of victory the nation should "reverently bow before the throne of divine grace and give devout praise to God, who holdeth the nations in the hollow of His hands and worketh upon them the marvels of His high will, and who has thus far vouchsafed to us the light of His face and led our brave soldiers and seamen to victory."

He called upon the nation to offer "thanksgiving to Almighty God" for "leading our hosts upon the waters to unscathed triumph," and concluded with these words:

> With the nation's thanks let there be mingled the nation's prayers that our gallant sons may be shielded from harm alike on the battlefield and in the clash of fleets, and be spared the scourge of suffering and disease while they are striving to uphold their country's honor; and withal let the nation's heart be stilled with holy awe at the thought of the noble men who have perished as heroes die, and be filled with compassionate sympathy for all those who suffer bereavement or endure sickness, wounds, and bonds by reason of the awful struggle. And above all, let us pray with earnest fervor that He, the Dispenser of All Good, may speedily remove from us the untold afflictions of war and bring to our dear land the blessings of restored peace and to all the domain now ravaged by the cruel strife the priceless boon of security and tranquillity.[12]

On October 28th, 1898, McKinley issued his second Thanksgiving proclamation. He referred to the "custom of our ancestors" of "giving thanks to Almighty God for all the blessings He has vouchsafed to us during the year." That year, he could not give thanks for peace with all nations; however, he said, "as we were compelled to take up the sword in the cause of humanity, we are permitted to rejoice that the conflict has been of brief duration and the losses we have had to mourn, though grievous and important, have been so few, considering the great results accomplished, as to inspire us with gratitude and praise to the Lord of Hosts." He encouraged the American people to laud and magnify God's name that a protracted war was avoided.

He continued:

> I do therefore invite all my fellow-citizens, as well those who may be at sea or sojourning in foreign lands as those at home, to set apart and observe Thursday, the 24th day of November, as a day of national thanksgiving, to come together in their several places of worship for a service of praise and thanks to Almighty God for all the blessings of the year, for the mildness of the seasons and the fruitfulness of the soil, for the continued prosperity of the people,

for the devotion and valor of our countrymen, for the glory of our victory and the hope of a righteous peace, and to pray that the divine guidance which has brought us heretofore to safety and honor may be graciously continued in the years to come.[13]

By his third Thanksgiving proclamation, issued on October 25, 1899, McKinley was able to include as an item of praise that an "honorable peace" had concluded the Spanish-American War and that the United States was "now on friendly relations with every power of earth." He urged that Thursday, November 30, be observed "as a day of general thanksgiving and prayer," by "all our people on this continent and in our newly acquired islands, as well as those who may be at sea or sojourning in foreign lands; and I advise that on this day religious exercises shall be conducted in the churches or meeting-places of all denominations, in order that in the social features of the day its real significance may not be lost sight of, but fervent prayers may be offered to the Most High for a continuance of the Divine Guidance without which man's efforts are vain, and for Divine consolation to those whose kindred and friends have sacrificed their lives for country."[14]

On October 29, 1900, McKinley issued his fourth and last Thanksgiving proclamation. In it, he set Thursday, November 29, as a "day of thanksgiving and praise to Him who holds the nations in the hollow of His hand." He recommended that Americans again "gather in their several places of worship and devoutly give Him thanks for the prosperity wherewith He has endowed us, for seed-time and harvest, for the valor, devotion and humanity of our armies and navies, and for all His benefits to us as individuals and as a nation; and that they humbly pray for the continuance of His Divine favor, for concord and amity with other nations, and for righteousness and peace in all our ways."[15]

On September 6, 1901, McKinley was shot. The Secret Service quickly caught the assassin. As McKinley was helped to a chair, he saw someone hit the assassin in the face. "Seeing this," biographer Charles Olcott said, "the spirit of the Master, whom he had served all his life, came upon the stricken President, and he cried in a tone of pity, 'Don't let them hurt him.' "[16] McKinley publicly forgave his assassin.[17]

At first, it was hoped that McKinley would recover from his wounds. Surgeons decided to attempt an operation. Biographer Charles Olcott described the scene immediately before the surgery:

From the time he was ten years old, President McKinley had unreservedly, but without ostentation, put his trust in God. It was the richest, deepest thought of his inner soul, and now, as he closed his eyes, realizing that he was about to sleep, perhaps to wake no more, his lips began to move and his wan face lighted with a smile. It was the same trust that now supported him. "Thy kingdom come, thy will be done," he murmured. The surgeons paused. Tears came into the eyes of those about the table. "For thine is the kingdom, and the power, and the glory, forever, Amen." With these words he passed into unconsciousness, while the earnest surgeons sought with all their skill to prolong his life.[18]

After the surgery, he survived for several more days. However, he died on September 14, 1901. Shortly before his death, he quoted the words to the hymn "Nearer, My God, to Thee."[19] His last words were: "It is God's way. His will, not ours, be done."[20]

Dr. Roswell Park did all he could to save McKinley's life. He witnessed McKinley's final moments. Remembering the scene, he observed, "Up to this time, I'd never really believed that a man could be a good Christian and a good politician."[21]

HISTORICAL CONTROVERSIES

Did McKinley make his "fellow-men for whom Christ also died" statement on Philippines policy?

On November 21, 1899, McKinley received the General Missionary Committee of the Methodist Episcopal Church. He talked to them about United States involvement in the Philippines. As they prepared to leave, he made one further statement to them.

Accounts of this final statement agree in most details. A standard version is found in McKinley's authorized biography, *The Life of William McKinley* by Charles Olcott:

Hold a moment longer! Not quite yet, gentlemen! Before you go I would like to say just a word about the Philippine business. I have been criticized a good deal about the Philippines, but don't deserve it. The truth is I did n't [sic] want the Philippines, and when they came to us, as a gift from the gods, I did not know what to do with them. When the Spanish War broke out, Dewey was at Hong-kong, and I ordered him to go to Manila and to capture or destroy the Spanish fleet, and he had to; because, if defeated, he had no place to refit on that side of the globe, and if the Dons were victorious, they would likely cross the Pacific and ravage our Oregon and California coasts. And so he had to destroy the Spanish fleet, and did it! But that was as far as I thought then.

When next I realized that the Philippines had dropped into our laps I confess I did not know what to do with them. I sought counsel from all sides – Democrats as well as Republicans – but got little help. I thought first we would take Manila; then Luzon; then other islands, perhaps, also. I walked the floor of the White House night after night until midnight, and I am not ashamed to tell you, gentlemen, that I went down on my knees and prayed to Almighty God for light and guidance more than one night. And one night it came to me this way – I don't know how it was, but it came: (1) That we could not give them back to Spain – that would be cowardly and dishonorable; (2) that we could not turn them over to France or Germany – our commercial rivals in the Orient – that would be bad business and discreditable; (3) that we could not leave them to themselves – they were unfit for self-government – and they would soon have anarchy and misrule over there worse than Spain's was; and (4) that there was nothing left for us to do but to take them all, and to educate the Filipinos, and uplift and civilize and Christianize them, and by God's grace to do the very best we could by them, as our fellow-men for whom Christ also died. And then I went to bed, and went to sleep, and slept soundly, and the next morning I sent for the chief engineer of the War Department (our map-maker), and I told him to put the Philippines on the map of the United States [pointing to a large map on the wall of his office], and there they are, and there they will stay while I am President![22]

Several phrases have been rendered in different ways in different sources. Instead of Olcott's "when they came to us, as a gift from the gods," Josephus Daniels quotes McKinley as saying "when they came to us, as a gift from God."[23]

Daniels' account was abridged; his much shorter account read: "The truth is I did not want the Philippines and when they came to us as a gift from God, I did not know what to do with them. I walked the floor of the White House night after night, until midnight, and I am not ashamed to tell you, gentlemen, that I went down on my knees and prayed to Almighty God for light and guidance more than one night. And one night it came to me that there was nothing left for us to do but take them all, and to educate the Filipinos and uplift and civilize and Christianize them, and by God's grace to do the very best we could by them as our fellowmen for whom Christ also died. And then I went to bed, and went to sleep and slept soundly."[24]

In absence of an authoritative version, I have followed the longer version.

Disputes over the wording of a phrase are minor details (though possibly significant here). The more serious controversy is over whether McKinley ever made the statement at all.

McKinley scholar Lewis Gould thinks there is a "possibility" that McKinley's statement was either not authentic or exaggerated. In *The Presidency of William McKinley*, he cited the following facts:

The account was written by General James F. Rusling and was published "more than three years after the Methodists had gone to the White House."[25]

In an 1899 book, Rusling stated that Abraham Lincoln said the following words to him in 1863: "I went to my room one day and got down on my knees and prayed Almighty God for victory at Gettysburg." Gould continued quoting, "After thus wrestling with the Almighty in prayer, I don't know how it was, and it is not for me to explain but, somehow or other, a sweet comfort crept into my soul[.]"[26]

The Lincoln and McKinley statements share the words "down on my knees and prayed Almighty God for" and "I don't know how it was."

Because of the similarity of the accounts and the fifteen shared words, Gould concludes that "in the face of two such similar accounts, there is the possibility that Rusling improved on McKinley's words with a device that had served him once before."[27]

That is a possibility, and Gould's speculation contains a surface plausibility. But the evidence shows that this is speculation and there is little ground for even this.

Three arguments against the supposition merit serious consideration:

First, the supposition rests on the argument that the parallel was intentional. Though the accounts have similar ideas, Lincoln and McKinley are not the only two presidents who have prayed while in office. (They are also not alone in telling their friends of their prayers.) Though the accounts have similar wording, a parallel of fifteen words in two phrases is not proof of plagiarism. If this were the only argument that could be made against Gould's supposition, the two accounts would be equally probable. But two other important pieces of evidence remain.

Second, the account was not based on Rusling's word alone. In Olcott's authorized *Life of William McKinley*, volume 2, he stated that the account was "from a report of the interview written by General James F. Rusling, and confirmed by the others who were present. Reprinted by permission from the *Christian Advocate*, January 22, 1903."[28] The other members of the delegation present at that meeting were Bishop Thomas Bowman, Bishop John F. Hurst, Dr. Samuel F. Upham, and Dr. John M. Buckley. Thus, there was not one witness to the truth of Rusling's account but five. Though any could have forgotten the precise wording, at least one of them would have noticed any serious error in fact.

Third, the account of Lincoln praying for victory at Gettysburg was well known before Rusling's 1899 book. William McKinley himself told the story in an 1892 speech—seven years before Rusling's book was published, and nine years before the meeting in question.[29]

When I read Gould's suggestion, I investigated the question for myself. As a preliminary step, I decided to see if the story was well known before Rusling used it. If it was, then McKinley could have heard the story. I did not expect to find that McKinley had not only read but also used the story himself.

Incidentally, I did not have to make a long search to find McKinley's quotation. Lewis Gould referred to it himself in a footnote reference after the passage in *The Presidency of William McKinley* where he discussed the possible unreliability of the verse. Thus, Gould was aware that McKinley knew about the passage. Perhaps he had already formulated his theory, and maintained it in the face of strongly opposing evidence.

Intentional similarity has not been proven; in the face of firsthand testimony, any argument against the statement is, at best, an unlikely possibility. If there was any intentional similarity between the statements, it was likely on McKinley's part.

CONCLUSION

McKinley was one of our most devout presidents. After his salvation at a camp-meeting revival at age ten, he remained committed to Christianity and to his church for the rest of his life. His orthodox religious beliefs had a large and crucial influence on his life and his presidency.

NOTES

1. Charles Sumner Olcott, *The Life of William McKinley,* vol. 2 (Boston and New York: Houghton Mifflin, 1916), 368.

2. Margaret Leech, *In the Days of McKinley* (New York: Harper & Bros., 1959), 11.

3. Ibid., 12.

4. Olcott, *The Life of William McKinley,* vol. 2, 368; Edmund Fuller and David E. Green, *God in the White House: The Faiths of American Presidents* (New York: Crown Publishers, 1968), 159.

5. McKinley, March 4, 1897. First inaugural address.

6. Ibid.

7. McKinley, March 4, 1901. Second inaugural address.

8. Leech, *In the Days of McKinley,* 133.

9. Lewis L. Gould, *The Presidency of William McKinley* (Lawrence: University Press of Kansas, 1980), 242.

10. Olcott, *The Life of William McKinley,* vol. 2, 368.

11. McKinley, *Public Papers of the Presidents: William McKinley, 1897.* Washington, DC: Government Printing Office. October 29, 1897. A Thanksgiving proclamation.

12. Ibid., July 8, 1898. Address for thanksgiving and prayer.

13. Ibid., October 28, 1898. A Thanksgiving proclamation.

14. Ibid., October 25, 1899. A Thanksgiving proclamation.

15. Ibid., October 29, 1900. A Thanksgiving proclamation.

16. Olcott, *The Life of William McKinley,* vol. 2, 316.

17. Daniel G. Reid, et al., *A Concise Dictionary of Christianity in America* (Downers Grove, IL: InterVarsity Press, 1995), 212.

18. Olcott, *The Life of William McKinley,* vol. 2, 318.

19. Gould, *The Presidency of William McKinley,* 252.

20. Benjamin Weiss, *God in American History: A Documentation of America's Religious Heritage* (Grand Rapids: Zondervan, 1966), 114.

21. Cranston Jones, *Homes of the American Presidents* (New York: Bonanza Books, 1962), 159.

22. Olcott, *The Life of William McKinley,* vol. 2, 109–11.

23. Josephus Daniels, *The Wilson Era: Years of Peace—1910–1917* (Chapel Hill: University of North Carolina Press, 1944), 169.

24. Ibid.

25. Gould, *The Presidency of William McKinley,* 141.

26. Ibid. Cited James Fowler Rusling, *Men and Things I Saw in Civil War Days* (New York: Eaton & Mains, 1899), 15.

27. Gould, *The Presidency of William McKinley,* 141.

28. Olcott, *The Life of William McKinley,* vol. 2, 111n.

29. Gould, *The Presidency of William McKinley,* 266.

CHAPTER 20

BENJAMIN HARRISON

BENJAMIN HARRISON was born on August 20, 1833, in North Bend, Ohio. He was raised in a godly household, where the Bible was read, hymns were sung, and the family members prayed together. Harrison's father, John Scott Harrison, made a formal confession of faith on October 8, 1849, and encouraged his son to do the same.

The Harrison family scrupulously observed the Sabbath every Sunday. The nearest Presbyterian church was in Cleves, Ohio. Though services were held there every other week, the Harrisons did not always attend due to poor road conditions. However, every Sunday they sang hymns "from four o'clock until bed-time."[1] Later in life, when Benjamin Harrison had married and had children, he continued to celebrate the Sabbath (on Sunday) with his family and faithfully observed it to the end of his life.

Harrison attended Miami University in Oxford, Ohio. Though the school was a public institution, every president until 1873 was a Presbyterian clergyman.[2] During the time that Harrison attended, most of the professors and trustees were also Presbyterians. School days at the university started with Bible reading and prayer.[3]

While Harrison attended the university, the Reverend Dr. Joseph Claybaugh was professor of Hebrew language and Oriental literature. In a series of revival meetings Claybaugh conducted on the campus in late 1850, Harrison was converted. After he wrote home telling his family about this decision, his sister Sallie wrote back: "Pa received your letter of a few days ago, and you cannot conceive what ineffable delight we all felt, to learn that you intended to connect your self with the church. May you never have cause to regret this step, it is indeed, a great privilege to be members with Christ's followers."[4] After this decision, Harrison regularly attended "prayer meetings and other devotional exercises."[5] Although he eventually decided to enter the legal profession, he did not do so without first devoting serious thought to becoming a minister.[6]

Harrison married Caroline Lavinia Scott on October 20, 1853. Biographer Harry Sievers stated that before "their nuptial vows they had dedicated themselves as formal communicants in the faith of Calvin and of Knox."[7]

In 1854, when he was twenty-one, Benjamin and Caroline Harrison moved to Indianapolis, Indiana, and joined the First Presbyterian Church. In 1925, the church published a *Centennial Memorial*. It said of Harrison: "When he came to this place in 1854 at the age of twenty-one he lost no time in uniting with this church and taking up such work as he found to do. He became a teacher in the Sabbath School, he was constant in his attendance on church meetings; his voice was heard in prayer meetings; he labored for and with young men, especially in the Y.M.C.A. And in whatever way opened, whether public or private, he gave testimony for his faith and the lordship of his Master."[8]

In 1857, Harrison became a deacon in his church. In 1861, he was elected to the position of elder and remained an elder in the First Presbyterian Church for forty years.[9] He also taught the young men's class in the Sabbath (Sunday) school for years.[10]

In the Civil War Harrison entered as a colonel in the Indiana infantry and was promoted to brigadier general. He wrote his wife in the early days of training:

> I hope you all remember us at home and that many prayers go up to God daily for my Regiment and for me. Ask Him for me in prayer, my dear wife, first that He will enable me to bear myself as a good soldier of Jesus Christ; second, that He will give me valor and skill to conduct myself so as to honor my country and my friends; and lastly, if consistent with His holy will, I may be brought "home again" to the dear loved ones, if not, that the rich consolation of His grace may be made sufficient for me and for those who survive.[11]

On May 13, 1864, Harrison wrote a letter to his wife while preparing for a battle. In the letter, he said:

> May God in His great mercy give us a great victory and may the nation give Him the praise. . . .
>
> I am thinking much of you and the dear children and my whole heart comes out towards you in tenderness and love and many earnest prayers will I send up to God this night, should you lose a husband and they a father in the fight, that in His grace you may find abundant consolation and in His providence abundant temporal comfort and support. I know you will not forget me, "should I be numbered among the slain," but let your grief be tempered by the consolation that I died for my country and in Christ.[12]

Harrison believed that men must trust God's decisions to be the best for their lives, whether they liked them or not. Years later in an 1887 letter to his son, Russell, he wrote: "I hope you will renew your Christian faith and duties. It is a great comfort to trust God—even if His providence is unfavorable. Prayer steadies one when he is walking in slippery places—even if things asked for are not given."[13]

After the Civil War, Harrison again taught the young men in his church and continued teaching "regular Bible classes" for decades.[14]

After First Presbyterian's pastor, Reverend Jeremiah P. E. Kumler, left in 1875, Harrison led the committee that sought his replacement. Though the task took two years, the committee eventually found and hired Dr. Myron W. Reed.[15]

Biographer Harry Sievers stated that "while religion had always played a significant role in the General's life, it took on a new depth under the influence of Myron W. Reed, one of the most popular preachers Indianapolis ever had. . . . Reed exerted a strong influence on Harrison."[16]

Harrison led an effort to plant another church in Indianapolis; the "missionary effort" resulted in the Ninth Presbyterian Church of Indianapolis.[17]

In 1876, he ran for governor of Indiana but lost the election. Democrats called him "cold as an iceberg" because his personality was reserved.[18] Biographer Harry Sievers chose another word to describe Harrison, stating that "he was shy; nevertheless, he brought himself to

unbend as the occasion required." Harrison would "sit for hours with
a party of men who are telling good stories and laugh heartily at every
one."[19]

In 1880, Harrison was elected U.S. senator.

He was elected president in 1888 and served for one term. In his
inaugural address, he said:

> My promise is spoken; yours unspoken, but not the less real and
> solemn. The people of every State have here their representatives.
> Surely I do not misinterpret the spirit of the occasion when I
> assume that the whole body of the people covenant with me and
> with each other to-day to support and defend the Constitution
> and the Union of the States, to yield willing obedience to all the
> laws and each to every other citizen his equal civil and political
> rights. Entering thus solemnly into covenant with each other, we
> may reverently invoke and confidently expect the favor and help
> of Almighty God—that He will give to me wisdom, strength, and
> fidelity, and to our people a spirit of fraternity and a love of right-
> eousness and peace.[20]

Harrison's proclamations and speeches as president are replete with
religious references. One of his first acts was to issue a proclamation
commemorating the centennial of the formal organization of the
United States government when George Washington took the oath of
office. That morning, Harrison stated, "All the churches of the city"
prayed for "God's blessing on the Government and its first President."
He then said:

> In order that the joy of the occasion may be associated with a deep
> thankfulness in the minds of the people for all our blessings in the
> past and a devout supplication to God for their gracious continu-
> ance in the future, the representatives of the religious creeds, both
> Christian and Hebrew, have memorialized the Government to des-
> ignate an hour for prayer and thanksgiving on that day.
>
> Now, therefore, I, Benjamin Harrison, President of the United
> States of America, in response to this pious and reasonable request,
> do recommend that on Tuesday, April 30, at the hour of 9 o'clock
> in the morning, the people of the entire country repair to their
> respective places of divine worship to implore the favor of God

that the blessings of liberty, prosperity, and peace may abide with us as a people, and that His hand may lead us in the paths of right-eousness and good deeds.[21]

During Harrison's presidency, there were eight seats on the cabi-net. He selected a Presbyterian to fill every seat.[22]

On June 7, 1889, Harrison issued a directive to the Army and Navy urging them to observe Sunday, quoting and reinforcing Abraham Lincoln's 1862 directive to that effect. The statement read:

In November, 1862, President Lincoln quoted the words of Washington to sustain his own views, and announced in a general order that—

The President, Commander in Chief of the Army and Navy, desires and enjoins the orderly observance of the Sabbath by the officers and men in the military and naval service. The importance for man and beast of the prescribed weekly rest, the sacred rights of Christian soldiers and sailors, a becoming deference to the best sentiment of a Christian people, and a due regard for the divine will demand that Sunday labor in the Army and Navy be reduced to the measure of strict necessity.

The truth so concisely stated can not be too faithfully regarded, and the pressure to ignore it is far less now than in the midst of war. To recall the kindly and considerate spirit of the orders issued by these great men in the most trying times of our history, and to promote contentment and efficiency, the President directs that Sunday-morning inspection will be merely of the dress and gen-eral appearance, without arms; and the more complete inspection under arms, with all men present, as required in paragraph 950, Army Regulations, 1889, will take place on Saturday.[23]

President Harrison issued four Thanksgiving proclamations during his presidency. In his first, issued on November 1, 1889, he said:

A highly favored people, mindful of their dependence on the bounty of Divine Providence, should seek fitting occasion to testify gratitude and ascribe praise to Him who is the author of their many blessings. It behooves us, then, to look back with thankful hearts over the past year and bless God for His infinite mercy in vouchsafing to our land enduring peace, to our people freedom from pestilence and famine, to our husbandmen abundant harvests, and to them that labor a recompense of their toil.

Now, therefore, I, Benjamin Harrison, President of the United States of America, do earnestly recommend that Thursday, the 28th day of this present month of November, be set apart as a day of national thanksgiving and prayer, and that the people of our country, ceasing from the cares and labors of their working day, shall assemble in their respective places of worship and give thanks to God, who has prospered us on our way and made our paths the paths of peace, beseeching Him to bless the day to our present and future good, making it truly one of thanksgiving for each reunited home circle as for the nation at large.[24]

On November 8, 1890, President Harrison issued his second Thanksgiving proclamation. In it he called on Americans to "meet in their accustomed houses of worship, and to join in rendering gratitude and praise to our beneficent Creator for the rich blessings He has granted to us as a nation and in invoking the continuance of His protection and grace for the future."[25]

His third Thanksgiving proclamation (1891) called for "a day of joyful thanksgiving to God for the bounties of His providence, for the peace in which we are permitted to enjoy them, and for the preservation of those institutions of civil and religious liberty which He gave our fathers the wisdom to devise and establish and us the courage to preserve."[26]

On June 29, 1892, Harrison issued a proclamation commemorating the four hundredth anniversary of Columbus's discovery of America. He said: "In the churches and in the other places of assembly of the people let there be expressions of gratitude to Divine Providence for the devout faith of the discoverer and for the divine care and guidance which has directed our history and so abundantly blessed our people."[27]

On November 4, 1892, President Harrison issued his fourth and last Thanksgiving proclamation. It said:

The gifts of God to our people during the past year have been so abundant and so special that the spirit of devout thanksgiving awaits not a call, but only the appointment of a day when it may have a common expression. He has stayed the pestilence at our door; He has given us more love for the free civil institutions in the creation of which His directing providence was so conspicuous; He has awakened a deeper reverence for law; He has widened our philanthropy by a call to succor the distress in other lands; He has blessed our schools and is bringing forward a patriotic and God-fearing generation to execute His great and benevolent designs for our country; He has given us great increase in material wealth and a wide diffusion of contentment and comfort in the homes of our people; He has given His grace to the sorrowing.

Wherefore, I, Benjamin Harrison, President of the United States, do call upon all our people to observe, as we have been wont, Thursday, the 24th day of this month of November, as a day of thanksgiving to God for His mercies and of supplication for His continued care and grace.[28]

Shortly after Harrison's 1888 election, Republican Matt Quay of Pennsylvania traveled to Indiana to congratulate Harrison. Quay, who had worked in the campaign, apparently had too high an opinion of himself; when Harrison said, "Providence has given us the victory," Quay grumbled to a Pennsylvania newspaper reporter that "he ought to know that Providence hasn't had a _____ thing to do with it."[29]

While Harrison continued believing that God's will directed the elections, Quay continued disbelieving. When Harrison and Quay later talked about the upcoming 1892 presidential election, Harrison said that God had "put him where he was." To this Quay responded: "Let God re-elect you then" and left the White House and the campaign.[30] Though Harrison did lose the 1892 campaign, it was not due to a lack of reliance on God.

In 1889, when the Church of the Covenant (since renamed The National Presbyterian Church) held its first service, President Benjamin Harrison was present. In *Churches of the Presidents in Washington*, Olga Jones stated that President and Mrs. Harrison attended "church with much regularity" while in Washington.[31]

After Caroline Harrison died, Benjamin Harrison married Mary Scott Lord.

He served several times in the Presbyterian Church's general assembly, supporting, in the words of Edmund Fuller and David Green, "liberalizing, or 'modernist' church policies."[32]

He died on March 13, 1901, in Indianapolis, Indiana.

CONCLUSION

Harrison's conversion at Miami University and his decision to join the Presbyterian Church commenced a lifelong commitment to Christianity. His religious beliefs influenced his presidency and the rest of his career.

NOTES

1. Harry J. Sievers and Katherine Speirs, *Benjamin Harrison*, vol. 1, *Hoosier Warrior: Through the Civil War Years, 1833–1865*, 2nd ed., rev. (New York: University Publishers, 1960), 28.

2. Ibid., 59.

3. Ibid., 49.

4. Ibid., 59.

5. Ibid., 60.

6. Homer E. Socolofsky and Allan B. Spetter, *The Presidency of Benjamin Harrison* (Lawrence: University Press of Kansas, 1987), 7.

7. Sievers and Speirs, *Benjamin Harrison*, 112.

8. Ibid., 113; Edmund Fuller and David E. Green, *God in the White House: The Faiths of American Presidents* (New York: Crown Publishers, 1968), 154.

9. Sievers and Speirs, *Benjamin Harrison*, vol. 1, 113.

10. Socolofsky and Spetter, *The Presidency of Benjamin Harrison*, 7.

11. Fuller and Green, *God in the White House*, 155.

12. Sievers and Speirs, *Benjamin Harrison*, vol. 1, 246.

13. Sievers and Speirs, *Benjamin Harrison*, vol. 2, *Hoosier Statesman: From the Civil War to the White House, 1865–1888* (New York: University Publishers, 1959), 309–10.

14. Ibid., 8, 75.

15. Ibid., 76–77.

16. Ibid., 163.

17. Ibid.

18. Fuller and Green, *God in the White House*, 155.

19. Sievers and Speirs, *Benjamin Harrison*, vol. 1, 114.

20. Harrison, March 4, 1889. Inaugural address.

21. Harrison, *Messages and Papers of the Presidents: Benjamin Harrison, 1889.* April 4, 1889. A proclamation commemorating the April 30 centennial of the formal organization of the United States government.

22. Socolofsky and Spetter, *The Presidency of Benjamin Harrison*, 23.

23. Harrison, *Messages and Papers*, June 7, 1889. A directive to the Army and Navy.

24. Ibid., November 1, 1889. A Thanksgiving proclamation.

25. Ibid., November 8, 1890. A Proclamation.

26. Ibid., November 13, 1891. A Thanksgiving proclamation.

27. Ibid., June 28, 1892. On the 400th anniversary of Columbus's discovery of America.

28. Ibid., November 13, 1892. A Thanksgiving proclamation.

29. Paul F. Boller Jr., *Presidential Campaigns* (New York and Oxford: Oxford University Press, 1984), 161.

30. Ibid., 165.

31. Olga Anna Jones, *Churches of the Presidents in Washington: Visits to Fifteen National Shrines* (New York: Exposition Press, 1954), 20.

32. Fuller and Green, 156.

CHAPTER 21

GROVER CLEVELAND

STEPHEN GROVER CLEVELAND was born on March 18, 1837, in Caldwell, New Jersey. His father, Richard Falley Cleveland, was a Presbyterian clergyman. Richard Cleveland's family clearly understood that one day of the week was to be devoted to the Lord. As a child, Grover attended all the church's services, beginning with a sermon, Sunday school, another sermon, and an afternoon prayer meeting. After the children went to sleep, the parents went to church for a final evening service.[1]

While Reverend Cleveland was pastor of a Presbyterian church in Fayetteville, New York, Grover became a communicant. Even when he later lived in Buffalo, New York, "he kept his name on the roll of his father's old church in Fayetteville."[2] He was a communicant in the Presbyterian Church throughout his life.

After his father died, Grover supported his mother and his younger siblings. His two older brothers served in the Civil War; but Grover paid a substitute to go in his place so he could remain home and help the family.

Cleveland entered politics by serving as the sheriff of Erie County, New York. In this position, he was the hangman at the execution of two murderers.

Cleveland served as the twenty-second and twenty-fourth president of the United States from 1885 to 1889 and from 1893 to 1897. He married Frances Folsom on June 2, 1886, during his first term.

He concluded his first inaugural address by urging his listeners to "not trust to human effort alone, but humbly acknowledging the power and goodness of Almighty God, who presides over the destiny of nations, and who has at all times been revealed in our country's history, let us invoke His aid and His blessings upon our labors."[3]

Cleveland issued eight Thanksgiving proclamations as President. On November 2, 1885, he issued his first (and longest) Thanksgiving proclamation. It said:

> The American people have always abundant cause to be thankful to Almighty God, whose watchful care and guiding hand have been manifested in every stage of their national life, guarding and protecting them in time of peril and safely leading them in the hour of darkness and of danger.
>
> It is fitting and proper that a nation thus favored should on one day in every year, for that purpose especially appointed, publicly acknowledge the goodness of God and return thanks to Him for all His gracious gifts.
>
> Therefore, I, Grover Cleveland, President of the United States of America, do hereby designate and set apart Thursday, the 26th day of November instant, as a day of public thanksgiving and prayer, and do invoke the observance of the same by all the people of the land.
>
> On that day let all secular business be suspended, and let the people assemble in their usual places of worship and with prayer and songs of praise devoutly testify their gratitude to the Giver of Every Good and Perfect Gift for all that He has done for us in the year that has passed; for our preservation as a united nation and for our deliverance from the shock and danger of political convulsion; for the blessings of peace and for our safety and quiet while wars and rumors of wars have agitated and afflicted other nations of the earth; for our security against the scourge of pestilence, which in other lands has claimed its dead by thousands and filled the streets with mourners; for plenteous crops which reward the labor of the husbandman and increase our nation's wealth, and for the contentment throughout our borders which follows in the train of prosperity and abundance.
>
> And let there also be on the day thus set apart a reunion of families, sanctified and chastened by tender memories and associations; and let the social intercourse of friends, with pleasant

reminiscence, renew the ties of affection and strengthen the bonds of kindly feeling.

And let us by no means forget while we give thanks and enjoy the comforts which have crowned our lives that truly grateful hearts are inclined to deeds of charity, and that a kind and thoughtful remembrance of the poor will double the pleasures of our condition and render our praise and thanksgiving more acceptable in the sight of the Lord.[4]

His second Thanksgiving proclamation, issued on November 1, 1886, recounted the blessings of God and called on Americans to "acknowledge the goodness and mercy of God and to invoke His continued care and protection." He said: "And while we contemplate the infinite power of God in earthquake, flood, and storm, let the grateful hearts of those who have been shielded from harm through His mercy be turned in sympathy and kindness toward those who have suffered through His visitations.

"Let us also in the midst of our thanksgiving remember the poor and needy with cheerful gifts and alms so that our service may by deeds of charity be made acceptable in the sight of the Lord."[5]

On October 25, 1887, Cleveland issued his third Thanksgiving proclamation. He urged the people to suspend secular work and employment, assembling "in their accustomed places of worship and with prayer and songs of praise give thanks to our Heavenly Father for all that He has done for us, while we humbly implore the forgiveness of our sins and a continuance of His mercy."[6]

He issued his fourth Thanksgiving proclamation on November 1, 1888. He urged the American people to acknowledge all that God had done for them as a nation and encouraged them to "suspend their ordinary work and occupations, and in their accustomed places of worship, with prayer and songs of praise, [and] render thanks to God for all His mercies[.]" He added: "And mindful of the afflictive dispensation with which a portion of our land has been visited, let us, while we humble ourselves before the power of God, acknowledge His mercy in setting bounds to the deadly march of pestilence, and let our hearts be chastened by sympathy with our fellow-countrymen who have suffered and who mourn.

"And as we return thanks for all the blessings which we have received from the hands of our Heavenly Father, let us not forget that He has enjoined upon us charity; and on this day of thanksgiving let us generously remember the poor and needy, so that our tribute of praise and gratitude may be acceptable in the sight of the Lord."[7]

After a four-year hiatus, Cleveland returned to the presidency in 1893. He began his second inaugural address by saying: "In obedience of the mandate of my countrymen, I am about to dedicate myself to their service under the sanction of a solemn oath. Deeply moved by the expression of confidence and personal attachment which has called me to this service, I am sure my gratitude can make no better return than the pledge I now give before God and these witnesses of unreserved and complete devotion to the interests and welfare of those who have honored me."[8]

He concluded the address with these words: "Above all, I know there is a Supreme Being who rules the affairs of men and whose goodness and mercy have always followed the American people, and I know He will not turn from us now if we humbly and reverently seek His powerful aid."[9]

On November 3, 1893, he issued his fifth Thanksgiving proclamation, the first of his second term. The proclamation said:

> While the American people should every day remember with praise and thanksgiving the divine goodness and mercy which have followed them since their beginning as a nation, it is fitting that one day in each year should be especially devoted to the contemplation of the blessings we have received from the hand of God and to the grateful acknowledgment of His loving kindness.
>
> Therefore, I, Grover Cleveland, President of the United States, do hereby designate and set apart Thursday, the 30th day of the present month of November, as a day of thanksgiving and praise to be kept and observed by all the people of our land. On that day let us forego our ordinary work and employments and assemble in our usual places of worship, where we may recall all that God has done for us and where from grateful hearts our united tribute of praise and song may reach the Throne of Grace. Let the reunion of kindred and the social meeting of friends lend cheer and enjoyment to the day, and let generous gifts of charity for the relief of the poor and needy prove the sincerity of our thanksgiving.[10]

His sixth Thanksgiving proclamation, issued on November 1, 1894, encouraged the American people to "gratefully render thanksgiving and praise to the Supreme Ruler of the Universe, who has watched over them with kindness and fostering care during the year that has passed; they should also with humility and faith supplicate the Father of All Mercies for continued blessings according to their needs, and they should by deeds of charity seek the favor of the Giver of Every Good and Perfect Gift." As in his other proclamations, he concluded by urging Americans to remember the poor and needy: "Surely He who has given us comfort and plenty will look upon our relief of the destitute and our ministrations of charity as the work of hearts truly grateful and as proofs of the sincerity of our thanksgiving."[11]

On November 4, 1895, he issued his seventh Thanksgiving proclamation. Besides urging Americans to give thanks, he urged them to pray that God would not forsake the United States. He said: "And with our thanksgiving let us humbly beseech the Lord to so incline the hearts of our people unto Him that He will not leave us nor forsake us as a nation, but will continue to us His mercy and protecting care, guiding us in the path of national prosperity and happiness, enduing us with rectitude and virtue, and keeping alive within us a patriotic love for the free institutions which have been given to us as our national heritage."[12]

On November 4, 1896, he issued his eighth and final Thanksgiving proclamation:

> The people of the United States should never be unmindful of the gratitude they owe the God of Nations for His watchful care, which has shielded them from dire disaster and pointed out to them the way of peace and happiness. Nor should they ever refuse to acknowledge with contrite hearts their proneness to turn away from God's teachings and to follow with sinful pride after their own devices.
>
> To the end that these thoughts may be quickened it is fitting that on a day especially appointed we should join together in approaching the Throne of Grace with praise and supplication.
>
> Therefore, I, Grover Cleveland, President of the United States, do hereby designate and set apart Thursday, the 26th day of the present month of November, to be kept and observed as a day of thanksgiving and prayer throughout our land.
>
> On that day let all our people forego their usual work and occupation, and, assembled in their accustomed places of worship, let

them with one accord render thanks to the Ruler of the Universe for our preservation as a nation and our deliverance from every threatened danger, for the peace that has dwelt within our boundaries, for our defense against disease and pestilence during the year that has passed, for the plenteous rewards that have followed the labors of our husbandmen, and for all the other blessings that have been vouchsafed to us.

And let us, through the mediation of Him who has taught us how to pray, implore the forgiveness of our sins and a continuation of heavenly favor.

Let us not forget on this day of thanksgiving the poor and needy, and by deeds of charity let our offerings of praise be made more acceptable in the sight of the Lord.[13]

While president, Grover Cleveland attended the First Presbyterian Church in Washington, DC, later known as the National Presbyterian Church. During Cleveland's time, Reverend Byron Sunderland was the church's pastor.[14]

On January 7, 1904, Cleveland's oldest daughter, Ruth, died at 12 years of age. After her death, he wrote a letter about the event to a friend and said:

I had a season of great trouble in keeping out of my mind the idea that Ruth was in the cold, cheerless grave instead of in the arms of her Saviour. It seems to me I mourn our darling Ruth's death more and more. So much of the time I can only think of her as dead, not joyfully living in heaven. God has come to my help and I have been able to adjust my thought to dear Ruth's death with as much comfort as selfish humanity will permit. One thing I can say: not for a moment since she left us has a rebellious thought entered my mind.[15]

During the spring of 1908, Cleveland's health went into decline. His sister, Mrs. E. B. Yeomans, wrote: "During these last weeks, he sent to his old home for one of the worn hymn books that were used at family prayers in his boyhood."[16] A longtime friend, St. Clair McKelway, wrote: "As weakness more encroached, he faced the inevitable with trust in the Almighty and with good will to mankind. The intent look which often came into his face was not due to misapprehension."[17]

Cleveland died on June 24, 1908, in Princeton, New Jersey. One of his sisters wrote that "his boyhood's faith brightened his dying hours."[18]

In recent years, Cleveland biographer Richard E. Welch Jr. has portrayed Cleveland as a man who "possessed no religious world view"[19] and who "largely shed the Presbyterian dogma of his boyhood." However, Welch cited no evidence to support these revisionist claims, besides that Cleveland "exhibited little or no religious prejudice."[20] However, exhibiting little or no religious prejudice hardly constitutes proof for the claim that Cleveland had no religious worldview and abandoned Presbyterian doctrine. In none of Cleveland's writings and statements—neither those quoted in this chapter nor any others I have encountered—have I found any evidence that Cleveland abandoned orthodox doctrine. Even Welch contradicts his previous statements, when he says that Cleveland "never saw reason to doubt the creed of his boyhood, and he expressed irritation with those who sought rationalist explanations of scriptural passages."[21]

Welch also claimed that the influence of Cleveland's Presbyterian upbringing has been exaggerated. If so, then Cleveland himself did the exaggerating, when he said that his upbringing as the son of a minister was "more valuable to me as a strengthening influence than any other incident in my life."[22]

CONCLUSION

Cleveland was a Presbyterian throughout his life. He was raised in the church, stayed a church member, and held to his faith in his final hours. While I found little in his public or private writings about his religious beliefs, what he did say was always in accordance with orthodox Christian doctrine.

NOTES

1. Robert M. McElroy, *Grover Cleveland: The Man and the Statesman: An Authorized Biography*, vol. 1 (New York: Harper & Bros., 1923), 6–7.

2. Franklin Steiner, *The Religious Beliefs of Our Presidents* (Girard, KS: Haldeman-Julius, 1936; repr., Amherst, NY: Prometheus Books, 1995), 47.

3. Cleveland, March 4, 1885. First inaugural address.

4. Cleveland, *Messages and Papers of the Presidents: Grover Cleveland, 1885*. November 2, 1885. A Thanksgiving proclamation.

5. Ibid., November 1, 1886. A Thanksgiving proclamation.

6. Ibid., October 29, 1887. A Thanksgiving proclamation.

7. Ibid., November 1, 1888. A Thanksgiving proclamation.

8. Cleveland, March 4, 1893. Second inaugural address.

9. Ibid.

10. Cleveland, *Messages and Papers,* November 3, 1893. A Thanksgiving proclamation.

11. Ibid., November 1, 1894. A Thanksgiving proclamation.

12. Ibid., November 4, 1895. A Thanksgiving proclamation.

13. Ibid., November 4, 1896. A Thanksgiving proclamation.

14. Allan Nevins, *Grover Cleveland: A Study in Courage to the End of a Career* (New York: Dodd, Mead, 1932), 301.

15. Steiner, *Religious Beliefs,* 49.

16. McElroy, *Grover Cleveland,* vol. 2, 385.

17. Ibid.

18. Steiner, *Religious Beliefs,* 49.

19. Richard E. Welch Jr., *The Presidencies of Grover Cleveland* (Lawrence: University Press of Kansas, 1988), 16.

20. Ibid., 74.

21. Ibid., 16. He referred to a May 23, 1888, speech, "Remarks before the Northern and Southern Presbyterian Assemblies at Philadelphia," reprinted in *Public Papers of Grover Cleveland, Twenty-second President of the United States, 1885–1889* (Washington, DC: Government Printing Office, 1889).

22. Richard G. Hutcheson Jr., *God in the White House: How Religion Has Changed the Modern Presidency* (New York: Macmillan, 1988), 56.

CHAPTER 22

CHESTER ALAN ARTHUR

CHESTER ALAN ARTHUR was born on October 5, 1829, in Fairfield, Vermont. His father, Reverend William Arthur, grew up as a Presbyterian but married Malvina Stone in an Episcopal church. Malvina Stone's uncle, John Stone, was a Baptist preacher.[1]

In 1827, William Arthur attended and was converted at a Freewill Baptist revival held in Burlington, Vermont. That same year he joined the Baptist clergy and was licensed to preach.[2]

After that, as one of his son's biographers says, "The following year he [William] switched to the larger 'regular' or 'close communion' sect, underwent a formal clerical examination, and was ordained May 8, 1828."[3] Within a month, William Arthur received a pastorate in Fairfield, Vermont, and moved there.[4] The next year, his son Chester was born.

Though Chester grew up in a church environment, he never personally committed his life to Christ. His biographer Thomas Reeves says: "While Chester, on occasion, attended a local church with Nell— a proper duty of proper people—he would never exhibit the personal commitment to the Gospel of Christ that would have pleased his father." Though his parents prayed that Chester and his brother William would believe in Christ, their request was apparently never granted. The two brothers' "hostility to the faith" eventually "estranged them from their parents."[5]

Their mother, Malvina, wrote letters to her sons, urging them to believe in Christ. One such letter to Chester's brother William read:

Dear William I am very much interested in your welfare as you well know and I pray God every day and all the time to bless you and keep you from temptation for I know that many surround you, that drunkenness, licentiousness, profane swearing, and gambling are to be found in the Army as much or more than anywhere else, I pray God to keep you from all those sins, and you may hate them all as God hates them. O that you would obey the commands of Christ to believe in him and be Baptized, for if you live or die, you will need religion more than all the world can give you. Dear Son, how long will you live in rebellion against God and refuse to obey his commandments? O that God would answer this my prayer, that before I am taken from life, you and Chester may come out publickly [sic], confess Christ, and be willing to be fools, for his sake. I know that he will lead you to everlasting life if you are willing.[6]

We do not know whether William ever responded to his mother's pleas and prayers; to the best of our knowledge, Chester never did.

While attending Union College, Chester Arthur wrote the following paper—one of only three of his college writings known to be extant:

A Brief Universal History from the Deluge to the Present Time

Moses being the only man that survived the distruction [sic] of earth's inhabitants by water, after living some time in the open air, set his son Nebudchadnezzar to build Solomon's temple. In the course of which happened the confusion of languages, and this was the cause why the temple was left unfinished. About this period Alexander the Great after a siege of some months, took the tower of Babel by storm, and put all its inhabitants to the sword. But soon after he was attacked with vertigo, and fell into the bullrushes, where he was found by Pharoh's daughter, to be taken care of.[7]

Was it written as a joke, as an early rebellion against his religious heritage, or simply a serious attempt at history by a confused young man? While his biographer Thomas Reeves thinks it was a joke, we simply do not know.

Arthur married Ellen Lewis Herndon on October 25, 1859. She attended an Episcopal church and sang in its choir.[8] Though Arthur attended the church with her, he never joined or made a public confession of faith.[9]

He rose in politics through the New York State Republican Party's spoils system. As a concession to the Stalwart wing of the party, he was nominated for the vice presidency in 1880.

Arthur became president when Garfield was assassinated. On September 22, 1881, shortly after he took office, Arthur issued a proclamation setting September 26th, the date Garfield's remains would be buried, as a "day of humiliation and mourning," earnestly recommending that the people "assemble on that day in their respective places of divine worship, there to render alike their tribute of sorrowful submission to the will of Almighty God and of reverence and love for the memory and character of our late Chief Magistrate."[10]

Arthur served as president from 1881 to 1885 and issued four Thanksgiving proclamations. The first, issued on November 4, 1881, expressed thanksgiving for the blessings of the year but also reflected the sadness over Garfield's death. Arthur said that though the nation lay "in the shadow of a great bereavement," yet "the countless benefits which have showered upon us during the past twelve months call for our fervent gratitude and make it fitting that we should rejoice with thankfulness that the Lord in His infinite mercy has most signally favored our country and our people."

Arthur called the nation to ascribe honor and praise "to Almighty God, whose goodness has been so manifest in our history and in our lives, and offering earnest prayers that His bounties may continue to us and to our children."[11]

In his second Thanksgiving proclamation, issued on October 25, 1882, he designated Thursday, November 30, 1882, as a day of public thanksgiving. He explained reasons that the nation had to be thankful: "[T]he peace and amity which subsist between this Republic and all the nations of the world," "the increasing friendship between different sections of the land," "liberty, justice, and constitutional government," and blessings closer to home, such as "the liberal return for the mechanic's toil affording a market for the abundant harvests of the husbandman." He concluded:

> Wherefore I do recommend that the day above designated be observed throughout the country as a day of national thanksgiving and prayer, and that the people, ceasing from their daily labors

and meeting in accordance with their several forms of worship, draw near to the throne of Almighty God, offering to Him praise and gratitude for the manifold goodness which He has vouchsafed to us and praying that His blessings and His mercies may continue.

And I do further recommend that the day thus appointed be made a special occasion for deeds of kindness and charity to the suffering and the needy, so that all who dwell within the land may rejoice and be glad in this season of national thanksgiving.[12]

He issued his third Thanksgiving proclamation on October 26, 1883. He acknowledged God as the "Giver of all Good" and recommended that on Thanksgiving Day "the people rest from their accustomed labors and, meeting in their several places of worship, express their devout gratitude to God that He hath dealt so bountifully with this nation and pray that His grace and favor abide with it forever."[13]

Arthur's fourth and final Thanksgiving proclamation was issued on November 7, 1884. In it, he urged the people "throughout the land" to "keep holiday at their several homes and their several places of worship, and with heart and voice pay reverent acknowledgment to the Giver of All Good for the countless blessings wherewith He hath visited this nation."[14]

After his wife Ellen's death, Chester Arthur gave a window in her memory to St. John's Episcopal Church in Washington, DC. He directed it to be placed on the south side of the building where it was visible from the White House.[15]

On July 5, 1882, Arthur's presidential checkbook records that he contributed funds for a Negro church.[16]

Arthur died on November 18, 1886, in New York City. His funeral services were held on Monday, November 22, 1886, in New York City's Church of the Heavenly Rest.[17]

CONCLUSION

Arthur received a godly upbringing from his father and his mother. However, to the best of our knowledge, he rejected this heritage. While he regularly attended church throughout his life, he never made a public profession of faith, never became a church member, and never (so far as we know) expressed belief in the doctrines of orthodox Christianity.

NOTES

1. George Frederick Howe, *Chester A. Arthur: A Quarter-Century of Machine Politics* (New York: Dodd, Mead, 1935), 3.

2. Thomas C. Reeves, *Gentleman Boss: The Life of Chester Alan Arthur* (New York: Knopf, 1975), 4.

3. Ibid., 5.

4. Howe, *Chester A. Arthur*, Howe notes that Henry Crocker's *History of the Baptists in Vermont* (pp. 371, 388, 390, 409, 444) and *Proceedings of the Fifth Annual Meeting of the Baptist Convention of the State of Vermont* both discuss William Arthur's "career as a Vermont clergyman."

5. Reeves, *Gentleman Boss*, 34.

6. Ibid., 35. Written on January 26, 1863. This is in the Arthur family papers in the Library of Congress.

7. Ibid., 9.

8. Edmund Fuller and David E. Green, *God in the White House: The Faiths of American Presidents* (New York: Crown Publishers, 1968), 146.

9. Ibid., 147.

10. Arthur, *Messages and Papers of the Presidents: Chester A. Arthur, 1881.* September 22, 1881.

11. Ibid., November 4, 1881. A Thanksgiving proclamation.

12. Ibid., October 25, 1882. A Thanksgiving proclamation.

13. Ibid., October 26, 1883. A Thanksgiving proclamation.

14. Ibid., November 7, 1884. A Thanksgiving proclamation.

15. Reeves, *Gentleman Boss*, 276.

16. Ibid., 312.

17. Ibid., 418.

CHAPTER 23

JAMES ABRAM GARFIELD

JAMES A. GARFIELD, the twentieth president of the United States, was born on November 19, 1831, in Orange, Ohio.

His parents, Abram and Eliza Garfield, converted to Christianity and joined a Disciples of Christ church when James was about two. After Abram died suddenly in 1833, Eliza remained in the church and continued to pass its teachings on to her children.

On March 3, 1850, James Garfield was converted. He came forward at the end of a camp meeting held by William Lillie, a Disciples of Christ preacher. Seven other young men from the area, including his good friend, Orrin Judd, were also saved.[1] He was baptized the next day. He noted in his diary entry for that day, March 4, "Today I was buried with Christ in baptism and arose to walk in newness of life."[2]

Garfield became a member of the Disciples of Christ. Alexander Campbell founded this denomination in 1809, with the assistance of his father Thomas. The denomination arose from the Restoration movement,[3] which sought to restore New Testament teaching.[4] The Christian Church (Disciples of Christ) was formed as a result of an 1831 merger of the Campbellite Disciples of Christ and Burton Stone's "Christians."[5] Alexander Campbell's emphasis was on the absence of creeds and denominations and on accepting all who had received Jesus as Savior and had been baptized by immersion. They also emphasized that, in the words of Thomas Campbell, "Where the Scripture speaks, we speak; where the Scriptures are silent, we are silent."[6] Thus, they shunned creeds and sought to base their theology on the Bible, to the best that they could understand it. Their doctrines include autonomy of local churches, plurality of eldership, weekly Sunday Communion, and admission to the church only after baptism by immersion.[7]

Garfield accepted these doctrines, such as the emphasis on the authority of the Bible over human traditions. He wrote in his diary: "I wish that men would let all human traditions alone and take the Bible alone as their guide."[8] He accepted other Disciples of Christ doctrines, such as that Christians should not take part in either war or in government, until his college years. Williams College was a Calvinistic school and his exposure there led him to change some of his views. (He became a general in the Civil War and a president of the United States because he did.) After exposure to Calvinist friends and their creeds, he argued the affirmative in a debate on the question, "Is War Justifiable?"[9]

In the spring of 1853, he began preaching at Disciples of Christ churches; by 1854 he preached nearly weekly. Before long, he spoke at two or more churches each Sunday.[10] Though he usually preached at Disciples of Christ congregations, he was invited at least once to preach to a "Free Will Baptist House" while he attended Williams College. (He described that occasion in these words: "I gave them the Division of the Word and the Setting up of the New Kingdom for an hour and a half and the old deacons said it was good Baptist doctrine, but I am afraid they could not adopt it and still hold their places in the F.W.B. fold."[11])

Biographer Allen Peskin stated that Garfield's sermons "stressed ethics rather than salvation; God's love rather than His wrath."[12] Garfield did believe in salvation, but according to Peskin, this was not his emphasis.

Garfield read the Bible daily. While still a student, he went on a mountain climb. At the end of the day, fellow climbers asked him to lead them in festivities. Instead he said, "Boys, I am accustomed to read a chapter with my absent mother every night: shall I read aloud?" Everyone permitted him.[13]

In the summer of 1851, Garfield visited a spiritualist session in Cleveland, Ohio, hosted by sisters Katie and Margaret Fox. Garfield asked for the spirit of his deceased father to be called up. He described the following communication:

> It (what professed to be it) responded by rapping. The rapping of
> no two spirits were alike. I asked my father his name. I called over
> several names and when the right one was called it rapped! In this

way it told me my own name, that I had one brother living, told me his name, said I had one brother in the spirit land, name given, age also, and told me how many years he (father) had been dead. There were many other tests and correct answers.[14]

Many other people in the area visited such sessions. According to one author, the spirit communications "undercut, and sometimes directly challenged, Christian doctrines about life after death,"[15] and in some areas of Northern Ohio "left behind a great deal of smoke and ashes where the inherited New England orthodoxy had been."

In May 1851, the atheist Joseph Treat held a series of talks on spirit rapping at the Hiram Methodist Church in Hiram, Ohio. He expressed a willingness to debate the issue.

After several days, Professor Thomas Munnell accepted the challenge. Munnell maintained the view that though the spirits were real, they were evil spirits. According to one Garfield biographer, Garfield "was not too sure that Munnell had taken the right tack on the spirit-rappings."[16]

After several days of debate between Munnell and Treat, students urged Garfield to replace Munnell, for they believed that the professor was too courteous to oppose a sarcastic atheist. Garfield accepted the responsibility and began to debate Treat. Corydon Fuller, a friend of Garfield, described one of Garfield's performances:

> Mr. Garfield arose and said that he had listened with great attention to the gentleman's speech, and hardly knew what to say in answer, but he would like to ask him one question. Would he be so kind as to tell the audience what was the present participle of the verb *to be*, in Greek, or, in other words, the Greek word to correspond with the English word "being"? Mr. Treat made no answer, and Mr. Garfield repeated his question and challenged him to answer, but *the poor man did not know*. Then, turning to his audience, he asked them what they thought of a man traveling over the country criticizing the work of the world's greatest scholars, when he did not know the very first thing the school-boy learned in his Greek grammar.[17]

After Treat regained his composure, the debate resumed. In a debate about a week later, Garfield defended the authority of the Bible.

He said that "truth is mighty, eternal, and the Bible firm as the Throne of God shall stand when kingdoms crumble and the planets crash."[18]

By the close of the debates, neither Garfield nor Treat would concede defeat. However, Treat left town afterward and, so far as is known, never returned.

In 1855, while Garfield was attending Williams College, the school was swept by revival. Though he disagreed with elements of the Baptist doctrine, he cooperated with them and kept his doctrinal differences to himself—in public. He did admit them in a letter sent to his future wife, Lucretia Randolph:

> They are having a great "Revival" in College now, and though I cannot subscribe to all the ways and means, yet I believe there is much good being done, and I can truly say I have never been among more spiritually minded Christians than those I find in Williams College. I am heartily cooperating with them in arousing the unconcerned to the interests of the Christian religion, but I let them have their way in reference to doctrine. I do not think I should be doing right to impose a discordant element at such a time as this, though I can hardly resist my desire to tell them what the Gospel is.[19]

In 1856, Garfield was debating what course he should follow in life. "I hope I am willing to follow the path of duty wherever it may lead," he wrote. He continued:

> I believe the first great duty of a Christian is to seek his own highest good by the highest and most harmonious activity of all the faculties of his body, mind, and heart. This work will include all his duties, to God and his fellow men, which grow out of his relations to them. As a prerequisite to this work, one must find his proper sphere in life, and fill that station to which he is best adapted.[20]

In 1857, Ohio, Garfield's home state, was swept by the final wave of the Great Awakening. During one two-week camp meeting, Garfield spoke nearly daily for two weeks and led forty people to the Lord.[21]

When he went to New England to attend Williams College, he preached among the Disciples of Christ in Vermont and New York.

By some accounts, Garfield stepped away from the pulpit after his college years. Though he did change his mind on some of the doctrines he held in early life (e.g., pacifism, a young earth,[22] and the role of Christians in politics), he never left the faith. Some of his sermons were published in B. A. Hinsdale's 1882 book *Garfield and Education*; others were in the Garfield *Papers, Public Addresses.*[23]

He married Lucretia Randolph on November 11, 1858.

In 1858, while Garfield was President of Hiram College, an early evolutionist named Denton came through Ohio and offered an open challenge for a debate on the origins of the earth. Denton took a "spontaneous generation and progressive development" stance; Garfield attempted to defend a more Biblical position.[24]

The debate lasted five days and nights and each debater delivered over 20 speeches. Although many of the spectators believed that Garfield won the debates, he made a crucial compromise. As early as 1854, Garfield had read Hugh Miller's gap theory, a compromise theory that proposed that the seven days of creation week were not days at all but rather were indeterminate lengths of time. Garfield defended the gap theory in this debate, abandoning the Biblical position of a young earth.[25]

In about 1850, Garfield noted in his diary that he had "engaged to support in debate the following proposition; viz., that Christians have no right to participate in human governments." Though he believed that the doctrine, which was taught by the Disciples of Christ, was unpopular, he "glor[ied] in defending unpopular truth against popular error."[26]

Over time, however, he changed his position—and decided to enter politics himself. An 1881 Garfield biography stated that he said the following words in 1859:

> The desire of brethren to have me preach and teach for them, a desire to do good in all ways I could, and to earn in noble callings, something to pay my way through a course of study, and to discharge debts, and the discipline and cultivation of mind in preaching and teaching, and the exalted topics for investigation in preaching and teaching, have led me into both callings. I have never intended to devote my life to either or both; although lately Providence seemed to be hedging my way and crowding me into the ministry. I have always intended to be a lawyer, and perhaps

to enter political life. Such has been my secret ambition since I thought of such things. I have been reading law for some time.[27]

When he was elected to the Ohio Senate in 1859, Isaac Errett, a leading member of the Disciples of Christ, asked him if "political honor [was] the highest honor." Errett said, "The truth, which he so well understood, and the Lord, whom he had so devotedly loved, had superior claims upon him, which no earthly temptation must lead him to compromise."[28]

Garfield chose to go to his elected post and enter, as one biographer described the perception of the denomination, the "sinful world of politics."[29] Though he did it without the blessing of his denomination, he felt confident that it was the right thing for him to do.

Garfield was a member of the United States House of Representatives for more than a decade. During those years and through his presidency, Garfield was a member of the National City Christian Church.[30] The church records state: "General James A. Garfield, Disciples Minister, elected to Congress, became a member of the local church."[31] According to Olga Jones in her book *Churches of the Presidents in Washington*, "reports show that he preached many a sermon for this congregation."[32]

One of Garfield's projects during his time as a Representative was to establish a Federal Department of Education. Due in large part to his sponsorship, the department was established as a sub-cabinet-level bureau.

During his youth, Garfield was opposed to the abolitionist movement, joining his denomination in holding that "the *simple relation* of master to slave is NOT UNCHRISTIAN."[33] However, over time, he came to believe that slavery was a national sin, and that the Civil War was punishment for this sin. Once the Civil War arrived, he came "nearer and nearer to downright Abolitionism." He even entered the Union Army, attaining military distinction as a general.

"Before God," he said one time, "I here record my conviction that the spirit of Slavery is the soul of the rebellion and the incarnate devil which must be cast out before we can trust in any peace as lasting and secure."[34]

Garfield was elected president of the United States in 1880 and took office the next year. He concluded his inaugural address with these words: "I shall greatly rely upon the wisdom and patriotism of Congress and of those who may share with me the responsibilities and duties of administration, and, above all, upon our efforts to promote the welfare of this great people and their Government I reverently invoke the support and blessings of Almighty God."[35]

In 1881, a would-be assassin named Charles Guiteau started stalking President Garfield. He even followed him to church. During one church service in June of 1881, he went to a service which Garfield attended, and concealed a revolver in a pocket. During the sermon, Guiteau interrupted the preacher by shouting, "What think ye of Christ?"[36] (Garfield made note of the interruption in his diary and referred to Guiteau as "a dull young man, with a loud voice."[37]) Guiteau decided to wait to shoot Garfield until the next week. By the next Sunday, Garfield had left town.

Guiteau shot Garfield on July 2, 1881. Guiteau wrote a letter explaining the assassination; he said, "I presume the President was a Christian and that he will be happier in Paradise than here." Though he claimed to have "no ill-will toward the President," Guiteau believed that the assassination "was a political necessity."[38]

Garfield died on September 19, 1881, in Elberon, New Jersey, only months into his term.

CONCLUSION

By his own testimony, James Garfield was a genuine Christian. He was not only one of the most evangelistic presidents our country has ever had, but he was also the only preacher to hold the office.

NOTES

1. Hendrik V. Booraem, *The Road to Respectability: James A. Garfield and His World, 1844–1852*. A Western Reserve Historical Society Publication. (Lewisburg, PA: Bucknell University Press, 1988/London: Associated University Presses, 1988), 124.

2. Edmund Fuller and David E. Green, *God in the White House: The Faiths of American Presidents* (New York: Crown Publishers, 1968), 139.

3. Daniel G. Reid, et al., *Concise Dictionary of Christianity in America* (Downers Grove, IL: InterVarsity Press, 1995), 75.

4. Ibid., 293.

5. Ibid., 74.

6. Ibid., 63.

7. The requirement of admission only after baptism has since been dropped in some Disciples of Christ churches.

8. Booraem, *Road to Respectability*, 128. From a May 17, 1850, diary entry.

9. Allan Peskin, *Garfield: A Biography* (Kent, OH: Kent State University Press, 1978), 43.

10. Ibid., 28–30.

11. James and Lucretia Garfield, *Crete and James: Personal Letters of James and Lucretia Garfield*, ed. John Shaw (East Lansing: Michigan State University Press, 1994), 56.

12. Peskin, *Garfield*, 48.

13. Ibid., 38.

14. Booraem, *The Road to Respectability*, 158.

15. Ibid., 188.

16. Ibid., 189.

17. Ibid.

18. Ibid., 190.

19. Garfield, *Crete and James*, 46. From a letter written to Lucretia Randolph by James Garfield, dated "Williamstown, March 6, 1855."

20. Ibid. From a letter written to Lucretia Randolph by James Garfield, dated "Williams College, March 16, 1856."

21. Peskin, *Garfield*, 48.

22. In 1858 while he was president of Hiram College, Garfield debated an early evolutionist named Denton. However, he compromised in so doing. Denton had come through Ohio in 1858, offering to debate anyone on the topic of origins, arguing for "spontaneous generation and progressive development" (Peskin, *Garfield*, 55). Garfield argued the biblical worldview with a crucial compromise. He conceded that in his opinion the world was millions of years old. He came to this conclusion trying to harmonize science with the Bible. Of course, Garfield did not have Christian Creationist scientists to show the logical holes in the semi-creation compromise theories (Peskin, *Garfield*, 56, whose sources were 1859 letters from S. W. Collins to Garfield and Garfield to J. H. Rhodes. Both letters are in the Library of Congress and cited in Theodore Smith, *The Life and Letters of James Abram Garfield*, vol. 1 [Hamden, CT: Archon Books, 1968], 26).

23. Robert Granville Caldwell, *James A. Garfield: Party Chieftain* (New York: Dodd, Mead, 1931), 50. It said that the Garfield public addresses included "two large volumes" of Garfield's sermons.

24. Peskin, *Garfield*, 55.

25. Ibid., 56.

26. John M. Taylor, *Garfield of Ohio: The Available Man* (New York: Norton, 1970), 37. Quoted Smith, *The Life and Letters of James Abram Garfield*, 89.

27. Franklin Steiner, *The Religious Beliefs of Our Presidents* (Girard, KS: Haldeman-Julius, 1936; repr., Amherst, NY: Prometheus Books, 1995), 147.

28. Peskin, *Garfield*, 65.

29. Ibid., 66.

30. Olga Anna Jones, *Churches of the Presidents in Washington: Visits to Fifteen National Shrines* (New York: Exposition Press, 1954), 62.

31. Ibid.

32. Ibid.

33. Peskin, *Garfield*, 19.

34. Peskin, *Garfield*, 140. From a letter Garfield wrote to J.H. Rhodes on May 1, 1862.

35. Garfield, *Messages and Papers of the Presidents: James A. Garfield, 1881.* March 9, 1881. Inaugural address.

36. Kenneth D. Ackerman, *Dark Horse: The Surprise Election and Political Murder of President James A. Garfield* (New York: Carroll & Graf, 2003), 356.

37. Ibid.

38. Taylor, *Garfield of Ohio*, 270; Ackerman, *Dark Horse*, 374.

CHAPTER 24

RUTHERFORD BIRCHARD HAYES

RUTHERFORD B. HAYES was born on October 4, 1822, in Delaware, Ohio. He never had the opportunity to meet his father, Rutherford Hayes Jr., who died on July 20, 1822. Both of Hayes's parents were members of the Presbyterian Church; his mother, Sophia Birchard Hayes, took him to a Presbyterian church throughout his childhood.[1]

From 1836 to 1838, Hayes attended the Methodist Academy in Norwalk, Ohio.[2] From 1838 through 1842, he attended Kenyon College, an Episcopalian school.[3]

In August 1839, a revival swept the Kenyon campus. Hayes stated that it was the "all-engrossing subject" on campus. In a letter to his mother, he described the state of the college and its students:

> There are now but ten in the whole college who are not changed. I am among the ten as yet... Every single one of my best friends are "gone," as it is called. I attend the meetings and read all the books that my friends request me to, but I find it is the loss of my friends which affects me more than anything else. When the revival began to take the "good" fellows as well as the "bad," I was frequently in company with five or six others, of whom I was the only one who would "acknowledge" my respect for religion, who are all "gone" but myself. I have but little hope I shall be among them.[4]

His writings give no evidence that he ever became a part of that revival.

Throughout his life, Hayes maintained a high respect for religion and for the Bible. In a June 19, 1841, entry, he decided to "put down a few of my present hopes and designs for the sake of *keeping* them *safe*." One of these was to "never do anything inconsistent with the character of a true friend and good citizen." He said, "To become such a man I shall necessarily have to live in accordance with the precepts of the Bible, which I firmly believe, although I have never made them strictly the 'rule of my conduct.' "[5]

On Sunday, April 24, 1853, he noted in his diary: "Have been reading Genesis for several days, not as a Christian reads for 'spiritual consolation,' 'instruction,' etc., not as an infidel reads to carp and quarrel and criticize, but as one who wishes to be informed and furnished in the earliest and most wonderful of all literary productions. The literature of the Bible should be studied as one studies Shakespeare, for illustration and language, for its true pictures of man and woman nature, for its early historical record."[6]

Through later life, Hayes maintained a high respect for the Bible. His October 15, 1884, diary entry read:

> Our County Bible Society holds its yearly meeting soon. As one of the vice-presidents of the general society of the country, as a nonchurch member, a non-professor of religion, I may say why men of the world, friends of their country and of their race, should support the religion of the Bible—the Christian religion. To worship— "the great Creator to adore"—the wish to establish relations with the Omnipotent Power which made the universe, and which controls it, is a deeply seated principle of human nature. It is found among all races of men. It is well-nigh universal. All peoples have some religion. In our day men who cast off the Christian religion show the same innate tendency by spending time and effort in spiritualism. If the God of the Bible is dethroned the goddess of reason is set up. Religion always has been, always will be. Now, the best religion the world ever had is the religion of Christ. A man or a community adopting it is virtuous, prosperous, and happy.
>
> Byron has said, "If our God was man—or man, God—Christ was both"; and continuing he said, "I never arraigned his creed, but the use—or abuse—made of it."

What a great mistake the man makes who goes about to oppose this religion! What a crime, if we may judge men's acts by their results! Nay, what a great mistake is made by him who does not support the religion of the Bible![7]

In his November 9, 1885, diary entry, he expressed similar sentiments:

Last night Rev. Mr. Prentiss gave us a good address on the Bible before the County Bible Society. I must sometime maintain my proposition that a non-professor of religion—"a mere man of the world"—who wishes well to his country and his fellow men ought actively to aid in the circulation of the Bible, and in adding to its influence. The general course of my argument is this: All peoples will have religion. Death leads the mind to consider the future, to a contemplation of Deity. Hence religion, or this is religion. Now, the best religion the world has ever known is the religion of the Bible. It builds up all that is good. It suppresses or diminishes all that is bad. With it men are happy and nations are prosperous. Where it is not found vice and crime prevail.[8]

On November 24, 1890, Hayes returned to the topic. "The religion of the Bible is the best in the world," he recorded in his diary. "I see the infinite value of religion. Let it be always encouraged. A world of superstition and folly have grown up around its forms and ceremonies. But the truth in it is one of the deep sentiments in human nature."[9]

From 1843 through 1845, Hayes attended the Harvard School of Law. While there, he purchased a New Testament and resolved to study it weekly. He also attended church regularly.[10] One of his longest religious statements—possibly his longest on a point of doctrine—was written during this time. In a diary entry on May 26, 1844, Hayes wrote:

I heard Dr. Walker preach this morning from the text, "Faith without works is dead." Luther found so much in the Epistle of James which conflicted with his own favorite doctrines, that he pronounced it "strange." And others have thought it of little worth because Christ is mentioned but once or twice and then coldly; because the doctrines of the resurrection and regeneration are scarcely noticed; and because it treats so much of the principles of mere morality. But these are not good reasons for putting one writer above another—Paul above James. It would rather seem wise to adopt views by which passages apparently conflicting may be harmonized and discrepancies explained and reconciled.

The great controversy concerning faith and works depends, in a great measure, for its origin and continuance on the ambiguity of the two words, *faith* and *works*. If by works is meant the mere outward act, there may be salvation without works, as a man may have great generosity without the opportunity or means of exhibiting it. So, on the other hand, the acts of generosity may be performed without merit. If by faith is meant only the intellectual acts of belief and approval of what is true and good, this without works is *dead*. But if by faith is meant the internal disposition, which will manifest itself in outward acts whenever opportunity occurs, this faith is essential to salvation. So that while Paul and James use different language, their doctrines are the same; they view the subject from different positions, but their views are the same. Paul looks to the origin of the act, James to the consummation of the disposition. It is interesting in this connection to trace the differences between the Jewish and the Christian disposition. That was a dispensation of works, this of faith. In that, the external rites and observance were the all important. In this, the feelings, the heart is regarded. In another aspect, the difference appears striking. The religion of the Bible is one of obedience and progress. The Old Testament contains a system of rules to be strictly followed in forms and ceremonies, suited to the childhood of our race in this respect. The New Testament looks to principles of action; if these are right all is right. But *rules* may be outgrown, while *principles* are eternal. So that while the Jewish dispensation, being temporary, has passed away, the Christian is eternal and must remain.

Now, in the use of the writings of the two apostles, we must consider the crying sin of the age in which we live and the people before whom we appear. If it is to speculation and mysticism, then the efficacy of works, as appears in the Epistle of James, should be preached; if to outward appearances, pompous ceremony, rites, etc., then justification by faith as declared by Paul should be proclaimed.[11]

This able commentary would do justice to a professional theologian. It shows a side of Hayes not seen in his other writings; he was able to set his doctrinal doubts aside and discuss a complex theological question in dispassionate language.

At this point in his life, Hayes's views were evidently influenced by deism. (Deism is the belief that a deity set up the world and left it to run itself.) In an April 15, 1845, diary entry, he commented on Merle d'Aubigné's *History of the Reformation* in these words:

> [According to] D'Aubigné's "History of the Reformation," Christianity has two features which especially distinguish it from all human systems: (1) That the only mediator between God and man is Jesus Christ. (2) That salvation is a *gift* of God—a matter of *grace*. . . . D'Aubigné constantly affirms that, in his opinion, the Reformation was the immediate work of the Divine hand.
>
> Now, it seems to me that Providence interferes no more in the greatest affairs of men than in the smallest, and that neither individuals nor nations are any more the objects of a special interposition of the Divine Ruler than the inanimate things of the world. The Creator gave to every creature of his hand its laws at the time of its creation and whatever can happen in accordance with those laws He doubtless foresaw, and it cannot be supposed that his laws are so imperfect that special interpositions are necessary to render then capable of fulfilling their design, nor is it possible for them to be violated. The Reformation like other revolutions was agreeable to principles which have existed since the world began.[12]

In 1847, after Hayes graduated from the Harvard School of Law, he set up a law practice in Lower Sandusky, Ohio.

In that same year, his uncle, Sardis Birchard, became influenced by Swedenborgianism. Swedenborgianism is based on the teachings of Emanuel Swedenborg, who lived from 1668 to 1772. According to the *Concise Dictionary of Christianity in America*, Swedenborg "apparently denied the orthodox doctrines of the Trinity, original sin, the vicarious atonement and the bodily resurrection."[13] The Church of the New Jerusalem, which was started by Robert Hindmarsh a few years after Swedenborg died, is founded on Swedenborg's doctrines.

In a February 1847 letter to his mother, Hayes stated that "Uncle has set all our heathens, who read anything except the *Statesman* and

Democrat, to reading Swedenborgian tracts and Professor Bush's writings. The views of the New Church are extremely popular. Men who were unwilling to believe their own existence, swallow these sublime mysteries without a 'strain.' We shall probably not build a church consecrated to the new views just yet; but we may come to that complexion hereafter. We shall be a pious folk when all our infidels and atheists become 'disciples.' "[14]

Had Hayes become a Swedenborgian? He did not say, though it could be argued that his words imply this. In the event that he did agree with Swedenborg's doctrines, he probably did not view this as being converted to a different religion. He more likely viewed this in the light of reading an author whose statements he found accurate.

Swedenborgianism resurfaced in his correspondence several months later. In a letter to his sister Fanny, he said: "I was thinking the other day of the tendency which some creeds have to cultivate a fondness for the horrible in religion as distinguished from the lovely—contrasting Methodism or Presbyterianism with Swedenborgianism. One sentence in Mother's last, which perhaps you did not see, struck me as illustrating this distinction. She says 'our soldiers *and all other persons* should be prepared for death *and all the other horrors* that await them!' "[15]

Except for passing references, this was the last time he mentioned Swedenborgianism. If asked later in life, he would not have described himself as a Swedenborgian. It would be revisionist history to maintain that he was a closet Swedenborgian throughout his life; however, it is quite possible that Swedenborg's doctrines influenced him, and this is worth keeping in mind.

In November 1849, Hayes prepared to set up a law practice in Columbus, Ohio. In a letter to his sister Fanny, he listed changes which he wanted to make in his life once he moved. He said: "When thinking of the great change which must come over my habits of life upon mingling in the throng of a great town, some fancies, or rather half-formed convictions of duty, force themselves upon me which have been absent from my thoughts since long, long ago. Believing in the essential verities of religion even with my weak, half-skeptical faith, there seems something inexcusable in neglecting this subject when seriously thought of. But I suppose that, instead of embracing the opportunity given me by a change of life and friends to attend to suggestions like these, they will as hitherto be postponed to a more convenient season."[16]

In May 1850, Hayes heard Ralph Waldo Emerson give a series of lectures in Cincinnati, Ohio. Hayes summarized Emerson's theology in his own words: "There is no *personal* creative God; but spirit which is diffused through all, which is a part of man and beast, *is God*. The highest manifestation of spirit is man. Man differs from mere matter in this: His spirit is self-conscious. Therefore, man is *nearer* than any other object in nature to an impersonation of Deity. And it may be said with more truth of *man* than of anything else, that he is God; there is *more God* in him than in anything else."[17] However, in a letter written thirty-nine years later, he said of Emerson: "He will not change our faith; he will not lead us to any faith."[18]

Knowing what he knew about Emerson's religion, he still named him as his favorite author. In a June 11, 1891, diary entry, he wrote: "Uncle Birchard read John Ruskin. He was the favorite author with him. Not with me. Mine is and for forty years has been Emerson. Ruskin says many good things—some that are worthy of Emerson. How apt for present purposes is this: 'Whenever in any religious faith, dark or bright, we allow our minds to dwell upon the points in which we differ from other people, we are wrong, and in the Devil's power. That is the essence of the Pharisee's thanksgiving,—"Lord, I thank thee that I am not as other men are"'—and so on for several sentences."[19]

In an August 1851 debate in Cincinnati on "Whether Christ Revealed Any New Truth," Hayes argued the negative. In his diary, he summarized his points: "Stated by the negative that various nations had just notions of a God; that the Pharisees believed in the immortality of the soul, future rewards, etc., resurrection, and final judgment; that most of the system of government, laws, etc., of Moses were taken from Egypt; that the Essenes asserted and practiced all those final moral precepts which Christ proclaimed—proved by Josephus, etc."[20]

Also in that month, he read *The Life and Works of Dr. Channing*, a man he described as "one of the noblest, purest men who ever lived."[21] In a letter to his future wife, Lucy Webb, he described his impressions of the book:

> The Doctor may be in error as to some doctrinal points, but the great features of his system are founded on the rock of truth. If ever I am made a Christian it will be under the influence of views like his. He says the test of Christianity is the state of the heart and affections, not the state of a man's intellectual belief. If a man feels

the humility becoming one prone to sinfulness, looks above for assistance, repents of what he does that is wrong, aspires to purity of intention and correctness of conduct in all the relations of life, such a man is a *Christian*, for he adopts the spirit of Christ's teachings and example,—this, too, in spite of his faith,—whether it be Calvinistic, Unitarian, Universalist, or Papist. That I can comprehend. The half of the orthodox creeds I don't understand and can't fully believe.[22]

As young men will do in letters of this sort, he put his views in the best light. He was somewhat more blunt in an August 18 diary entry:

[Quoting Channing:] "In my view, religion is but another name for happiness, and I am most cheerful when I am most religious." "Happiness is another name for love," etc.

What a pure, good man, so spiritual and spotless, Dr. Channing was. If I am ever to be a religious being, it must be with a faith not unlike his. The gloomy theology of the orthodox—the Calvinists—I do not, I cannot believe. Many of the notions—nay, most of the notions—which orthodox people have of the divinity of the Bible, I disbelieve. I am so nearly infidel in all my views, that, too, in *spite* of my wishes, that none but the most liberal doctrines can command my assent. Dr. Channing describes the effect which some of the terror-striking dogmas pronounced [by] a positive Calvinist had upon his feelings. "This can't be true," thought he. "If it were, all cheerfulness would be ended." But his religious uncle said, "Sound doctrine, all sound"; went home, took off his coat, and to read a newspaper and talk politics. He [Channing] then thought, this [doctrine] is *practically* disbelieved; and here began those reflections which ultimately led him to that catholic liberty of religious belief which in his after life he preached.[23]

In November 1852, Hayes attended lectures and a sermon by "the notorious Christian infidel, Theodore Parker, of Boston." In a letter to his sister Fanny, he summarized and commented on the main points of the sermon:

But *the talk* of all was his sermon. He gave us the notions entertained by all the early heathen peoples of God, showing them to be absurd enough; then, the Hebrew, Mosaic and patriarchal, idea of Divinity was a very narrow and perfect one. The God of the Old Testament is partial, revengeful, hating and loving without just cause, unmerciful, etc., etc.—which, *I think, he proved* by the books. The New Testament idea was higher, but still imperfect. For it represents Him as not perfect in love, justice, goodness, or even power. For it makes Him the author of *absolute* and *eternal evil*, viz.: a Devil and Hell and endless punishment, and represents Him as *compelled* to resort to suffering to save his creatures. The writers of the best religion found in literature, viz.: Fénelon, Swedenborg, William Law, Wordsworth, and Channing approach more nearly to the true idea, but yet their reflections are tinged with a *fear, an apprehension,* that God is as represented in the New Testament, wrathful; though not a full acknowledgement, but feeble denial rather, of this is found in their works. But the true idea now beginning to struggle with the popular theology is that God is a *perfect being* in love, justice, mercy, power, etc., etc.[24]

He does not say that he *believed* this in its entirety, nor does he say that he rejects any of the propositions. (When he disagreed with a preacher's sermon, he often noted the fact in his diary. He did not do so in this letter, though an argument either way is based on silence.)

After his December 30, 1852, marriage to Lucy Webb, he regularly attended the Methodist church with her.[25] Though he never joined the church he attended its service nearly every Sunday. He also supported it financially,[26] and became a member of its board of trustees.

Hayes served in the Civil War as an officer in the Ohio Twenty-third Regiment. His writings during this period of his life are interesting. He expressed the highest respect for orthodox Christianity, while not believing it. Though he stated unequivocally that he was not an orthodox Christian and once even used the term "unbeliever" to describe himself,[27] he also voiced a longing to one day believe with all his heart. In an October 1861 diary entry, his words were almost poetic. He said:

Queer world! We fret our little hour, are happy and pass away. Away! Where to? "This longing after immortality! These thoughts that wander through eternity!" I have been and am an unbeliever of all these sacred verities. But will I not take refuge in the faith of my fathers at last? Are we not all impelled to this? The great abyss, the unknown future,—are we not happier if we give ourselves up to some settled faith? Can we feel safe without it? Am I not more and more carried along, drifted, towards surrendering to the best religion the world has yet produced? It seems so. In this business, as I ride through the glorious scenery this loveliest season of the year, my thoughts float away beyond this wretched war and all its belongings. Some, yes many, glorious things, as well as all that is not so, [impress me]; and [I] think of the closing years on the down-hill side of life, and picture myself a Christian, sincere, humble, devoted, as conscientious in that as I am now in this—not more so. My belief in this war is as deep as any faith can be;—but thitherward I drift. I see it and am glad.[28]

His attitude toward Christianity is fascinating. He asked if one could feel safe without it; he referred to taking "refuge in the faith of my fathers"; he asked if those who give themselves up to "some settled faith" are not happier; he was "glad" to picture himself a Christian— yet he could not bring himself to make that step.

His attitude toward Christianity remained much the same throughout his adult life. Religion played an important part in his life; he attended church more frequently than some of our most orthodox presidents did. Yet until his final years, Hayes viewed Christianity from the outside—with the highest respect.

Hayes was elected president in a contested election in 1876. On February 25, 1877, Hayes wrote a proposed speech in his diary to be delivered if he was asked to give a speech concerning the disputed presidential election. The speech, which was never delivered, closed with these words: "We do not want a united North or a united South. We want a united country. And if the great trust shall devolve upon me, I fervently pray that the Divine Being, who holds the destinies of nations in His hands, will give me wisdom to perform its duties so as to promote the truest and best interests of the whole country."[29]

Hayes served one term as president. He concluded his inaugural address by referring to God in a generic way. He said:

Looking for the guidance of that Divine Hand by which the destinies of nations and individuals are shaped, I call upon you, senators, Representatives, judges, fellow-citizens, here and everywhere, to unite with me in an earnest effort to secure to our country the blessings, not only of material prosperity, but of justice, peace, and union—a union depending not upon the constraint of force, but upon the loving devotion of a free people; "and that all things may be so ordered and settled upon the best and surest foundations that peace and happiness, truth and justice, religion and piety, may be established among us for all generations."[30]

Hayes issued four Thanksgiving proclamations, one in each year of his presidency. In his first Thanksgiving proclamation, issued on October 29, 1877, he said that it was the season in which "a religious people celebrates with praise and thanksgiving the enduring mercy of Almighty God." He reminded the American people of the blessings that they had received that year. "[T]he experience of the last year," he said, "is conspicuously marked by the protecting providence of God and is full of promise and hope for the coming generations." He urged the American people: "Let us with one spirit and with one voice lift up praise and thanksgiving to God for His manifold goodness to our land, His manifest care for our nation" and to "give thanks and praise to Almighty God for His mercies and to devoutly beseech their continuance."[31]

On October 30, 1878, he issued his second Thanksgiving proclamation. He encouraged thankfulness for the blessings received; he also encouraged rejoicing for the "unity of spirit" with which the people of the United States had faced a widespread pestilence that year and again urged the American people to "meet together on that day in their respective places of worship, there to give thanks and praise to Almighty God for His mercies and to devoutly beseech their continuance."[32]

In his third Thanksgiving proclamation, issued on November 3, 1879, he said: "At no recurrence of the season which the devout habit of a religious people has made the occasion for giving thanks to Almighty God and humbly invoking His continued favor has the material prosperity enjoyed by our whole country been more conspicuous, more manifold, or more universal." He appointed Thursday, November 27, as "a day of national thanksgiving and prayer" and earnestly recommended that "withdrawing themselves from secular cares and labors, the people of the United States do meet together on that day in their respective places of worship, there to give thanks and praise to Almighty God for His mercies and to devoutly beseech their continuance."[33]

He issued his fourth and final Thanksgiving proclamation on November 1, 1880. He said that at no period since the formation of the United States had our people "had so abundant and so universal reasons for joy and gratitude at the favor of Almighty God or been subject to so profound an obligation to give thanks for His loving-kindness and humbly to implore His continued care and protection." He enumerated some of the blessings seen by the country and said: "[F]or all these let the thanks of a happy and united people, as with one voice, ascend in devout homage to the Giver of All Good."[34]

His observance of the external forms of religion was more consistent than the practice of many more orthodox believers. In an 1875 letter to his son Webb, he commented on regular church attendance in these words: "I hope you will be benefited by your churchgoing. Where the habit does not Christianize, it generally civilizes. That is reason enough for supporting churches, if there were no higher."[35]

Hayes held morning prayers with his family daily. He said that this involved "the reading of a chapter in the Bible, each one present reading a verse in turn, and all kneeling repeat the Lord's prayer."[36] According to one source, Rutherford and Lucy Hayes ended each day at the White House by singing hymns;[37] on some Sunday evenings, they invited others to come to their hymn sings. Attendees of the Sunday evening hymn sings included some of the most prominent politicians in the country.

While Hayes was president, the Hayes family attended the Foundry Methodist Church. In a March 1878 diary entry, Hayes stated that he had "gone to church at least once every Sunday since I became President."[38] In a May 22, 1892, diary entry, he noted that he missed church that day. He stated: "This long absence from church will not, I hope, be repeated. It is longer than ever before since the war—six weeks."[39] Thus, from 1865 through the last (full) year of his life, he never missed more than five consecutive Sunday services.

During his presidency, liquor was banned from the White House. This ban was chiefly symbolic; Rutherford Hayes would occasionally drink with fellow Civil War veterans (out of the White House), while Lucy sent gifts of wine to friends with wine cellars.

However, the Hayes family knew the power of the example the presidency could set, and, in Rutherford's words while governor of Ohio, too many "noble minds [were] rendered unfit to be trusted with public office because of drink.[40]

Some critics stated that alcoholic drinks were secretly slipped into White House drinks. Hayes responded, "The joke of the Roman punch oranges was not on us, but on the drinking people. My orders were to flavor them *rather strongly* with the same flavor that is found in Jamaica rum. This took! There was not a drop of spirits in them!"[41]

Once Hayes retired home to Fremont, Ohio, he resumed his connection with his local Methodist Episcopal church. In 1883, he participated in the church's effort to erect a new building. In a March 18, 1883, entry in his diary, he noted that he "proposed three ideas which were adopted." He then enumerated four: "1. Church not to cost exceeding fifteen thousand dollars complete. 2. No obligations to be incurred until four-fifths of the estimated cost has been secured in reliable subscriptions. 3. A committee on collections to proceed with a canvass for subscriptions as soon as plans are adopted. 4. A committee on plans; plan to be adopted by official board before a canvass for subscriptions is made."[42] Through the following months, he participated in the board of trustees meetings overseeing the project.[43]

After the cost of the project was raised to between $18,000 and $20,000, he pledged to pay one-quarter of the expenses himself.[44] The church was completed by February 27, 1885, though a debt of $8,300 remained. In a Feb. 28 diary entry, Hayes noted that he would make the following pledge: "In order to provide for the whole debt of the church, General and Mrs. Hayes will subscribe one-fourth of the amount due, provided enough is raised from others to pay off the indebtedness. In case a less sum is raised, they will subscribe one-fourth of the total sum raised."[45] A sufficient sum was raised the next day, March 1, and Hayes fulfilled his pledge.

Unfortunately, on February 6, 1888, this church building "burned completely."[46] That evening, Hayes met with the other members of the building committee "and resolved to rebuild at once; to take up subscriptions."[47]

Hayes was also involved in other church matters. In 1883, Reverend D.D. Mather, his pastor, was accused (Hayes described the accusations as "idle gossip") of "imprudent but not in the least licentious conduct with women."[48] Hayes either believed the rumors to be false or to be insignificant. He decided to stand with the pastor, and hoped that the division in the church would calm. He said: "This lack of unity and concord will continue until repentance and reparation do their work in behalf of our injured pastor or until time and changes in the leading influences of the church restore harmony. . . . I will not remain in a congregation so divided. If proper feeling is again restored, I will return. I prefer the Methodist Episcopal church, but I prefer still more peace. We have the congregations of other denominations with whom we can, I think, live in peace."[49] He wrote to Bishop Randolph Foster in Cleveland, Ohio, urging the retention of Rev. Mather.[50] Hayes lost the battle: In September 1884, he noted in his diary that Dr. Mather had preached his last sermon as the pastor of the Fremont Methodist Episcopal Church that morning. He said that Mather's "good gray head" was loved "by many; by none more than by this household."[51]

From his youth, Hayes attended revivals—and watched. An August 1839 revival on the Kenyon College campus has already been noted. Though it may have been the first revival he attended, it was certainly not the last. He described an April 1885 revival from the viewpoint of an interested observer. He wrote the following extensive comments in an April 2, 1885, diary entry:

> In the evening attended the revival meeting of the Methodist Episcopal church. These meetings have been held almost every night for six or eight weeks. The accessions to the church are over one hundred new converts, and perhaps forty or fifty others who have been at some time members but who have discontinued membership or attendance. The meetings will soon be discontinued. This, to enable our pastor, Mr. Prentiss, to recover his strength and to enable him to give attention to the general interests of the church. The new members must be allowed to settle down to plain duties as Christians. The excitement of their new situation must wear off and everyday life be resumed. This seems to be the view of Mr. Prentiss.
>
> The manner of the revival meetings is usually about this: Precisely at the appointed hour, the bell having ceased to ring, and the congregation being all seated and quiet, Mr. Prentiss takes his stand in front of the desk, near the altar rail, and announces from a small revival hymn-book the hymn. Miss Ickes at the small organ starts the tune. Mr. Prentiss who is a good singer begins, with his left hand beating time and walking along the platform, occupying in his walk ten or twelve feet in length along near the altar-rail. He sings with an earnest, strong, and good voice. The whole congregation rise and join in spirit. There is generally a chorus that is

repeated with increasing unction. "Bringing in the Sheaves" is a favorite hymn. Having finished the first hymn, a second, a third, and fourth immediately follow. The whole house soon enters into the spirit of it.

At the end of the fourth hymn Mr. Prentiss says, "Let us all now kneel and invoke the Divine assistance." He kneels at the altar-rail and in a short prayer, with much feeling, appeals for the coming of the Spirit to each heart. He next reads from the Scriptures—possibly with comments. Another hymn follows; then a short sermon, urging the necessity of prompt surrender or acceptance of the means of salvation. After the sermon he asks all to come forward, "the old and young in years, the old and young in Christ"; "and while we sing let all who desire Christ or the prayers of the church or who feel an interest in their soul's salvation come forward and kneel at the altar."

He then, as the members move towards the altar-rail, the whole congregation standing and singing, goes along the aisles and urges those whom he knows are thinking of joining the church or those whom he sees are deeply interested, to come forward. One and another comes forward and kneels. The example is contagious, and some evenings ten or fifteen new "converts" are seen "seeking their Saviour."

Members are called on for short prayers. Singing and praying continue twenty or thirty minutes. There is not much shouting, not many spontaneous "amens," but there is an occasional "Thank God" or sigh or groan. Mr. Prentiss himself is apt to interject frequently "Amen," "Thank God," "Yes," without regard to the sense of the prayer, thus giving vent to his feelings as the praying goes on. All the new converts are, while kneeling, encouraged by the older members who kneel by their sides, and affectionately urge them to go on and adopt "the new life." Ladies often pray in low sweet tones. There is nothing unseemly or boisterous. There is warm and deep emotion, without demonstration. A subdued excitement pervades the assembly. The converts are about equally male and female, young and old. For the most part they are of the middle and poorer classes.

When all have been talked with and recognized who came forward as converts, Mr. Prentiss says, "You will now all return to your places." A hymn, prayer, the doxology, and a benediction close the meeting.[52]

Hayes went to many of these meetings over the years but never went forward. In April 1886, when another series of revival meetings was being held, his son surprised him by going forward and joining "the list of pro- bationers."[53] In the same series of revival meetings, he was personally invited to give a public profession of faith. "A well-looking, modest young woman," he said," who knew me but who was a stranger, took me by the hand and earnestly asked: 'Do you love the Lord?' I talked kindly to her. She said a few words about the importance of my making a public pro- fession for the sake of the example."[54] He noted the advice in his diary and left it at that. (Incidentally, this was not the only time he was urged to make a public profession of faith in Christ. In his February 6, 1889, diary entry, he stated that Reverend Frederick Merrick had written him "a letter exhorting me for the sake of the example to 'make a public profession of faith in Christ.' "[55] Though he described President Merrick as "a noble, charitable, true Christian in the best sense" and as a "convert, in the usual sense," he did not choose to accept the advice.)

He described a March 1890 revival conducted by a Reverend Yatman as the "best and most enjoyable I ever attended."[56] About a year later in February 1891, he commented on another revival, the final to be noted in his diaries. He said: "Mr. Albritton is having a very suc- cessful 'season' of awakening in our church. He fills the church full. All of the backsliding or cold members seem to be interested, and many give their names to the church."[57]

On June 25, 1889, Lucy Hayes died. A few hours before her death, Hayes wrote about the impending event in his diary. "Who knows what the future might have brought to her? It is indeed hard—hard indeed— to part with her, but could I or should I call her back? Rather let me try to realize the truth of the great mystery. 'The LORD hath given, the LORD hath taken away; blessed be the name of the Lord.' "[58]

On May 17, 1890, Hayes wrote in his diary: "Writing a few words for Mohonk Negro Conference, I find myself using the word Christian. I am not a subscriber to any creed. I belong to no church. But in a sense satisfactory to myself and believed by me to be important, I try to be a Christian, or rather I want to be a Christian and to help do Christian work."[59]

In his March 13, 1892, diary entry, Hayes commented on Charles Dickens. He said: "Dean Stanley's sermon on Charles Dickens is given in Mackenzie's 'Life of Dickens.' It is so good. Read it, *my children.* Read also Dickens' will, where he speaks of his religion. I would say it, dear ones, with all my heart, ditto."[60] (Dickens's will concluded with the words: "I commit my soul to the mercy of God through our Lord and Saviour Jesus Christ, and I exhort my dear children humbly to try to guide themselves by the teachings of the New Testament in its broad spirit, and to put no faith in any man's narrow construction of its letter here or there."[61])

Yet to the end of his life, Hayes did not describe himself as an orthodox Christian. Though he never enumerated his beliefs point by point, he did comment on specific doctrines. In his November 19, 1892, diary entry, he noted: "Mr. Albritton preached a fine sermon on justification. I could not accept his doctrine, but the morality he would inculcate and the practical duties he insisted on were sound and well put."[62] In a September 4, 1892, diary entry, he commented on a lecture by Reverend Fitch, a missionary to Shanghai, China:

> In the evening we attended a lecture by [the] Rev. [Mr.] Fitch, a missionary for twenty years to China—the husband of our bright cousin, Mary McLelland. She is far the most interesting of the two. He is a Presbyterian. He had a good audience in our Methodist church. He spoke of the three hundred millions of people in China. Twelve million a year die in ignorance of the Bible—one million a month perishing without salvation! This to me seems monstrous. God, the Father of all, God, who is love, dooms millions of his creatures to eternal torment! This he did not say, but, of course, it is implied in what he did say. He gave very few facts, nothing new, and did it in a quiet, modest way, without egotism or pretension. One thinks well of his character but has a poor opinion of his ability and intelligence. He to bring a new religion to a quiet and cultured people![63]

Yet Hayes expressed hope somewhat later when he wrote a letter to Mary M. Fitch (his cousin and the wife of Reverend Fitch) several months before his death. He said: "The teachings of Christ, meaning his words as interpreted by Himself in his life and deeds, are in truth the way of salvation. Wishing and striving to do this [accepting Christ's teachings] I know that I am safe."[64]

On January 8, 1893, nine days before his death, Hayes attended his final church service. He noted in his diary that he had heard "a fair sermon by Presiding Elder Barnes." He also made his last written religious statement: "I am a Christian according to my conscience in belief, not of course in character and conduct, but in purpose and wish;—not of course by the orthodox standard. But I am content, and have a feeling of trust and safety."[65]

"Not of course by the orthodox standard"? This was a characteristic of Hayes' religion throughout his life. Authorized biographer Charles Williams stated that Hayes "felt himself to be a Christian in all essential respects," though "he never united with any church."[66]

This statement accurately encapsulates the evidence. In 1851, Hayes said: "The half of the orthodox creeds I don't understand and can't fully believe."[67] Hayes believed that Christ's teachings were the way of salvation. They are important—but did he include in those teachings the teachings of the cross, the atonement, and the resurrection? If Christ's words are accepted *along with* His atonement, they *are* the way of salvation—but if His words are accepted without His atonement, they do *not* provide salvation.

Hayes died on January 17, 1893, in Fremont, Ohio. His last recorded words were, "I know I am going where Lucy is."[68]

His funeral was held on January 20 at the Fremont Methodist Church. Biographer Charles Williams described the funeral in these words: "Thousands of people stood in the snow outside while the brief service was celebrated. This consisted of the reading of the Twenty-third Psalm by the Pastor of the Fremont Methodist Church, the singing of the hymn, 'It is Well With my Soul' by a Cleveland choir, assisted by Mrs. Fred H. Dorr of Fremont, a warm personal friend; an impressive prayer by President Bashford, of Ohio Wesleyan University; the favorite hymn 'God Be with You Till We Meet Again'; and the reciting by the entire company of the Lord's Prayer."[69]

President Benjamin Harrison, in his announcement of Hayes's death, paid tribute to his service to the country and described him as "a loyal comrade and friend, a sympathetic and helpful neighbor, and the honored head of a happy Christian home."[70]

The Sunday after Hayes's death, Reverend Washington Gladden delivered a memorial discourse at his church in Columbus, Ohio. He said of Hayes's religion:

I do not know that he formulated for himself any creed; he was content, probably, with a very short statement of some of the fundamental truths of religion. He was profoundly interested in the truth which constitutes the heart of all faiths. . . . He asked me, not long ago, if I knew of a certain minister of our communion. I replied that I had known him from his seminary days. "Well," he said, "I heard him preach last Sunday at Brattleboro, Vermont. You know," he added, with a humorous twinkle, "we always think that a man who agrees with us is an able man. But the text of this sermon was a striking one: 'The second is like unto it.' That was all there was of the text; but it was enough, I assure you, to furnish the foundation of a very strong discourse."

I could easily believe it. "The second is like unto it"—*equal* to it. It is what our Master says about the second great commandment of the law. The first great commandment is "Thou shalt love the Lord thy God with all thy heart;" the second is like unto it—equally binding, equally fundamental, equally religious—"Thou shalt love thy neighbor as thyself." The fact that had made its impression upon the President's mind was the equivalence of these commandments. That indicated his heart recognition of both of them. But I suppose if he had been challenged to confess his faith, it would have been uttered in the words of the beloved apostle, "He that loveth not his brother whom he hath seen, how can he love God whom he has not seen?" And if the word of that apostle is true—that "every one who loveth is begotten of God and knoweth God"—then the unselfish ministry of the last ten years would prove that the first great commandment was also the law of his life.[71]

HISTORICAL CONTROVERSIES

Did Hayes ever make the following quotation?

According to Federer's *America's God and Country* and Northrop's *A Cloud of Witnesses*, Hayes said: "I am a firm believer in the Divine teachings, perfect example, and atoning sacrifice of Jesus Christ. I believe also in the Holy Scriptures as the revealed Word of God to the world for its enlightenment and salvation."[72]

No other source is cited. I have not found this statement anywhere else. Where did it come from? Is it genuine? This question remains to be answered.

CONCLUSION

Opinions of biographers have ranged from descriptions of Hayes as a devout Methodist to a closet Unitarian.

Which view is true? The answer depends on what *parts* of the creeds Hayes had trouble believing. Further, did he have a hard time understanding them while feeling that they were accurate, or did he actually disbelieve them? There is a difference.

On the issue of his personal religious beliefs, Hayes was one of our more reticent presidents. Unless new research discloses new information, we must simply content ourselves with the accurate description of Hayes as a president who gave much thought to and cared deeply about religion and faithfully observed its outward forms.

NOTES

1. Charles Richard Williams, *The Life of Rutherford Birchard Hayes: Nineteenth President of the United States*, vol. 2 (Boston and New York: Houghton Mifflin, 1914), 436.

2. Hayes, *Diary and Letters of Rutherford Birchard Hayes*, ed. Charles Richard Williams, vol. 1 (Columbus: The Ohio State Archaeological and Historical Society, 1922), 11.

3. Williams, *Life of Rutherford Birchard Hayes*, vol. 2, 436.

4. Hayes, *Diary and Letters*, vol. 1, 36-37.

5. Ibid., 57; Williams, *Life of Rutherford Birchard Hayes*, vol. 1, 20.

6. Williams, *Life of Rutherford Birchard Hayes*, vol. 1, 72; Hayes, *Diary and Letters*, vol. 1, 449.

7. Hayes, *Diary and Letters*, vol. 4, 168.

8. Ibid., 347–48.

9. Ibid., 615.

10. Ibid., vol. 1, 145, 164.

11. Ibid., 152.

12. Ibid., 163.

13. Daniel G. Reid, et al., *Concise Dictionary of Christianity in America* (Downers Grove, IL: InterVarsity Press, 1995), 81.

14. Hayes, *Diary and Letters*, vol. 1, 196.

15. Ibid., 201–2.

16. Ibid., 272.

17. Ibid., 315. From a letter to his sister Fanny, dated "Cincinnati, June 12, 1850." He made clear that he had not heard Emerson say a word of this, "but if I could comprehend what he *would* have said if he had come down out of

the clouds or up out of the mists, the notions I have given you are *like* those he would have expressed."

18. Ibid., vol. 4, 527.

19. Ibid., vol. 5, 9.

20. Ibid., vol. 1, 385.

21. Ibid., 396.

22. Williams, *Life of Rutherford Birchard Hayes*, vol. 1, 79; Hayes, *Diary and Letters*, vol. 1, 389.

23. Hayes, *Diary and Letters*, vol. 1, 385–86.

24. Ibid., 431.

25. Williams, *Life of Rutherford Birchard Hayes*, vol. 1, 70.

26. Rexford G. Tugwell, *How They Became President: Thirty-five Ways to the White House* (New York: Simon & Schuster, 1964), 236.

27. Hayes, *Diary and Letters*, vol. 2, 128.

28. Ibid., 127–28.

29. Ibid., vol. 3, 421.

30. Hayes, March 5, 1877. Inaugural address.

31. Hayes, *Messages and Papers of the Presidents: Rutherford B. Hayes, 1877.* October 29, 1877. Thanksgiving proclamation.

32. Ibid., October 30, 1878. Thanksgiving proclamation.

33. Ibid., November 3, 1879. Thanksgiving proclamation.

34. Ibid., November 1, 1880. Thanksgiving proclamation.

35. Hayes, *Diary and Letters*, vol. 3, 82.

36. Ibid., 469; Edmund Fuller and David E. Green, *God in the White House: The Faiths of American Presidents* (New York: Crown Publishers, 1968), 136.

37. Joseph Nathan Kane, *Facts about the Presidents: From George Washington to Bill Clinton*, 6th ed. (New York: H. W. Wilson, 1993), 124–25.

38. Hayes, *Diary and Letters*, vol. 3, 470.

39. Ibid., vol. 5, 83.

40. Margaret Truman, *First Ladies: An Intimate Group Portrait of White House Wives* (New York: Random House, 1995), 47.

41. Fuller and Green, *God in the White House*, 136.

42. Hayes, *Diary and Letters*, vol. 4, 111.

43. Ibid., 113–114, 118, 133, 194-95.

44. Ibid., 133.

45. Ibid., 195.

46. Ibid., 369.

47. Ibid.

48. Ibid., 124.

49. Ibid.

50. Ibid., 124–25.

51. Ibid., 160–61. See diary entries for September 14 and September 16, 1884.

52. Ibid., 200.

53. Ibid., 281.

54. Ibid.

55. Ibid., 443.

56. Ibid., 554.

57. Ibid., 626.

58. Ibid., vol. 1, 474. Hayes did not quote the precise wording of the verse, a mistake understandable under the circumstances.

59. Williams, *Life of Rutherford Birchard Hayes,* vol. 2, 437: Hayes, *Diary and Letters,* vol. 4, 574.

60. Hayes, *Diary and Letters,* vol. 5, 64.

61. Williams, *Life of Rutherford Birchard Hayes,* vol. 2, 437.

62. Hayes, *Diary and Letters,* vol. 5, 124.

63. Ibid., 102.

64. Williams, *Life of Rutherford Birchard Hayes,* vol. 2, 436–37.

65. Hayes, *Diary and Letters,* vol. 5, 143.

66. Williams, *Life of Rutherford Birchard Hayes,* vol. 2, 436–37.

67. Ibid., vol. 1, 79.

68. Hayes, *Diary and Letters,* vol. 5, 145, 160.

69. Ibid., 159.

70. Harrison, *Messages and Papers,* January 18, 1893; Hayes, *Diary and Letters,* vol. 5, 161.

71. Williams, *Life of Rutherford Birchard Hayes,* vol. 2, 436–37.

72. William J. Federer, *America's God and Country: Encyclopedia of Quotations* (Coppel, TX: Fame Publishing, 1994), 286.

ULYSSES S. GRANT

ULYSSES GRANT was born on April 27, 1822, in Point Pleasant, Ohio. Bliss Isley, author of a book on the Christianity of the presidents of the United States, stated that Grant's "mother, a devoted Methodist, brought up her children to know the Bible."[1]

From the fall of 1838 until the spring of 1839, Grant attended the Presbyterian Academy in Ripley, Ohio.[2]

In 1839, Grant was appointed to and began attending West Point. In a September 1839 letter to his cousin, R. McKinstry Griffith, he grumbled about the school's policy of demerits for missing church services. He noted that another Ohio cadet, Elihu Grant, "was also put under arrest so he cannot leave his room perhaps fer a month, all this fer not going to Church. We are not only obliged to go to church but must *march* there by companys. This is not exactly republican. It is an Episcopal Church[.]"[3]

Grant knew Thomas J. Jackson at West Point; he later described Jackson (who eventually acquired the nickname "Stonewall") as "a religious man then, and some of us regarded him as a fanatic."[4]

Grant married Julia Boggs Dent on August 22, 1848.

After service in the Mexican War, Grant retired to private life. In 1860, he moved to Galena, Illinois, and took a job as a clerk. While there, he attended a Methodist Episcopal church, pastored by Reverend John H. Vincent.

During the Civil War, Grant and Vincent corresponded. One surviving letter is reproduced in Grant papers. Grant wrote Vincent: "Since we last met, and since I had the pleasure of listening to your feeling discourses from the pulpit, much has transpired to make or unmake men. . . . I was truly rejoiced at receiving a letter from you and hope it will not be the last. If you should make your expected trip to Palestine it would afford me the greatest pleasure to hear from you from that far off land and to reply punctually to your letters."[5]

In September 1861, while Grant was a brigadier general, he issued this order:

GENERAL ORDERS NO 9
   The President of the United States having appointed Thursday the 26th inst as a day of Humiliation, Prayer, and Fasting for all the people of the nation and recommend that if [sic] be observed and kept in all humility and with all religious solemnity to the end that the united prayer of the nation might ascend to the Throne of Grace and bring down plentiful blessings upon our own country;
   It is therefore ordered, That the day be properly observed by the several commands of this district that all military duty be suspended except such as may be forced upon us by unavoidable necessity, and the officers non commissioned officers and Privates according to their several creeds and modes of worship, unite in the offering of fervent supplications to almighty God for his blessings upon our beloved country.
                         By order of Brig Genl U. S. Grant
                         JNO. A. RAWLINS
                         Asst Adjt Genl[6]

Because the order was written down by Jno. Rawlins, though issued in Grant's name, it is impossible to determine how much influence Grant had over the precise wording of the order.

On November 23, 1861, Grant issued a similar statement:

Whereas the respective Governors of the States of Illinois, Missouri, and Kentucky, have appointed Thursday the 20th of November, inst., as a day of Thanksgiving and Prayer to Almighty God, the General Commanding this District, cheerfully and earnestly recommends to the Officers and men of his command, a proper observance of the day. All business will be suspended, so far as it may be compatible with the public service, and Chaplains, will hold appropriate religious services in their respective regiments.[7]

On November 3, 1862, Grant ordered that the "sympathizers with the rebellion" within the district he commanded ("Department of the Tennessee") would be responsible for relief of fellow-citizens in an impoverished state. He ordered that "a suitable Chaplain or other commissioned officer, will be appointed at each Post where it may be necessary to distribute supplies under this order, who shall have charge of the distribution of supplies and who shall be held responsible for the faithful performance of his duties, and that no supplies are unworthily discharged."[8]

On August 16, 1863, Grant was elected a member of the Methodist Missionary Society of the Cincinnati Conference. He wrote the society's secretary, Reverend J. F. Marlay, to express his gratitude. He said: "Through you permit me to express my thanks to the society of which you are the honored secretary, for the compliment they have seen fit to pay me by electing me one of its members. I accept the election as a token of earnest support, by members of the Methodist Missionary Society of the Cincinnati Conference, to the cause of our country in this hour of trial."[9]

On March 9, 1864, President Abraham Lincoln formally commissioned Grant as the lieutenant general in command of the armies of the United States. Lincoln said: "General Grant, the nation's appreciation of what you have done, and it's [sic] reliance upon you for what remains to do, in the existing great struggle, are now presented with this commission, constituting you Lieutenant General in the Army of the United States. With this high honor devolves upon you also, a corresponding responsibility. As the country herein trusts you, so, under God, it will sustain you. I scarcely need to add that with what I here speak for the nation goes my own hearty personal concurrence."[10]

"Mr. President," Grant responded, "I accept the commission with gratitude for the high honor conferred. With the aid of the noble armies that have fought on so many fields for our common country, it will be my earnest endeavor not to disappoint your expectations. I feel the full weight of the responsibilities now devolving upon me and know that if they are met, it will be due to those armies, and above all to the favor of that Providence which leads both nations and men."[11]

During an 1865 trip to Philadelphia, Grant donated $600 to the Spring Garden Street Methodist Episcopal Church.[12] Of the total donation, $500 was in his name and $100 was in his wife's name. After members of the church donated $1,000 more, a pew was permanently reserved for the Grant family.

In 1866, Baltimore resident Thomas Kelso wrote a letter to Grant, stating that he was a member of the Methodist Episcopal Church, "the Same church to which your honored Parents belong," and wanted to see a Methodist Episcopal Church building built in Washington, DC. He said, "I propose, General, by your leave, to give to Said church— *Five Thousand Dollars* in your Name—Designing in this way to Connect your name with this Godly undertaking: and also to evince the Gratitude—which in Common with all Loyal Citizens—I cherish toward you for the Signal Services, which, under God, you have rendered to our beloved Country."[13] Kelso therefore donated $5,000 in Grant's name and donated an additional $9,000 in his own name.

Grant was elected president in 1868. In his inaugural address, he said that "the greatest good to the greatest number is the object to be attained." He said: "This requires security of person, property, and religious and political opinions in every part of our common country, without regard to local prejudice."[14]

He closed the speech by asking the people to pray for the nation. "In conclusion I ask patient forbearance one toward another throughout the land, and a determined effort on the part of every citizen to do his share toward cementing a happy union; and I ask the prayers of the nation to Almighty God in behalf of this consummation."[15]

He was reelected in 1872. He began his second inaugural address by stating that "under Providence" he had been "called a second time to act as Executive over this great nation."[16] Later in the speech, he stated his opinion on the question of whether expanding a government's territory is detrimental to the country. He said, "I do not share in the apprehension held by many as to the danger of governments becoming weakened and destroyed by reason of their extension of territory. Commerce, education, and rapid transit of thought and matter by telegraph and steam have changed all this. Rather do I believe that our Great Maker is preparing the world, in His own good time, to become one nation, speaking one language, and when armies and navies will be no longer required."[17]

Grant regularly attended the Methodist church with his wife, who became a member. As president, he attended the Metropolitan Methodist Church and became a trustee, though not a member.[18] While he was president, he also paid $21 quarterly for a pew in the First Presbyterian Church in Washington.[19] It is not known how often he attended services in his pew, number 69.

During his presidency, Grant dealt several times with Indian affairs. In a draft for his 1870 annual message to Congress, he wrote the following words:

> Reform in the management of Indian Affairs has received the special attention of the Administration from its inauguration to the present day. The experiment of making it a missionary work was tried with a few agencies, given to the denomination of Friends and has been found to work most advantageously. All agencies and Superintendencies not so disposed of were given to Officers of the Army. The Act of Congress reducing the Army renders Army Officers ineligible for civil positions. Indian Agencies being civil Offices, I determined to give all the Agencies to such religious denominations as had heretofore established Missionaries among the Indians, and perhaps to other denominations who would undertake the work on the same terms, i.e., as a Missionary work. The societies selected are allowed to name their own agents and are expected to watch over them, and aid them, as missionaries, to Christianize and Civilize the Indian, and to train him in the arts of peace.[20]

In a message to Congress dated January 30, 1871, Grant informed them of a council of Indian tribes held in December 1870, at which they adopted a declaration of rights and a Constitution for their government. Grant commented: "This [is] the first indication of the aborigines desiring to [adopt] our form of government, and it [is] highly desirable that they become self sustaining, self relying, Christianized and Civilized."[21]

On October 15, 1874, Grant made a speech at the dedication of the Lincoln Monument in Oak Ridge Cemetery, Springfield, Illinois. He said: "During those years of doubting and despondency among the many patriotic men of the country, Abraham Lincoln never for a moment doubted but that the final result would be in favor of peace, union and freedom to every race in this broad land. His faith in an All Wise Providence directing our arms to this final result was the faith of the christian that his Redeemer liveth."[22]

As president, Grant issued eight Thanksgiving proclamations. In his first, issued on October 5, 1869, he recounted the many blessings that America had received in the course of the year. He then said: "It becomes a people thus favored to make acknowledgment to the Supreme Author from whom such blessings flow, of their gratitude and their dependence, to render praise and thanksgiving for the same, and devoutly to implore a continuance of God's mercies."[23]

In his second Thanksgiving proclamation, issued on October 21, 1870, he urged the American people to give thanks for the bounty of God. He said that "it behooves a people sensible of their dependence on the Almighty publicly and collectively to acknowledge their gratitude for his favors and mercies and humbly to beseech for their continuance[.]"[24]

Grant issued his third Thanksgiving proclamation on October 28, 1871. He urged thankfulness for the blessings and sympathy for those who had calamities in the previous year. He recommended that "on Thursday, the 30th day of November next, the people meet in their respective places of worship and there make the usual annual acknowledgments to Almighty God for the blessings He has conferred upon them, for their merciful exemption from evils, and invoke His protection and kindness for their less fortunate brethren, whom in His wisdom He has deemed it best to chastise."[25]

On October 11, 1872, Grant issued his fourth Thanksgiving proclamation. He reminded Americans that if any one people had "more occasion than another" to "thank the Almighty for His mercies and His blessings," it was the people of the United States, who during that year had been blessed with civil and religious freedom, equality before the law, and had "enjoyed exemption from any grievous or general calamity."[26]

On October 14, 1873, Grant issued his fifth Thanksgiving proclamation, offering thanks for the fact that the nation was gradually but surely "recovering from the lingering results of a dreadful civil strife."[27]

Grant issued his sixth Thanksgiving proclamation on October 27, 1874. He recommended to all citizens "to assemble in their respective places of worship on Thursday, the 26th day of November next, and express their thanks for the mercy and favor of Almighty God, and, laying aside all political contentions and all secular occupations, to observe such day as a day of rest, thanksgiving, and praise."[28]

On October 27, 1875, Grant called the nation to a "humble expression of our thanks to Almighty God." He said: "Amid the rich and free enjoyment of all our advantages, we should not forget the source from whence they are derived and the extent of our obligation to the Father of All Mercies." He acknowledged that civil and religious liberty, peace, and security were from God's "continuing mercy."[29]

On October 26, 1876, he issued his eighth and last Thanksgiving proclamation. He stated that Americans should be grateful for their individual blessings, then added these words:

> In addition to these favors accorded to us as individuals, we have especial occasion to express our hearty thanks to Almighty God that by His providence and guidance our Government, established a century ago, has been enabled to fulfill the purpose of its founders in offering an asylum to the people of every race, securing civil and religious liberty to all within its borders, and meting out to every individual alike justice and equality before the law.
>
> It is, moreover, especially our duty to offer our humble prayers to the Father of All Mercies for a continuance of His divine favor to us as a nation and as individuals.[30]

In this proclamation, he referred to America's centennial, celebrated that year. Grant issued a proclamation commemorating the centennial on June 26, 1876. It read:

> The centennial anniversary of the day on which the people of the United States declared their right to a separate and equal station among the powers of the earth seems to demand an exceptional observance.
>
> The founders of the Government, at its birth and in its feebleness, invoked the blessings and the protection of a Divine Providence, and the thirteen colonies and three millions of people have expanded into a nation of strength and numbers commanding the position which then was asserted and for which fervent prayers were then offered.
>
> It seems fitting that on the occurrence of the hundredth anniversary of our existence as a nation a grateful acknowledgment should be made to Almighty God for the protection and the bounties which He has vouchsafed to our beloved country.
>
> I therefore invite the good people of the United States, on the approaching 4th day of July, in addition to the usual obser-

vances with which they are accustomed to greet the return of the day, further, in such manner and at such time as in their respective localities and religious associations may be most convenient, to mark its recurrence by some public religious and devout thanksgiving to Almighty God for the blessings which have been bestowed upon us as a nation during the century of our existence, and humbly to invoke a continuance of His favor and of His protection.[31]

Grant served as president until 1877.

In a September 29 speech to the 1875 Army of the Tennessee reunion, he said:

> Let us all labor to add all needful guarantees for the more perfect security of Free Thought, Free speech, a Free Press, Pure Morals, Unfettered Religious sentiment, and of Equal Right & Privileges to all men irrespective of Nationality, Color or Religion. Encourage free schools and resolve that not one dollar of money appropriated to their support no matter how raised, shall be appropriated to the support of any sectarian school. Resolve that either the state or Nation, or both combined, shall support institutions of learning sufficient to afford to every child growing up in the land the opportunity of a good common school education, unmixed with sectarian, pagan, or atheistical tenets. Leave the matter of religion to the family circle, the church & the private school supported entirely by private contribution. Keep the church and the state forever separate, With these safeguards I believe the battles which created us 'the Army of the Tennessee' will not have been fought in vain.[32]

Interestingly enough, in the same paragraph where Grant said that "not one dollar" should be appropriated to support a "sectarian school," he also said that the institutions funded in the land must be "unmixed with sectarian, pagan, or atheistical tenets." Thus, while he would not have approved government funding of Roman Catholic and Protestant schools, he would also have opposed the modern public school system, which, in the interest of "multiculturalism," permits the teaching of any pagan religion and the observance of every religion except Christianity.

By April 1885, it became evident that Grant was near death. His family summoned the Reverend J. P. Newman. Newman baptized Grant (by sprinkling) shortly before Grant's death; however, some historians (and some of Grant's relatives) have stated that the sprinkling took place while Grant was asleep or unconscious and that he was unaware of it. (This debate is discussed later in the chapter.)

Days before his death, on July 8, 1885, a Catholic clergyman from Baltimore visited Grant and told him that everyone was praying for him. Grant, unable to speak due to the progression of his throat cancer, responded in writing:

> Yes, I know, and I feel very grateful to the Christian people of the land for their prayers in my behalf. There is no sect or religion, as shown in the Old or the New Testaments, to which this does not apply. Catholics, Protestants, and Jews, and all the good people of the Nation, of all politics as well as of religions, and of all nationalities, seem to have united in wishing or praying for improvement. I am a great sufferer all the time, but the facts I have related are compensation for much of it. All that I can do is to pray that the prayers of all these good people may be answered so far as to have us all meet in another and a better world. I cannot even speak in a whisper.
>
> "July 8, 1885. (Signed,) U. S. Grant."[33]

Grant died on July 23, 1885, in Mount McGregor, New York.

The popular image of Ulysses S. Grant is that of a cigar-smoking, cold-hearted, irreligious general. Every previous book on the Christianity of the presidents has helped to reinforce that image.

However, there is another side to the story. While William Makepeace Thayer was researching his 1885 book, *From Tannery to the White House: The Life of Ulysses S. Grant*, he interviewed Dr. O. H. Tiffany,[34] who, in Thayer's words, "was General Grant's pastor in Washington at one time." Dr. Tiffany related Grant's response to one of his sermons in these words:

> He was a man of religious habit and thoroughly honest and earnest in his belief in a Superintending Providence, regarding certain facts in history as inexplicable without this, and admiring the firm faith of a devoted sister, and reverencing with a sacredness

that was beautiful in its exhibition the piety of his parents. He made a visit of a week to Martha's Vineyard, which was then as now my summer home. I preached a sermon on the victory of faith, from the text: "They overcame him by the blood of the Lamb." He was more moved than I had ever seen him under a discourse, and, at the close of the sermon, at his suggestion, we wandered away from the crowd and engaged in earnest and serious conversation. He said: "Why is there so much stress laid upon the blood in your preaching and in the New Testament?" I explained to him in the simplest terms the doctrine of atonement, and he seemed fully to comprehend it. The giving up of life as a test of love was an incontrovertible argument to a man who had led thousands through death to victory, and I have always had a strong confidence that on that day the General had a personal realization of the truth as it is in Jesus.[35]

Many historians and biographers ignore this account and continue to portray Grant as an irreligious man until his death. (Part of their evidence is the diary of Senator Chaffee, whose testimony is offered as evidence to contradict Reverend Newman's deathbed baptism account.)

Apparently, Grant did not make an outright statement of faith in his conversation with Dr. Tiffany. However, if this account is accurate, Dr. Tiffany clearly explained the doctrine of atonement and Grant "seemed fully to comprehend it." Whether or not he confessed with his mouth that Jesus Christ is Lord, he apparently had at least this chance to understand the basic doctrines of salvation.

Grant said, "I believe in the Holy Scriptures, and whoso lives by them will be benefited thereby. Men may differ as to the interpretation, which is human, but the Scriptures are man's best guide."[36]

HISTORICAL CONTROVERSIES

Was Ulysses S. Grant baptized shortly before his death?
By April 1885, it became evident that Grant was terminally ill. His family, knowing that Grant had never to their knowledge professed faith in Christ, summoned the well-known Methodist minister J. P. Newman. In *God in the White House: The Faiths of American Presidents*, authors Edmund Fuller and David Green wrote:

Without impugning the sincerity of Newman's faith, it is certainly true that he hoped to gain the fame of converting General Grant. For his part, the laboring, dying man said brusquely that he didn't care how much praying went on around him if it consoled his wife and children. Newman hovered in constant attendance from April until Grant's death on July 23, 1885.[37]

Grant's son, Ulysses Grant Jr., had married the daughter of former Senator Jerome Chaffee. During the period when Grant's health was in decline and Reverend Newman was visiting him, Chaffee wrote:

There has been a good deal of nonsense in the papers about Dr. Newman's visits. General Grant does not believe that Dr. Newman's prayers will save him. He allows the doctor to pray simply because he does not want to hurt his feelings.[38]

Though some have said Grant was never baptized, the statement is technically incorrect, for Grant was sprinkled with water shortly before his death. However, Edmund Fuller and David Green stated that the baptism was, in effect, a farce. They described the scene in these words:

Once Grant was propped in his chair, in the sleep not far from a coma, and the Rev. Mr. Newman sprinkled him with water and baptized him. Grant was roused by the drops of water and the words. Told what had happened, he replied simply, "You surprise me." He made no acknowledgment of the rite, but Newman informed the press that Grant had been converted and baptized in the Methodist faith.[39]

CONCLUSION

Grant lived much of his life without much more than casual respect for Christianity. Toward the end of his life, there is some reason to believe that he thought more about spiritual matters. Two pastors, Dr. O. H. Tiffany and Dr. J. P. Newman, both stated that they helped lead him to Jesus. Dr. Tiffany's account is more credible, especially because it is an incontestable fact that Grant had full awareness of his surroundings and actions when the conversation with Tiffany occurred. While Grant never made a public profession of faith, he may have accepted salvation while talking with his pastor, Dr. Tiffany.

NOTES

1. Bliss Isley, *The Presidents: Men of Faith* (Boston: W. A. Wilde, 1953), 140.

2. Ulysses S. Grant, *The Papers of Ulysses S. Grant,* ed. John Y. Simon (Carbondale and Edwardsville, IL: Southern Illinois University Press, 1967), xxxvii.

3. Ibid., vol. 1, 7.

4. Ibid., vol. 5, 294. Cited John Russell Young and Michael Fellman, eds., *Around the World with General Grant,* vol. 2 (1879), 210.

5. Ibid., vol. 5, 132. Simon stated that Vincent "claimed to have seen him frequently in church," citing the *Directory of American Biography* (New York: 1928–36), vol. 19, 277–79.

6. Ibid., vol. 2, 305–6.

7. Ibid., vol. 3, 406.

8. Ibid., vol. 6, 252.

9. Ibid., vol. 6, 643. Simon quoted from Julian K. Larke, *General Grant and His Campaigns* (New York: 1864), 433. On December 9, Reverend Lewis R. Dunn (of the Methodist Episcopal Church in Morristown, NJ) wrote a letter to Grant's headquarters, informing him that he had been made a life director of that church's missionary society. Brig. Gen. James H. Wilson acknowledged the letter.

10. Benjamin P. Thomas, *Abraham Lincoln: A Biography* (New York: Knopf, 1952; repr., New York: Barnes and Noble Books, 1994), 418.

11. Ibid.

12. Grant, *The Papers of Ulysses S. Grant,* ed. Simon, vol. 15, 529. See Philadelphia's *Daily Evening Bulletin* (June 26, 1865) and *Inquirer* (June 26, 1865). John Simon, editor of the papers, cautioned that Grant "reportedly" made the donation. He was evidently unable to confirm the donation in other sources.

13. Ibid., vol. 16, 348. Simon cited the February 1, 1866, *Boston Sun* and the July 27, 1878, *New York Times.*

14. Ibid., vol. 19, 140.

15. Grant, March 4, 1869. First inaugural address.

16. Grant, March 4, 1873. Second inaugural address.

17. Ibid.

18. Olga Anna Jones, *Churches of the Presidents in Washington: Visits to Fifteen National Shrines* (New York: Exposition Press, 1954), 100.

19. Ibid., 24.

20. Grant, *The Papers of Ulysses S. Grant*, ed. Simon, vol. 21, 41.

21. Ibid., 152.

22. Ibid., vol. 25, 259.

23. Ibid., vol. 19, 250–51; Grant, *Messages and Papers of the Presidents: Ulysses S. Grant, 1869*. October 5, 1869. A Thanksgiving proclamation.

24. Grant, *Messages and Papers*, October 21, 1870. A Thanksgiving proclamation.

25. Ibid., October 28, 1871. A Thanksgiving proclamation.

26. Ibid., October 11, 1872. A Thanksgiving proclamation.

27. Ibid., October 14, 1873. A Thanksgiving proclamation.

28. Ibid., October 27, 1874. A Thanksgiving proclamation.

29. Ibid., October 27, 1875. A Thanksgiving proclamation.

30. Ibid., October 26, 1876. A Thanksgiving proclamation.

31. Ibid., June 26, 1876. On America's centennial.

32. Grant, *Papers of Ulysses S. Grant*, ed. Simon, vol. 26, 343–44.

33. William M. Thayer, *From Tannery to the White House: The Life of Ulysses S. Grant: His Boyhood, Youth, Manhood, Public and Private Life and Services* (Chicago: Albert Whitman, 1927), 456.

34. The interview occurred in 1885. Thayer stated that the interview took place "since the General's [Grant's] decease," and the book was published later in the year.

35. Thayer, *From Tannery to the White House*, 464–65.

36. William J. Federer, ed., *America's God and Country: Encyclopedia of Quotations*, 8th ed. (Cappel, TX: Fame Publishing, 1994), 265. Quoted in James Penny Boyd, *Military and Civil Life of General Ulysses S. Grant* (Garretson, 1885), 709–10.

37. Edmund Fuller and David E. Green, *God in the White House: The Faiths of American Presidents* (New York: Crown Publishers, 1968), 129.

38. Ibid., 129–30.

39. Fuller and Green, *God in the White House*, 129.

CHAPTER 26

ANDREW JOHNSON

ANDREW JOHNSON was born on December 29, 1808, in Raleigh, North Carolina. He married Eliza McCardle on May 17, 1827. She was a member of the Methodist Episcopal Church. Though Johnson was not a member, he attended church with her.[1]

Johnson became a tailor, settling in Greeneville, Tennessee.

On May 12, 1843, the mechanics of Greeneville unanimously adopted an address, urging the state of Tennessee to employ its prisoners in various mechanic trades. Andrew Johnson was on the five-member committee appointed to draw it up; he said that he "drew up every word of it" himself.[2] The report argued that there would never be "any system better calculated to restrain immoral conduct, or that will approach nearer perfection, than the theocracy instituted for the government of the children of Israel." It proceeded to cite Exodus 22:1–3, which provided that criminals restore what they had taken as well as other passages instituting appropriate recompense for actions.

Johnson then argued: "It appears satisfactory to our minds, from reading the above recited passages from Holy Writ, that GOD himself intended that the punishment should be commensurate with the crime committed. By turning to the New Testament, we find those very principles recognised and sustained by our Saviour. St. Matthew, chapter V, verse 17, 'Think not that I am come to destroy the law or the prophets, I am not come to destroy, but to fulfil.' In the same, chapter XXVI, verse 52, 'Then said Jesus unto him, put up again thy sword into its place: for all they that take the sword, shall perish with the sword.' "

Johnson said: "The committee have neither the time nor inclination to enter into an elaborate, argument upon the subject; but are willing to adopt the rules and regulations laid down by Moses, acting under the immediate direction of God himself, and afterwards sustained and recognised by Him that suffered crucifixion, to make the redemption of man possible."[3] This is Johnson's earliest known reference to Jesus. His second came later in the same report, where he said: "We are informed that Joseph, the husband of Mary, the mother of Jesus, was a carpenter by trade, and the probability is strong, that our Saviour followed it himself."[4]

In 1843, while Johnson was a state senator, he opposed daily prayers in the Tennessee Senate. His political opponent William G. Brownlow said that Johnson was an "avowed infidel."[5] However, in the fall of 1849, when the United States House of Representatives was deadlocked in a race for speaker of the house, Johnson offered, in the words of biographer Hans Trefousse, "a resolution for prayer in Congress to help speed the termination of the contest."[6]

In 1844, in a speech as a U.S. representative, Johnson said he was a "member of a Protestant church."[7] To the best of my knowledge, this statement has not yet been verified.

In 1845, Johnson's Whig opponents stated and attempted to prove that he was an infidel. On October 15, 1845, he issued a rebuttal entitled, "To the Freemen of the First Congressional District of Tennessee." This is an in-depth discussion of his faith, from his own pen. He knew if it could be proven he was an infidel, his political career would be over. Therefore, he discussed his religious views openly in this article.

The Whigs had claimed that Johnson publicly stated that Jesus was an illegitimate child, and that Mary was "a strumpet" (old term for a prostitute). Johnson replied: "This base and malignant charge, from beginning to end, is utterly and absolutely false; and there is not a man or woman, boy or child, white or black, living or dead, that ever heard me make use of any such expression, or any thing like it, in disrespect or in contempt of the Saviour of lost and ruined man."[8]

He was also accused of stating that Jesus was a usurer and a swindler. In the same rebuttal, he replied: "I feel well assured, too that there is nothing in all this that charges our Saviour with being an unlawful usurer, or of "practising the doctrine or of being a swindler." Such a thought never entered my head–such an expression I know never escaped my lips; and there is not a man living, be his station high or low, that ever heard me make use of any such language, or any thing like it, in connexion with the name of Jesus Christ."[9]

When he was accused of being an infidel, he replied that the charge was "without the shadow of foundation in truth."[10] He defined the term "infidel" as "an unbelief in the divine authenticity of the Bible— a disbelief in a future state of rewards and punishments—or, in other words, one who believes there is no such place as a hell to punish sinners in, as declared in the Holy Bible,"[11]and declared he did not fit this description.

He added, "I think it proper to repeat what I have again and again said on previous occasions, THAT THE CHARGE OF INFIDELITY, AS PREFERRED AGAINST ME IN THE LATE CANVASS, IS UTTERLY AND ABSOLUTELY FALSE FROM BEGINNING TO END; AND THAT, SO FAR AS THE DOCTRINES OF THE BIBLE ARE CONCERNED, OR THE GREAT SCHEME OF SALVATION, AS FOUNDED, TAUGHT, AND PRACTISED BY JESUS CHRIST HIMSELF, I NEVER DID ENTERTAIN A SOLITARY DOUBT."[12]

He concluded by repeating once more that he held "A belief in the pure and unadulterated principles of Democracy, is a belief in the religion of our Saviour, as laid down while here upon earth himself— rewarding the virtuous and meritorious without any regard to station, to wealth, or to distinction of birth."[13]

During the early years of his political career, Andrew Johnson referred to or quoted the Bible frequently.[14] For whatever reason, the number of references and quotes in his surviving speeches and papers decreased as he climbed the political ladder. Possibly, he felt less need to establish himself in the eyes of the electorate as a man sufficiently religious to be an acceptable representative.

On December 19, 1845, Johnson introduced this resolution into the Tennessee House of Representatives: "Resolved by this House— That the ministers of the different Churches of *God*, be and they are hereby most respectfully invited, and earnestly requested to attend every morning and open the proceedings of Congress with *sincere* prayer to the giver of all good, for a continuance of his benedictions upon this nation, and that it shall be done upon the terms as laid down in the Gospel of Jesus Christ—'without money and without price'—except such amounts as may be voluntarily contributed by the members of this house individually[.]"[15] Though the resolution did not pass, it may have helped Johnson escape the charge of atheism.[16]

In a May 1852, speech to New York Land Reformers, Johnson described a homesteader who was criticized as being a leveler. Johnson said that "[t]he Savior of Man came down from Heaven to elevate the multitude to the honorable condition of men and angels, and if he who shed his blood on Calvary was considered a leveler, so was he."[17]

On October 17, 1853, Johnson made his first inaugural address as governor of Tennessee. In the address, he made the case that because man "partakes most highly of the nature and character of Him in whose image he is made," he used the term "the *Divinity of Man*." He said: "It is the business of the Democratic party to progress in the work of work of increasing this principle of Divinity, or Democracy, and thereby elevate and make man more perfect. I hold that the Democratic party proper, of the whole world, and especially of the United States, has undertaken the *political redemption of man*, and sooner or later, the great work will be accomplished."[18]

Johnson believed that the "work of progress and elevation" would one day be finished: "The Church Militant will cease to exist, and the Church Triumphant begin: at the same point, Democracy progressive will give way and cease to exist, and Theocracy begin."[19] He continued:

> "The divinity of man being now fully developed,—it may now be confidently and exultingly asserted that the *voice of the people is the voice of God*; and proclamation be made, that the millenial morning has dawned, when the Lion and the Lamb shall lie down together; when the 'voice of the turtle' shall be 'heard in our land;' when 'the suckling child shall play upon the hole of the asp,' and the 'weaned child put its hand upon the cockatrice's den,' and the glad tidings shall be proclaimed throughout the land, of man's political and religious redemption, and that there is 'on earth, peace, good will toward men.'
>
> "It will be readily perceived by all discerning young men, that Democracy is a ladder, corresponding in politics, to the one spiritual which Jacob saw in his vision: one up which all, in proportion to their merit, may ascend."[20]

This speech used dramatic phrases; in all probability, it was well received by its audience. But the theology it reveals is rather unorthodox. In orthodox Christianity, man is not viewed as divine, and the millennium comes with the return of Jesus, not through man being declared divine. (Orthodox Christians' interpretations of future prophetic events differ primarily in interpretation of timing. Most Christians agree there will be a tribulation and a millennium and merely disagree in details such as length of the tribulation and timing of Jesus' return.)

On his second inaugural address as governor of Tennessee, delivered on October 23, 1855, Johnson said: "It is important, therefore, always to bear in mind, that whatever tends substantially to benefit the common people, will generally be viewed with hostility by the pseudo aristocracy of the country. Hence, genuine Christianity and Democracy, both originate with, and have mainly been supported by, men of humble origin, circumstances, and situations, whom those puffed up with undue wealth, assumed learning, power, rank, and authority, generally profess to despise for their low birth, poverty, and ignorance."[21]

Johnson was elected to the United States Senate. On February 17, 1858, he made a speech on the Senate floor on "Maintaining Federal Authority in Utah." In the speech, he said: "Sir, in the midst of all this delusion, while we pursue the career upon which we intend to enter against the Mormons, we should act as Christians; and with the Light of Christianity, with the Bible before us, we should endeavor to correct and reform that misguided and deluded people."[22]

On the next day, Johnson spoke again on the same topic: "I am willing to be tolerant. Standing upon these great principles laid down and inculated in the constitutions of all the States, I think that we should adopt other means, we should act towards the Mormons as Christians ought to act—go with the Bible in one hand and the torch of reason in the other, and dissuade them if we could from their course."[23]

When the southern states seceded, Johnson was the only Southern senator to remain loyal to the Union and to retain his seat. Tennessee had a sizable loyal population and was internally torn throughout the Civil War.

On January 31, 1862, Johnson made a speech on the expulsion of Indiana's Senator Jesse Bright. In the speech he said: "Let us look forward to the time when we can take the flag, the glorious flag of our country, and nail it below the Cross, and there let it wave as it waved in the olden times, and let us gather around it, and inscribe as our motto: 'Liberty and Union, one and inseparable, now and forever.' Let us gather around it, and while it hangs floating beneath the cross, let us exclaim, 'Christ first, our country next!' "[24]

Later in 1862, Senator Johnson was appointed the provisional governor of his home state of Tennessee, which had been captured from the Confederates. Nashville was then under siege by the Confederate forces. Abraham Lincoln told painter Frank Carpenter about a conversation that Johnson had with Methodist chaplain Granville Moody during the siege:

> Johnson, manifesting intense feeling . . . said, "Moody, we are sold out. Buell is a traitor! He is going to evacuate the city, and in forty-eight hours we shall be in the hands of the Rebels!" Then he commenced pacing the floor again, twisting his hands, and chafing like a caged tiger, utterly insensible to his friend's entreaties to become calm. Suddenly he turned and said, "Moody, can you pray?" "That is my business, sir, as a minister of the Gospel," returned the Colonel. "Well, Moody, I wish you would pray," said Johnson; and instantly both went down on their knees, at opposite sides of the room. As the prayer waxed fervent, Johnson began to respond in true Methodist style. Presently he crawled over on his hands and knees to Moody's side, and put his arm over him, manifesting the deepest emotion. Closing the prayer with a hearty "Amen" from each, they arose. Johnson took a long breath, and said, with emphasis, "Moody, I feel better!" Shortly afterwards he asked, "Will you stand by me?" "Certainly I will," was the answer. "Well, Moody, I can depend on you; you are one in a hundred thousand!" He then commenced pacing the floor again. Suddenly he wheeled, the current of his thought having changed, and said, "Oh! Moody, I don't want you to think I have become a religious man because I asked you to pray. I am sorry to say, but I am not, and have never pretended to be, religious. No one knows this better than you; but Moody, there is one thing about it—I DO believe in ALMIGHTY GOD! And I believe also in the Bible, and I say 'd——' me, if Nashville shall be surrendered!"[25]

Nashville was not surrendered.

On January 21, 1864, when Unionists in Tennessee's Hall of Representatives endorsed resolutions calling for the restoration of Tennessee and its state government, they saw Governor Johnson "in an obscure corner"[26] and called for him to make a speech. In the speech, he talked about God's dealings with nations. He said:

The ways of Providence are incomprehensible to short-sighted, erring man. In the various periods of the world's history there have been manifestations of a power incomprehensible to us, and I believe that there is a direct and important connection between the moral and physical world, and the one is affected more or less by the other in bringing about great events. Going back to the history of the world, we find events and signs have preceded final results. This nation, many think, has been involved in a great sin. Nations as well as individuals must sooner or later be overtaken for their transgressions. Perhaps this rebellion will result in great good; the nation will become chastened and the sin removed. Who can tell?[27]

After citing examples of nations from history that had fallen, he stated:

"I will not say whether these were special interpositions of Providence or the results of a Divine law, but they are great facts."

I might take you to Jerusalem, and tell of the persecution by the Jews of Christ, and his crucifixion upon the cross, and now their dispersion to all parts of the globe. I will not assume that it was an interposition of Divine Providence, or the result of a general law, but it is a great fact, and the Jews have been dispersed and rebuked. There are many ways in which the Almighty manifests his power. He sometimes unlocks the winds, and rends the forests, and stands whole navies upon the hidden rocks and desert shores. Sometimes He manifests His power in the forked lightning's glare, and sometimes His mutterings are heard in distant though threatening peals of thunder. Sometimes He lets the comet loose, which sweeps from one extreme of the universe to another, shaking from its fiery tail pestilence and death. There are

Signs sent by God to mark the will of Heaven—
Signs which bid nations weep and be forgiven.

Does not the mind irresistibly come to the conclusion that this great sin must be gotten clear of, or result in the overthrow and destruction of this nation? I say, then, remove the evil, obey the laws of Heaven, and always reach a right conclusion.[28]

In 1864, Johnson was elected vice president of the United States on the Union Party ticket. After Abraham Lincoln died on April 15, 1865, Johnson became president.

Chief Justice Salmon P. Chase administered Johnson's oath of office. After Johnson took the oath, he kissed the Bible upon which he was sworn. Several days later, Chief Justice Chase sent Johnson the Bible upon which the oath was administered and noted that Johnson had kissed the Bible at Ezekiel 11:21,[29] "But as for them whose heart walketh after the heart of their detestable things and their abominations, I will recompense their way upon their own heads, saith the Lord GOD."[30]

On April 17, two days later, nearly sixty ministers from churches in the District of Columbia gathered and prepared a joint message for President Johnson. Upon receiving the message, he asked to see them immediately. They came to him, and he spoke to them for several minutes, saying:

> My whole life has been based on the profound belief, in which I have never wavered, that there is a great principle of right which lies at the basis of all things. I have always trusted to that principle as the certain support of all who abide by it—the great principle of right and justice and truth. I shall trust to it, and guide the administration of public affairs in conformity to it. I should feel anxious for the future, but I have an abiding confidence in the strength of that principle *and in Him who founded it.* I thank you for the assurance which you have been pleased to offer me. . . .
>
> We mourn together to-day over the calamity that has fallen upon the country. I feel that our beloved country will pass through the trouble of the present. I say again that I put my trust in the great principle which underlies all our institutions, and believe that we shall come out of the struggle to a better and higher life. The country has not accomplished her mission; but under the benignant smile of the Almighty she will yet fulfill it. The country will triumph in the end, and these great principles will be firmly established.[31]

While he was president, Johnson sometimes attended St. Patrick's Roman Catholic cathedral, because he admired the preaching of Father Maguire.[32] Based on this, one author has concluded that "deep in his heart," Johnson "was a Roman Catholic."[33] The evidence extant does not support this theory. He certainly had no objection to Catholicism; I have not yet found anything in writing to support the theory that he preferred the Catholic church above all others. He simply liked Father Maguire's preaching. He also attended the Methodist church at times with his wife.

One of Johnson's first acts as President was to issue a proclamation (dated April 25, 1865) setting May 25 as a day of mourning for Lincoln. In it he said:

> Whereas our country has become one great house of mourning, where the head of the family has been taken away, and believing that a special period should be assigned for again humbling ourselves before Almighty God, in order that the bereavement may be sanctified to the nation:
>
> Now, therefore, in order to mitigate that grief on earth which can only be assuaged by communion with the Father in heaven, and in compliance with the wishes of Senators and Representatives in Congress, communicated to me by resolutions adopted at the National Capitol, I, Andrew Johnson, President of the United States, do hereby appoint Thursday, the 25th day of May next, to be observed, wherever in the United States the flag of the country may be respected, as a day of humiliation and mourning, and I recommend my fellow-citizens then to assemble in their respective places of worship, there to unite in solemn service to Almighty God in memory of the good man who has been removed, so that all shall be occupied at the same time in contemplation of his virtues and in sorrow for his sudden and violent end.[34]

When he was informed that he had made a mistake, scheduling the day of mourning on Ascension Day, he issued a second proclamation. He said that as the day he had named was "sacred to large numbers of Christians as one of rejoicing for the ascension of the Savior," he would reschedule the day of humiliation and prayer to June 1.[35]

Johnson made several speeches in which he defended his policy of leniency to former Confederates. In two of these speeches, he cited Jesus' example of mercy toward sinners as his example. The first of these two speeches was delivered on February 22, 1866, and said:

> We must conform our actions and our conduct to the example of Him who founded our holy religion. Not that I would make such a comparison on this occasion[36] in any personal aspect. I came into

the place under the Constitution of the country and by the approbation of the people, and what did I find? I found eight millions
of people who were in fact condemned under the law, and the
penalty was death. Was I to yield to the spirit of revenge and
resentment, and declare that they should all be annihilated and
destroyed? How different would this have been from the example
set by the holy founder of our religion, the extreme points of
whose divine arch rests upon the horizon, and whose span
embraces the universe;—he who founded this great scheme came
into the world and found man condemned under the law, and his
sentence was death. What was his example? Instead of condemning the world or even a nation to death, he died upon the cross,
attesting by his wounds and his blood that he died that mankind
might live. Let those who have erred repent—let them acknowledge their allegiance—let them become loyal, willing supporters
and defenders of our glorious stripes and stars, and of the
Constitution of our country—let the leaders, the conscious, intelligent traitors, be punished and subjected to the penalties of the
law; but to the great mass, who have been forced into this rebellion, in many instances, and in others have been misled, I say
extend leniency, kindness, trust, and confidence.[37]

On August 29, 1866, Johnson again defended leniency to former
Confederates in a speech he made in New York. He said:

I am not for destroying all men, or condemning to total destruction all men who have erred once in their lives. I believe in the
memorable example of Him who came with peace and healing on
his wings; and when he descended and found men condemned
unto the law, instead of executing it, instead of shedding the blood
of the world, he placed himself on the cross, and died that men
might be saved. If I have pardoned many, I trust in God that I
have erred on the right side. If I have pardoned many, I believe it
is all for the best interests of the country; and so believing and convinced that our Southern brethren were giving evidence by their
practice and profession that they were repentant, in imitation of
Him of old who died for the preservation of men. I exercised that
mercy which I believed to be my duty.[38]

Johnson issued several Thanksgiving proclamations as president. His first, issued on October 28, 1865, gave thanks for the end of the Civil War and for peace with foreign nations. He reminded the nation that "righteousness exalteth a nation, while sin is a reproach to any people," and recommended that the American people "make confession of our national sins against His infinite goodness, and with one heart and one mind implore the divine guidance in the ways of national virtue and holiness."[39]

In his second Thanksgiving proclamation, issued on October 8, 1866, he expressed thanks that the "civil war that so recently closed among us has not been anywhere reopened," and recommended that the American people devoutly implore that God would "grant to our national councils and to our whole people that divine wisdom which alone can lead any nation into the ways of all good."[40]

Johnson's 1867 Thanksgiving proclamation urged the American people to rest and refrain "from secular labors" on Thanksgiving Day. He urged them to "reverently and devoutly give thanks to our Heavenly Father for the mercies and blessings with which He has crowned the now closing year" and to "implore Him that the same divine protection and care which we have hitherto so undeservedly and yet so constantly enjoyed may be continued to our country and our people throughout all their generations forever."[41]

Johnson served as president until 1869.

On April 3, 1869, Johnson made a speech at Knoxville, Tennessee. He said that he would rather be in their midst, "privileged to advocate the principles of the Constitution, than to be inaugurated President." He also said: "I had rather be in your midst to unfurl the banner of peace and fasten it below the cross, with the inscription, 'God first and my country next.' "[42]

On June 29, 1873, Johnson made a note about death. He probably expected to die shortly; he had contracted cholera. He said:

All seems gloom and dispair [sic]
I have performed my duty to my God, my country and my family. I have nothing to fear. Approaching death to me is the mere shadow of God's protecting wing. Beneath it I feel almost sacred. Here I know can no evil come. Here I will rest in quiet and peace beyond the reach of calumny's poisoned shaft—the influence of

envy and jealous enemies, where Treason and Traitors in state, back sliders and hypocrits [sic] in church can have no place—where the greatest fact will be realized *that* GOD IS TRUTH and *gratitude*, the *highest attribute of man.*

Adieu—Sic iter ad astra. Such is the way to the stars or immortality.[43]

However, he did not die for another two years.

On October 23, 1873, he made a speech in Washington, DC, and said: "I have never been a partisan in politics, nor have I been a fanatic in religion. My religion has been co-extensive with my race, and my politics have corresponded with the boundary of the nation. I have felt that every man, acting upon principle, and upon the principles laid down in the Constitution, let him be far or near, was my brother—speaking, in other language, the same idea that the world is my home, and every honest man my brother."[44]

On July 29, 1875, he had a stroke and his family gathered at his house. The nearby Elizabethton, Tennessee, Masonic fraternity also gathered to help care for him as he neared death. After suffering a second stroke the next day, he died on July 31.

The Masonic fraternity took charge of Johnson's body and placed a guard around it until the funeral several days later. The funeral was conducted with full Masonic rites.

CONCLUSION

Johnson was a religious man. He was a "Christian" in the generic sense of one who attends a Christian church and generally agrees with many of the things taught; however, his surviving writings and speeches suggest that he held some doctrines that were not in accordance with orthodox Christianity.

NOTES

1. Lately Thomas, *The First President Johnson: The Three Lives of the Seventeenth President of the United States of America* (New York: William Morrow, 1968), 49.

2. Johnson, *The Papers of Andrew Johnson, 1860–1861*, eds. Leroy P. Graf and Ralph W. Haskins, vol. 1 (Knoxville: University of Tennessee Press, 1967, 1976), 250.

3. Ibid.

4. Ibid.

5. Hans L. Trefousse, *Andrew Johnson: A Biography* (New York and London: Norton, 1989), 49.

6. Ibid., 75.

7. Edmund Fuller and David E. Green, *God in the White House: The Faiths of American Presidents* (New York: Crown Publishers, 1968), 118.

8. Johnson, *The Papers of Andrew Johnson*, eds. Graf and Haskins, vol. 1, 222.

9. Ibid., 228–29.

10. Ibid., 221.

11. Ibid., 233.

12. Ibid., 240.

13. Ibid.

14. Among others, he quoted, paraphrased, or alluded to the following passages: Gen. 4:22; 9:6; Exod. 7:12; Lev. 25:23; Deut. 5:16; Ruth 1:16; 1 Sam. 9:2; Prov. 6:10; 30:15; Jonah 4:6–7; Matt. 8:20; Acts 12:22–23; James 1:27.

15. Johnson, *The Papers of Andrew Johnson*, eds. Graf and Haskins, vol. 1, 278.

16. Thomas, *The First President Johnson*, 60.

17. Johnson, *The Papers of Andrew Johnson*, eds. Graf and Haskins, vol. 2, 59.

18. Ibid., 176.

19. Ibid.

20. Ibid., 176–77.

21. Ibid., 343.

22. Ibid., vol. 3, 28.

23. Ibid., 39.

24. Ibid., vol. 5, 132. Quoted in William J. Federer, ed., *America's God and Country: Encyclopedia of Quotations* (Coppell, TX: Fame Publishing, 1994), 334; John Savage, *The Life and Public Services of Andrew Johnson: Seventeenth President of the United States* (Auburn, ME: Derby & Miller, 1866), 274.

25. Trefousse, *Andrew Johnson,* 160–61.

26. *Nashville Dispatch*, January 22, 1864.

27. Johnson, *The Papers of Andrew Johnson*, eds. Graf and Haskins, vol. 6, 584–85.

28. Ibid., 585–86.

29. Ibid., vol. 7, 672.

30. Ibid., 673.

31. Ibid., 576.

32. Fuller and Green, *God in the White House*, 123.

33. John McCollister, *So Help Me God: The Faith of America's Presidents*

(Louisville: Westminster/John Knox Press, 1991), 95.

34. Johnson, *Messages and Papers of the Presidents: Andrew Johnson, 1865.* April 25, 1865.

35. Ibid., April 29, 1865.

36. The speech was made on George Washington's birthday; he was defending his (Johnson's) policy of leniency to Confederates.

37. Johnson, *The Papers of Andrew Johnson,* ed. Bergeron, vol. 10, 148–49. This account of the speech was printed in the February 23, 1866, *New York Times.*

38. Ibid., vol. 11, 163–64. The August 30, 1866, *World* provided this account of Johnson's speech, which had not been prepared in advance.

39. Johnson, *Messages and Papers,* October 28, 1865. A Thanksgiving proclamation.

40. Ibid., October 8, 1866. A Thanksgiving proclamation.

41. Ibid., October 26, 1867. A Thanksgiving proclamation.

42. Johnson, *The Papers of Andrew Johnson,* ed. Bergeron, vol. 15, 574.

43. Ibid., vol. 16, 430.

44. Ibid., 466.

CHAPTER 27

ABRAHAM LINCOLN

A BRAHAM LINCOLN was born on February 12, 1809, in Hardin County, Kentucky.

His father, Thomas Lincoln, joined the Pigeon Creek Baptist Church by letter on June 7, 1823. Sarah Bush Johnston Lincoln (Abraham's stepmother) also became a member, but Abraham Lincoln did not. Thomas Lincoln was an active member, serving as trustee for several years, attending a church conference as a representative, and acting on a number of committees."[1]

Lincoln's youngest stepsister, Matilda Johnston (Moore), remembered that when Thomas and Sarah Lincoln would travel the one and a half miles to their church, the children would stay home. "When they were gone," she remembered, "Abe would take down the Bible, read a verse, give out a hymn, and we would sing. [We] were good singers." During this time, Abraham Lincoln was "about 15 years of age."

"He would preach and we would do the Crying," she said. "Sometimes he would join in the Chorus of Tears."[2]

Early in his adult life, Abraham Lincoln settled in New Salem, Illinois. Though the village had no church, it did have a minister, the Reverend John Berry. Additionally, circuit riders, such as Peter Cartwright, visited upon occasion.[3]

On December 13, 1836, Lincoln wrote Mary Owens a letter. In it he said:

> There is great strife and struggling for the office of U.S. Senator here at this time. It is probable we shall ease their pains in a few

days. The opposition men have no candidate of their own, and consequently they smile as complacently at the snarls of the contending Van Buren candidates and their respective friends, as the christain [sic] does at Satan's rage.[4]

On April 15, 1837, Lincoln moved from New Salem to Springfield, Illinois. Three weeks later, he wrote Mary Owens, saying: "I am quite as lonesome here as [I] ever was anywhere in my life. I have been spoken to by but one woman since I've been here, and should not have been by her, if she could have avoided it. I've never been to church yet, nor probably shall not be soon. I stay away because I am conscious I should not know how to behave myself."[5]

He married Mary Todd on November 4, 1842.

In an 1843 congressional campaign, Lincoln found himself embroiled in a religious controversy. In a letter to his friend Martin M. Morris the next year, Lincoln described it:

There was, too, the strangest combination of church influence against me. Baker is a Campbellite; and therefore, as I suppose, with few exceptions got all that church. My wife has some relations in the Presbyterian churches, and some with the Episcopal churches; and therefore, wherever it would tell, I was set down as either the one or the other, while it was everywhere contended that no Christian[6] ought to go for me, because I belonged to no church, was suspected of being a deist, and had talked about fighting a duel. With all these things, Baker, of course, had nothing to do. Nor do I complain of them. As to his own church going for him, I think that was right enough, and as to the influences I have spoken of in the other, though they were very strong, it would be grossly untrue and unjust to charge that they acted upon them in a body or were very near so. I only mean that those influences levied a tax of a considerable per cent. upon my strength throughout the religious controversy.[7]

In 1846, Lincoln again ran for a seat in the U.S. House of Representatives. He was opposed by Peter Cartwright, the frontier preacher. A religious controversy arose when Cartwright openly called Lincoln an infidel. To counteract the charge, Lincoln published a statement of his religious beliefs in Lacon's *Illinois Gazette* on August 15, 1846.[8] It read:

A charge having got into circulation in some of the neighborhoods of the District, in substance that I am an open scoffer at Christianity, I have by the advice of some friends concluded to notice the subject in this form. That I am not a member of any Christian Church, is true; but I have never denied the truth of the Scriptures; and I have never spoken with intentional disrespect of religion in general, or of any denomination of Christians in particular. It is true that in early life I was inclined to believe in what I understand is called the "Doctrine of Necessity"—that is, that the human mind is impelled to action, or held in rest by some power, over which the mind itself has no control; and I have sometimes (with one, two, or three, but never publicly) tried to maintain this opinion in argument. The habit of arguing thus, however, I have, entirely left off for more than five years. And I add here, I have always understood this same opinion to be held by several of the Christian denominations. The foregoing is the whole truth, briefly stated, in relation to myself, upon this subject.

I do not think I could myself, be brought to support a man for office, whom I knew to be an open enemy of, and scoffer at, religion. Leaving the highest matter of eternal consequences between him and his Maker, I still do not think any man has the right thus to insult the feelings, and injure the morals, of the community in which he may live. If, then, I was guilty of such conduct, I should blame no man who should condemn me for it; but I do blame those, whoever they may be, who falsely put such a charge in circulation against me.[9]

Lincoln won the election. In 1847, he went to Washington, DC to begin his term. Biographer Benjamin Thomas notes that "the city had thirty-seven churches of eight denominations, though no record exists of Lincoln's attending any of them during his Congressional term."[10]

He was elected president in 1860. When he left Springfield to go to Washington, DC, he said:

I now leave, not knowing when, or whether ever, I may return, with a task before me greater than that which rested upon Washington. Without the assistance of that Divine Being who ever attended him, I cannot succeed. With that assistance I cannot fail.

Trusting in Him who can go with me, and remain with you and be everywhere for good, let us confidently hope that all will yet be well. To His care commending you, as I hope in your prayers you will commend me, I bid you an affectionate farewell.[11]

He served as President from 1861 to 1865. In his first inaugural address, he said: "Why should there not be a patient confidence in the ultimate justice of the people? Is there any better or equal hope in the world? In our present differences, is either party without faith of being in the right? If the Almighty Ruler of Nations, with His eternal truth and justice, be on your side of the North, or on yours of the South, that truth and that justice will surely prevail by the judgment of this great tribunal of the American people." He added: "Intelligence, patriotism, Christianity, and a firm reliance on Him who has never yet forsaken this favored land are still competent to adjust in the best way all our present difficulty."[12]

Throughout the year 1862, Lincoln was pressured to issue an emancipation proclamation. He responded that he was seeking God's will on the matter. For example, when the religious denominations of Chicago joined together to ask him to issue an emancipation proclamation, he responded in these words:

The subject presented in the memorial is one upon which I have thought much for weeks past, and I may even say for months. I am approached with the most opposite opinions and advice, and that by religious men, who are equally certain that they represent the Divine will. I am sure that either the one or the other class is mistaken in that belief, and perhaps in some respects both. I hope it will not be irreverent for me to say that if it is probable that God would reveal his will to others, on a point so connected with my duty, it might be supposed he would reveal it directly to me; for, unless I am more deceived in myself than I often am, it is my earnest desire to know the will of Providence in this matter. And if I can learn what it is I will do it! These are not, however, the days of miracles, and I suppose it will be granted that I am not to expect a direct revelation. I must study the plain physical facts of the case, ascertain what is possible, and learn what appears to be wise and right.

The subject is difficult, and good men do not agree. For instance, the other day, four gentlemen of standing and intelligence from New York called as a delegation on business connected with the war; but before leaving two of them earnestly besought me to proclaim general emancipation, upon which the other two at once attacked them. You know also that the last session of Congress had a decided majority of antislavery men, yet they could not unite on this policy. And the same is true of the religious people. Why, the rebel soldiers are praying with a great deal more earnestness, I fear, than our own troops, and expecting God to favor their side: for one of our soldiers who had been taken prisoner told Senator Wilson a few days since that he met nothing so discouraging as the evident sincerity of those he was among in their prayers.[13]

Lincoln ended up deciding to issue the Emancipation Proclamation on January 1, 1863.

On November 15, 1862, Lincoln issued this "General Order Respecting the Observance of the Sabbath Day in the Army and Navy." It read:

> The President, Commander in Chief of the Army and Navy, desires and enjoins the orderly observance of the Sabbath by the officers and men in the military and naval service. The importance for man and beast of the prescribed weekly rest, the sacred rights of Christian soldiers and sailors, a becoming deference to the best sentiment of a Christian people, and a due regard for the divine will demand that Sunday labor in the Army and Navy be reduced to the measure of strict necessity.
>
> The discipline and character of the national forces should not suffer nor the cause they defend be imperiled by the profanation of the day or name of the Most High. "At this time of public distress," adopting the words of Washington in 1776, "men may find enough to do in the service of God and their country without abandoning themselves to vice and immorality." The first general order issued by the Father of his Country after the Declaration of Independence indicates the spirit in which our institutions were rounded and should ever be defended:
>
> "The General hopes and trusts that every officer and man will endeavor to live and act as becomes a Christian soldier defending the dearest rights and liberties of his country."[14]

Assistant Adjutant General T. M. Vincent said that he took this order in Stanton's handwriting to Abraham Lincoln, who approved it without suggesting a change.[15] Therefore, if Vincent's statement is accurate, Stanton wrote the original words but Abraham Lincoln approved of them and was willing to issue them under his name.

On March 30, 1863, Abraham Lincoln issued this call for a day of national prayer and humiliation:

> Whereas the Senate of the United States, devoutly recognizing the supreme authority and just government of Almighty God in all the affairs of men and of nations, has by a resolution requested the President to designate and set apart a day for national prayer and humiliation; and
>
> Whereas it is the duty of nations as well as of men to own their dependence upon the overruling power of God, to confess their sins and transgressions in humble sorrow, yet with assured hope that genuine repentance will lead to mercy and pardon, and to recognize the sublime truth, announced in the Holy Scriptures and proven by all history, that those nations only are blessed whose God is the Lord;
>
> And, insomuch as we know that by His divine law nations, like individuals, are subjected to punishments and chastisements in this world, may we not justly fear that the awful calamity of civil war which now desolates the land may be but a punishment inflicted upon us for our presumptuous sins, to the needful end of our national reformation as a whole people? We have been the recipients of the choicest bounties of Heaven; we have been preserved these many years in peace and prosperity; we have grown in numbers, wealth, and power as no other nation has ever grown. But we have forgotten God. We have forgotten the gracious hand which preserved us in peace and multiplied and enriched and strengthened us, and we have vainly imagined, in the deceitfulness of our hearts, that all these blessings were produced by some superior wisdom and virtue of our own. Intoxicated with unbroken success, we have become too self-sufficient to feel the necessity of redeeming and preserving grace, too proud to pray to the God that made us.
>
> It behooves us, then, to humble ourselves before the offended Power, to confess our national sins, and to pray for clemency and forgiveness.

Now, therefore, in compliance with the request, and fully concurring in the views of the Senate, I do by this my proclamation designate and set apart Thursday, the 30th day of April, 1863, as a day of national humiliation, fasting, and prayer. And I do hereby request all the people to abstain on that day from their ordinary secular pursuits, and to unite at their several places of public worship and their respective homes in keeping the day holy to the Lord and devoted to the humble discharge of the religious duties proper to that solemn occasion.

All this being done in sincerity and truth, let us then rest humbly in the hope authorized by the divine teachings that the united cry of the nation will be heard on high and answered with blessings no less than the pardon of our national sins and the restoration of our now divided and suffering country to its former happy condition of unity and peace. In witness whereof I have hereunto set my hand and caused the seal of the United States to be affixed.[16]

On July 15, 1863, President Lincoln issued a proclamation for thanksgiving. It read:

It has pleased Almighty God to hearken to the supplications and prayers of an afflicted people, and to vouchsafe to the army and navy of the United States victories on land and on the sea so signal and so effective as to furnish reasonable grounds for augmented confidence that the union of these States will be maintained, their Constitution preserved, and their peace and prosperity permanently restored. These victories have been accorded not without sacrifices of life, limb, health, and liberty, incurred by brave, loyal, and patriotic citizens. Domestic affliction in every part of the country follows in the train of these fearful bereavements.

It is meet and right to recognize and confess the presence of the Almighty Father, and the power of his hand equally in these triumphs and in these sorrows.

Now, therefore, be it known that I do set apart Thursday, the 6th day of August next, to be observed as a day for national thanksgiving, praise, and prayer, and I invite the people of the United States to assemble on that occasion in their customary places of worship, and, in the forms approved by their own consciences, render the homage due to the Divine Majesty for the wonderful things he has done in the nation's behalf, and invoke the influences of his Holy Spirit to subdue the anger which has produced and so long sustained a needless and cruel rebellion, to change the hearts of the insurgents, to guide the counsels of the government with wisdom adequate to so great a national emergency, and to visit with tender care and consolation throughout the length and breadth of our land all those who, through the vicissitudes of marches, voyages, battles, and sieges have been brought to suffer in mind, body, or estate, and finally to lead the whole nation through the paths of repentance and submission to the Divine Will back to the perfect enjoyment of union and fraternal peace.[17]

General Daniel E. Sickles quoted Lincoln as telling him that before the battle of Gettysburg, "oppressed by the gravity of our affairs, I went to my room one day, and I locked the door, and got down on my knees before Almighty God, and prayed to him mightily for victory." Carl Sandburg believed that this was not an accurate quote; that opinion was based on Sandburg's perception of the way he believed Lincoln usually prayed rather than any doubts as to General Sickles' credibility.[18]

In 1863, President Lincoln considered a homestead law. He commented that he desired friendly relationships with the Indian tribes and hoped that attention would be paid "above all, to that moral training which, under the blessing of Divine Providence, will confer upon them the elevated and sanctifying influences, the hopes and consolations, of the Christian faith."[19]

Lincoln sought God's guidance for many important decisions in the Civil War; he believed that for these decisions he must answer to God. A case in point was the use of black soldiers. He said: "At the beginning of the war, and for some time, the use of colored troops was not contemplated; and how the change of purpose was wrought I will not now take time to explain. Upon a clear conviction of duty I resolved to turn that element of strength to account; and I am responsible for it to the American people, to the Christian world, to history, and in my final account to God."[20]

Abraham Lincoln had a strong belief that God governed the world. He earnestly sought God's guidance for the many decisions he faced as president and as commander in chief of the nation's military:

I am glad of this interview, and glad to know that I have your sympathy and prayers. We are indeed going through a great trial, a fiery trial. In the very responsible position in which I happen to be placed, being a humble instrument in the hands of our Heavenly Father as I am, and as we all are, to work out His great purposes, I have desired that all my works and acts may be according to His will, and that it might be so I have sought His aid; but if, after endeavoring to do my best in the light which he affords me, I find my efforts fail, I must believe that for some purpose unknown to me, He wills it otherwise. If I had had my way, this war would never have been commenced. If I had been allowed my way, this war would have been ended before this; but we find it still continues, and we must believe that He permits it for some wise purpose of His own, mysterious and unknown to us; and though with our limited understandings we may not be able to comprehend it, yet we cannot but believe that He who made the world still governs it.[21]

I do not consider that I have ever accomplished anything without God, and if it is His will that I must die by the hand of an assassin, I must be resigned. I must do my duty as I see it, and leave the rest to God.[22]

I can only say in this case, as in so many others, that I am profoundly grateful for the respect, given in every variety of form in which it can be given, from the religious bodies of the country. I saw, upon taking my position here, that I was going to have an Administration, if an Administration at all, of extraordinary difficulty. It was, without exception, a time of the greatest difficulty that this country ever saw. I was early brought to a living reflection that nothing in my power whatever, in others to rely upon, would succeed without the direct assistance of the Almighty - but all must fail.

I have often wished that I was a more devout man than I am. Nevertheless, amid the greatest difficulties of my administration, when I could not see any other resort, I would place my whole reliance in God, knowing that all would go well, and that He would decide for the right.

I thank you, gentlemen, in the name of the religious bodies which you represent, and in the name of the Common Father, for this expression of your respect, I can say no more.[23]

In 1864, a story of a delegation headed by a minister visiting President Lincoln became circulated, including in the *Charleston Mercury*. The minister told Lincoln that he "hoped the Lord is on our side."

Lincoln said, "I don't agree with you. I am not at all concerned about that, for we know that the Lord is always on the side of the right. But it is my constant anxiety and prayer that I and this nation should be on the Lord's side."[24]

Lincoln believed that God's will would be accomplished through the Civil War. Iowa Congressman James F. Wilson was a member of a delegation that called on Abraham Lincoln. One member of this delegation said, "Slavery must be stricken down wherever it exists. If we do not do it right I believe God will let us go our own way to our ruin. But if we do right, I believe He will lead us safely out of this wilderness, crown our arms with victory, and restore our now disseevered Union."

Lincoln said he agreed with the role of God and Providence but responded, "My faith is greater than yours. . . . But I also believe He will compel us to do right in order that He may do these things, not so much because we desire them as that they accord with His plans of dealing with this nation, in the midst of which He means to establish justice. I think He means that we shall do more than we have yet done in furtherance of His plans, and He will open the way for our doing it. I have felt His hand upon me in great trials and submitted to His guidance, and I trust that as He shall further open the way I will be ready to walk therein, relying on His help and trusting in His goodness and wisdom."[25]

Lincoln also firmly believed that God willed the Civil War and would only permit it to continue for as long as He chose:

> The will of God prevails. In great contests each party claims to act in accordance with the will of God. Both *may* be, and one *must* be, wrong. God cannot be *for* and *against* the same thing at the same time. In the present civil war it is quite possible that God's purpose is something different from the purpose of either party; and yet the human instrumentalities, working just as they do, are the best adaptation to effect this purpose. I am almost ready to say that this is probably true; that God wills this contest, and wills that it shall not end yet. By his mere great power on the minds of the now contestants, he could either have *saved* or *destroyed* the Union

without a human contest. Yet the contest began. And having begun, he could give the final victory to either side any day. Yet the contest proceeds.[26]

In all it has been your purpose to strengthen my reliance on God. I am much indebted to the good Christian people of the country for their constant prayers and consolations; and to no one of them more than yourself. The purposes of the Almighty are perfect, and must prevail, though we erring mortals may fail to accurately perceive them in advance. We hoped for a happy termination of this terrible war long before this; but God knows best, and has ruled otherwise. We shall yet acknowledge his wisdom, and our own error therein. Meanwhile we must work earnestly in the best lights he gives us, trusting that so working still conduces to the great end he ordains. Surely he intends some great good to follow this mighty convulsion, which no mortal could make, and no mortal could stay.[27]

Lincoln was reelected in 1864. His second inaugural address is a classic of American literature. In this speech, which is perhaps the most widely quoted inaugural address of all time, Lincoln addressed and described both parties in the conflict, the North and the South:

Both read the same Bible and pray to the same God, and each invokes His aid against the other. It may seem strange that any men should dare to ask a just God's assistance in wringing their bread from the sweat of other men's faces, but let us judge not, that we be not judged. The prayers of both could not be answered. That of neither has been answered fully. The Almighty has His own purposes. "Woe unto the world because of offenses! For it must needs be that offenses come: but woe to that man by whom the offense cometh!" If we shall suppose that American slavery is one of those offenses which, in the providence of God, must needs come, but which, having continued through His appointed time, He now wills to remove, and that He gives to both North and South this terrible war as the woe due to those by whom the offense came, shall we discern therein any departure from those divine attributes which the believers in a living God always ascribe to Him? Fondly do we hope, fervently do we pray, that this mighty scourge of war may speedily pass away. Yet, if God wills that it continue until all the wealth piled by the bondsman's two hundred and fifty years of unrequited toil shall be sunk, and until every drop of blood drawn with the lash shall be paid by another drawn with the sword, as was said three thousand years ago, so still it must be said "the judgments of the LORD are true and righteous altogether."

With malice toward none, with charity for all, with firmness in the right as God gives us to see the right, let us strive on to finish the work we are in, to bind up the nation's wounds, to care for him who shall have borne the battle and for his widow and his orphan, to do all which may achieve and cherish a just and lasting peace among ourselves and with all nations.[28]

On September 7, 1864, a committee of black people from Baltimore presented Lincoln with a Bible. He responded:

I can only say now, as I have often said before, it has always been a sentiment with me, that all mankind should be free. So far as I have been able, so far as came within my sphere, I have always acted as I believed was just and right, and done all I could for the good of mankind. I have, in letters sent forth from this office, expressed myself better than I can now.

In regard to the great Book, I have only to say it is the best gift which God has ever given to man. All the good from the Saviour of the world is communicated to us through this Book. But for that Book, we could not know right from wrong. All those things desirable to man are contained in it. I return you sincere thanks for this very elegant copy of this great Book of God which you present.[29]

In Abraham Lincoln's visit to Richmond after the city fell into Union hands, a group of Negroes kneeled around him to kiss his shoes. He responded, "Don't kneel to me. This is not right. You must kneel to God only, and thank Him for the liberty you will hereafter enjoy. I am but God's humble instrument, but you may rest assured that, as long as I live, no one shall put a shackle to your limbs, and you shall have all the rights which God has given to every other free citizen of this Republic."[30]

While president, Lincoln regularly attended the New York Avenue Presbyterian Church in Washington, DC.[31] The church's pastor was Reverend Phinias Gurley.

Lincoln had and paid rent for a pew in the church; however, due to the number of people who wanted to talk to him after the services, he "usually sat alone in the pastor's room from which he could hear the service without being seen." According to Olga Jones in her book *Churches of the Presidents in Washington,* "reliable sources hold that Abraham Lincoln had definitely planned to become a member of this church on Easter Sunday morning, 1865."[32]

This intention was publicly known by Lincoln's death. In a funeral sermon preached the Sunday after Lincoln's death, Reverend Joseph P. Thompson said: "It is said upon good authority, that had he lived he would have made a public profession of his faith in Christ."[33]

At this church, it was the custom to sit in pews during prayer. Lincoln stood. When a parishioner asked why Lincoln stood, he said: "When my generals visit the White House, they stand when their commander-in-chief enters the Oval Office. Isn't it proper, then, that I stand for *my* commander-in-chief?"[34]

On April 11, 1865, Lincoln and a group of friends at the White House were discussing dreams. He talked about several dreams mentioned in the Bible, and stated, "If we believe the Bible, we must accept the fact that, in the old days, God and his angels came to men in their sleep and made themselves known in dreams." He said he had recently had a dream that had haunted him ever since.

In the dream, he heard "subdued sobs, as if a number of people were weeping." In the dream, he went into the East Room, and "met with a sickening surprise. Before me was a catafalque, on which rested a corpse in funeral vestments. Around it were stationed soldiers who were acting as guards; and there was a throng of people, some gazing mournfully upon the corpse, whose face was covered, others weeping pitifully."

When he asked one of the soldiers who was dead in the White House, the soldier said, "The President. He was killed by an assassin."

Lincoln then told his friends: "After it occurred, the first time I opened the Bible, strange as it may appear, it was at the twenty-eighth chapter of Genesis, which relates the wonderful dream Jacob had. I turned to other passages, and seemed to encounter a dream or a vision wherever I looked. I kept turning the leaves of the old book, and everywhere my eyes fell upon passages recording matters strangely in keeping with my own thoughts—supernatural visitations, dreams, visions, and so forth."[35]

His wife was understandably shocked by the dream. Lincoln said, "Well, let it go. I think the Lord in His own good time and way will work this out all right. God knows what is best."[36]

Three days later, of course, he was shot. He died the next day, April 15, 1865. His last words were a wish to visit the Holy Land. His wife, Mary Lincoln, stated: "He said he wanted to visit the Holy Land and see those places hallowed by the footprints of the Saviour. He was saying there was no city he so much desired to see as Jerusalem. And with the words half spoken on his tongue, the bullet of the assassin entered the brain, and the soul of the great and good President was carried by the angels to the New Jerusalem above."[37]

Bishop Matthew Simpson, a Methodist preacher, preached a funeral sermon for Lincoln in Springfield, Illinois. He said:

> Abraham Lincoln was a good man. He was known as an honest, temperate, forgiving man, a just man, a man of noble heart in every way; as to his religious experience I cannot speak definitely, because I was not privileged to know much of his private sentiments. My acquaintance with him did not give me the opportunity to hear him speak on this topic. I know, however, he read the Bible frequently; loved it for its great truths and for its profound teachings; and he tried to be guided by its precepts. He believed in Christ, the Savior of sinners, and I think he was sincerely trying to bring his life into the principles of revealed religion.[38]

HISTORICAL CONTROVERSIES

Was Abraham Lincoln a Christian?

That question is disputed so heatedly that while writing this book, I seriously considered including no Chapter 27.

There are three main schools of thought. Some hold that Abraham Lincoln was always an infidel. (I call this the "always lost" position.) Some hold that he was always a Christian. (I call this the "always saved" position.) Some hold that he was not a Christian until some point in his presidency.[39] (I call this the "conversion" position.)[40]

Numerous people who knew Abraham Lincoln before his presidency state that he held unorthodox doctrines and was not a Christian then. Many of these witnesses, as well as the people who adopt their side of the debate, extrapolate their information through the rest of Lincoln's life and hold the belief that he never changed his views. The historians who hold this position often discredit all contrary accounts.

Numerous people who knew Abraham Lincoln during his presidency state that his doctrines changed and that he moved much closer to Christianity and, according to some, became a Christian. Some of these witnesses extrapolate their information backwards into an earlier time in Lincoln's life and discredit all contrary accounts.

Unless several dozen witnesses lied, Abraham Lincoln was not an orthodox Christian before his presidency. But unless several dozen other witnesses lied, neither was he an atheist or a person who did not care about religion.

Lincoln knew that Christians believed that Jesus came to earth to die for sinful men. As he said in an 1842 temperance speech:

> "But," say some, "we are no drunkards, and we shall not acknowledge ourselves such by joining a reformed drunkard's society, whatever our influence might be." Surely no Christian will adhere to this objection. If they believe as they profess, that Omnipotence condescended to take on himself the form of sinful man, and as such to die an ignominious death for their sakes, surely they will not refuse submission to the infinitely lesser condescension, for the temporal, and perhaps eternal, salvation of a large, erring, and unfortunate class of their fellow-creatures. Nor is the condescension very great.[41]

Lincoln believed that the "days of miracles" had passed and even said so in a statement given to the religious denominations of Chicago.[42] Whether intentionally or unintentionally, a statement that the "days of miracles" have passed implies a belief that there once were "days of miracles."

Lincoln once told Congressman Henry C. Deming (Connecticut) why he had never joined a church: "I have never united with any church, because I have found difficulty in giving my assent without mental reservations to the long, complicated statements of Christian doctrine which characterizes their articles of belief and confession of faith. When any church will inscribe over its altars its sole qualification for membership the Saviour's condensed statement of both law and gospel, *Thou shalt love the Lord thy God with all thy soul, and with all thy mind; and thy neighbor as thyself,* that church I will join with all my heart and all my soul."[43]

These quotes are generally undisputed.

After Lincoln's death, his former law partner, atheist William Herndon, made it his life's work to prove that Lincoln was not a Christian. He found several of Lincoln's friends from his Illinois days who stated that he was not a Christian when they knew him. This testimony is invariably weakened by the witnesses' attempt to extrapolate Lincoln's beliefs when they knew him to his beliefs during his presidency.

Herndon's controversial work makes a reasonably weighty case for his contention that Lincoln was not an orthodox Christian during his law years.

In September 1866, Herndon conducted his only interview with Mary Todd Lincoln. In his notes on the interview he claimed she said:

> Mr. Lincoln had no hope & no faith in the usual acceptation of those words: he never joined a Church: he was a religious man always, as I think: he first thought – to say think – about this subject was when Willie died – never before. he felt religious More than Ever about the time he went to Gettysburg: he was not a technical Christian: he read the bible a good deal about 1864.[44]

However, Mary Todd Lincoln and Herndon differed in their recollections. Herndon gave his material to Ward Hill Lamon for Lamon's *Life of Abraham Lincoln* (1872).

On December 12, 1873, in a lecture Herndon gave in Springfield, he said that both Lincoln and he were infidels and quoted Mrs. Lincoln as saying that her husband was not a "technical Christian."[45]

According to the *Illinois State Journal* on December 19, 1873, Mrs. Lincoln "denies unequivocally that she had the conversation with Mr. Herndon, as stated by him." Mrs. Lincoln then stated that she had not denied the conversation; in the words of Paul Boller, "she had denied the way he had interpreted her remarks."[46]

She said: "I told him in positive words that my husband's heart was naturally religious." In the words of Paul Boller, she said "that he often turned to the Bible for comfort and frequently attended church with her, though not a member." She added: "What more can I say to this man, who when my heart was broken with anguish, issued falsehoods against me & mine, which were enough to make Heaven blush?"[47]

Thus, we see that Herndon's testimony was likely embellished, if not fabricated, at times. Few of his witnesses had any contact with Lincoln outside of his Illinois years. For that reason, I have not devoted pages to reprinting Herndon's accusations. They can easily be found in other books. Herndon's carelessness and embellishment does not incline me to grant his accusations further circulation than they have already received. In addition, it is probable that Lincoln's views changed after the point that his Illinois friends described.

Additionally, some accounts contradict the statements of Herndon's friends. Herndon sent a letter in 1867 to Reverend Dr. James Smith, pastor of Springfield's First Presbyterian Church, which the Lincoln family attended. Smith replied:

> I beg leave to say it is a very easy matter to prove that while I was pastor of the First Presbyterian Church of Springfield, Mr. Lincoln did avow his belief in the divine authority and inspiration of the Scriptures. . . . It was my honour to place before Mr. Lincoln arguments designed to prove the divine authority and inspiration of the Scriptures, accompanied by arguments of infidel objectors in their own language. To the arguments on both sides, Mr. Lincoln gave a most patient and searching investigation. To use his own language, he examined the arguments as a lawyer who is anxious to reach the truth investigates testimony. The result was the announcement by himself that the argument in favour of the divine authority and inspiration of the Scriptures was unanswerable. I could say much more on the subject, but as you are the person addressed, for the present I decline. The assassin Booth, by his diabolical act, unwittingly sent the illustrious martyr to glory, honour, and immortality, but his false friend has attempted to send him down to posterity with infamy branded on his forehead, as a man who, notwithstanding all he suffered for his country's good, was destitute to those feelings and affections without which there can be no excellency of character.[48]

Witnesses who knew Lincoln in Washington said that the death of his son William profoundly influenced his religious beliefs and brought them more in line with orthodox Christianity.

One of these witnesses was Reverend Dr. Francis Vinton, rector of Trinity Church, New York. He met Abraham Lincoln about two weeks after William died. Biographer Francis B. Carpenter later wrote this account of the conversation:

> "Your son," said Dr. Vinton, "is *alive*, in Paradise. Do you remember that passage in the Gospels: 'God is not the God of the *dead* but of the living, for *all* live unto him'?"
>
> The President had listened as one in a stupor, until his ear caught the words, "Your son is alive." Starting from the sofa, he exclaimed, "Alive! *alive!* Surely you mock me."
>
> "No, sir, believe me," replied Dr. Vinton; "it is a most comforting doctrine of the church, founded upon the words of Christ himself."
>
> Mr. Lincoln looked at him a moment, and then, stepping forward, he threw his arm around the clergyman's neck, and laying his head upon his breast, sobbed aloud. "*Alive? alive?*" he repeated.
>
> "My dear sir," said Dr. Vinton, greatly moved, as he twined his own arm around the weeping father, "believe this, for it is God's most precious truth. Seek not your son among the dead; he is not here; he lives to-day in Paradise! Think of the full import of the words I have quoted. The Sadducees, when they questioned Jesus, had no other conception than that Abraham, Isaac, and Jacob were dead and buried. Mark the reply: 'Now that the dead *are* raised, even Moses showed at the bush when he called the Lord the God of Abraham, the God of Isaac, and the God of Jacob. For he is not the God of the dead, but of the living, *for all live unto him!*' Did not the aged patriarch mourn his sons as dead?—'Joseph is not, and Simeon is not, and ye will take Benjamin also.' But Joseph and Simeon were both living, though he believed it not. Indeed, Joseph being taken from him, was the eventual means of the preservation of the whole family. And so God has called your son into his upper kingdom—a kingdom and an existence as real, more real, than your own. It may be that he too, like Joseph, has gone, in God's good providence, to be the salvation of *his* father's household. It is a part of the Lord's plan for the ultimate happiness of you and yours. Doubt it not. I have a sermon," continued Dr. Vinton, "upon this subject, which I think might interest you."

Mr. Lincoln begged him to send it at an early day—thanking him repeatedly for his hopeful and cheering words. The sermon was sent, and read over and over by the President, who caused a copy to be made for his own private use before it was returned. Through a member of the family, I have been informed that Mr. Lincoln's views in relation to spiritual things seemed changed from that hour. Certain it is, that thenceforth he ceased the observance of the duty of the day of the week upon which his son died, and gradually resumed his accustomed cheerfulness.[49]

Biographers, including those like Carl Sandburg who had no particular objective to paint him as a Christian or as an agnostic, generally agree that this meeting probably happened. The only objection usually made against it is that some think it was "colored." They feel that Lincoln could not have been this emotional or distraught.

While it is possible that details of the account are exaggerated and that another person who saw the scene might have described it in different terms, these criticisms overlook a crucial fact: The death of a child can cause even the most stoic parent to display emotion. Lincoln, though perhaps undemonstrative at times, was an extraordinarily sensitive man. It is highly improbable that he would display no emotion at his son's death, for he could well have displayed emotion in private meetings such as this one.

One weakness of accounts on each side of the debate is that they were made years after the fact; critics observe that the witnesses' memories could have faded, or they could have adapted their stories to please a certain audience. To sidestep this problem, I consulted a book called *Our Martyr President, Abraham Lincoln: Voices from the Pulpit of New York and Brooklyn*, published in 1865. This book is a collection of sermons paying tribute to Lincoln given Easter Sunday, the Sunday after his death.

I found that two stories had gained significant circulation. Different ministers told the stories with slight differences. Reverend James Eells said:

A well known Christian lady was asked by him, about a year ago, what were the simplest proofs of change of heart, and as she spoke particularly of faith in the Lord Jesus Christ, and renunciation of self, and comfort in prayer, he delighted her with the reply: "Then I may believe that I am really a Christian."

And you, no doubt, will call to mind his answer to the man who closed a business interview with the direct question, "Mr. President, before we part, will you permit me to ask you, do you love Jesus?" Mr. Lincoln rested his head on his hand a moment, then said: "When I left my home for Washington, I was not then a Christian, though I desired the prayers of God's people; when my little son died—the heaviest affliction of my life—I was not a Christian, though I deeply felt the need of grace and comfort. But when I walked among the graves of the thousands, who at Gettysburg had been swept into eternity, I resolved to give my heart to God; and since then I do love Jesus!"[50]

Reverend Charles S. Robinson told the Gettysburg story, with slightly different wording:

So much, then, is true; "he was a good man, and a just." But there is a question, which our intelligent Bible-reading people are wont to ask, when any one of their great men dies—was he a Christian man? There is no reason why we should turn away, unanswered, an inquiry like this. It is not an impertinent and obtrusive investigation of his interior life. He made no mystery of his faith. His own tale of his religious experience is something like this—coming in more than one way, and attested with more than one witness:

"When I left Springfield, I felt my utter dependence upon God. The responsibility weighed heavily upon my heart. I knew I should fail without a divine help. But I was not then a Christian. When my child died, I felt that I needed the comfort of the Gospel. It was the severest affliction that ever fell upon me. Then I wanted to be a Christian. But never did I feel that I reached that point, till I wandered one day, alone, among the graves of the boys that fell at Gettysburg. There, when I read the inscriptions, so full of hope and faith, I began to think I loved and trusted Jesus as my Saviour."[51]

In these two accounts, Lincoln covers the same three events—leaving Springfield, his son's death, and Gettysburg. However, the accounts differ enough that it appears he expressed similar sentiments to at least two different people. (This is supported by Reverend Robinson's statement that the story came to him "in more than one way, and attested with more than one witness.")

A third pastor, Reverend Robert Lowry, referred to the same stories. However, in the Gettysburg story, he did not quote Lincoln's words. Lowry said:

> When little Willie Lincoln passed from earth, the mind of the bereaved father was deeply affected by thoughts of death. But the vortex of public duties held him from pursuing the serious thoughts to which his mind had been directed. But when he stood on the battle-field of Gettysburg, and beheld the graves of the brave men who had gone down to death for the principles of which he was the exponent, such a sense of the presence of God and of his own worthiness took possession of his soul, as to overwhelm him. From that day he dated his entrance into a new life.
>
> I am told that, a few months ago, a lady, visiting the Presidential mansion, was invited to a seat in the family carriage. In the course of the ride, the conversation turned on the subject of religion. The President was deeply interested, and begged the visitor to describe, as possible, what was that peculiar state of mind in which one might know himself to be a Christian. She repeated to him the simple story of the cross; and explained, that when a poor sinner, conscious that he could not save himself, *looked to Jesus*, and saw in his death a *full atonement* for the sinner's sins, and *believed* that Christ's death was accepted *as a substitute* for the sinner's death, he felt himself to have been delivered from Divine wrath, and to be "at peace with God through our Lord Jesus Christ." The President replied, in a tone of satisfaction, "*That is just the way I feel.*"[52]

I have found no reason to discount these stories. They appear to be accurate reflections of Lincoln's religious beliefs during the last year of his life. It is worth noting that the first minister stated that his congregation would recall the Gettysburg story, implying that they had heard it; the second minister said that he had received it from several sources; and, the third minister stated it as known fact.

CONCLUSION

Lincoln was probably an agnostic during most or all of his career as a lawyer. While he might have believed parts of the Christian religion, he probably did deny others.

His writings and conversations as president, however, lead me to conclude that he did, indeed, draw closer to God. He recognized God's role in governing the nations, and came closer to a personal belief in Christianity. His son's death sparked in him an interest in life in Christ. If accounts widely circulated by his death are to be believed, he made the final step into the kingdom and became a Christian.

NOTES

1. Benjamin P. Thomas, *Abraham Lincoln: A Biography* (New York: Knopf, 1952; repr., New York: Barnes and Noble Books, 1994), 12.

2. Douglas L. Wilson and Rodney O. Davis, *Herndon's Informants: Letters, Interviews, and Statements about Abraham Lincoln* (Urbana and Chicago: University of Illinois Press, 1998), 107. From an interview Herndon conducted with Matilda Johnston Moore on September 8, 1865.

3. Thomas, *Abraham Lincoln*, 25.

4. Ibid., 57.

5. Ibid., 67.

6. Some authors have Lincoln not capitalizing "Christian." (Thomas, *Abraham Lincoln*, 103, is an example.)

7. Lincoln, *Writings of Abraham Lincoln*, vol. 1. From a letter written to Martin M. Morris on March 26, 1843, from Springfield, Illinois.

8. Some, such as Nathaniel Wright Stephenson (in *Lincoln: An Account of His Personal Life, Especially of Its Springs of Action as Revealed and Deepened by the Ordeal of War*), state that Lincoln met Cartwright's charge of infidelity with silence. This is not accurate; however, Lincoln's refutation was lost and forgotten for some time.

9. Thomas, *Abraham Lincoln*, 108–9.

10. Ibid., 115.

11. Ibid., 239.

12. Lincoln, March 4, 1861. First inaugural address.

13. Lincoln, *Writings of Abraham Lincoln*, vol. 6, September 13, 1862. Reply to a committee from the religious denominations of Chicago, asking that the president issue a proclamation of emancipation.

14. Lincoln, *Messages and Papers of the Presidents: Abraham Lincoln, 1862.* November 15, 1862. "General Order Respecting the Observance of the Sabbath Day in the Army and Navy," Lincoln's "General Order Respecting the

Observance of the Sabbath Day in the Army and Navy." Quoted by Sandburg, *Abraham Lincoln: The War Years,* vol. 3, 374.

15. Carl Sandburg, *Abraham Lincoln: The War Years,* vol. 3 (New York: Harcourt, Brace, & World, 1939), 374–75.

16. Lincoln, *Messages and Papers,* March 30, 1863. Proclamation for a Day of Fasting and Prayer.

17. Sandburg, *Abraham Lincoln,* vol. 2, 358–59.

18. Ibid., vol. 3, 378.

19. Ibid., vol. 2, 482.

20. Lincoln, *Writings of Abraham Lincoln,* vol. 7; Sandburg, *Abraham Lincoln,* vol. 3, 42.

21. Lincoln, *Writings of Abraham Lincoln,* vol. 7, 50–51. The quote is from a September 1862 address given to a group of Quakers.

22. Jim Bishop, *The Day Lincoln Was Shot* (New York: Random House/ Gramercy, 1984), 105.

23. Sandburg, *Abraham Lincoln,* vol. 3, 370. Told to a delegation of the Baltimore (Old School) Presbyterian Synod in October 1863.

24. Ibid., 346.

25. Ibid., 380.

26. Ibid., 590. Lincoln wrote this paragraph in September 1862. His secretary, John Hay, found it there and copied it.

27. Ibid., 225. Written to a Quaker, Eliza Gurney.

28. Lincoln, March 4, 1865. Second inaugural address.

29. Lincoln, *Writings of Abraham Lincoln,* vol. 7, September 7, 1864.

30. Bishop, *The Day Lincoln Was Shot,* 45.

31. Sandburg, *Abraham Lincoln,* vol. 3, 368.

32. Olga Anna Jones, *Churches of the Presidents in Washington,* (New York: Exposition Press, 1954), 47.

33. George Bancroft, Bishop Simpson, and R. S. Storrs Jr., *Our Martyr President, Abraham Lincoln: Lincoln Memorial Addresses* (New York: Tibbals and Whiting, 1865), 202.

34. John McCollister, *So Help Me God: The Faith of America's Presidents* (Louisville: Westminster/John Knox Press, 1991), 87.

35. Bishop, *The Day Lincoln Was Shot,* 55–56. He was quoting Lamon, who, he said, "remembered this dialogue almost word for word."

36. Ibid., 58. Part of the quote appears in Winik, *April 1865,* pages 205–6.

37. Federer, *America's God and Country,* 391; John Wesley Hill, *Abraham Lincoln: Man of God* (New York: G. P. Putnam's Sons, 1926), 432. Shortly after the assassination, Mary Lincoln told the story to Reverend N. W. Miner, a Springfield pastor who participated in Lincoln's burial service. The account is found in the *Lincoln Scrapbook,* 52. The scrapbook was located in the Library of Congress in Washington, DC.

38. Franklin Steiner, *The Religious Beliefs of Our Presidents* (Girard, KS: Haldeman-Julius, 1936; repr., Amherst, NY: Prometheus Books, 1995), 128–29.

39. Some believe Lincoln became a Christian slightly before his presidency, perhaps in 1858. I count this view as a slight variation of the conversion view.

40. Because there is no evidence to support it, no one holds that he was a Christian who apostatized from the faith.

41. Lincoln, *Writings of Abraham Lincoln*, vol. 1, February 22, 1842. Address before the Springfield Washingtonian Temperance Society.

42. Ibid., vol. 6, September 13, 1862. Reply to a committee from the religious denominations of Chicago, asking that the president issue a proclamation of emancipation.

43. Bliss Isley, *The Presidents: Men of Faith* (Boston: W. A. Wilde, 1953), 127. Isley quoted William E. Barton, *The Soul of Abraham Lincoln.*

44. Wilson and Davis, *Herndon's Informants,* 360. From a September 1866 interview with Mary Todd Lincoln.

45. Paul F. Boller Jr., *Presidential Wives: An Anecdotal History* (New York and Oxford: Oxford University Press, 1998), 126.

46. Ibid., 127.

47. Ibid. He cited Goetz, *Incidents,* 27–28, and Randall, *Mary Lincoln,* 425–29.

48. Hill, *Abraham Lincoln: Man of God,* 291–92.

49. Sandburg, *Abraham Lincoln,* 379–80.

50. Bancroft et al., *Our Martyr President,* 231–32.

51. Ibid., 89.

52. Ibid., 309–10.

CHAPTER 28

JAMES BUCHANAN

JAMES BUCHANAN was born on April 23, 1791, in Cove Gap, Pennsylvania. His parents were Presbyterians and brought him up in that faith. In 1796, when Buchanan was five years old, his family moved to Mercersburg, Pennsylvania, and attended Mercersburg's Presbyterian Church. Dr. John King, the pastor of the church, had a strong impact on James Buchanan in his youth; later in his life, Buchanan stated that he had "never known any human being for whom I felt greater reverence than for Dr. King."[1]

In 1840, James Buchanan took his nephew, James Buchanan Henry, into his house. Since both of Henry's parents (Reverend Robert & Harriet Buchanan Henry) had passed away, James Buchanan, as the executor of his sister Harriet's will, became Henry's guardian.

Years later after Buchanan died, Henry sent thoughts on his uncle's religious faith to George Ticknor Curtis, author of the 1883 *Life of James Buchanan*. Henry wrote:

> Mr. Buchanan's parents were Presbyterians, and he always evinced a preference for that form of worship. He was a regular attendant upon church services, both at Washington and in Lancaster, being a pew holder and an always generous contributor to both the building and maintenance of Christian worship. I have known him to give a thousand dollars at a time in aid of building funds for churches of all denominations, and many of his most faithful

friends were members of the Roman Catholic communion. He was, to my knowledge, always a sincere believer in all the cardinal doctrines of Christianity, had no eccentricities of religious belief, but accepted Christianity as a divine revelation and a simple rule for the conduct of human life, and relied upon it for the guidance of his own life. He certainly always pressed their force upon my cousin and myself, in our family intercourse under his roof, as his wards. I remember that she and I always hid away our secular newspaper or novel on Sunday if we heard him approaching, as we were otherwise pretty sure to get a mild rebuke for not better employing our time on Sunday, either in good works, or at least in better reading.[2]

The cousin to which Henry referred was Harriet Lane. Buchanan enabled Lane, an Episcopalian, to attend the Georgetown Convent of the Visitation in Washington, DC, and even rented a pew (Pew 21) for her at the St. James Episcopal Church in Lancaster, Pennsylvania.

Throughout Buchanan's entire public service career, his inherited faith influenced his thinking, but not as much as it would in later life. While a United States government minister to Russia, Buchanan wrote the following to his brother, Edward (who was an Episcopalian minister): "I can sincerely say for myself that I desire to be a Christian, and I think I could withdraw from the vanities and follies of the world without suffering many pangs. I have thought much upon the subject since my arrival in this strange land and sometimes almost persuade myself that I am a Christian; but I am often haunted by the spirit of skepticism. My true feeling upon many occasions is: 'Lord, I would believe; help thou my unbelief.' Yet I am far from being an unbeliever."[3]

In a February 29, 1844, letter to his brother, Buchanan said: "I am a believer, but not with that degree of firmness of faith calculated to exercise a controlling influence on my conduct. I ought constantly to pray, 'Help Thou my unbelief.' I trust that the Almighty Father, through the merits and atonement of His Son, will yet vouchsafe me to a clearer and stronger faith than I possess."[4]

In an 1839 letter written to General Andrew Jackson, Buchanan said: "Although not a member of any church myself; yet I was gratified to learn, both for your own sake and that of example, that you had borne a public testimony to the truth and power of religion. It can alone convert the inevitable ills attendant upon humanity into positive blessings and thus wean us from this world; and make death itself the portal to another and a better state of existence."[5]

Buchanan was elected president in 1856 and served one term. His first act as president was to ask for God's help in executing his duties. He began his inaugural address by saying: "Fellow-citizens: I appear before you this day to take the solemn oath 'that I will faithfully execute the office of President of the United States and will to the best of my ability preserve, protect, and defend the Constitution of the United States.' In entering upon this great office I must humbly invoke the God of our fathers for wisdom and firmness to execute its high and responsible duties in such a manner as to restore harmony and ancient friendship among the people of the several States and to preserve our free institutions throughout many generations."[6]

He concluded his inaugural address with these words: "I shall now proceed to take the oath prescribed by the Constitution, whilst humbly invoking the blessing of Divine Providence on this great people."[7]

In each of James Buchanan's four annual messages, he thanked God for the blessings that He had given to the nation. In the first three annual messages, the acknowledgement and thanksgiving began the speech. In the fourth, as the storm clouds of the Civil War approached, the thanksgiving was more subdued, yet still evident.

He began his first annual message by saying that "our thanks are due to Almighty God for the numerous benefits which He has bestowed upon this people, and our united prayers ought to ascend to Him that He would continue to bless our great Republic in time to come as He has blessed it in time past."[8]

In his second annual message, he said that "we have much reason for gratitude to that Almighty Providence which has never failed to interpose for our relief at the most critical periods of our history."[9]

He began his third annual message by expressing "deep and heartfelt gratitude" to "that Almighty Power which has bestowed upon us such varied and numerous blessings throughout the past year." He added:

> We have much reason to believe from the past events in our history that we have enjoyed the special protection of Divine Providence ever since our origin as a nation. We have been exposed to many threatening and alarming difficulties in our progress, but on each successive occasion the impending cloud has been dissipated at the moment it appeared ready to burst upon our head,

and the danger to our institutions has passed away. May we ever be under the divine guidance and protection.[10]

But by the time he was preparing his fourth annual message, he could see the storm clouds of Civil War ahead on the horizon. His words were more subdued and cautious. He stated his belief that the immediate peril to the country was due to the abolition agitation inspiring slaves with "vague notions of freedom," giving the South "apprehensions of servile insurrections." In this message, he asked God to preserve the Constitution and the Union. He added:

> Self-preservation is the first law of nature, and has been implanted in the heart of man by his Creator for the wisest purpose; and no political union, however fraught with blessings and benefits in all other respects, can long continue if the necessary consequence be to render the homes and the firesides of nearly half the parties to it habitually and hopelessly insecure. Sooner or later the bonds of such a union must be severed. It is my conviction that this fatal period has not yet arrived, and my prayer to God is that He would preserve the Constitution and the Union throughout all generations.[11]

As his life progressed, Buchanan grew more interested in matters of faith. By 1860, he had decided to join the Presbyterian Church when his term as president ended. He talked about this decision and about other matters of religion with the Reverend William M. Paxton, D.D., pastor of New York City's First Presbyterian Church. After Buchanan's death, Paxton wrote an account of these conversations. He said:

> In the month of August, in the year 1860, Mr. Buchanan, then President of the United States, visited the Bedford Springs, in the State of Pennsylvania. I happened to be present when the stage arrived, and having had a previous personal acquaintance with him, was one of the first to bid him welcome.
>
> A day or two afterwards, as he passed me in the hall, he stopped and said, "May I take the liberty of sending for you to come to my room, when I can find leisure for a conversation?" To this I replied that it would give me great pleasure to obey such a call. The next day the invitation came, through his private secre-

tary, and when we were seated alone, he turned to me and said, "I sent for you to request that you will favor me with a conversation upon the subject of religion. I knew your father and mother in early life, and, as you have some knowledge of my family, you are aware that I was religiously educated. But for some years I have been much more thoughtful than formerly upon religious subjects. I think I may say that for twelve years I have been in the habit of reading the Bible and praying daily. I have never had any one with whom I have felt disposed to converse, but now that I find you here, I have thought that you would understand my feelings, and that I would venture to open my mind to you upon this important subject, and ask for an explanation of some things that I do not clearly understand." When I had assured him that I would be gratified to have such a conversation, he began immediately by asking, "Will you be good enough to explain what an experience of religion is?" In answer, I opened to him the Bible account of our sinful estate, and of the necessity of regeneration by the Spirit of God, and of atonement through the sacrifice of our Lord Jesus Christ. He then began to question me, as closely as a lawyer would question a witness, upon all the points connected with regeneration, atonement, repentance, and faith. What surprised me was that his questions were not so much of a doctrinal as of an experimental character. He seemed anxious to understand how a man might know that he was a Christian, and what conscious experiences entered into the exercises of repentance and faith. It is needless for me to detail the particulars of the conversation. It gave me an opportunity of speaking to him in the most simple and familiar way. When I related the experience of some eminent Christian, or used a simple illustration, such as I have employed in Sabbath school addresses, he seemed much gratified, and proceeded to put his questions to draw out still more definite explanations. He particularly was anxious to understand how faith receives and appropriates the Lord Jesus Christ, and how a man may know that he believes. He put himself in the position of a little child, and asked questions in the simplest manner. Sometimes he asked me to go over an explanation a second time, as if he wished to fix it upon his memory. His manner was so earnest, and his mind was evidently so deeply engaged, that I was strongly impressed with the conviction of his entire sincerity.

After the more experimental points had been disposed of, he asked a few purely doctrinal questions, the answers to which he received without any disposition to enter upon a discussion. At the close of the conversation, he asked particularly what were the conditions of membership in the Presbyterian Church, and what were the points upon which an applicant for admission would be examined. The conversation lasted, probably, from two to three hours. After sitting quiet for a few minutes, he said, "Well, sir, I thank you. My mind is now made up. I hope that I am a Christian. I think I have much of the experience which you describe, and, as soon as I retire from my office as President, I will unite with the Presbyterian Church." To this, I replied, "Why not *now*, Mr. President? God's invitation is *now*, and you should not say *tomorrow*." To this he answered, with deep feeling, and with a strong gesture, "I must delay, for the *honor of religion*. If I were to unite with the Church *now*, they would say hypocrite from Maine to Georgia." I felt the truth of his answer, and did not continue my urgency.

This closed our conversation, but, as Mr. Buchanan remained at the Springs for some time, he seemed to seize every opportunity, when he met me in the hall or in the parlor, to ask some question which he had been pondering, or to repeat some passage of Scripture upon which his mind had been dwelling, and ask how I understood it. For example, meeting me in the passage, he asked me the meaning of the verse, "The bruised reed he will not break: the smoking flax he will not quench;" and when I explained the figures, and showed how beautifully they expressed the tenderness of our Lord, he seemed to exhibit the most simple-hearted gratification.

I take pleasure in giving these recollections for the record, because I have never entertained a doubt of the entire honesty of Mr. Buchanan's religious impressions. I did not agree with him in politics, or feel any sympathy with his public career; but I think that he is entitled to this testimony from one who was placed in circumstances to judge fairly of the reality of his religious convictions. The purpose which President Buchanan expressed to me of uniting with the Church was fulfilled. He connected himself with the Presbyterian Church in Lancaster, Pa., immediately after his retirement from the Presidential chair.[12]

Buchanan followed through, and did apply for membership in the Presbyterian Church. However, possibly due to his political or theological views, and possibly due to the fact that longtime political foe Thaddeus Stephens was a member of the church, his application was denied. On September 23, 1865, after the Civil War ended, the elders of the Presbyterian Church examined his "experimental evidence of piety," found it satisfactory, and admitted him into the church membership.[13]

His niece, Annie Buchanan, described his religion at this point in his life. She said:

As long as I can remember my uncle, he was a religious man, becoming more and more so as his life drew near its close. His knowledge of the scriptures was very thorough, and whatever doubts he may have had in his earlier life, had been dissipated by the rays of the Sun of Righteousness. He was, certainly, during the latter years of his life, a strong and firm believer in Jesus Christ as his Savior. It was his constant habit, after his return from Washington, to read daily in the New Testament, and a large part of Sunday he spent in studying that and books founded upon its teachings. A devotional book, Jay's Morning and Evening Exercises, was his constant companion, and he read a great deal in the sermons of the great French preacher, Massillon, a French copy of which he had and often quoted. He conversed much about the Gospel and its teachings, and one could easily tell that he was deeply interested in the subject.

It was his practice, during all his life, to attend church on Sunday morning, and some effect of his early teaching, which very strongly inculcated the hallowing of the Lord's day, was shown when he was in St. Petersburg. It was the custom there for even the most devout, after they had attended services through the day, to go to balls and festivities in the evening of Sunday. My uncle thought that he could not be excused from attending the Emperor's balls, but made it a rule never to dance on Sunday evening, and so caused great surprise to some of his friends there, especially when he explained to them that in America the manner prevalent in Russia of spending Sunday evening would be thought quite shocking.

To show how much my uncle respected the religious sense of the community, I will mention, that when the Prince of Wales was visiting him in Washington, and when a large company had been invited to do the Prince honor, my uncle would not consent to having any dancing at it. He took this position, not that he disapproved himself of dancing, but that he thought that it would cause scandal to the religious people of the country if there were to be a dance there in the White House. "I am the servant of the people," was his motto, and with this feeling in his mind he toiled, he lived and acted, always trying to prevent anything from being done which would give offence to that people.

I remember dining with him, in company with a lady who seemed to be a thoroughly worldly woman, one whose life had been spent in public and among worldly people. I do not remember the whole conversation, or how my uncle came to say it, but I remember his remark, "I say my prayers every day of my life." The lady looked up at him in surprise, and questioned, thinking he was jesting. "No," said my uncle, "I am not jesting, I have always said my prayers." I will only add, while on this subject, that not only did my uncle attend church constantly on Sundays, but he was very particular to omit his ordinary avocations, and to make it a day of rest, through all his life.

There was one thing very noticeable in my uncle's conversation during those years which he spent at Wheatland, after his return from Washington. He conversed very little on the political matters of the day, and, particularly, he showed remarkably little bitterness towards those whose indifference and even hatred towards himself showed themselves so strongly when power and influence had passed out of his hands. Occasionally, certainly, he could not help speaking his mind about one or two particularly flagrant cases, but as a general thing he passed over their conduct in silence. He was not fond of picking people to pieces, and his inclination was rather to speak and think kindly of his neighbors.[14]

Shortly before his death, Buchanan talked about Christianity with his friend and executor, Mr. Swarr. In what his pastor labeled a "dying testimony," Buchanan said: "The principles of the Christian religion were instilled into my mind in my youth; and from all I have observed and experienced in the long life Providence has vouchsafed to me, I have only become more strengthened in the conviction of the Divine character of the Saviour, and the power of atonement through His redeeming grace and mercy."[15]

His friend, Reverend Dr. John Williamson Nevin, described Buchanan's religion near the end of his life in these words:

> There was no reserve or hesitation in his manner. His habitual diplomatic caution was gone. At the same time there was no excitement or agitation in his mind. He was perfectly calm, and had no fear of death whatever. Still it was full before him, and he had no disposition to hide from himself its awful presence. He wished to be talked with as a man who felt himself to be on the borders of the eternal world, and who was fully awake to the dread issues of the life to come. But with all this, his spirit abode in quiet confidence and peace, and the ground of his trust throughout was the mercy of God through the righteousness of Jesus Christ. There was nothing like enthusiasm, of course, in his experience; the general nature of the man made that impossible. His religion showed itself rather in the form of fixed trust in God, thankfulness for His past mercy, and general resignation to His holy will. In these twilight hours, thus circumstanced, it could not be but that central regard was had continually to the person of Jesus Christ, and the significance of the Christian redemption as comprehended in the idea of His coming in the flesh. This at least it had not taken hold of his mind, as he confessed, in the same manner before. Now, however, it gave him great satisfaction, and he considered it one special benefit of his sickness, that it had taught him to see in the simple exercise of "looking to Jesus" what he found to be, for himself, at least, the most consoling and the most strengthening practice of Christian faith.[16]

Buchanan died on June 1, 1868, in Lancaster, Pennsylvania. He had never married; his will, along with bequests to his niece, the poor living in his city, and the servants at his house, included a generous bequest to his church.[17]

Dr. Nevin, Buchanan's pastor, preached the funeral sermon. He chose the text, "I would not have you to be ignorant, brethren, concerning them which are asleep, that ye sorrow not, even as others which have no hope. For if we believe that Jesus died and rose again, even so them also which sleep in Jesus will God bring with him" (1 Thess. 4:13–14).

In his sermon, he talked in depth about Buchanan's commitment to Christianity. He said:

Where are the voices that, thirty or forty years ago, filled our Congressional halls and electrified the land with their eloquent words? Kings and Presidents, the princes of the earth—terrestrial gods, as they are sometimes called—die like other men. "All flesh is as grass, and all the glory of man as the flower of grass; the grass withereth, and the flower thereof falleth away, but the word of the Lord endureth forever." And where do we find this enduring word of the Lord in full presence and power, save in the Logos Incarnate, our Lord Jesus Christ, who is the Alpha and Omega of the whole creation, the same yesterday, today and forever?

Happily, the venerable sage of Wheatland, as he has sometimes been called, sought and found here what he himself was ready to acknowledge as something better than all the greatness of the world; an humble but strong trust in the atoning righteousness of Christ, which brightened the whole evening of his life, which proved to be the strength of his spirit, when heart and flesh began to fail, and which now makes his death but the quiet sleep that precedes the morning of the resurrection. He died in the Lord; this is our great comfort in following him to the grave. We sorrow not as those who have no hope. "For if we believe that Jesus died and rose again, even so them also which sleep in Jesus will God bring with him."

In some sense, Mr. Buchanan was a religious man, we may say, all his life. Brought into the Presbyterian church by baptism in his infancy, he enjoyed at the same time the unspeakable advantage of an early Christian training, which made itself felt more or less sensibly on all his character and conduct in later years. In serious conversation with me on this subject less than a year ago, he referred, with moistened eyes and faltering voice, to the lessons that had been instilled into him as a boy, especially by his pious mother. She had taught him to pray; and her presence, as an invisible ministering spirit, seemed to hold him to the duty, as it were in spite of himself, through the whole of his subsequent public life. Whatever of worldliness there might be in his thoughts and ways otherwise, his conscience would not allow him to give up the outward exercise, at least, of some private as well as public, forms of devotion.

He made it a point to read the bible [sic], honored the Sabbath, and observed more or less faithfully stated times for secret prayer.

His general character, at the same time, was always good. Those who stood nearest to him in his public life, and who knew him best, have ever united in bearing the most favorable testimony to what he was in this view. He has been known and spoken of on all sides as a true gentlemen of the old school, distinguished for his personal integrity, a man of honorable spirit, upright in his deportment, and beyond the common measure virtuous in his manners. He was unquestionably one of the purest in mind, and most exemplary in life belonging to the generation of public men, which has now come to a close in his death. It is, indeed, something wonderful, that in his peculiar circumstance he should have been able to pass through such a long life of exposure to all forms of corruption and sin, so generally unscathed as he seems to have been by the fiery ordeal. In this respect, he is worthy of lasting admiration, and may well be held up as an example for the study and imitation of younger candidates for political distinction coming after his day. When will all our public men lay to heart, as they ought, that true oracle of the olden time: "The memory of the just is blessed; but the name of the wicked shall rot?"

All this, however, Mr. Buchanan himself very well knew, fell short of what was required to make him a Christian in the full sense of the term; and as he advanced in life accordingly, he seems to have turned his mind more and more seriously to the necessity of becoming a follower of the Saviour in a more inward and strict way. This practical discipleship he believed himself to have reached in some measure years before he withdrew from political life. Yet, he made then no open profession of faith, in the way of what is commonly called joining the church, under the idea that there was some reason for postponing it in the peculiar circumstances in which he stood as a public man. That idea, of course, was a serious mistake, as he himself acknowledged it to be afterwards, when earnestly spoken with on the subject. He ought to have joined the church sooner, he said, and especially before he left Washington. As it was, he took this important step in due course of time, subsequently, after full serious consideration, by connecting himself in form with the Presbyterian church of Lancaster, which had been his regular place of worship previously, where he continued to worship afterwards, and in communion with which he has now departed this life, "looking for the general resurrection in the last day, and the life of the world to come."

It was my privilege to converse with him frequently on religious subjects, during these last years, and I can say his mind seemed to be always clear and remarkably firm, as well as consistent, in the apprehension of Christianity, under its simplest and most commonly acknowledged evangelical form. He had studied carefully, I may be allowed to state, the Heidelberg Catchecism (that most œcumenical, and in some respects most genial of all the Reformed Protestant Confessions), and he was accustomed to speak highly of it at all times, as being a summary of religious truth, to which he cordially subscribed as the full expression of his theological faith.

More particularly, however, it was during the last summer, that I had the opportunity of coming to the most intimate knowledge of his Christian views and hopes, on the occasion of his returning home from Cape May, under an attack of a strange sickness which threatened at the time to carry him to the grave. The sickness was attended with but little bodily pain, and it left his mind perfectly clear and free, while yet it was of such a character as to produce in his own mind the strong impression that it would end in his death. In these solemn circumstances, I had interviews with him day after day for some time, in which I talked with him, and prayed with him, as a dying man; and in which he talked also most freely himself with regard to his own condition, giving utterance to his views and feelings in a way which furnished the most satisfactory and pleasing evidence that religion had become with him, indeed, a deeply-settled principle in the soul, and such a conviction of faith as could not be shaken by the powers either of earth or hell. Let it be sufficient here to say, that he was able to resign himself with full filial confidence and trust into the hands of God as a faithful Creator and Saviour, and that he found Him an all sufficient help in his time of need. At the same time, his faith was far more than a vague trust merely in God's general goodness and mercy. It was most explicitly the humble, penitent reliance of one who knew himself to be a sinner, on the mercy of God secured to men through His Son Jesus Christ. At this time, especially, more than before, he was brought to see and feel the importance of simply looking to Jesus (in the spirit of St. John's gospel and of the Apostle's Creed), as being Himself the sum and substance of the whole Christian salvation. His mind fastened with peculiar interest on the text: "Lord to whom shall we go? Thou hast the words of eternal life. And we believe and are sure that Thou art that Christ the Son of the living God."

Altogether it was a death-bed experience, full of tranquil light and peace, the calm evening sunset of a long life, which seemed to be itself but the brightening promise of a new and far better life beyond the grave.

His late sickness, which has now terminated in his death, was more prostrating for him throughout, both in body and in mind, than that of which I have just spoken. Through it all, however, his views and feelings in regard to religion he declared to be, in the prospect of quitting this world, just what he had over and over again witnessed them to be before. He bowed with entire submission to his Heavenly Father's will. His last intelligible word, indeed, whispered in the ear of anxious affection bending over him, as was turned somewhat painfully upon his bed, and felt, no doubt, that the end had come—after which he fell away into the gentle sleep that some hours later closed the scene—was the short Christian prayer: "O Lord, God Almighty, as Thou Wilt!" Thus he passed away. His trust was in Christ crucified and risen from the dead, and in Christ alone. He died in the full faith of the gospel, and in the joyful hope of having part at last in the resurrection of the body and in the life everlasting.

He sleeps in Jesus. Be this his epitaph; the last and crowning honor of his long, illustrious life; the richest ornament of his public, no less than of his private memory and name. Be this also the consolation of his sorrowful friends as they look upon that venerable majestic form lying in state before us, and are called now to follow it in slow melancholy procession to the grave. We sorrow not as others, which have no hope; for if Jesus died and rose again, them also which sleep in Jesus God will bring with Him. The aged statesman has been gathered to his fathers full of years, like a shock of corn fully ripe and laden with fruit; he has served his country well, and enjoyed its honors largely, in his generation; he has left behind him a fair example of justice, benevolence, integrity and truth, a bright record indeed, of honorable and virtuous character in all respects. In all this we find matter for thankful satisfaction, and occasion for bowing in meek submission to the Divine will, which has now at last removed him from our sight. But, through all this, at the same time, we triumph and rejoice most of all, as Christians, in what we know to have been his Christian death, and in the assurance that we have, therefore, of his being still with us, and near to us, in Christ.

To Whom, now let us offer our united and unfeigned thanks for that victory over death and the grave, which he has obtained for us and for all who sleep in Him, while we pray also for power to follow the faith of those who have gone before us, "that we may enter at death into their joy, and so abide with them in rest and peace, till both they and we shall reach our common consummation of redemption and bliss in the glorious resurrection of the last day." *Amen.*[18]

George Ticknor Curtis's two-volume *Life of James Buchanan,* for which the above accounts by Reverend Paxton, Annie Buchanan, and Reverend Dr. Nevin were written, is the primary source for the first-hand accounts of those individuals who observed Buchanan's Christianity. As this book is well over a century old and is rare and difficult to find, I have reproduced these accounts in full for two reasons: First, so that the readers of this book can read the same firsthand evidence I had access to. Second, in the event that copies of the old volumes become difficult or impossible to find, I want to ensure that the accounts are preserved for future generations of scholars.

One more question must be answered before I conclude this chapter. In Buchanan's funeral sermon, his pastor said that Buchanan "cordially subscribed" to the doctrines taught in the Heidelberg Catechism "as the full expression of his theological faith." What are the doctrines of the Heidelberg Catechism?

The Heidelberg Catechism is a succinct explanation of Christianity from a Calvinist perspective. It contains 129 questions and answers on various matters related to Christian doctrine. Some questions most relevant to the study of Buchanan's religion—those that deal most directly with a person's beliefs about the central doctrines of Christianity—are reproduced below:

Q. 22. What is then necessary for a Christian to believe?

A. All things promised us in the gospel, which the articles of our catholic undoubted Christian faith briefly teach us.

Q. 23. What are these articles?

A. 1. I believe in God the Father, Almighty, Maker of heaven and earth:

2. And in Jesus Christ, his only begotten Son, our Lord:

3. Who was conceived by the Holy Ghost, born of the Virgin Mary:

4. Suffered under Pontius Pilate; was crucified, dead, and buried: He descended into hell:

5. The third day he rose again from the dead:

6. He ascended into heaven, and sitteth at the right hand of God the Father Almighty:

7. From thence he shall come to judge the quick and the dead:

8. I believe in the Holy Ghost:

9. I believe a holy catholic church: the communion of saints:

10. The forgiveness of sins:

11. The resurrection of the body:

12. And the life everlasting.

Q. 60. How are thou righteous before God?

A. Only by a true faith in Jesus Christ; so that, though my conscience accuse me, that I have grossly transgressed all the commandments of God, and kept none of them, and am still inclined to all evil; notwithstanding, God, without any merit of mine, but only of mere grace, grants and imputes to me, the perfect satisfaction, righteousness and holiness of Christ; even so, as if I never had had, nor committed any sin: yea, as if I had fully accomplished all that obedience which Christ has accomplished for me; inasmuch as I embrace such benefit with a believing heart.

Q. 61. Why sayest thou, that thou art righteous by faith only?

A. Not that I am acceptable to God, on account of the worthiness of my faith; but because only the satisfaction, righteousness, and holiness of Christ, is my righteousness before God; and that I cannot receive and apply the same to myself any other way than by faith only.

CONCLUSION

James Buchanan honored his Presbyterian heritage throughout his life. During this time, he could best be described as moderately religious. However, in his years of retirement, he made a public commitment to Christianity. Numerous sources testify of his private devotion and his firm belief in Christ's atoning sacrifice.

Near the end of his life, Buchanan testified: "I have only become more strengthened in the conviction of the Divine character of the Saviour, and the power of atonement through His redeeming grace and mercy."[19]

In the words of his niece, Annie Buchanan, her uncle James was "a strong and firm believer in Jesus Christ as his Savior."[20]

NOTES

1. Philip S. Klein, *President James Buchanan: A Biography* (Pennsylvania State University Press, 1962), 7.

2. George Ticknor Curtis, *Life of James Buchanan: Fifteenth President of the United States,* vol. 2 (New York: Harper and Brothers, 1883), 672.

3. Edmund Fuller and David E. Green, *God in the White House: The Faiths of American Presidents* (New York: Crown Publishers, 1968), 98.

4. William J. Federer, ed., *America's God and Country: Encyclopedia of Quotations* (Coppel, TX: Fame Publishing, 1994), 80.

5. Quoted in William U. Hensel's paper "The Religious Convictions and Character of James Buchanan." Hensel's paper was delivered at the Bellevue Presbyterian Church in Gap, Pennsylvania, on November 10, 1911. A published version was issued by the Lancaster Intelligencer Print in 1912; this quotation is found on pages 14–15 of that version.

6. Buchanan, *Messages and Papers of the Presidents: James Buchanan, 1857.* March 4, 1857. Inaugural address.

7. Ibid.

8. Ibid., December 8, 1857. First annual message.

9. Ibid., December 6, 1858. Second annual message.

10. Ibid., December 19, 1859. Third annual message.

11. Ibid., December 3, 1860. Fourth annual message.

12. Curtis, *Life of James Buchanan*, vol. 2, 670–71.

13. Klein, *President James Buchanan*, 427.

14. Curtis, *Life of James Buchanan*, vol. 2, 678–79.

15. Ibid., 684.

16. Ibid.

17. Klein, *President James Buchanan*, 428.

18. Curtis, *Life of James Buchanan*, vol. 2, 682–86.

19. Ibid., 684.

20. Ibid., 678.

CHAPTER 29

FRANKLIN PIERCE

FRANKLIN PIERCE was born on November 23, 1804, in Hillsborough, New Hampshire. In 1820, he entered Bowdoin College in Brunswick, Maine. He was soon befriended by a fellow student named Zenas Caldwell, "a most devoted Christian of the Methodist persuasion."[1] Pierce described Caldwell as "a man of well-considered and firmly established religious opinions and . . . one of the truest followers of the Blessed Redeemer."[2]

Pierce also said, "While we occupied the same room he was on his knees every night and I by his side praying for himself and me. He conquered me by his faith and Christian life."[3] Pierce biographer Roy Nichols commented that "while it [Caldwell's example] did not impel him to make open profession of religion it made a lasting impression."[4] Pierce told Caldwell that he was not a religious skeptic, but yet he had not been able to experience rebirth.[5]

At their college graduation, Pierce told Caldwell that "he had not yet been reborn, although he thought of religion a great deal."[6] Caldwell died shortly after college, having planted seeds in Pierce's life that would come to fruition decades later.

Pierce married Jane Means Appleton on November 10, 1834. The Pierces generally attended the South Congregational Church in Concord, New Hampshire. The church was Jane's church; however, one early campaign biographer said that, due to Caldwell's influence, "his sympathies are with the Methodists."[7] While his wife was alive, he attended church with her when her health was good enough; when it was not, he walked to church on his own.

Though he knew many fundamentals of the Christian faith and the rebirth, Pierce had not yet made a public confession of faith. This is not to say that he did not ponder and struggle with that and surrounding issues. In 1839, while a Senator in Washington, DC, Pierce wrote his wife: "I have dwelt somewhat more this winter upon the truths of Divine revelation than usual and perhaps have struggled somewhat harder to think and act in conformity with the precepts and commandments of the New Testament than ever before—but with indifferent success as every man must who is not a humble and devoted Christian to which character I can, I regret to say, make no pretension."[8]

Nichols commented about Pierce's spiritual state at this point: "He had no doubts as to the fundamental truths which could be revealed only through the Gospel, but the consciousness of salvation did not come to him, invite it as he would."[9]

Both Franklin and Jane Pierce were understandably crushed when their son Frank died on November 14, 1843. Just before his son died, Pierce wrote:

> We are commanded to set up no idol in our hearts and I am conscious that within the last two years particularly my prevailing feeling has been that we were living for our children. In all my labors, plans and exertions in them was the center of all my hopes, they were in all my thoughts. We should have lived for God and have left the dear ones to the care of Him who is alone able to take care of them and us. I think I have experienced as thoroughly as most men the unsatisfying character of the mere things of this world. My mind has long been impressed with the fact that if our present life is not probationary in character, if we are not placed here, as the blessed word of God teaches, to prepare for another and more exalted state of being, we are destined to waste our energies upon things that are unsubstantial, fleeting, passing away and that can bring no permanent peace—can give no calm hope that is an anchor to the soul. And yet with that conviction constantly recurring few have been more entirely absorbed in the whirl of business and cares purely of a worldly character than I have.[10]

On their son's gravestone, Pierce and his wife wrote: "A loved and precious treasure lost to us here but safe in the Redeemer's care."[11]

In 1852, Pierce reluctantly accepted the Democratic nomination for president of the United States. As frequently happened in the presidential campaigns of the era, campaign biographies were written. At least four were written about Pierce and published during the 1852 campaign. One of these was D.W. Bartlett's *The Life of General Franklin Pierce*. He said of Pierce's religion: "You can always find him in his place at church on Sundays, and on week-days he is ever ready to assist the poor and unfortunate with his money and his talents."[12]

Bartlett also said, "In his habits he is strict and severe. In several conversations with him, we could not fail to observe with what solemnity and reverence he alluded to the hand of Providence in all things. He is not a member of any Church, but generally attends worship at the Congregational Church in Concord."[13]

Pierce was elected president in 1852. Just after the election, his son Benjamin was killed in an accident. Both President and Mrs. Pierce were stricken with grief. Nichols says:

> She [Mrs. Pierce] sought consolation in her religion, and her husband was much influenced by her ideas. Together for many a day they submitted themselves to a rigorous Calvinistic self-questioning, and sought to solve the riddle of their sorrow by discovering the purpose in this stern decree of a just God. Pierce had never experienced signs of grace and was now more than ever conscious of faults and weaknesses which bore the marks of sin. Might not this bereavement be punishment for his transgressions? Mrs. Pierce may have felt the force of his suggestion, but she did not adopt it. She found her solace in a most destructive solution of the problem. God, said she, had taken their boy so that Pierce might have no distraction, caused by his preoccupation with the child's welfare, to interfere with his attention to the great responsibilities which were to be his. His high honor had been purchased at the price of his son's sacrifice.
>
> It is difficult to express adequately the effect which this interpretation of the tragedy worked upon the President-elect. It became the fact of greatest importance in his life, troubling his conscience, unsettling him almost completely, and weakening his self-confidence

for many months to come. . . . Much of the difficulty which he experienced in administration during the next four years may be attributed to this terrible tragedy and its long-continued after effects.[14]

During his presidency, Pierce remained faithful to the outward duties of a Christian. He read prayers to the White House servants every morning and prayed before meals. He and his wife attended church on Sundays; they attended Reverend Byron Sunderland's Four and a Half Street Church at times and the Presbyterian Ninth Street Church at other times. The White House conducted no business on Sundays.[15]

Pierce's presidential writings contain many references to God. He began his second annual message summarizing the previous year and said: "In the present, therefore, as in the past, we find ample grounds for reverent thankfulness to the God of grace and providence for His protecting care and merciful dealings with us as a people."[16]

He concluded that message with these words: "Under the solemnity of these convictions the blessing of Almighty God is earnestly invoked to attend upon your deliberations and upon all the counsels and acts of the Government, to the end that, with common zeal and common efforts, we may, in humble submission to the divine will, cooperate for the promotion of the supreme good of these United States."[17]

During Pierce's presidency, the slavery debate raged. He concluded his third annual message with a discussion of the debate and an appeal that God would preserve the Union. "I rely confidently on the patriotism of the people, on the dignity and self-respect of the States, on the wisdom of Congress, and, above all, on the continued gracious favor of Almighty God to maintain against all enemies, whether at home or abroad, the sanctity of the Constitution and the integrity of the Union."[18]

Yet the Union dissolved and civil war came. During the Civil War, on December 2, 1863, Jane Pierce died. Though the Pierces had attended the South Congregational Church for years, Franklin's attendance became infrequent when the preacher, Reverend Henry E. Parker, began to preach against slavery.

He knew the pastor of St. Paul's Episcopal Church in Concord, the Reverend Dr. Eames. Because Eames "did not preach on politics" like Parker did, Pierce began attending the Episcopal church.[19]

For decades, Pierce had given much thought to religion but had not made a firm commitment. Although he acknowledged that Zenas Caldwell had planted within him a seed of faith, the seed did not grow to fruition for decades. His wife, Jane, cared deeply about religion, as did her relatives; Pierce's relatives, however, cared little for religion.

Nichols says that for forty years Pierce "professed to be an orthodox believer, but moving experience, which would lead to public confession, he seems never to have felt; nor did he have the willingness or the confidence to accept the discipline. He did his best to invite the experience, was regular in his church attendance, and especially after the death of his boy he became even more observant as his White House customs show."[20] Yet he did not make a public confession of faith for all the years of his marriage.

While attending St. Paul's Episcopal Church in Concord, he became friends with the Reverend Dr. Eames. Eames successfully influenced him to make a public profession of faith on Sunday, December 3, 1865. He stated that he would "renounce the devil and all his works, the vain pomp and glory of the world, with all covetous desires of the same and the sinful desires of the flesh, to no longer follow nor be led by them, and to obediently keep God's holy will and commandments and to walk in the same all the days of his life."[21] He was then baptized on the same day by the Reverend Dr. Eames.

In the spring of 1866 Bishop Chase confirmed him in the Episcopal faith,[22] and Pierce became a communicant in the Episcopal Church.[23]

He died on October 8, 1869, in Concord, New Hampshire.

CONCLUSION

From his college years through his wife's death, Franklin Pierce knew about religion and acknowledged many of its truths. However, he admitted that he had not yet been reborn. After his wife's death, he made a public profession of faith, was baptized, and confirmed in the Episcopal Church.

NOTES

1. D. W. Bartlett, *The Life of General Franklin Pierce of New Hampshire* (Auburn, ME: Derby & Miller, 1852), 24.

2. Roy Franklin Nichols, *Franklin Pierce: Young Hickory of the Granite Hills* (Philadelphia: University of Philadelphia Press), 25.

3. Ibid.

4. Ibid.

5. Ibid., 30.

6. Edmund Fuller and David E. Green, *God in the White House: The Faiths of American Presidents* (New York: Crown Publishing, 1968), 93.

7. Bartlett, *The Life of General Franklin Pierce*, 25.

8. Nichols, *Franklin Pierce*, 106–7.

9. Ibid., 107.

10. Ibid., 124–25.

11. Ibid., 125.

12. Bartlett, *The Life of General Franklin Pierce*, 241.

13. Ibid.

14. Nichols, *Franklin Pierce*, 226.

15. Ibid., 243.

16. Pierce, *Messages and Papers of the Presidents: Franklin Pierce, 1854.* December 4, 1854. Second annual message.

17. Ibid.

18. Ibid., December 31, 1855. Third annual message.

19. Fuller and Green, *God in the White House,* 95.

20. Nichols, *Franklin Pierce*, 527–28.

21. Ibid., 528.

22. Fuller and Green, *God in the White House,* 95.

23. Franklin Steiner, *The Religious Beliefs of Our Presidents* (Girard, KS: Haldeman-Julius, 1936; repr., Amherst, NY: Prometheus Books, 1995), 66.

CHAPTER 30

MILLARD FILLMORE

MILLARD FILLMORE was born on January 7, 1800, in Cayuga County, New York. He married Abigail Powers on February 2, 1826. Powers's father, the Reverend Lemuel Powers, was a Baptist minister who died while Abigail was an infant; however, her mother, Abigail Newland Powers, raised her in the Baptist faith.

When Millard Fillmore and Abigail Powers were married, an Episcopalian minister performed the ceremony in the home of Abigail's brother.[1]

In the spring of 1830, the Fillmores moved to Buffalo, New York. Millard's cousin, Reverend Glezen Fillmore, was a Methodist circuit rider and had organized the first Methodist church there. However, Millard and Abigail did not attend that church.[2]

Instead, they became charter members of Buffalo's first Unitarian society. In 1834, the association built a church, which the Fillmores attended. Fillmore biographer Robert Rayback believed that Fillmore's decision to join the Unitarian church was based not on the church's doctrine but on its emphasis on reason:

> To a man of Fillmore's temperament, the Unitarian rejection of the Trinity was of less significance than its rejection of all dogma that offended reason. When, in conformity to this, the Unitarians replaced the angry God of the Calvinists with a benevolent one and a sinful mankind with a virtuous one, and thereby embraced the idea of progress, they magnified the attraction of their church for Fillmore.[3]

When he applied for membership in the American Unitarian Association in Boston, his membership was denied. He only remained in Buffalo's Unitarian church because of his friendship with its pastor, G. W. Hosmer.[4]

When President Zachary Taylor died on July 9, 1850, Vice President Millard Fillmore became president. He issued a proclamation announcing Taylor's death, which said:

> Fellow-Citizens of the Senate and House of Representatives:
>
> I have to perform the melancholy duty of announcing to you that it has pleased Almighty God to remove from this life Zachary Taylor, late President of the United States. He deceased last evening at the hour of half-past 10 o'clock, in the midst of his family and surrounded by affectionate friends, calmly and in the full possession of all his faculties. Among his last words were these, which he uttered with emphatic distinctness:
>
> "I have always done my duty. I am ready to die. My only regret is for the friends I leave behind me."[5]

Fillmore served as president from 1850 until 1853. In his first annual message, he began by stating that he had been suddenly called "in the midst of the last session of Congress by a painful dispensation of Divine Providence to the responsible station which I now hold[.]"[6]

By his second annual message, the nation had recovered from the shock of having two presidents die in office within recent memory. His introduction was more upbeat; he said: "None can look back to the dangers which are passed or forward to the bright prospect before us without feeling a thrill of gratification, at the same time that he must be impressed with a grateful sense of our profound obligations to a beneficent Providence, whose paternal care is so manifest in the happiness of this highly favored land."[7]

In his third (and final) annual message, he expressed thanks to an "all-merciful Providence," saying: "Our grateful thanks are due to an all-merciful Providence, not only for staying the pestilence which in different forms has desolated some of our cities, but for crowning the labors of the husbandman with an abundant harvest and the nation generally with the blessings of peace and prosperity."[8]

Biographer Robert Rayback believed that either Fillmore was unfamiliar with the Bible's contents or else he chose not to use or allude to it often in his speeches.[9] He would refer to Providence from time to time, but few if any instances survive of biblical references or quotations.

On March 30, 1853, Abigail Powers Fillmore died. On February 10, 1858, Fillmore married Caroline Carmichael McIntosh. After his Unitarian pastor, G. W. Hosmer, retired, Fillmore attended a Baptist church with his wife.[10] He also attended an Episcopal church upon occasion.[11]

Fillmore became a member of the American Sunday School Union, after the $50 membership fee was paid by the Brick Church of Rochester while he was president. He said, "This is an unexpected and I fear an undeserved honor, so delicately and modestly conveyed that it could not fail to reach the heart."[12]

Fillmore died on March 8, 1874, in Buffalo, New York. In Fillmore's funeral, three ministers—a Baptist, an Episcopalian, and a Presbyterian— shared in the ceremonies.

CONCLUSION

Fillmore was an intellectual. In his younger years, he preferred the Unitarian church because of their intellectualism; in old age, he retained affinity with that church while attending other churches. While we know little about Fillmore's religious beliefs, the little we do know suggests that he agreed with the unorthodox doctrines of the Unitarians.

NOTES

1. Robert J. Rayback, *Millard Fillmore: Biography of a President* (Buffalo, NY: Buffalo Historical Society/Henry Stewart, 1959), 45–46.

2. Ibid., 45.

3. Ibid., 46.

4. Edmund Fuller and David E. Green, *God in the White House: The Faiths of American Presidents* (New York: Crown Publishers, 1968), 91.

5. Taylor, *Messages and Papers of the Presidents: Zachary Taylor, 1850.* July 10, 1850. Message announcing the death of Zachary Taylor.

6. Fillmore, *Messages and Papers of the Presidents: Millard Fillmore, 1850.* December 2, 1850. First annual message.

7. Ibid., December 2, 1851. Second annual message.

8. Ibid., December 6, 1852. Third annual message.

9. Rayback, *Millard Fillmore,* 45.

10. Fuller and Green, *God in the White House,* 91.

11. Bliss Isley, *The Presidents: Men of Faith* (Boston: W. A. Wilde, 1953), 104.

12. Ibid.

★

CHAPTER 31

ZACHARY TAYLOR

ZACHARY TAYLOR was born on November 24, 1784, in Orange County, Virginia. He married Margaret Mackall Smith on June 21, 1810. Smith was a devout Episcopalian.[1]

For most of his military life, Taylor did not attend church regularly. When he did, he attended a Protestant Episcopal church with his wife. In the words of presidential Christianity authors Edmund Fuller and David Green, Taylor was "commonly but misleadingly listed as an Episcopalian," but "belonged to no church and never made any recorded profession of faith. More so than with Harrison, his religion was in his wife's name during his forty years of married life."[2] However, author Bliss Isley looked at the opposite side of the coin, stating that "Taylor was an adherent, though not in full communion." Isley cited a statement by Taylor's daughter as evidence that though Taylor "took only a passive interest in the affairs of the denomination" he "was a diligent Bible student."[3]

Possibly the only surviving statement on Taylor's religion (certainly the only statement known to biographers and authors on presidential Christianity) was made by Taylor's daughter, White House hostess Elizabeth (Betty) Bliss. She said of her father: "He was a constant reader of the Bible and practiced all its precepts, acknowledging his responsibility to God."[4]

Taylor was elected president in 1849 and served until 1850. During his brief presidency, he attended St. John's Episcopal Church in Washington, DC, with his wife.

Taylor's few references to Christianity in his presidential writings and speeches were mostly to that general term for a deity, "Divine Providence."

In his inaugural address on March 5, 1849, he congratulated his fellow citizens "upon the high state of prosperity to which the goodness of Divine Providence has conducted our common country."[5]

On March 3, 1849, he wrote: "Our Government can only be preserved in its purity by the suppression and entire elimination of every claim or tendency of one coordinate branch to encroachment upon another. With the strict observance of this rule and the other injunctions of the Constitution, with a sedulous inculcation of that respect and love for the Union of the States which our fathers cherished and enjoined upon their children, and with the aid of that overruling Providence which has so long and so kindly guarded our liberties and institutions, we may reasonably expect to transmit them, with their innumerable blessings, to the remotest posterity."[6]

In his first and only annual message, on December 4, 1849, Taylor said that in the past year the nation had been "blessed by a kind Providence with an abundance of the fruits of the earth." He added that "although the destroying angel for a time visited extensive portions of our territory with the ravages of a dreadful pestilence, yet the Almighty has at length deigned to stay his hand and to restore the inestimable blessing of general health to a people who have acknowledged His power, deprecated His wrath, and implored His merciful protection."[7]

Though Taylor thanked God "for his manifold blessings" in private correspondence, he did not choose to issue Thanksgiving proclamations during his term of office. He did not state that he was unable to do so due to any separation of church and state: In a November 1849 letter, he instead cited the custom of the time:

> Sir: Your communication of Oct. 6th in relation to a proclamation for a day of National Thanksgiving was duly received, and, with many others of the same import, has been considered with the attention which its importance demands. While uniting cordially in the universal feeling of thankfulness to God for his manifold blessings, and especially for the abatement of pestilence which so lately walked in our midst, I have yet thought it most proper to leave the subject of a Thanksgiving Proclamation where custom in many parts of the country has so long consigned it, in the hands

of the Governors of the several States. This decision has been strengthened by the consideration that this is the season usually set apart for that purpose, and that several of the Governors have already issued their annual proclamations accordingly.[8]

Taylor died on July 9, 1850, in Washington, DC. His funeral service was conducted at his church, St. John's Episcopal Church, and the funeral sermon was preached by the church's rector, Reverend Dr. Pyne.

CONCLUSION

Zachary Taylor and James Monroe are, perhaps, the two presidents of whose religious beliefs we know the least. We do not know that Taylor's religious beliefs, such as they were, were orthodox, but we do not know that they were not. However orthodox they may have been, though, his religious convictions were evidently not strong enough to prompt him to join a church.

NOTES

1. Edmund Fuller and David E. Green, *God in the White House: The Faiths of American Presidents* (New York: Crown Publishers, 1968), 87.

2. Ibid.

3. Bliss Isley, *The Presidents: Men of Faith* (Boston: W. A. Wilde, 1953), 95.

4. Fuller and Green, *God in the White House*, 87.

5. Taylor, *Messages and Papers of the Presidents: Zachary Taylor, 1849.* March 5, 1949. Inaugural address.

6. Ibid., March 3, 1849.

7. Ibid., December 4, 1849. First annual message.

8. Franklin Steiner, *The Religious Beliefs of Our Presidents* (Girard, KS: Haldeman-Julius, 1936; repr. Amherst, NY: Prometheus Books, 1995), 186.

CHAPTER 32

JAMES KNOX POLK

JAMES KNOX POLK was born on November 2, 1795, in Mecklenburg City, North Carolina.

When Polk's parents took him to be baptized, the local Presbyterian minister, Reverend James Wallis, required that they first make a public confession of faith. When Polk's father, Sam Polk, would not do this, baptism was denied.

Neither Sam Polk nor his father, Ezekiel Polk, was an orthodox Christian. However, Sam Polk left the religious education of his ten children up to his wife, Jane Knox Polk, so James Polk's early life had the strong influence of orthodox Christianity. Jane regularly attended church and took James with her. He received his earliest religious instruction there.

Jane Knox Polk was a Presbyterian, as her family had been for generations. The "Knox" middle name that she passed on to her son had also been in the family for generations. In fact, Jane was a great-grandniece of John Knox, the Scottish Presbyterian reformer.[1] For her, the Christian faith was not merely a heritage; it was who she was. She delighted in "the Bible, the Confession of Faith, the Psalms and Watt's Hymns."[2]

James Knox Polk lived his early years in the midst of a religious controversy, and he was caught in the crossfire. After his grandmother, Maria Polk, died, his grandfather, Ezekiel Polk, remarried. Every one of the children born to this marriage either was stillborn or did not survive infancy.[3]

In his grief over the deaths of the children, the Presbyterian doctrine of infant condemnation was cited as evidence that the babies were not in heaven. Ezekiel Polk did not want to believe that—but his violent reaction stunned the community. He rejected Christianity and began publicly defending deism and circulating deistic literature.[4] Two local ministers, the Reverends James Wallis and Samuel C. Caldwell, countered his attacks and defended Christianity.

The contest ended in the early 1800s. Revival swept the area, and about five thousand people attended one 1802 camp meeting. Since some of Ezekiel Polk's strongest allies were converted, he gave up and left the area the next year.

When James Polk was almost eleven, his family moved to Tennessee. He attended a school sponsored by the Zion Church in Columbia, Tennessee, for a year. The schoolmaster was Reverend Robert Henderson, who stated that Polk read "the usual course of Latin authors, part of the Greek testament and a few of the dialogues of Lucian." He said that Polk's "moral conduct was unexceptionable and unexemplary."[5]

After a year in that school, he attended Samuel P. Black's school in Murfreesboro, Tennessee. His teachers at each school were Calvinists who passed their values on to Polk.[6]

In 1816, he was admitted to the University of North Carolina at Chapel Hill, where the president was Presbyterian minister Reverend Robert Chapman.[7] One of Polk's chief religious influences was the mathematics professor, Dr. Joseph Caldwell.[8] The school's education had a religious foundation. Polk biographer John Siegenthaler describes the school's atmosphere: "Bible study was at the base of all other instruction at the university, moral philosophy serving as the foundation upon which the school determined that an informed young man would build a career."[9]

Biographer Charles Sellers describes Polk's response to the teachings of the college:

> Jim seems to have found the Witherspoon-Caldwell system convincing; at any rate he never betrayed a sign of dissent from the orthodoxy it expounded. Yet the common sense philosophy seems to have had the effect of discouraging personal religious sentiment, even while it was indoctrinating against heretical ideas. Answering questions and quieting doubts on the intellectual plane, its net result was often to file the concerns of religion and philosophy

away into that area of consciousness reserved for problems settled and closed. Caldwell himself was suspected by his ministerial brethren of a loss of genuine piety, while his young student from Tennessee, though to outward appearance scrupulously orthodox, would never feel himself strongly enough "convicted" to join a church.[10] [Note: The last phrase of the final sentence is only partially true. See later in this chapter for further discussion.]

Polk married Sarah Childress, a devout Presbyterian,[11] on January 1, 1824. After their marriage, Polk purchased a pew in the Presbyterian church of Columbia, Tennessee. The Polks attended its services faithfully; James Polk was there "every Sunday that he was in town."[12]

Polk ran for Congress shortly thereafter and made his first speech to Congress in 1826. He said: "From my earliest infancy I have been taught to believe that from the fall of our first great parent until the present hour, man has been depraved, frail and impure."[13]

One day, after attending a Baptist church, Polk wrote that the preacher "enforced the doctrine of predestination more strongly than I had heard it for many years, and perhaps in my life."[14] This is in spite of the fact that Polk spent most of his life in a Presbyterian church.

In August 1833, Polk attended a Methodist camp meeting conducted by Reverend John McFerrin, who later became the Methodist bishop of Tennessee. McFerrin described for his audience the "inheritance incorruptible, and undefiled, and that fadeth not away, . . . reserved in heaven for you."[15] In *The Presidents: Men of Faith*, Bliss Isley stated that until that meeting Polk "sat erect in his pew each Sunday, little thinking that his soul had any special need of salvation." Isley described Polk's response to McFerrin's preaching in these words:

Never before had Polk been so profoundly moved. As he listened to McFerrin, he understood why Methodism had gained six thousand converts in a single year in Tennessee's Cumberland District. In his own heart he arraigned himself before the judgment bar of God and convicted himself of sin.

He felt the impulse to rush forward with the others, but a counteracting force held him back. It must have been the thought that his wife and mother would be shocked, should he accept conversion at a noisy camp meeting. Suppressing his impulse, he withdrew.[16]

Though he did not make a commitment to Christianity for decades, a seed had been planted that would grow into fruition near the end of his life.

In 1844, Sarah Childress Polk decided to join the Presbyterian Church.[17] (Though she had regularly attended up until that time, she had not become a member.) James Polk attended Presbyterian churches with her for the rest of his life.

After fourteen years in the United States House of Representatives, several of which were spent as speaker of the house, Polk ran for governor of Tennessee and won the election. At his inaugural, he asked a Methodist bishop to deliver the invocation.[18]

During his term as governor, Polk talked with Reverend McFerrin frequently about religion. Author Bliss Isley expressed his opinion that it was "possible that the governor would have joined the Methodist Church during his second term, had there been a second term."[19]

Polk was elected president in 1844 and served one term (1845–49). In his inaugural address, on March 5, 1845, he invoked God's aid:

In assuming responsibilities so vast I fervently invoke the aid of that Almighty Ruler of the Universe in whose hands are the destinies of nations and of men to guard this Heaven-favored land against the mischiefs which without His guidance might arise from an unwise public policy. With a firm reliance upon the wisdom of Omnipotence to sustain and direct me in the path of duty which I am appointed to pursue, I stand in the presence of this assembled multitude of my countrymen to take upon myself the solemn obligation "to the best of my ability to preserve, protect, and defend the Constitution of the United States."[20]

He concluded his inaugural address by again invoking God's aid:

Confidently relying upon the aid and assistance of the coordinate departments of the Government in conducting our public affairs, I enter upon the discharge of the high duties which have been assigned me by the people, again humbly supplicating that Divine Being who has watched over and protected our beloved country from its infancy to the present hour to continue His gracious benedictions upon us, that we may continue to be a prosperous and happy people.[21]

Polk referred to God several times in his presidential speeches. In his first annual message, Polk stated: "I am happy that I can congratulate you on the continued prosperity of our country. Under the blessings of Divine Providence and the benign influence of our free institutions, it stands before the world a spectacle of national happiness."[22]

He also expressed his gratitude to God in his fourth annual message, which began with these words: "Under the benignant providence of Almighty God the representatives of the States and of the people are again brought together to deliberate for the public good. The gratitude of the nation to the Sovereign Arbiter of All Human Events should be commensurate with the boundless blessings which we enjoy."[23]

While he was president, Polk kept a diary. In an entry written on his fiftieth birthday, November 2, 1845, he wrote:

Attended the Methodist church (called the Foundry Church) today, in company with my private secretary, J. Knox Walker. It was an inclement day, there being rain from an early hour in the morning; and Mrs. Polk and the ladies of my household did not attend church today. Mrs. Polk being a member of the Presbyterian Church I generally attend that church with her, though my opinions and predilections are in favor of the Methodist Church.

This day my birthday, being fifty years old, having been born according to the family register in the family Bible, corroborated by the account given me by my mother, on the 2d of November, 1795.

The text today was from the Acts of Apostles, Ch. 15, v.31— "Because he hath appointed a day, in the which he will judge the world in righteousness, by the man whom he hath ordained." It was communion day in the church, and the sermon was solemn and forcible. It awakened the reflection that I had lived fifty years, and that before fifty years more would expire, I would be sleeping with the generations which have gone before me. I thought of the vanity of this world's honors, how little they would profit me half a century hence, and that it was time for me to be "putting my house in order."[24]

Polk rarely missed church services at Washington's First Presbyterian Church; he attended 147 of the 183 Sundays mentioned in his diary while president. When he missed, he was kept home by either illness or bad weather.[25] On several occasions, he paid the First Presbyterian Church $6.50 for pew rent.

One Sunday, he attended services at the Capitol. He mentioned the service in his diary, saying: "The subject of the discourse was the Cross of Christ, a noble theme. The minister laboured very much and seemed to be making a very great effort. There was nothing solemn or impressive in the manner or matter of the sermon; and the idea was constantly in mind that the minister was endeavouring to make a display of eloquence & learning, in which I think he failed."[26]

Polk was tolerant of members of other denominations, so long as they were not fanatics. His October 14, 1846, diary entry is devoted to an account of an interview he had with a Presbyterian pastor, Reverend William L. McCalla. Reverend McCalla came with letters of introduction from several people who promised to attack Polk for attacking several Roman Catholic chaplains unless Polk appointed McCalla as a chaplain. Polk stated: "I felt great contempt for Mr. McCalla and his religion and gave him my mind freely. I told him that, thank God, under our Constitution there was no connection between church and state, and in my action as President of the United States I recognized no distinction between creeds in my appointments to office."[27]

Polk summed up his impressions of Reverend McCalla in these words: "I consider him either a knave without vital reason or a fanatic without reason. I have met with no man during my administration, among the numerous office-seekers who have beset me, for whom I have so profound a contempt. To attempt to connect me with religious feuds between sects, either for the purpose of coercing me to give him an office or to give him a pretext to attack me upon affected or pretended religious grounds if I did not, proves him to be a man destitute of both religion and principle."[28]

On November 2, 1848, Polk made a birthday entry in his diary. He noted that he turned fifty-three that day. He said: "Upon each recurrence of my birthday I am solemnly impressed with the vanity and emptiness of worldly honours and worldly enjoyments, and of the wisdom of preparing for a future estate. In four months I shall retire from public life forever. I have lived three-fourths of the period ordinarily allotted to man on earth. I have been highly honoured by my fellowmen and have filled the highest station on earth, but I will soon go the way of all the earth. I pray God to prepare me for the great event."[29]

When it was evident that he was approaching death, his mother urged him to be baptized and join the Presbyterian Church. She even brought a Presbyterian minister to baptize him.[30] However, Polk had already decided that when he joined the church, he wanted Reverend John McFerrin to baptize him.[31] So Polk was baptized on June 9, 1849, by the same pastor who had conducted the 1833 camp meeting where Polk had been spiritually moved.[32] Polk joined the Methodist Church then and died a few days later, on June 15, 1849, in Nashville, Tennessee.

CONCLUSION

Polk grew up and lived his life as a churchgoing Presbyterian. He apparently believed the doctrines of Christianity throughout his life. At a Methodist camp meeting, he was challenged to receive Christ as his personal Savior, yet was too fearful of his family's probable reaction to make a commitment. So he spent the rest of his life as a mere churchgoer. However, when he knew that his death was approaching, he asked the same pastor who had conducted the camp meeting to baptize him. He then joined the Methodist Church.

Like other presidents, including William Henry Harrison, he decided to wait until his deathbed to commit himself to Christianity; however, unlike Harrison, God let Polk live long enough to follow through with his decision.

NOTES

1. John Seigenthaler, *James K. Polk*, (New York: Times Books, 2003) 12.

2. Charles G. Sellers, *James K. Polk, Jacksonian: 1795–1843* (Princeton, NJ: Princeton University Press, 1957), 23.

3. Ibid., 21.

4. Ibid., 24–25.

5. Eugene Irving McCormac, *James K. Polk: A Political Biography to the End of a Career, 1845–1849* (New York: Russell and Russell, 1965), 3.

6. Paul H. Bergeron, *The Presidency of James K. Polk* (Lawrence: University Press of Kansas, 1987), 10.

7. Seigenthaler, *James K. Polk*, 21.

8. Sellers, *James K. Polk*, 45.

9. Seigenthaler, *James K. Polk*, 21.

10. Sellers, *James K. Polk*, 46.

11. Carl Sferazza Anthony, *First Ladies: The Saga of the Presidents' Wives and Their Power, 1789–1961* (New York: Morrow, 1990), 133.

12. Sellers, *James K. Polk*, 94.

13. Bergeron, *The Presidency of James K. Polk*, 240.

14. Ibid., 244.

15. Sellers, *James K. Polk*, 210.

16. Bliss Isley, *The Presidents: Men of Faith* (Boston: W. A. Wilde, 1953), 84.

17. Sellers, *James K. Polk*, 211.

18. Isley, *The Presidents*, 85.

19. Ibid.

20. Polk, March 5, 1845. Inaugural address.

21. Ibid.

22. Polk, *Messages and Papers of the Presidents: James K. Polk, 1845.* December 2, 1845. First annual message.

23. Ibid., December 5, 1848. Fourth annual message.

24. Allan Nevins, *Polk: The Diary of a President, 1845–1849* (London, New York, and Toronto: Longmans, Green, 1929, 1952), 23–24. Quoted in McCormac, *James K. Polk*, 721.

25. Bergeron, *The Presidency of James K. Polk*, 239.

26. Ibid., 242.

27. Nevins, *Polk: The Diary of a President*, 157.

28. Ibid., 158.

29. Ibid., 350–51. Quoted in part in Bergeron, *The Presidency of James K. Polk*, 243.

30. Isley, *The Presidents*, 87.

31. McCormac, *James K. Polk*, 721.

32. Benjamin Weiss, *God in American History: A Documentation of America's Religious Heritage* (Grand Rapids: Zondervan, 1966), 82.

CHAPTER 33

JOHN TYLER

JOHN TYLER was born on March 29, 1780, in Greenway, Virginia. He married Letitia Christian on March 29, 1813.

He was a member of the Protestant Episcopal Church.[1]

Vice President Tyler came to the presidency upon William Henry Harrison's 1841 death and filled out the rest of the term. Tyler issued this proclamation after Harrison died:

> When a Christian people feel themselves to be overtaken by a great public calamity, it becomes them to humble themselves under the dispensation of Divine Providence, to recognize His righteous government over the children of men, to acknowledge His goodness in time past, as well as their own unworthiness, and to supplicate His merciful protection for the future.
>
> The death of William Henry Harrison, late President of the United States, so soon after his elevation to that high office, is a bereavement peculiarly calculated to be regarded as a heavy affliction and to impress all minds with a sense of the uncertainty of human things and of the dependence of nations, as well as individuals, upon our Heavenly Parent.
>
> I have thought, therefore, that I should be acting in conformity with the general expectation and feelings of the community in recommending, as I now do, to the people of the United States of every religious denomination that, according to their several modes and forms of worship, they observe a day of fasting and

prayer by such religious services as may be suitable on the occasion; and I recommend Friday, the 14th day of May next, for that purpose, to the end that on that day we may all with one accord join in humble and reverential approach to Him in whose hands we are, invoking Him to inspire us with a proper spirit and temper of heart and mind under these frowns of His providence and still to bestow His gracious benedictions upon our Government and our country.[2]

In each of his four annual messages, Tyler expressed thanks to God, using a different name for God each time. In his first annual message, he thanked "Divine Providence" and called the Senate and House of Representatives to renew their devotion to their "Heavenly Parent."[3] In his second annual message, he referred to God as the "Great Creator of All Things" and as "that great Being who made us and who preserves us as a nation."[4] In his third annual message, he called on the people of the country to render up thanks to the "Supreme Being." He also referred to God as an "overruling Providence."[5] In his fourth annual message, he stated that they had cause for expressing gratitude to the "Supreme Ruler of the Universe."[6]

While president, he had a family pew in St. John's Church, a Protestant Episcopal church in Washington, DC.[7]

On September 10, 1842, his wife Letitia died in the White House. About a year and a half later, on June 26, 1844, he married Julia Gardiner.

After his term ended, he retired to his home, Sherwood Forest in Charles City, Virginia. Biographer Oliver Perry Chitwood says that "there is evidence to indicate that in his declining years he was blessed with an experiential knowledge of real religion."[8]

He died on January 18, 1862, in Richmond, Virginia. In his funeral service, Bishop Johns, of the Episcopal Diocese of Virginia, delivered the sermon. He said:

It is comforting to know that the great work of eternity had not been neglected. His gifted mind held fast as a foundation of its faith and hope to the oracles of God. He was long accustomed to meditate on the things of eternity; and when, a few years ago, he was prostrated by illness and impressed by the idea of approaching dissolution, the testimony of the pastor whose service he was so fond of attending in the Church he had so reverently joined, shows the brightness of the faith in which he died.[9]

Chitwood stated that Tyler's "theological opinions seem not to have been in any way at variance with the orthodoxy of his day." Tyler once said, "My life has always been illuminated by a bright faith in the Christian religion."[10]

In his writings, Tyler expressed a belief in a caring God. In 1832, while in the Senate, Tyler wrote the following in a letter to his daughter, Mary: "The person who is a stranger to sickness is equally a stranger to the highest enjoyments of health. So that I have brought myself to believe that the variableness in the things of the world are designed by the Creator for the happiness of His creatures. In truth, what exists but for some wise purpose? All our crosses and the numerous vexations which assail us are designed to improve our moral condition."[11]

Governor Henry Wise, who knew Tyler well, said this about Tyler's religion: "He was a firm believer in the atonement of the son of God, and in the efficacy of his blood to wash away every stain of mortal sin. He was by faith and heirship a member of the Episcopal Church, and never doubted Divine Revelation."[12]

After his death, his widow, Julia Gardiner Tyler, converted to Roman Catholicism. She made her decision to do so in March 1872 and formally joined the church the following month.[13]

CONCLUSION

Testimony, both by Tyler himself and by those who knew him well, points to the fact that Tyler was an orthodox Christian. His faith was not, by all appearances, a topic he frequently discussed; however, when he did discuss religion, his beliefs were orthodox.

NOTES

1. Oliver Perry Chitwood, *John Tyler: Champion of the Old South* (New York: Russell and Russell, 1939, 1964), 434.

2. Harrison, *Messages and Papers of the Presidents: William Henry Harrison, 1841*. April 13, 1841.

3. Tyler, *Messages and Papers of the Presidents: John Tyler, 1841*. December 7, 1841. First annual address.

4. Ibid., December 6, 1842. Second annual address.

5. Ibid., December 1843. Third annual address.

6. Ibid., December 3, 1844. Fourth annual address.

7. Chitwood, *John Tyler*, 434.

8. Ibid., 435.

9. Franklin Steiner, *The Religious Beliefs of Our Presidents* (Girard, KS: Haldeman-Julius, 1936; repr., Amherst, NY: Prometheus Books, 1995), 96.

10. John McCollister, *So Help Me God: The Faith of America's Presidents* (Louisville: Westminster/John Knox Press, 1991), 58; Chitwood, *John Tyler,* 435.

11. Robert Seager II, *And Tyler Too: A Biography of John and Julia Gardiner Tyler* (New York: McGraw-Hill, 1963), 109; Chitwood, *John Tyler*, 434–35.

12. Steiner, *Religious Beliefs of Our Presidents*, 96; Bliss Isley, *The Presidents: Men of Faith* (Boston: W. A. Wilde, 1953), 77. Isley's version reads, "Episcopal Church of Christ, and he never doubted Divine Revelation."

13. Seager, *And Tyler Too*, 538–39.

CHAPTER 34

WILLIAM HENRY HARRISON

WILLIAM HENRY HARRISON was born on February 9, 1773, in Berkeley, Virginia.

He married Anna Tuthill Symmes on November 25, 1795. He attended a Protestant Episcopal church regularly on Sunday mornings and attended a Presbyterian church on some Sunday evenings. For at least part of his life, his churchgoing was due to his wife's influence. When Harrison was asked why he did not conduct business on Sundays, he said: "I have too much respect for the religion of my wife to encourage violation."[1]

Harrison helped build a church in Cleves, Ohio. One author said that "William Henry Harrison's 1,500 feet of lumber helped build the structure[.]"[2]

After Reverend Timothy Flint, a Congregational minister, visited Harrison's house, he wrote: "I could desire no attentions, no facilities for discharging my duty, which he did not constantly proffer me. His house was opened for public worship. He kept an open table to which every visitor was welcomed."[3] On May 18, 1817, while Harrison was in Cincinnati, he was one of the sponsors at the founding of Christ Church (Episcopal) and was named a vestryman.[4]

Harrison's attitude toward Christianity warmed as he aged. In 1840, while Harrison was president-elect, newspaper reporters found him in a Pittsburgh hotel room reading the Bible. He said that he had made it a fixed habit to read his Bible every night before he went to sleep. Though at first he read it as "a matter of duty," he said, "it has now become a pleasure."[5]

His inaugural address contained several religious statements and references. The three that are most pertinent to his religious beliefs are quoted below:

> However strong may be my present purpose to realize the expectations of a magnanimous and confiding people, I too well understand the dangerous temptations to which I shall be exposed from the magnitude of the power which it has been the pleasure of the people to commit to my hands not to place my chief confidence upon the aid of that Almighty Power which has hitherto protected me and enabled me to bring to favorable issues other important but still greatly inferior trusts heretofore confided to me by my country. . . .
>
> Caesar became the master of the Roman people and the senate under the pretense of supporting the democratic claims of the former against the aristocracy of the latter; Cromwell, in the character of protector of the liberties of the people, became the dictator of England, and Bolivar possessed himself of unlimited power with the title of his country's liberator. There is, on the contrary, no instance on record of an extensive and well-established republic being changed into an aristocracy. The tendencies of all such governments in their decline is to monarchy, and the antagonist principle to liberty there is the spirit of faction—a spirit which assumes the character and in times of great excitement imposes itself upon the people as the genuine spirit of freedom, and, like the false Christs whose coming was foretold by the Savior, seeks to, and were it possible would, impose upon the true and most faithful disciples of liberty. . . .
>
> I deem the present occasion sufficiently important and solemn to justify me in expressing to my fellow-citizens a profound reverence for the Christian religion and a thorough conviction that sound morals, religious liberty, and a just sense of religious responsibility are essentially connected with all true and lasting happiness; and to that good Being who has blessed us by the gifts of civil and religious freedom, who watched over and prospered the labors of our fathers and has hitherto preserved to us institutions far exceeding in excellence those of any other peo-

ple, let us unite in fervently commending every interest of our beloved country in all future time.[6]

The day after his inauguration, Harrison "walked out into the city and purchased a Bible and a Prayer Book for the use of Presidents."[7] During the brief period between his inauguration and his death, he attended St. John's Church Lafayette Square (Episcopal), occupying pew 45.[8]

Freeman Cleaves, author of *Old Tippecanoe*, the definitive biography of Harrison, stated that after he purchased the Bible, he "had announced his intention of becoming a communicant when he caught a severe cold."[9] This statement was corroborated by St. John's rector, the Reverend Mr. Hawley. (Though unchallenged for nearly a century, the statement has since become the source of a historical controversy. This is discussed in more detail below.)

Unfortunately, Harrison died on April 4, 1841, a few days before he could fulfill his resolution to join the church. Five members of his Cabinet (one of whom was Daniel Webster) prepared a brief notice of the arrangements for Harrison's funeral. The notice began:

> The circumstances in which we are placed by the death of the President render it indispensable for us, in the recess of Congress and in the absence of the Vice-President, to make arrangements for the funeral solemnities. Having consulted with the family and personal friends of the deceased, we have concluded that the funeral be solemnized on Wednesday, the 7th instant, at 12 o'clock. The religious services to be performed according to the usage of the Episcopal Church, in which church the deceased most usually worshiped.[10]

HISTORICAL CONTROVERSIES

Did William Henry Harrison intend to join the Episcopal church?

Until the 1930s, nobody questioned that he did, but since that time arguments have been made supporting and opposing the account.

William Henry Harrison died on April 4, 1841, Palm Sunday. At the funeral, held on Wednesday, April 7, Harrison's pastor, the Reverend Mr. Hawley, read the traditional Episcopal service for funerals. He also spoke briefly about Harrison. Meticulous diarist (and former president)

John Quincy Adams attended the funeral and described it in his diary with these words:

> *April 7*—Funeral of W. H. Harrison, President of the United States. This ceremony was performed in a decent and unostentatious manner, with proper religious solemnity, and with the simplicity congenial to our republican institutions. A quarter before twelve, noon, I attended at the President's house, where, in the centre of the East Room, the coffin, covered with a black velvet pall, was placed on a plain table, by the side and crosswise of which was another, at which the Rev. Mr. Hawley, rector of St. John's Church, read the Episcopal funeral service, with a very brief additional statement of two facts. The first, that the day after General Harrison entered the President's house, he walked out into the city and purchased a Bible and Prayer-book, both of which were on the table, and were exhibited to the assembled auditory by the officiating divine, who said that it had been the daily habit of the late President to commence the day by reading in the Bible. The other fact was, that he had expressed regret at not having joined in full communion with the Church, and that it was his intention to have done so at the ensuing Easter-day–next Sunday.[11]

Montgomery's *Life of Harrison* recorded the same event, with slightly different wording:

> At half past 11 o'clock, the Rev. Mr. Hawley, Rector of St. John's Church arose, and observed that he would mention an incident connected with the Bible, which lay on the table before him (covered with black silk velvet). "This Bible," said he, "was purchased by the President on the fifth of March. He has since been in the habit of daily reading it. He was accustomed not only to attend church, but to join audibly in the services, and to kneel humbly before his maker."
>
> Dr. Hawley stated that had the President lived, and been in health, he intended on the next Sabbath to become a communicant at the Lord's table.[12]

In his book *The Presidents: Men of Faith*, Bliss Isley wrote: "Upon arrival in Washington, Harrison arranged to unite with the St. John's

Church on Easter Sunday. In preparation he bought a new Bible and prayer book and prepared for membership."[13]

Freeman Cleaves, author of the definitive Harrison biography, *Old Tippecanoe*, wrote that this statement was not a surprise when Dr. Hawley announced it. He said: "He [Harrison] had purchased a new Bible and had announced his intention of becoming a communicant when he caught a severe cold."[14] The cold led to his death.

For the next two generations, neither scholars nor the general public doubted these statements. The first known questioning of the account was by the agnostic author Franklin Steiner in his book *The Religious Beliefs of Our Presidents*. Since Steiner challenged or minimized most other conversion accounts, his claim can be questioned. Since then, several authors who referenced Steiner's book in their research have questioned the Reverend Mr. Hawley in a similar way. Steiner and those who follow his revisionist interpretation make two arguments against the account. They say:

1. The conversion does not fit what we know of Harrison.

2. If Harrison truly intended to join the church, he would have done so at an earlier date.

Let us look at each argument.

First, let us consider the argument that a conversion to Christianity does not fit what we know of Harrison.

What do we know of Harrison? We know from sources recorded before his presidency that he observed the Sabbath, that he helped a local church construct its building with his lumber, that he sponsored the founding of an Episcopal church in Cincinnati and was named a vestryman in that church, and that he read the Bible for twenty years leading up to his death, first as a matter of duty but eventually as a matter of pleasure. Through his wife's influence and his regular reading of the Bible, he was moving toward Christianity. What we know of Harrison casts no doubts on Reverend Hawley's account.

Second, let us consider the argument that if Harrison had truly believed the Episcopal church's doctrines, he would have joined the church earlier in life, and thus Reverend Hawley must have fabricated his account.

This argument does not hold. A person can be convicted of the truth at any point in his life. Additionally, many people like Harrison have observed outward forms of religion (such as observing the Sabbath, attending church, and reading the Bible) throughout their lives, though they have not made formal connections to any church. These people know the truth in their hearts, but either do not want to join a church at the present moment or feel no urgency to do so. Some people who know the truth but do not act on it wait to make a public profession of faith and join a church until the end of their lives.

Since Harrison read the Bible, observed the Sabbath, and attended church, he knew the truth. For him, preparing to meet his Maker would naturally involve acting upon what he already knew to be true.

No valid arguments can be made against Reverend Hawley's funeral sermon. However, several strong points attest to its veracity. First, additional documentation has been discovered to corroborate the first of Reverend Hawley's statements, that General Harrison purchased a Bible and a prayer book. In Olga Jones's book *Churches of the Presidents in Washington*, she quotes a document found in St. John's Church Lafayette Square's archives that confirms this. "It is noted in a document in this historic shrine," Jones wrote, "that 'the day after General Harrison entered the President's House, he walked out into the city and purchased a Bible and a Prayer Book' for the use of Presidents."[15]

Second, Reverend Hawley would have known if President Harrison wanted to join the church in one week. Certain preparations would have been made for such an event. Decisions to join a church were rarely if ever made on the spur of a moment. In most denominations, the pastor of the church goes over the basics of the Christian faith and the doctrine of the church with those intending to join. Reverend Hawley either made up the story or simply stated what he knew to be true.

Third, according to biographer Freeman Cleaves, Harrison announced his intentions before his death, and therefore his family and close friends knew that he intended to join the church. If what Reverend Hawley said was incorrect, any one of them could have publicly or privately stated the truth. By their silent acquiescence, they were either participating in a deception or simply acknowledging the truth. With all the friends, family, political connections, and enemies that a president of the United States has, at least one person would have noted in a diary if Reverend Hawley concocted the story to comfort the nation.

Fourth, Reverend Hawley's statements went unchallenged for decades. As already mentioned, the first known person to question the account came about a century after the fact, and was an agnostic atheist freethinker with the ulterior motive of proving that no early presidents were Christians. Others since have followed his lead, using his reasons or similar ones, while not carefully investigating the reliability of the source of the historical revision.

Fifth, Reverend Hawley's statement that Harrison intended to join on Easter Sunday is in keeping with an early church tradition that members were frequently or exclusively admitted on Easter and Pentecost. If Harrison's church maintained this practice, the first occasion he could have joined the church after his move to Washington, DC, would have been Easter Sunday.

We have no reason to doubt Harrison's intentions to join the Episcopal Church. Yet another question remains. Why did he express this intention? It could have been due to the urging of his wife. Even though other factors likely entered in, his wife's constant Christian example was probably no small part of the reason that he drew closer to the kingdom of God.

It could also have been a realization that he needed assistance and Divine guidance to do his duties. Though Harrison's decision may have been a combination of these or other factors, likely the biggest motivation was that he realized he was sick and might not have much time left on earth.

In the absence of any evidence to the contrary, I conclude that Harrison sincerely intended to join the Episcopal Church.

CONCLUSION

Through his married life, William Henry Harrison respected his wife's faith, observed the Sabbath, and read the Bible. His statement shortly before he took office that reading the Bible had become a pleasure suggests he was turning toward Christianity.

In the light of this statement, he probably did state his intentions to join the Episcopal Church. Though we cannot know with certainty, his decision apparently reflected a sincere belief in the truth of Christianity. No man knows how long he has to live; Harrison died days before he was to become a church member and a publicly professed Christian.

I see no valid reason to doubt that his intent to join the church was sincere and reflected a belief in the essential doctrines of Christianity.

NOTES

1. Carl Sferazza Anthony, *First Ladies: The Saga of the Presidents' Wives and Their Power, 1789–1961* (New York: Morrow, 1990), 120.

2. Harry J. Sievers and Katherine Speirs, *Benjamin Harrison*, vol. 1, *Hoosier Warrior: Through the Civil War Years, 1833–1865*, 2nd ed., rev. (New York: University Publishers, 1960), 28.

3. Freeman Cleaves, *Old Tippecanoe: William Henry Harrison and His Time* (New York: Charles Scribner's Sons, 1939), 230; Bliss Isley, *The Presidents: Men of Faith* (Boston: W. A. Wilde, 1953), 70.

4. Cleaves, *Old Tippecanoe*, 244. He referred to W. H. Venable, *Centennial History of Christ Church, Cincinnati*, 1917, 11–12.

5. Cleaves, *Old Tippecanoe*, 332. He quoted from the April 13, 1841, *National Intelligencer*. Edmund Fuller and David E. Green, *God in the White House: The Faiths of American Presidents* (New York: Crown Publishers, 1968), 74.

6. Harrison, *Messages and Papers of William Henry Harrison, 1841*, March 4, 1841. Inaugural address.

7. Olga Anna Jones, *Churches of the Presidents in Washington: Visits to Fifteen National Shrines* (New York: Exposition Press, 1954), 27.

8. Cleaves, *Old Tippecanoe*, 341.

9. Ibid.

10. Harrison, *Messages and Papers*, April 4, 1841.

11. John Quincy Adams, *The Diary of John Quincy Adams, 1794–1845*, ed. Allan Nevins (New York: Longmans, Green, 1929; repr., New York: Charles Scribners, 1951), 521. Fuller and Green, *God in the White House*, 76. Elsewhere in Adams' diary, we find other statements made by Reverend Hawley, such as this one made twenty years before on December 23, 1821: "Mr. Sparks, the Unitarian, preached for the first time at the Capitol, to a crowded auditory. His election as chaplain to the House of Representatives occasioned much surprise and has been followed by unusual symptoms of intolerance. Mr. Hawley, the Episcopal preacher at St. John's Church, last Sunday preached a sermon of coarse invective upon the House, who, he said, by this act had voted Christ out-of-doors; and he enjoined upon all the people of his flock not to set their feet within the Capitol to hear Mr. Sparks" (Adams, *The Diary of John Quincy Adams*, 271–72).

12. Franklin Steiner, *The Religious Beliefs of Our Presidents* (Girard, KS: Haldeman-Julius, 1936; repr., Amherst, NY: Prometheus Books, 1995), 68.

13. Isley, *The Presidents*, 72.

14. Cleaves, *Old Tippecanoe*, 340.

15. Jones, *Churches of the Presidents*, 27.

CHAPTER 35

MARTIN VAN BUREN

MARTIN VAN BUREN was born on December 5, 1782, in Kinderhook, New York. His parents were Abraham and Maria Van Buren. According to Van Buren biographer Dennis Lynch, Maria was a "devout little woman" with a "simple faith." "It now seemed as though they had never wanted for anything," Lynch said, "but then no one ever does who has trust in the Lord."[1]

During his youth, Martin Van Buren was a member of Kinderhook Reformed Church. He continued to attend this church throughout his entire life.

In their book *God in the White House,* Edmund Fuller and David Green said that though the Dutch Reformed faith was "part of the pattern of Van Buren's life" and he was "known always as a good churchman," "he never showed a deep interest in theological affairs."[2]

Lynch said that Van Buren "left us only two quotations from the Bible, one a brief line, and the other five verses from the Acts."[3] The five verses were Acts 23:6–10. In the passage, when Paul was before the Sanhedrin, he said that the conflict was over the Pharisaical doctrine of the resurrection. This action divided the Sanhedrin into parties and probably saved Paul's life. Van Buren cited it in the context of James Madison's maneuvering to make his political enemies fight each other.[4]

Though we may know little of his theological beliefs, we do know he was an enthusiastic singer. As biographer Lynch put it, "Crowded though the church might be, and every voice raised in song, Van Buren's rendering of the hymn could be heard above the rest."[5]

Van Buren married Hannah Hoes on February 21, 1807.

He was elected president in 1836 and served from 1837 until 1841. He concluded his inaugural address by saying:

> In receiving from the people the sacred trust twice confided to my illustrious predecessor, and which he has discharged so faithfully and so well, I know that I can not expect to perform the arduous task with equal ability and success. But united as I have been in his counsels, a daily witness of his exclusive and unsurpassed devotion to his country's welfare, agreeing with him in sentiments which his countrymen have warmly supported, and permitted to partake largely of his confidence, I may hope that somewhat of the same cheering approbation will be found to attend upon my path. For him I but express with my own the wishes of all, that he may yet long live to enjoy the brilliant evening of his well-spent life; and for myself, conscious of but one desire, faithfully to serve my country, I throw myself without fear on its justice and its kindness. Beyond that I only look to the gracious protection of the Divine Being whose strengthening support I humbly solicit, and whom I fervently pray to look down upon us all. May it be among the dispensations of His providence to bless our beloved country with honors and with length of days. May her ways be ways of pleasantness and all her paths be peace![6]

In his official messages and papers, Van Buren made only one other religious statement. In his second annual message, delivered on December 3, 1838, he said: "All forms of religion have united for the first time to diffuse charity and piety, because for the first time in the history of nations all have been totally untrammeled and absolutely free."[7]

While he was president, he attended St. John's Church Lafayette Square (Episcopal), as there was no Dutch Reformed church was in Washington at the time.[8]

During the last years of her life, Hannah Hoes Van Buren became a Presbyterian. Though Martin Van Buren remained in the Dutch Reformed Church, at times he attended a Presbyterian church with her until her death on February 5, 1819.[9]

He died on July 24, 1862, in Kinderhook, New York. His funeral was held at the Kinderhook Reformed Church; the hymn "O God, Our Help in Ages Past" was the only music played.[10]

William Federer's book, *America's God and Country*, stated that Martin Van Buren made a confession of faith on his deathbed, stating that "the atonement of Jesus Christ is the only remedy and rest for my soul."[11] Since I have found no mention of this in any other account of his death, I have been unable to confirm or refute the accuracy of the report.

HISTORICAL CONTROVERSIES

Was Van Buren a member of the Dutch Reformed Church?

In his book *The Religious Beliefs of Our Presidents*, agnostic writer Franklin Steiner admitted that Van Buren attended Kinderhook Reformed Church in Kinderhook and St. John's Episcopal Church in Washington, but stated that he could "find no positive evidence that he was a communicant in either Church, or that he took any interest in religious subjects other than conventional adherence."[12] While Van Buren might not have been a communicant, Steiner's wording implies that he was not a church member at all. This was not the case.

Several sources have stated that Martin Van Buren was a member of the Dutch Reformed Church. In his book, *The Presidents: Men of Faith*, Bliss Isley stated: "Van Buren was a member of the Dutch Reformed Church, a regular attendant at services throughout his life, and probably he was a student of the Scriptures. It is known that he always kept a Bible on a cabinet in his room for ready reference."[13] In *Churches of the Presidents in Washington*, Olga Jones noted that Van Buren was "recorded as being a member of the Dutch Reformed Church."[14] Tom Martino, a ranger at the Martin Van Buren National Historic Site (Lindenwald), stated that Van Buren was a member of the Kinderhook Reformed Church in his youth.[15]

CONCLUSION

We know less about Van Buren's religious beliefs than about the beliefs of most other presidents. We do know he was a longtime member of his church and by all accounts was an active participant in its services.

NOTES

1. Dennis Tilden Lynch, *An Epoch and a Man: Martin Van Buren and His Times* (New York: Horace Liveright, 1929), 128.

2. Edmund Fuller and David E. Green, *God in the White House: The Faiths of American Presidents* (New York: Crown Publishers, 1968), 69.

3. Lynch, *An Epoch and a Man,* 128.

4. Ibid.

5. Ibid., 531.

6. Van Buren, March 4, 1837. Inaugural address.

7. Van Buren, *Messages and Papers of the Presidents: Martin Van Buren, 1838.* December 3, 1838. Second annual message.

8. Lynch, *An Epoch and a Man,* 446.

9. Ibid., 308.

10. Ibid., 545.

11. William J. Federer, ed., *America's God and Country: Encyclopedia of Quotations* (Coppel, TX: Fame Publishing, 1994), 621.

12. Franklin Steiner, *The Religious Beliefs of Our Presidents* (Girard, KS: Haldeman-Julius, 1936; repr., Amherst, NY: Prometheus Books, 1995), 95.

13. Bliss Isley, *The Presidents: Men of Faith* (Boston: W. A. Wilde, 1953), 64.

14. Olga Anna Jones, *Churches of the Presidents in Washington: Visits to Fifteen National Shrines* (New York: Exposition Press, 1954), 79. This statement was included in a chapter on Grace Reformed Church in Washington (T. Roosevelt's church). Jones stated that Van Buren's church membership "was long before Grace Reformed Church had been organized."

15. From a telephone conversation with Ranger Tom Martino, 2004. The National Park Service maintains the Martin Van Buren National Historic Site.

CHAPTER 36

ANDREW JACKSON

ANDREW JACKSON was born on March 15, 1767, in Waxhaw, South Carolina. His father died before he was born.[1] His mother, Betty Jackson, raised Jackson in the Presbyterian Church and taught him the Westminster Catechism.[2] She even hoped that he would become a Presbyterian minister.[3]

In 1791, Andrew Jackson married Rachel Donelson. While her previous husband had said that he would divorce her, he did not do so until after this wedding. So, on January 17, 1794, after Donelson's divorce was finalized, Jackson and Donelson married a second time.

During Rachel's lifetime, Jackson attended her Presbyterian church. He even built a chapel at his estate, The Hermitage, for her. But when she urged him to join the Presbyterian Church, he responded, "My dear, if I were to do that now, it would be said, all over the country, that I had done it for the sake of political effect. My enemies would all say so. I can not do it *now*, but I promise you that when once more I am clear of politics I will join the church."[4]

While he did not feel comfortable making a public profession of faith, he did maintain a habit of daily Bible reading, reading three chapters of the Bible every day throughout most of his married life.[5]

In 1828, Jackson mounted a successful campaign for the presidency. During the campaign, Martin Van Buren, one of Jackson's campaign managers, decided to make an issue of the candidates' religious beliefs. John Quincy Adams was a Unitarian, and Jackson attended a Presbyterian church, so Van Buren thought he could portray Jackson as "a more orthodox believer."[6] Van Buren wrote New York publisher James Hamilton, saying: "Does the old gentleman have prayers in his own House? If so, mention it modestly." In response, Hamilton printed that Jackson was "a sincere believer in the Christian religion, and performs his devotions regularly with his family in his own House, and in a Presbyterian Church in his neighborhood."[7]

Jackson won the election. On December 22 of that year, Rachel died. Though heartbroken, Jackson took office in 1829. He concluded his first inaugural address with these words: "And a firm reliance on the goodness of that Power whose providence mercifully protected our national infancy, and has since upheld our liberties in various vicissitudes, encourages me to offer up my ardent supplications that He will continue to make our beloved country the object of His divine care and gracious benediction."[8]

He expressed similar sentiments in the conclusion of his second inaugural address: "Finally, it is my most fervent prayer to that Almighty Being before whom I now stand, and who has kept us in His hands from the infancy of our Republic to the present day, that He will so overrule all my intentions and actions and inspire the hearts of my fellow-citizens that we may be preserved from dangers of all kinds and continue forever a united and happy people."[9]

Although Jackson publicly and privately expressed his reliance upon and thanksgiving to God, he did not feel that it was within the powers of his office to set a date for Americans to express Thanksgiving to God. Thus, he did not issue any Thanksgiving proclamations.

During his two terms, Jackson faithfully attended a Presbyterian church and paid his pew rent regularly.[10]

In 1833, Jackson's friend General John Coffee died. Jackson sent a letter of condolences to the family, which biographer Robert Remini quoted from and summarized in these words:

> "He is gone from us, and we cannot recall him. we [sic] must follow him . . . and it becomes our duty to prepare for this event." It is religion alone, he said, "that can give peace to us here, and happiness beyond the grave." Only religion can support us in our dying years. All else is "vanity and vexation of spirit." On his dying bed, Coffee had expressed regret that he had not joined the church and he admonished his family not to follow his example.

This "admonition," Jackson added in his letter to the family, "ought to be cherished by you all, and practiced upon." Apparently, Coffee had also asked for Jackson's prayers for his wife and children, and Old Hickory acknowledged that "they will be constantly offered up at the throne of grace for you all." Rely on "our dear Savior," he wrote; He will be father to the fatherless and husband to the widow. Trust in the mercy and goodness of Christ, and "always be ready to say with heartfelt resignation, 'may the Lord's will be done.' "[11]

He wrote a similar letter about a year later, to console his grand-nephew Andrew Jackson Hutchings and his wife Mary after their baby died. The letter, dated January 25, 1835, said:

I am truly happy to find that you both have met this severe bereavement with that christian [sic] meekness & submission as was your duty. This charming babe was only given you from your great creator and benefactor, it is probable you doated [sic] upon him too much, to the neglect of him who gave the boon, & he has taken him from you, to bring to your view that to him your first love is due, and by this chastisement, to bring you back to your duty to god [sic]—it is to him we owe all things—it is he that giveth, and he has a right to take away, and we ought humbly to submit to his will, and be always ready to say, blessed be his name. We have one consolation under this severe bereavement, that this babe is now in the boosom [sic] of its saviour, a sweet little angel in heaven, free from all the temptation, pains & evils of this world and we ought to prepare to unite with him & other sorts [saints] who have gone before us to those mansions of bliss, where the weary are at rest—Then let us not mourn for the dead but for the living, and prepare to follow him to the mansions of bliss.[12]

Jackson had promised his wife that he would join the Presbyterian Church after he returned to private life; he fulfilled this promise on July 15, 1838. He said in a letter a month later, "I would long since have made this solemn public dedication to Almighty God, but knowing the wretchedness of this world, and how prone many are to evil, that the scoffer of religion would have cried out—'hypocrisy! he has joined the church for political effect,' I thought it best to postpone this public act until my retirement to the shades of private life, when no false imputation could be made that might be injurious to religion."[13]

Two clergymen, Reverend James Smith and Reverend Dr. John Todd Edgar played a role in his decision to make a public profession of faith. Reverend Smith was pastor of the Hermitage Church, a church Jackson had constructed on his estate. Reverend Dr. Edgar was pastor of the First Presbyterian Church of Nashville.[14]

Reverend Smith had been reluctant to admit Jackson to the church, because of his beliefs on election and possibly other doctrines. Reverend Dr. Edgar wanted to admit Jackson and his daughter, Sarah. As an inducement for them to join, Edgar declined to baptize Sarah Jackson's child unless she joined the church.

When biographer James Parton was researching his 1859–60 three-volume biography of Jackson, Edgar, who at that time was still the pastor of the First Presbyterian Church of Nashville, sent him an account of Jackson's conversion.

Edgar's firsthand account, as rendered by Parton, is the only original source known to be extant on Jackson's conversion. Because it is only found in a rare book nearly 150 years old, I decided to reprint the account here. Parton wrote:

> Ere long a "protracted meeting" was held in the little church on the Hermitage farm. Dr. Edgar conducted the exercises, and the family at the Hermitage were constant in their attendance. The last day of the meeting arrived, which was also the last day of the week. General Jackson sat in his accustomed seat, and Dr. Edgar preached. The subject of the sermon was the interposition of Providence in the affairs of men, a subject congenial with the habitual tone of General Jackson's mind. The preacher spoke in detail of the perils which beset the life of man, and how often he is preserved from sickness and sudden death. Seeing General Jackson listening with rapt attention to his discourse, the eloquent preacher sketched the career of a man who, in addition to the ordinary dangers of human life, had encountered those of the wilderness, of war, and of keen political conflict; who had escaped the tomahawk of the savage, the attack of his country's enemies, the privations and fatigues of border warfare, and the aim of the assassin. How is it, exclaimed the preacher, that a man endowed with reason and gifted with intelligence can pass through such scenes

as these unharmed, and not see the hand of God in his deliverance? While enlarging on this theme, Dr. Edgar saw that his words
were sinking deep into the General's heart, and he spoke with
unusual animation and impressiveness.

The service ended, General Jackson got into his carriage, and
was riding homeward. He was overtaken by Dr. Edgar on horse-
back. He hailed the Doctor, and said he wished to speak with him.
Both having alighted, the General led the clergyman a little way
into the grove.

"Doctor," said the General, "I want you to come home with
me to-night."

"I can not to-night," was the reply; "I am engaged elsewhere."

"Doctor," repeated the General, "I want you to come home
with me tonight."

Dr. Edgar said that he had promised to visit that evening a sick
lady, and he felt bound to keep his promise. General Jackson, as
though he had not heard the reply, said a third time, and more
pleadingly than before:

"Doctor, I *want* you to come home with me to-night."

"General Jackson," said the clergyman, "my word is pledged;
I can not break it; but I will be at the Hermitage to-morrow
morning very early."

The anxious man was obliged to be contented with this
arrangement, and went home alone. He retired to his apartment.
He passed the evening and the greater part of the night in meditation, in reading, in conversing with his beloved daughter, in
prayers. He was sorely distressed. Late at night, when his daughter left him, he was still agitated and sorrowful. What thoughts
passed through his mind as he paced his room in the silence of the
night, of *what* sins he repented, and what actions of his life he
wished he had not done, no one knows, or will ever know.

But the value of this upheaving of the soul depends upon that.
There is a repentance which is radical, sublime, regenerating. There
is a repentance which is shallow and fruitless. Conversion means a
turning. It is only when we know from what a man turns, and to
what he turns, that we can know whether his turning is of any benefit to him. There is such a thing as a man's emancipating himself,
in one night of agony and joy, in one thrilling instant of time, from
the domination of pride and desire. He who is walking along the

plain can not reach the mountain top in a moment; but in a moment he can set his face toward it, and begin to scale the height. Touching the nature and worth of this crisis in General Jackson's life I know nothing, and can say nothing. We shall soon have an opportunity of observing whether the *spirit* of the man had changed, or whether to the last he remained what we have seen him hitherto.

As the day was breaking, light seemed to dawn upon his troubled soul, and a great peace fell upon him.

To Dr. Edgar, who came to him soon after sunrise, General Jackson told the joyful history of the night, and expressed a desire to be admitted into the church with his daughter that very morning. The usual questions respecting doctrine and experience were satisfactorily answered by the candidate. Then there was a pause in the conversation. The clergyman said at length:

"General, there is one more question which it is my duty to ask you. Can you forgive all your enemies?"

The question was evidently unexpected, and the candidate was silent for a while.

"My political enemies," said he, "I can freely forgive; but as for those who abused me when I was serving my country in the field, and those who attacked me *for* serving my country—Doctor, that is a different case."

The Doctor assured him that it was not. Christianity, he said, forbade the indulgence of enmity absolutely and in all cases. No man could be received into a Christian church who did not cast out of his heart every feeling of that nature. It was a condition that was fundamental and indispensable.

After a considerable pause the candidate said that he thought he could forgive all who had injured him, even those who had assailed him for what he done for his country in the field. The clergyman then consented to his sharing in the solemn ceremonial of the morning, and left the room to communicate the glad tidings to Mrs. Jackson [Jackson's daughter in law]. She hastened to the General's apartment. They rushed with tears into each other's arms, and remained long in a fond and silent embrace.

The Hermitage church was crowded to the utmost of its small capacity; the very windows were darkened with the eager faces of the servants. After the usual services, the General rose to make the required public declaration of his concurrence with the doctrines, and his resolve to obey the precepts, of the church. He leaned heavily upon his stick with both hands; tears rolled down his cheeks. His daughter, the fair, young matron, stood beside him. Amid a silence the most profound, the General answered the questions proposed to him. When he was formally pronounced a member of the church, and the clergyman was about to continue the services, the long restrained feeling of the congregation burst forth in sobs and exclamations, which compelled him to pause for several minutes. The clergyman himself was speechless with emotion, and abandoned himself to the exultation of the hour. A familiar hymn was raised, in which the entire assembly, both within and without the church, joined with an ecstatic fervor which at once expressed and relieved their feelings.[15]

Reverend Smith, the regular pastor at the Hermitage, was disappointed and perhaps somewhat miffed to hear that Edgar had admitted Jackson. Smith vented his feelings on paper. He stated: "To be honest and candid, I *do regret* that General Jackson joined the church when he did and as he did," adding that he would "not have accepted General Jackson into our church."[16]

Yet whatever Reverend Smith's cautions were, Jackson went through the ceremony wholeheartedly. In the words of biographer Remini, he "rose in his place to announce he desired to join the church. He further declared his belief in its doctrines, and his resolve to obey its precepts."[17]

For the rest of his life, President Jackson was an active Christian. He regularly attended church, read his Bible (with Scott's *Commentaries* and his hymn book) every day, and held nightly meetings for his family and servants. In these meetings, he read prayers and sometimes expounded Bible verses.[18]

After his conversion, the Hermitage Church began organizing regular meetings. General Jackson was nominated to be a ruling elder of the church. He said: "No, the Bible says, 'Be not hasty in laying on of hands.' I am too young in the church for such an office. My countrymen have given me high honors, but I should esteem the office of ruling elder in the church of Christ, a far higher honor than any I have ever received."[19] He proposed two other men for the position.

Although Jackson believed many of the Presbyterian doctrines, he apparently had a hard time accepting the doctrine of election, holding instead to the doctrine that all men could be saved. As he once asked a Presbyterian clergyman, "Brother Bain, do you mean to tell me that when my Saviour said 'Come unto me, *all* ye who labor and are heavy laden,' he didn't mean what he said?"[20]

In 1838, when a friend, Ralph Earl, suddenly died, Jackson wrote: "I must soon follow him, and hope to meet him and those friends who have gone before me in the realms of bliss thro the mediation of a dear redeemer, Jesus Christ."[21]

In spring 1845, Jackson approached death. He was visited by many friends who wanted to bid him farewell. One of these was General Thomas Jessup. Jackson told Jessup: "Sir, I am in the hands of a merciful God. I have full confidence in his goodness and mercy. . . . The Bible is true. . . . I have tried to conform to its spirit as near as possible. Upon that sacred volume I rest my hope for eternal salvation, through the merits and blood of our blessed Lord and Saviour, Jesus Christ."[22]

Jackson died on June 18, 1845. His will, completed in 1843, began with these words: "*First*, I bequeath my body to the dust whence it comes, and my soul to God who gave it, hoping for a happy immortality through the atoning merits of our Lord Jesus Christ, the Savior of the world."[23]

CONCLUSION

Through Jackson's public life, he read his Bible and maintained the outward forms of religion. In all likelihood, he believed most of the essential doctrines of Christianity through those years. Once he retired from public life, he made a public confession of faith—a confession that, to the best we can determine from eyewitness accounts, was not a mere form but was one that reflected a heartfelt conviction and belief in Jesus Christ.

NOTES

1. Hendrik Booraem, *Young Hickory: The Making of Andrew Jackson* (Dallas: Taylor Trade Publishing, 2001), 19.

2. Ibid., 20–21.

3. Robert V. Remini, *Andrew Jackson and the Course of American Democracy, 1833–1845* (New York: Harper & Row, 1984), 7.

4. Paul F. Boller Jr., *Presidential Campaigns* (New York and Oxford: Oxford University Press, 1984), 52.

5. Jackson stated that for the thirty-five years preceding his presidency, it was his habit to read three chapters of the Bible every day. Thus, he started about 1793.

6. Boller, *Presidential Campaigns*, 51.

7. Ibid.

8. Jackson, *Messages and Papers of the Presidents: Andrew Jackson, 1829*. March 4, 1829. First inaugural address.

9. Ibid., March 4, 1833. Second inaugural address.

10. Olga Anna Jones, *Churches of the Presidents in Washington: Visits to Fifteen National Shrines* (New York: Exposition Press, 1954), 24.

11. Remini, *Andrew Jackson*, 91.

12. Ibid., 226.

13. James Parton, *Life of Andrew Jackson*, vol. 3 (Boston and New York: Houghton Mifflin, 1860), 643.

14. Ibid., 644.

15. Ibid., 644–48.

16. Remini, *Andrew Jackson*, 446–47.

17. Ibid., 447.

18. Ibid. Remini said that Jackson "read prayers in the presence of his family and servants, and sometimes he offered short homilies of his own." Remini also noted that Jackson read through "Scott's Bible" twice before his death.

19. Parton, *Life of Andrew Jackson*, vol. 3, 648.

20. Remini, *Andrew Jackson*, 444.

21. Ibid., 448.

22. Ibid., 519.

23. Parton, *Life of Andrew Jackson*, vol. 3, 650; Joseph N. Kane, *Facts About the Presidents: A Compilation of Biographical and Historical Data*, 1st ed. (New York: H. W. Wilson, 1959), 61.

CHAPTER 37

JOHN QUINCY ADAMS

JOHN QUINCY ADAMS was born on July 11, 1767, in Braintree, Massachusetts.

He married Louisa Catherine Johnson on July 26, 1797.

In 1812, Adams began writing letters about the Bible to his son, George Washington Adams. He finished the series on September 14, 1813.[1]

In 1816, John Quincy Adams was the U. S. Minister to Great Britain. His father wrote asking John Quincy to debate whether the Bible was fallible with him. John Quincy Adams responded that he did not want to debate the topic, since he was "not called upon to be its judge."[2] When John Adams persisted, John Quincy, in the words of biographer Paul Nagel, "conceded that he cautiously followed the doctrines of Trinitarianism and Calvinism, although, he added, 'I do not approve of their intolerance.' "[3] John Quincy Adams did not approve of Unitarianism or of Joseph Priestley, one of the movement's leaders. He "challenged his father to read Bishop Massillon's sermon on the divinity of Christ, 'after which you can be a Socinian if you can.' " John Quincy concluded, "I hope you will not think me in danger of perishing everlastingly, for believing too much."[4]

In June and July of 1817, Adams sailed home to take the position of secretary of state. On the voyage, he explained to a scoffer his reasons for holding "the faith that is within me."[5] According to biographer Nagel, this "encounter set Adams to wondering why others could not accept that the entire Bible was a succession of miracles from beginning to end, 'and that if any one of them is admitted, it is dealing with trifles to contend about any other.' "[6]

While secretary of state, Adams was elected president of the American Bible Society. He accepted the office because "he had become alarmed by two developments in the nation's religious attitude: the contrasting appeals of Unitarianism and Evangelicalism," Nagel said. "These schools of thought challenged the very personal spiritual views he had adopted while in Europe. Consequently, after 1817 his diary began featuring rebuttals of genial Unitarianism and of intolerant Fundamentalism, both of which he considered to be threats to republican society."[7]

He disliked Unitarianism because it considered religion "as merely a system of morals." He cited as a disturbing example Henry Clay's comment after a Unitarian church service that Clay was "much pleased with this system of religion that the clergymen of Boston are now getting up [underlining in original]."[8]

Adams' diary establishes beyond doubt that he was not a deist—that he believed in a God who still directed the courses of people and of nations. An entry commemorating the end of the year 1812 reads:

> *Dec.* 3—I offer to a merciful God at the close of this year my humble tribute of gratitude for the blessings with which He has in the course of it favored me and those who are dear to me, and I pray for a continuance of his goodness. Above all, I pray that He who worketh in us both to will and to do, may grant to me and mine that temper of heart and that firmness of soul which are best adapted daily to receive all his dispensations, whether joyous or afflictive. It has pleased Him in the course of this year to lay his chastening hand on me, and to try me with bitter sorrow. My endeavors to quell the rebellion of the heart have been sincere, and have been assisted with the blessing from above. As I advance in life its evils multiply, the instances of mortality become more frequent, and approach nearer to myself. The greater is the need of fortitude to encounter the woes that flesh is heir to, and of religion to support pains for which there is no other remedy. Religious sentiments become from day to day more constantly habitual to my mind.[9]

In 1814, when Adams was chosen to negotiate with Great Britain to end the War of 1812, he wrote in his April 22 diary entry: "The weight of the trust committed, though but in part, to me, the difficulties, to all human appearance insuperable, which forbid the hope of success, the universal gloom of the prospect before me, would depress a mind of more sanguine complexion than mine. On the providence of God alone is my reliance. The prayer for light and vigilance, and presence of mind and fortitude and resignation, is fine, for strength proportioned to my trial, is incessant upon my heart. The welfare of my family and country, with the interests of humanity, are staked upon the event. To Heaven alone it must be committed."[10]

Several years later, after negotiating a treaty with Spain over Florida, he wrote a message to his sons in a February 22, 1821, diary entry: "Let my sons, if they ever consult this record of their father's life, turn back to the reflections of the journal of that day [the day the Florida treaty was signed]. Let them meditate upon all the vicissitudes which have befallen the treaty, and of which this diary bears witness, in the interval between that day and this. Let them remark the workings of private interests, of perfidious fraud, of sordid intrigues, of royal treachery, of malignant rivalry, and of envy masked with patriotism, playing to and fro across the Atlantic into each other's hands, all combined to destroy this treaty between the signature and the ratification, and let them learn to put their trust into the overruling providence of God."[11]

During his earlier years, Adams wrote several pieces of poetry. He set several psalms to music, including the Twenty-third Psalm:

> My shepherd is the Lord on high;
> His hand supplies me still;
> In pastures green He makes me lie,
> Beside the rippling rill.
> He cheers my soul, relieves my woes,
> His glory to display;
> The paths of righteousness He shows
> And leads me in His way.[12]

Adams was elected president in 1824 and served one term. He concluded his inaugural address by asking for God's help: "To the guidance of the legislative councils, to the assistance of the executive and subordinate departments, to the friendly cooperation of the respective State governments, to the candid and liberal support of the people so far as it may be deserved by honest industry and zeal, I shall look for whatever success may attend my public service; and knowing that "except the Lord keep the city the watchman waketh but in vain," with fervent supplications for His favor, to His overruling providence I commit with humble but fearless confidence my own fate and the future destinies of my country."[13]

On July 4, 1828, John Quincy Adams participated in the groundbreaking ceremonies for the Erie Canal. In his speech for the occasion, he said that the American vision was developed in three stages. The first was marked by the Declaration of Independence; the second was marked by the Constitution. He said that the third, national improvement, began then. The preeminent purpose of the canal, he believed, was a step in fulfilling God's command to "replenish the Earth, and subdue it."[14]

During Adams' earlier years in Washington, his church attendance was sporadic. An 1819 diary entry states: "Since I have now resided at Washington I have not regularly attended at any church—partly because I have permitted the week to encroach too much upon the Sabbath, and have not been sufficiently attentive to the duties of the day, but chiefly because, although the churches here are numerous and diversified, not one of them is of the Independent Congregational class to which I belong, the church to which I was bred, and in which I will die."[15]

By the time he was elected president, however, Adams attended three churches—Unitarian, Episcopal, and Presbyterian—every Sunday, in the morning, afternoon, and evening.[16] Until his 1827 death, Robert Little was the pastor of the Unitarian church Adams attended during his presidency and congressional service. The church was located at Sixth and D Streets, N.W., in Washington, DC. On Sunday afternoons, he attended the Second Presbyterian Church, where the pastor was Reverend Daniel Baker.[17] Adams was a trustee there.

After his father's death in July 1826, Adams told Peter Whitney, the pastor of the Unitarian Church of Quincy, that he wanted to join. On October 1, according to biographer Samuel Flagg Bemis, "The pastor asked each of those present who wished to express a belief in the divine mission of Christ, and who had a fixed purpose to live according to the rules of his gospel, to rise."[18] Along with several others, Adams rose and formally joined the church.[19]

After his term as president, Adams embarked on what was perhaps the most illustrious portion of his public career—service in the United States House of Representatives. Adams was one of the earliest and most vocal supporters of the abolitionist cause. He expressed his views on whether a representative was to strictly follow the wishes of his electorate in these words: "The magistrate is the servant not... of the people but of his God."[20]

Adams used biblical arguments in an 1845 debate over the nation's right to the Oregon Territory, a territory also claimed by Great Britain. He asked the clerk to read from Genesis 1:26–28, which, he said, was the "foundation of our title."

The clerk read: "And God said, Let us make man in our image, after our likeness: and let them have dominion over the fish of the sea, and over the fowl of the air, and over the cattle, and over all the earth, and over every creeping thing that creepeth upon the earth. So God created man in his own image, in the image of God created He him; male and female created He them. And God blessed them, and God said unto them, Be fruitful, and multiply, and replenish the earth, and subdue it: and have dominion over the fish of the sea, and over the fowl of the air, and over every living thing that moveth upon the earth."

Adams declared: "There, sir, in my judgment, is the foundation not only of our title to Oregon but the foundation of all human title to all human possessions." He said that he could not cite the Bible if the controversy was with a non-Christian, but that "It is between Christian nations that the foundation of title to land is laid in the first chapter of Genesis, and it is in this book that the title to jurisdiction, to eminent domain, has its foundation."

He then asked the clerk to read Psalm 2:8: "Ask of me, and I shall give *thee* the heathen *for* thine inheritance, and the uttermost parts of the earth *for* thy possession," and concluded that God wanted the territory to belong to the United States, because "We claim that country to make the wilderness blossom, to establish laws, to increase . . . and to subdue the earth, which we are commanded to do by the first behest of God Almighty. She [Great Britain] claims it . . . for navigation, for her hunters to hunt the wild beast. There is the difference between our claims."[21]

Adams won his case; the House voted to withdraw from the treaty by which the United States and Great Britain agreed to govern the territory jointly. The Senate also voted to withdraw, and the process was set in place that led to Oregon's admission to the Union.

On April 30, 1829, John Quincy and Louisa's son, George Washington Adams, died on a steamer in Long Island Sound. Some suspected that George had committed suicide. The parents were devastated. The tragedy drew them nearer to each other. Louisa said that John Quincy became "a ministering angel, always at my side."[22] According to Margaret Truman's book on *First Ladies*, "They read comforting passages in their Bibles to each other." She also quoted from a letter John Quincy wrote another son, Charles: "We are in great distress. But the first Shock of this heavy dispensation of Providence is past, and your Mother and myself, relying on him who chastiseth in Mercy, still look for consolation in the affectionate kindness of our remaining sons."[23]

Early in his life, Adams began a lifelong practice of daily Bible reading. In an 1809 diary entry describing a typical day, he stated that he woke up "about six o'clock, often earlier," and "read ten or fifteen chapters in the Bible."[24] Beginning in about 1801 and continuing for the remainder of his life, he also read sermons by John Tillotson, the archbishop of Canterbury from 1691 to 1694.[25]

Adams read through the Bible every year. From time to time, he would read the Bible in a foreign translation. His March 13, 1812, diary entry stated:

> *March* 13—This morning I finished the perusal of the German Bible, which I began 20th June last. There are many differences of translation from either the English or the French translation— some of which I have compared in the three versions. Many passages, obscure and even unintelligible to me in the English, are clear in the French and German. Of the three, the German, I think, has the fewest of these obscurities. But the eloquence of St. Paul strikes me as more elevated and sublime in the English than in either of the others.[26]

During his presidency, Adams rose at five, read two chapters of Scott's *Bible and Commentary*, "and the corresponding Commentary of Hewlett."[27]

How orthodox were Adams' religious beliefs? Edmund Fuller and David Green stated that John Quincy Adams rejected orthodox Calvinism and moved toward Unitarianism.[28] On the other hand, biographer Bemis stated that there "was always a 'smack of orthodoxy' about Adams."[29]

Let us look at his views on different doctrines. In 1846, he wrote down his mental debate over whether Christ was sent by God to atone for the sins of mankind. Biographer Nagel states: " 'I cannot believe it,' he said of atonement. 'It is not true. It is hateful. But how shall I contradict St. Paul?' "[30] He knew that what Paul wrote was in the Bible. Adams also said what he did believe: "I reverence God as my creator. As creator of the world. I reverence him with holy fear. I venerate Jesus Christ as my redeemer; and, as far as I can understand, the redeemer of the world. But this belief is dark and uncertain."[31]

Once, when Adams was asked whether he was a Trinitarian or a Unitarian, he answered: "I believe in one God, but His nature is incomprehensible to me, and of the question between the Unitarians and the Trinitarians I have no definite belief, because no definite understanding."[32]

At another time, Daniel Baker asked him for his views on the topic. He answered: "I am not either a Trinitarian or a Unitarian. I believe the nature of Jesus Christ is superhuman; but whether he is God, or only the first of human beings, is not clearly revealed to me in the Scriptures."[33]

Biographer Bemis stated that Adams was not "sure about the virgin birth or miracles." Bemis also said that Adams "held that the Bible, despite numerous allegorical passages, was in essence divine revelation."[34] Concerning references to the supernatural, Bemis stated: "The Bible bothered him with its literal statements. How about the miracles? He did not believe that they were beyond the power of an almighty Creator, but he had come to doubt the *facts* as related in the Scriptures."[35]

Yet Adams retained some belief in God. In about 1845, he wrote: "For I believe there is a god [sic] who heareth prayer, and that honest prayers to him will not be in vain."[36]

John Quincy Adams died on February 23, 1848.

CONCLUSION

Adams was raised in an essentially orthodox environment. Later in life, he struggled with what he could not know and prove. Rather than accepting the unknowable on faith and on the Bible's authority, he chose to doubt whether various doctrines were true. His eternal destiny was decided by his conclusions, which we will not know this side of eternity.

NOTES

1. Paul C. Nagel, *John Quincy Adams: A Public Life, A Private Life* (New York: Knopf, 1997), 203.

2. Ibid., 124.

3. Ibid., 231.

4. Ibid.

5. Ibid., 235.

6. Ibid.

7. Ibid., 260.

8. Ibid., 261. It was not Adams's custom to underline passages in his diary, so this shows particular concern.

9. John Quincy Adams, *The Diary of John Quincy Adams, 1794–1845*, ed. Allan Nevins (New York: Longman, Green, 1929; repr., New York: Charles Scribners, 1951), 103.

10. Ibid., 119.

11. Ibid., 255.

12. Leonard Falkner, *The President Who Wouldn't Retire: John Quincy Adams, Congressman from Massachusetts* (New York: Coward-McCann, 1967), 38.

13. Adams, March 4, 1825. Inaugural address.

14. Mary W. M. Hargreaves, *The Presidency of John Quincy Adams* (Lawrence: University Press of Kansas, 1985), 178.

15. Adams, *The Diary of John Quincy Adams*, 217.

16. Nagel, *John Quincy Adams*, 308.

17. Samuel Flagg Bemis, *John Quincy Adams and the Union* (New York: Knopf, 1956), 103.

18. Ibid., 111.

19. Hargreaves, *The Presidency of John Quincy Adams*, 114.

20. John Fitzgerald Kennedy, *Profiles in Courage* (New York: Harper & Brothers, 1955, 1964, 2006), 31.

21. Falkner, *The President Who Wouldn't Retire*, 294–96.

22. Margaret Truman, *First Ladies: An Intimate Group Portrait of White House Wives* (New York: Random House, 1995), 285.

23. Ibid.

24. Adams, *The Diary of John Quincy Adams*, 61.

25. Nagel, *John Quincy Adams*, 124.

26. Adams, *The Diary of John Quincy Adams*, 91.

27. Ibid., 345.

28. Edmund Fuller and David E. Green, *God in the White House: The Faiths of American Presidents* (New York: Crown Publishers, 1968), 58.

29. Samuel Flagg Bemis, *John Quincy Adams and the Foundations of American Foreign Policy* (New York: Knopf, 1949), 8.

30. Nagel, *John Quincy Adams,* 407.

31. Ibid.

32. Adams, *Memoirs of John Quincy Adams, Comprising Portions of His Diary from 1795 to 1848,* ed. Charles Francis Adams, vol. 7 (Philadelphia, 1874–77, 12 vol.), 324.

33. Ibid., 477.

34. Bemis, *John Quincy Adams and the Foundations,* 7.

35. Bemis, *John Quincy Adams and the Union,* 105. Italics in the original.

36. Nagel, *John Quincy Adams,* 405. He was an old man by this writing, and his handwriting was deteriorating. The lack of capitalization of God's name may not have been intentional.

CHAPTER 38

JAMES MONROE

JAMES MONROE was born on April 28, 1758, in Westmoreland County, Virginia. His parents were Scottish Presbyterians.[1]

He married Elizabeth Kortright on February 16, 1786.

He was elected president in 1816 and served two terms. In his first inaugural address, he paid tribute to our nation's religious liberty, asking: "On whom has oppression fallen in any quarter of our Union? Who has been deprived of any right of person or property? Who restrained from offering his vows in the mode which he prefers to the Divine Author of his being? It is well known that all these blessings have been enjoyed in their fullest extent."[2]

He also recognized God's hand guiding the country. "If we persevere in the career in which we have advanced so far and in the path already traced, we can not fail, under the favor of a gracious Providence, to attain the high destiny which seems to await us." He concluded: "I enter on the trust to which I have been called by the suffrages of my fellow-citizens with my fervent prayers to the Almighty that He will be graciously pleased to continue to us that protection which He has already so conspicuously displayed in our favor."[3]

In Monroe's second inaugural address, he said that the "happiness of our country will always be the object of my most fervent prayers to the Supreme Author of All Good." He concluded: "With full confidence in the continuance of that candor and generous indulgence from my fellow-citizens at large which I have heretofore experienced, and with a firm reliance on the protection of Almighty God, I shall forthwith commence the duties of the high trust to which you have called me."[4]

Another religious statement Monroe made while President was in his eighth annual message. After discussing the condition of the United States, he said: "For these blessings we owe to Almighty God, from whom we derive them, and with profound reverence, our most grateful and unceasing acknowledgments."[5]

While president, Monroe attended St. John's Church Lafayette Square "with regularity." Yet Monroe was "not a member of any given church," and a paper in the St. John's Church archives stated that Monroe "agreed with Jefferson that religion is 'a matter between our Maker and ourselves.' "[6]

He died on July 4, 1831, in New York City.

CONCLUSION

Monroe believed that religion was a private matter and did not discuss his religious beliefs in preserved correspondence. Historians researching his religion have little information and cannot form conclusions on the topic.

NOTES

1. E. Stacy Matheny, *American Patriotic Devotions* (New York: Association Press, 1932), 118.

2. Monroe, *Messages and Papers of the Presidents: James Monroe, 1817.* March 4, 1817. First inaugural address.

3. Ibid.

4. Ibid., March 5, 1821. Second inaugural address.

5. Ibid., December 7, 1824. Eighth annual address.

6. Olga Anna Jones, *Churches of the Presidents in Washington: Visits to Fifteen National Shrines* (New York: Exposition Press, 1954), 27.

CHAPTER 39

JAMES MADISON

JAMES MADISON was born on March 16, 1751, in Port Conway, Virginia. His parents, James and Molly Conway Madison, were devout Episcopalians; James (the father) was even a vestryman in the St. Thomas parish. They had James baptized when he was twenty-one days old.[1] Madison eventually became a communicant in the Episcopalian church.

In 1772, Madison wrote his friend William Bradford: "[A] watchful eye must be kept on ourselves lest while we are building ideal monuments of Renown and Bliss here we neglect to have our names enrolled in the Annals of Heaven."[2] When Bradford decided against entering the ministry, Madison expressed a hope that Bradford might someday become "a fervent advocate in the cause of Christ."[3]

James Madison studied theology at Princeton University in preparation for entering the ministry. In 1910, Bishop William Meade wrote: "During his stay at Princeton a great revival took place, and it was believed that he partook of its spirit. On his return home he conducted worship in his father's house. He soon after offered for the Legislature, and it was objected to him, by his opponents, that he was better suited to the pulpit than to the legislative hall."[4]

Biographer Ralph Ketcham noted that through Madison's university career, "every one of Madison's teachers, as far was we know, was either a clergyman or a devoutly orthodox Christian layman."[5] He also said:

> Though much of the Christian aspect of Madison's schooling was relatively perfunctory and he seems never to have been an ardent

believer himself, he nonetheless year after year undertook his studies from a Christian viewpoint. Furthermore, he never took an
antireligious or even an anti-Christian stance, and he retained the
respect and admiration of the devoutly orthodox young men with
whom he studied at Princeton. It seems clear he neither embraced
fervently nor rejected utterly the Christian base of his education.
He accepted its tenets generally and formed his outlook on life
within its world view.[6]

Ketcham added: "Though he did not long continue to express
them [the essentials of Christian morality and social theory] in the same
way as his teachers, it is not possible to understand the purpose and
earnestness of Madison's public life without sensing its connection with
the Christian atmosphere in which he was raised."[7]

William Rives wrote in his *History of the Life and Times of James
Madison*: "After the manner of the Bereans he seems to have searched
the Scriptures daily and diligently. . . . He explored the whole history
and evidences of Christianity on every side, through clouds of witnesses
and champions for and against, from the Fathers and schoolmen down
to the infidel philosophers of the eighteenth century. No one not a professed theologian, and but few even of those who are, have ever gone
through more laborious and extensive inquiries to arrive at the truth."[8]

We do not know what conclusions he arrived at. Bishop Meade,
author of *Old Churches, Ministers, and Families of Virginia*, stated: "I
was never at Mr. Madison's but once, and then our conversation took
such a turn—though not designed on my part—as to call forth some
expressions and arguments which left the impression on my mind that
his creed was not strictly regulated by the Bible."[9]

However, Madison did not express hostility to Christianity. Bishop
Meade added: "Whatever may have been the private sentiments of Mr.
Madison on the subject of religion, he was never known to declare any
hostility to it. He always treated it with respect, attended public worship in his neighborhood, invited ministers of religion to his house, had
family prayers on such occasions—though he did not kneel himself at
prayers. Episcopal ministers often went there to see his aged and pious
mother and administer the Holy Communion to her."[10]

Madison was elected a delegate to Virginia's convention in 1776.
On June 12, the convention proclaimed a "Declaration of Rights."
Madison only spoke once during the Convention. His one motion was

to amend the religious freedom clause; where it had previously stated that "all men should enjoy the fullest toleration in the exercise of religion," Madison offered the phrase "all men are equally entitled to the full and free exercise of it [religion]."[11] Though not adopted, this was an early articulation of Madison's belief that religion should not be compulsory. Where the wording "toleration" was used, religious liberty was viewed as a revocable privilege. Madison's amendment, if accepted, would have declared religious liberty an irrevocable right.

Madison married a Quaker widow, Dolley Dandridge Payne, on September 15, 1794. (Since Madison was not a Quaker, Dolley was read out of the Quaker faith for marrying outside the denomination.[12])

In 1784, Madison made a speech in opposition to a bill that would assess citizens for the support of religious teachers. He argued that religion was "not within [the] purview of civil authority." He said that the bill at hand had a tendency to establish Christianity, and the progress of the general assessment proved the tendency.

"[There is a] Difference between establish[in]g and tolerating error," his shorthand notes read. The "True question [was] not, 'Is Relig[ion] necess[ar]y,' but 'Are Rel[igious] Estab[lishmen]ts necess[ary] for religion?" To this he answered, "No."

He stated that there was a "Propensity of man to Religion" and argued that "Experience [showed that] relig[ion was] corrupted by Estab[lishmen]ts."

He said that the true remedies were not establishing the church, but "Laws to cherish virtue," "Administration of justice," and "Personal example," among others.

He also pointed out specific defects in the bill at hand. "What is Christianity?" he asked. Under this bill, the "courts of law [had] to decide."

"Is it Trinitarianism, arianism, socinianism? Is it salvation by faith, or works also? &c., &c., &c." It "Ends in what is orthodoxy, what Heresy;" it "Dishonors [C]hristianity."[13]

Madison drafted the Virginia Guarantee of Religious Liberty.[14]

Madison was elected president in 1808 and served two terms. He concluded his first inaugural address with:

> But the source to which I look or the aids which alone can supply my deficiencies is in the well-tried intelligence and virtue of my fellow-citizens, and in the counsels of those representing them in

the other departments associated in the care of the national interests. In these my confidence will under every difficulty be best placed, next to that which we have all been encouraged to feel in the guardianship and guidance of that Almighty Being whose power regulates the destiny of nations, whose blessings have been so conspicuously dispensed to this rising Republic, and to whom we are bound to address our devout gratitude for the past, as well as our fervent supplications and best hopes for the future.[15]

During his first term, the War of 1812 threatened the nation's independence. After Congress recommended that Madison set aside a day "to be observed by the people of the United States with religious solemnity as a day of public humiliation and prayer," Madison issued a proclamation setting aside August 3, 1812, as a day "to be set apart for the devout purposes of rendering the Sovereign of the Universe and the Benefactor of Mankind the public homage due to His holy attributes; of acknowledging the transgressions which might justly provoke the manifestations of His divine displeasure; of seeking His merciful forgiveness and His assistance in the great duties of repentance and amendment, and especially of offering fervent supplications that in the present season of calamity and war He would take the American people under His peculiar care and protection; that He would guide their public councils, animate their patriotism, and bestow His blessing on their arms; that He would inspire all nations with a love of justice and of concord and with a reverence for the unerring precept of our holy religion to do to others as they would require that others should do to them; and, finally, that, turning the hearts of our enemies from the violence and injustice which sway their councils against us, He would hasten a restoration of the blessings of peace."[16]

Madison was reelected in 1812. He began his second inaugural address by discussing the solemnity of his duties. He said: "From the weight and magnitude now belonging to it I should be compelled to shrink if I had less reliance on the support of an enlightened and generous people, and felt less deeply a conviction that the war with a powerful nation, which forms so prominent a feature in our situation, is stamped with that justice which invites the smiles of Heaven on the means of conducting it to a successful termination."[17]

In 1813, Madison issued a proclamation calling for a day of public humiliation and prayer. He called on the people to give thanks for their many domestic blessings, and add to the expressions of devout thankfulness "supplications to the same Almighty Power that He would look down with compassion on our infirmities; that He would pardon our manifold transgressions and awaken and strengthen in all the wholesome purposes of repentance and amendment; that in this season of trial and calamity He would preside in a particular manner over our public councils and inspire all citizens with a love of their country and with those fraternal affections and that mutual confidence which have so happy a tendency to make us safe at home and respected abroad; and that as He was graciously pleased heretofore to smile on our struggles against the attempts of the Government of the Empire of which these States then made a part to wrest from them the rights and privileges to which they were entitled in common with every other part and to raise them to the station of an independent and sovereign people, so He would now be pleased in like manner to bestow His blessing on our arms in resisting the hostile and persevering efforts of the same power to degrade us on the ocean, the common inheritance of all, from rights and immunities belonging and essential to the American people as a coequal member of the great community of independent nations; and that, inspiring our enemies with moderation, with justice, and with that spirit of reasonable accommodation which our country has continued to manifest, we may be enabled to beat our swords into plowshares and to enjoy in peace every man the fruits of his honest industry and the rewards of his lawful enterprise."

He concluded the proclamation with a reminder that public humiliation, to be worthy of the regard of God, must be voluntary: "If the public homage of a people can ever be worthy the favorable regard of the Holy and Omniscient Being to whom it is addressed, it must be that in which those who join in it are guided only by their free choice, by the impulse of their hearts and the dictates of their consciences; and such a spectacle must be interesting to all Christian nations as proving that religion, that gift of Heaven for the good of man, freed from all coercive edicts, from that unhallowed connection with the powers of this world which corrupts religion into an instrument or an usurper of the policy of the state, and making no appeal but to reason, to the heart, and to the conscience, can spread its benign influence everywhere and can attract to the divine altar those freewill offerings of humble supplication, thanksgiving, and praise which alone can be acceptable to Him whom no hypocrisy can deceive and no forced sacrifices propitiate."[18]

Continuance of the war prompted another proclamation the next year. On November 16, 1814, he issued a proclamation calling for another day of public humiliation and fasting, calling on the people to confess "their sins and transgressions," strengthen their vows of "repentance and amendment," and mingle with their devout thankfulness "supplications to the Beneficent Parent of the Human Race that He would be graciously pleased to pardon all their offenses against Him[.]"[19]

The return of peace gave a whole different tenor to his next proclamation, a thanksgiving proclamation issued on March 14, 1815. He called on the nation to give thanks for the end of the conflict, "which is now so happily terminated by a peace and reconciliation with those who have been our enemies."[20]

In 1825, after Madison had retired to private life, the Reverend F. Beasley sent him a tract proving the existence of God and discussing His attributes. Madison responded by stating that he was not able to bestow enough critical attention to do the tract justice. He stated:

> And the belief in a God, all powerful, wise, and good, is so essential to the moral order of the world, and to the happiness of man, that arguments which enforce it cannot be drawn from too many sources, nor adapted with too much solicitude to the different characters and capacities to be impressed with it.
>
> But whatever effect may be produced on some minds by the more abstract train of ideas which you so strongly support, it will probably always be found that the course of reasoning, from the effect to the cause, "from nature to nature's God," will be the more universal and more persuasive application.
>
> The finiteness of the human understanding betrays itself on all subjects, but more especially when it contemplates such as involve infinity. What may safely be said seems to be, that the infinity of time and space forces itself on our conception, a limitation of either being inconceivable; that the mind prefers at once the idea of a self-existing cause to that of an infinite series of cause and effect, which augments, instead of avoiding the difficulty; and that it finds more facility in assenting to the self-existence of an invisible cause, possessing infinite power, wisdom, and goodness, than to the self-existence of the universe, visibly destitute of those attributes, and which may be the effect of them. In this comparative facility of conception and belief, all philosophical reasoning on the

subject must, perhaps, terminate. But that I may not get farther beyond my depth, and without the resources which bear you up in fathoming efforts, I hasten to thank you for the favor which has made me your debtor, and to assure you of my esteem and my respectful regards.[21]

Madison wrote a manuscript including a commentary on parts of the Bible. The manuscript is in the possession of the Library of Congress.[22]

Biographer Ralph Ketcham said of Madison's religion: "Though not inclined to religious speculations, Madison adhered to a calm faith in a moral, orderly universe presided over by a God beyond the limited capacity of man to fully conceive or understand."[23]

J. Eidsmoe's summary of Madison's religion is well-taken: "If Madison ever rejected the fundamental doctrines of the Christian faith, he never said so in writing that has survived to date. And throughout his life he remained friendly and respectful toward Christianity and toward the Church.

"Was Madison a believer in Jesus Christ? Did he remember, in the phrase he used to his youthful friend in 1772, to have his name 'enrolled in the Annals of Heaven?' We must leave that question to God, and to Madison himself.

"But this much is very clear: The Christian religion, and particularly Reverend Witherspoon's Calvinism, strongly influenced Madison's views of law and government."[24]

Madison died on June 28, 1836, in Montpelier, Virginia.

CONCLUSION

Madison had a strong influence from orthodox Christianity in his youth and apparently never turned his back on this heritage. Though we know little of his specific doctrines, we do know that he was not a deist. He believed in the "Almighty Being whose power regulates the destiny of nations."

NOTES

1. Tim LaHaye, *Faith of Our Founding Fathers* (Brentwood, TN: Wolgemuth and Hyatt, 1987), 127.

2. Ralph Ketcham, *James Madison: A Biography* (Charlottesville and London: University Press of Virginia, 1971, 1990, 1998), 52. From a letter to

William Bradford written on November 9, 1772. Found in *The Papers of James Madison*, vol. 1, 74–76. The six-volume set was edited by William T. Hutchinson, W. M. E. Rachal, and others, and was published in Chicago from 1962 through 1969.

3. Ibid., 55.

4. William Meade, *Old Churches, Ministers, and Families of Virginia*, vol. 2 (Baltimore: Genealogical Publishing, 1995), 99.

5. Ketcham, *James Madison*, 46.

6. Ibid., 46–47.

7. Ibid., 48.

8. William Rives, *History of the Life and Times of James Madison*, vol. 1 (1859), 33–34. Quoted in LaHaye, *Faith of Our Founding Fathers*, 129–130.

9. Quoted in Irving Brant, *James Madison: The Virginia Revolutionist, 1751–1780* (Indianapolis: Bobbs-Merrill, 1941), 113.

10. Ibid.

11. Gaillard Hunt, *Life of James Madison* (Library Reprints, 2002), 8–9.

12. Carl Sferazza Anthony, *First Ladies: The Saga of the Presidents' Wives and Their Power, 1789–1961* (New York: Morrow, 1990), 56.

13. Madison, *Writings of James Madison, 1772–1836*, vol. 1 (1836; repr., Library of America, 1999). Notes of a speech made by Madison in the House of Delegates of Virginia at the autumnal session of 1784, in opposition to the general assessment bill for support of religious teachers. Only notes for the speech have survived. I have used brackets to indicate the missing letters in many abbreviated words.

14. Benjamin Weiss, *God in American History: A Documentation of America's Religious Heritage* (Grand Rapids: Zondervan, 1966), 64.

15. Madison, March 4, 1809. First inaugural address.

16. Madison, *Messages and Papers of the Presidents: James Madison, 1812*. July 9, 1812. A proclamation.

17. Ibid., March 4, 1813. Second inaugural address.

18. Ibid., July 23, 1813. A proclamation.

19. Ibid., November 16, 1814. A proclamation.

20. Ibid., March 4, 1815. A proclamation.

21. Madison, *Writings of James Madison, 1772–1836*, vol. 3. November 20, 1825. Letter to the Reverend F. Beasley.

22. Bliss Isley, *The Presidents: Men of Faith* (Boston: W. A. Wilde, 1953), 31.

23. Ketcham, *James Madison*, 667.

24. John Eidsmoe and D. James Kennedy, *Christianity and the Constitution: The Faith of Our Founding Fathers* (Grand Rapids: Baker Book House, 1987), 13. Quoted in LaHaye, *Faith of Our Founding Fathers*, 132.

CHAPTER 40

THOMAS JEFFERSON

THOMAS JEFFERSON was born on April 13, 1743, in Albemarle County, Virginia. According to a family legend, he read all of his father's books, including his Bible, by the time he turned five.[1] In 1757, his father, Peter Jefferson, died. For the next two years, Jefferson spent weekdays boarding at the residence of Anglican clergyman James Maury.[2] Maury taught Jefferson Greek and Latin. By one account, Jefferson's lifelong distrust of the clergy began during those two years.[3]

In one of his earliest surviving letters written to John Page on December 25, 1762, Jefferson described his dissatisfaction with the school he was attending in these dramatic terms: "This very day, to others the day of greatest mirth and jollity, sees me overwhelmed with more and greater misfortunes than have befallen a descendant of Adam's for these thousand years past I am sure; and perhaps, after excepting Job, since the creation of the world. I think his misfortunes were somewhat greater than mine: for although we may be pretty nearly on a level in other respects, yet I thank my God I have the advantage of brother Job in this, that Satan has not as yet put forth his hand to load me with bodily afflictions."[4]

This seems to reflect an early orthodoxy in several areas; Jefferson referred to (1) the creation of the world, (2) Job, (3), Satan, and even (4) to God as "my God."

In another letter to John Page, this one written on July 15, 1763, Jefferson expressed opinions in surprising concordance with the Calvinistic doctrine of predestination:

Perfect happiness I beleive [sic] was never intended by the deity to be the lot of any one of his creatures in this world; but that he has very much put in our power the nearness of our approaches to it, is what I as stedfastly [sic] beleive [sic]. The most fortunate of us all in our journey through life frequently meet with calamities and misfortunes which may greatly afflict us: and to fortify our minds against the attacks of these calamities and misfortunes should be one of the principal studies and endeavors of our lives. The only method of doing this is to assume a perfect resignation to the divine will, to consider that whatever does happen, must happen, and that by our uneasiness we cannot prevent the blow before it does fall, but we may add to it's force after it has fallen. These considerations and others such as these may enable us in some measure to surmount the difficulties thrown in our way, to bear up with a tolerable degree of patience under this burthen of life, and to proceed with a pious and unshaken resignation till we arrive at our journey's end, where we may deliver up our trust into the hands of him who gave it, and receive such reward as to him shall seem proportioned to our merit.[5]

This, again, reflects a rather orthodox concept of God and His workings in this life. However, as theologians will quickly note, Jefferson appeared even at this early stage in his religious development to view salvation as merit-based ("receive such reward as to him shall seem proportioned to our merit")—a common fallacy but a fallacy nonetheless.

Later in life, Jefferson adopted religious views that were not orthodox. When considering these, though, it must be remembered that throughout most of his life, he was an active member of his Episcopalian church, even becoming a vestryman—giving neighbors no reason to suspect that he had adopted unorthodox doctrines (if, indeed, he had in his earlier years). Even his family knew him as a regular churchgoer; his oldest grandson, Thomas Jefferson Randolph, remembered him in these words: "He was regular in his attendance [at] church, taking his prayer book with him. He drew the plan of the Episcopal church in Charlottesville, was one of the largest contributors to its erection, and contributed regularly to the support of its minister."[6]

Thomas Jefferson Randolph referred to an agreement that Jefferson drafted and signed in February 1777, after the Episcopal church was disestablished in Virginia. Jefferson organized a group of people who voluntarily agreed to support their local minister. He drafted a document whereby he and his fellow subscribers declared themselves to be "desirous of encouraging and supporting the Calvinistical Reformed Church, and of desiring to our selves, through the ministry of it's [sic] teachers, the benefits of Gospel knolege [sic] and religious improvement." They agreed to pay Reverend Charles Clay a set sum, in consideration of which they expected him to preach regular sermons in their parish.[7]

Jefferson's work in his parish was not limited to monetary support. In June or July 1774, he joined John Walker (a fellow member of both the Virginia House of Burgesses and of the parish of St. Anne) in issuing the following proclamation:

To the Inhabitants of the Parish of St. Anne.

The members of the late House of Burgesses having taken into their consideration the dangers impending over British America from the hostile invasion of a sister colony, thought proper that it should be recommended to the several parishes in this colony that they set apart some convenient day for fasting, humiliation and prayer devoutly to implore the divine interposition in behalf of an injured and oppressed people; and that the minds of his majesty, his ministers, and parliament, might be inspired with wisdom from above, to avert from us the dangers which threaten our civil rights, and all the evils of civil war. We do therefore recommend to the inhabitants of the parish of St. Anne that Saturday the 23d instant be by them set apart for the purpose aforesaid, on which day will be prayers and a sermon suited to the occasion by the reverend Mr. Clay at the new church on Hardware river, which place is thought the most centrical to the parishioners in General.[8]

On August 3, 1771, Jefferson wrote a letter to Robert Skipwith, who had asked Jefferson to send a list of recommended books for starting a private library. Interestingly, though Jefferson named books by Seneca, Epictetus, Antoninus, Xenophon, Locke, and Hume in his list of books on religion, he mentioned the Bible in his list of books on ancient history.[9]

Jefferson married Martha Wayles Skelton on January 1, 1772.

Much has been made of Jefferson's refusal to issue thanksgiving proclamations as president.[10] He did not, however, decline to issue them while governor of Virginia. On November 11, 1779, he issued the following proclamation:

> WHEREAS the Honourable the General Congress, impressed with a grateful sense of the goodness of the Almighty God, in blessing the greater part of this extensive continent with plentiful harvests, crowning our arms with repeated successes, conducting us hitherto safely through the perils with which we have been encompassed and manifesting in multiplied instances his divine care of these infant states, hath thought proper by their act of that Thursday the 9th of December next be appointed a day of publick and solemn thanksgiving and prayer, which act is in these words, to wit.
>
> "Whereas it becomes us humbly to approach the throne of Almighty God, with gratitude and praise, for the wonders which his goodness has wrought in conducting our forefathers to this western world; for his protection to them and to their posterity, amidst difficulties and dangers; for raising us their children from deep distress, to be numbered among the nations of the earth; and for arming the hands of just and mighty Princes in our deliverance; and especially for that he hath been pleased to grant us the enjoyment of health and so to order the revolving seasons, that the earth hath produced her increase in abundance, blessing the labours of the husbandman, and spreading plenty through the land; that he hath prospered our arms and those of our ally, been a shield to our troops in the hour of danger, pointed their swords to victory, and led them in triumph over the bulwarks of the foe; that he hath gone with those who went into the wilderness against the savage tribes; that he hath stayed the hand of the spoiler, and turned back his meditated destruction; that he hath prospered our commerce, and given success to those who sought the enemy on the face of the deep; and above all, that he hath diffused the glorious light of the gospel, whereby, through the merits of our gracious Redeemer, we may become the heirs of his eternal glory. Therefore,
>
> ["]Resolved, that it be recommended to the several states to appoint THURSDAY the 9th of December next, to be a day of publick and solemn THANKSGIVING to Almighty God, for his mercies, and of PRAYER, for the continuance of his favour and protection to these United States; to beseech him that he would be

graciously pleased to influence our publick Councils, and bless them with wisdom from on high, with unanimity, firmness and success; that he would go forth with our hosts and crown our arms with victory; that he would grant to his church, the plentiful effusions of divine grace, and pour out his holy spirit on all Ministers of the gospel; that he would bless and prosper the means of education, and spread the light of christian [sic] knowledge through the remotest corners of the earth; that he would smile upon the labours of his people, and cause the earth to bring forth her fruits in abundance, that we may with gratitude and gladness enjoy them; that he would take into his holy protection, our illustrious ally, give him victory over his enemies, and render him finally great, as the father of his people, and the protector of the rights of mankind; that he would graciously be pleased to turn the hearts of our enemies, and to dispence the blessings of peace to contending nations.

["]That he would in mercy look down upon us, pardon all our sins, and receive us into his favour; and finally, that he would establish the independence of these United States upon the basis of religion and virtue, and support and protect them in the enjoyment of peace, liberty, and safety."

I do therefore by authority from the General Assembly issue this my proclamation, hereby appointing Thursday the 9th day of December next, a day of publick and solemn thanksgiving and prayer to Almighty God, earnestly recommending to all the good people of this commonwealth, to set apart the said day for those purposes, and to the several Ministers of religion to meet their respective societies thereon, to assist them in their prayers, edify them with their discourses, and generally to perform the sacred duties of their function, proper for their occasion.

Given under my hand and the seal of the commonwealth, at Williamsburg, this 11th day of November, in the year of our Lord, 1779, and in the fourth of the commonwealth.

THOMAS JEFFERSON[11]

Although Jefferson was merely adopting the words of the Continental Congress for the main body of the text, he evidently either endorsed their sentiments or did not see fit to make any protest public. Whatever his views on the topic, it is interesting that he endorsed a document this religious in his official duties as governor.

In 1787, Jefferson wrote a letter to Peter Carr, making suggestions as to how Carr could best embark on a systematic study of religion. This advice sheds an interesting light on Jefferson's own religious opinions. Jefferson encouraged Carr to indulge novelty and singularity of opinion "in any other subject rather than that of religion." But then he added: "On the other hand, shake off all the fears and servile prejudices, under which, weak minds are servilely crouched. Fix reason firmly in her seat, and call to her tribunal every fact, every opinion. Question with boldness even the existence of a God; because, if there be one, he must more approve of the homage of reason, than that of blindfolded fear."

He encouraged Carr to examine first "the religion of your own country," Christianity. But this, too, came with a caveat: "But those facts in the Bible which contradict the laws of nature, must be examined with more care, and under a variety of faces. Here you must recur to the pretensions of the writer to inspiration from God. Examine upon what evidence his pretensions are founded, and whether that evidence is so strong, as that its falsehood would be more improbable than a change in the laws of nature, in the case he relates."

When examining the New Testament, Jefferson said to "Keep in your eye the opposite pretensions: 1, of those who say he was begotten by God, born of a virgin, suspended and reversed the laws of nature at will, and ascended bodily into heaven; and 2, of those who say he was a man of illegitimate birth, of a benevolent heart, enthusiastic mind, who set out without pretensions to divinity, ended in believing them, and was punished capitally for sedition[.]"

He concluded: "Do not be frightened from this inquiry by any fear of its consequences. If it ends in a belief that there is no God, you will find incitements to virtue in the comfort and pleasantness you feel in its exercise, and the love of others which it will procure you. If you find reason to believe there is a God, a consciousness that you are acting under his eye, and that he approves you, will be a vast additional incitement; if that there be a future state, the hope of a happy existence in that increases the appetite to deserve it; if that Jesus was also a God, you will be comforted by a belief of his aid and love."[12]

Jefferson's religious belief was a controversial issue during the 1800 presidential election. In 1800, the Reverend John Mason of New York published a book called *The Voice of Warning, to Christians, on the Ensuing Election of a President of the United States.* He said that Jefferson was a man "who writes against the truths of God's word; who makes not even a profession of Christianity; who is without Sabbaths; without the sanctuary, without so much as a decent external respect for the faith and worship of Christians."[13] Others countered these charges with statements that whatever his personal beliefs were, Jefferson attended church services.

Jefferson was elected president in 1800 and served two terms. In his first inaugural address, he addressed the topic of what was needed to make Americans a prosperous and happy people. He said:

> Kindly separated by nature and a wide ocean from the exterminating havoc of one quarter of the globe; too high-minded to endure the degradations of the others; possessing a chosen country, with room enough for our descendants to the thousandth and thousandth generation; entertaining a due sense of our equal right to the use of our own faculties, to the acquisitions of our own industry, to honor and confidence from our fellow-citizens, resulting not from birth, but from our actions and their sense of them; enlightened by a benign religion, professed, indeed, and practiced in various forms, yet all of them inculcating honesty, truth, temperance, gratitude, and the love of man; acknowledging and adoring an overruling Providence, which by all its dispensations proves that it delights in the happiness of man here and his greater happiness hereafter—with all these blessings, what more is necessary to make us a happy and a prosperous people? Still one thing more, fellow-citizens—a wise and frugal Government, which shall restrain men from injuring one another, shall leave them otherwise free to regulate their own pursuits of industry and improvement, and shall not take from the mouth of labor the bread it has earned. This is the sum of good government, and this is necessary to close the circle of our felicities.[14]

Jefferson concluded his speech with these words: "Relying, then, on the patronage of your good will, I advance with obedience to the work, ready to retire from it whenever you become sensible how much better choice it is in your power to make. And may that Infinite Power which rules the destinies of the universe lead our councils to what is best, and give them a favorable issue for your peace and prosperity."[15]

Jefferson believed that whatever a president's personal religious beliefs, he was to set an example for the American people by attending church. A stranger once asked Jefferson why he went to church, as he thought Jefferson did not "believe a word of it."

Jefferson responded, "Sir, no nation has yet existed or been governed without religion. I, as the Chief Magistrate of this nation, am bound to give it the sanction of my example."[16]

He regularly attended Sunday services in the hall of the House of Representatives. Sermons were preached by either the chaplain or a visiting minister.[17]

He also made religious statements in private correspondence during his presidency. In a December 5, 1801, letter to Reverend Isaac Story, Jefferson wrote: "When I was young I was fond of speculations which seemed to promise some insight into that hidden country, but . . . I have for very many years ceased to read or to think concerning them, and have reposed my head on that pillow of ignorance which a benevolent Creator has made so soft for us. . . . I have thought it better, by nourishing good passions and controlling the bad, to merit an inheritance in a state of being of which I can know so little, and to trust for the future in Him who has been so good for the past."[18]

In 1804, when his daughter, Mary Jefferson Eppes, was ailing and near death, Jefferson was observed to be reading the Bible.[19]

Jefferson was reelected in 1804. In his second inaugural address, he said: "In matters of religion I have considered that its free exercise is placed by the Constitution independent of the powers of the General Government. I have therefore undertaken on no occasion to prescribe the religious exercises suited to it, but have left them, as the Constitution found them, under the direction and discipline of the church or State authorities acknowledged by the several religious societies."[20]

He also said that he would need "the favor of that Being in whose hands we are, who led our fathers, as Israel of old, from their native land and planted them in a country flowing with all the necessaries and comforts of life; who has covered our infancy with His providence and our riper years with His wisdom and power, and to whose goodness I ask you to join in supplications with me that He will so enlighten the minds of your servants, guide their councils, and prosper their measures that whatsoever they do shall result in your good, and shall secure to you the peace, friendship, and approbation of all nations."[21]

Thomas Jefferson summed up his beliefs about Christianity and about Jesus in a book he called *The Philosophy of Jesus of Nazareth, extracted from the account of his life and teachings as given by Matthew,*

Mark, Luke and John. Being an abridgement of the New Testament for the use of the Indians, unembarrassed with matters of fact or faith beyond their comprehension. It is more briefly called *The Jefferson Bible.*

In two letters, one to John Adams and the other to Charles Thomson, he discussed the ideas behind this book. To Adams he said:

> In extracting the pure principles which he taught, we should have to strip off the artificial vestments in which they have been muffled by priests, who have travestied them into various forms as instruments of riches and power for themselves. . . . We must reduce our volume to the simple evangelists, select even from them, the very words of Jesus, paring off the amphibologisms into which they have been led by forgetting often, or not understanding, what had fallen from him. . . . There will be found remaining the most sublime and benevolent code of morals which has ever been offered to man.
>
> I have performed this operation for my own use, by cutting verse by verse out of the printed book, and arranging the manner which is evidently his, and which is as easily distinguishable as diamonds in a dunghill. The result is an octavo of forty-six pages of pure and unsophisticated doctrines, such as were professed and acted on by the *unlettered* Apostles, the Apostolic Fathers, and the Christians of the First Century. Their Platonizing successors, indeed, in after times, in order to legitimate the corruptions which they had incorporated into the doctrines of Jesus, found it necessary to disavow the primitive Christians, who had taken their principles from the mouth of Jesus himself, of his Apostles, and the Fathers contemporary with them. They excommunicated their followers as heretics."[22]

"Diamonds in a dunghill"? That was not a mere whim or slip of his pen. He repeated the phrase in another letter to Adams:

> In the New testament there is internal evidence that parts of it have proceeded from an extraordinary man; and that other parts of the fabric of very inferior minds. It is as easy to separate those parts, as to pick out diamonds from dunghills. The matter of the first was such as would be preserved in the memory of the hearers, and handed on by tradition for a long time; the latter such

stuff as might be gathered up, for imbedding it, any where, and at any time.[23]

He believed that the parts he believed of the New Testament were diamonds, and what he did not believe was as a dunghill. (He removed everything that was supernatural—the virgin birth, the Resurrection, and Jesus' miracles.)

Jefferson sent Adams a copy of this book.[24]

To Charles Thomson, secretary of the Continental Congress, he wrote:

> I, too, have made a wee little book from the same materials, which I call the Philosophy of Jesus; it is a paradigma of His doctrines made by cutting the texts out of the book, and arranging them on the pages of a blank book in a certain order of time or subject. A more beautiful or precious morsel of ethics I have never seen; it is a document in proof that I am a real Christian, that is to say, a disciple of the doctrines of Jesus, very different from the Platonists, who call me infidel and themselves Christians and preachers of the gospel, while they draw all their characteristic dogmas from what its author never said or saw. They have compounded from the heathen mysteries a system beyond the comprehension of man, of which the great reformer of the ethics and deism of the Jews, were he to return to earth, would not recognize one feature.[25]

So what did this book, of which he spoke so much, contain? It contained some moral teachings of Jesus and some actions such as His chasing the money changers from the temple. In the words of Fuller and Green in *God in the White House*, "He reduced the narrative to the sparsest bones, omitted all supernatural statements, miracles, and claims of divinity. . . The Passion story is included, but ends with the entombment."[26]

Thomas Jefferson's oldest grandson, Thomas Jefferson Randolph, remembered this about the book: "His codification of the morals of Jesus was not known to his family before his death, and they learned from a letter addressed to a friend that he was in the habit of reading nightly from it before going to bed."[27]

In Jefferson's letters, he said that what he left out of his book—the supernatural events, the claims to divinity, and the Resurrection—was a "dunghill," and referred to these doctrines as "beyond the comprehension of man."

In about 1801, he wrote his *Syllabus of the Doctrines of Jesus, Compared with Those of Others*. One biographer described it in these words: "The *Syllabus* said in brief, I am a good Christian, a man who reveres Jesus, though I cannot accept his godhood. Still, I accept his moral system as being better than either that of the ancient philosophers or that of the ancient Jews."[28]

Jefferson believed that religion was a private matter. "I have ever thought religion a concern purely between our God and our consciences, for which we were accountable to Him and not to the priests. I never told my own religion, nor scrutinized that of another. I never attempted to make a convert nor wished to change another's creed. I have ever judged of the religion of others by their lives, . . . for it is in our lives, and not from our words, that our religion must be read. By the same test the world must judge me."[29]

In a January 11, 1817, letter to John Adams, he said: "One of our fan-colouring biographers, who paints small men as very great, enquired of me lately, with real affection too, whether he might consider as authentic, the change in my religion spoken of in some circles. Now this supposed that they knew what my religion had been before, taking for it the word of their priests, whom I certainly never made the confidants of my creed. My answer was 'say nothing of my religion. It is known to my god and myself alone. It's evidence before the world is to be sought in my life. If that has been *honest and dutiful to society*, the religion which has regulated it cannot be a bad one.' "[30]

What was Jefferson's religion?

He made several positive statements about Christianity. "I hold the precepts of Jesus, as delivered by himself, to be the most pure, benevolent, and sublime which have ever been preached to man."[31]

In an 1803 letter, he wrote: "His system of morality was the most benevolent and sublime probably that has been ever taught, and consequently more perfect than those of any of the ancient philosophers. . . . [He was] the most innocent, the most benevolent, the most eloquent and sublime character that ever has been exhibited to man."[32]

In 1814, he wrote: "There never was a more pure and sublime system of morality delivered to man than is to be found in the four Evangelists."[33]

Yet he believed that Christianity had been perverted and that the diamonds of moral instruction needed to be weeded out of the dunghill of miracles, resurrections, and the supernatural. In a March 21, 1801, letter to English author Joseph Priestley, Jefferson referred to the "Christian Philosophy" as "the most sublime and benevolent, but the most perverted System that ever shone on Man."[34]

There are abundant proofs showing Jefferson believed that Christianity had been perverted:

> I am a real Christian, that is to say, a disciple of the doctrines of Jesus-very different from the Platonists, who call me infidel and themselves Christians and preachers of the gospel, while they draw all their characteristic dogmas from what its Author never said nor saw. They have compounded from the heathen mysteries a system beyond the comprehension of man, of which the great Reformer of the vicious ethics and deism of the Jews, were He to return on earth, would not recognize one feature.[35]

> My views of are the result of a life of inquiry and reflection, and very different from that anti-Christian system imputed to me by those who know nothing of my opinions. To the corruptions of Christianity I am indeed opposed; but not to the genuine precepts of Jesus himself. I am a Christian, in the only sense in which he wished anyone to be—sincerely attached to his doctrines in preference to all others.[36]

> I hold the precepts of Jesus, as delivered by Himself, to be the most pure, benevolent, and sublime which have ever been preached to man. I adhere to the principles of the first age, and consider all subsequent innovations as corruptions of His religion, having no foundation in what came from Him. . . . If the freedom of religion guaranteed to us by law in theory can ever rise in practice under the overbearing inquisition of public opinion, truth will prevail over fanaticism, and the genuine doctrines of Jesus, so long perverted by His pseudo-priests, will again be restored to their original purity. This reformation will advance with the other improvements of the human mind, but too late for me to witness it.[37]

> Happy in the prospect of a restoration of primitive Christianity, I must leave to younger athletes to encounter and lop off the false

branches which have been engrafted into it by the mythologists of the middle and modern ages.[38]

I concur with the author [of a recent sermon] in considering the moral precepts of Jesus as more pure, correct, and sublime than those of the ancient philosophers; yet I do not concur with him in the mode of proving it. He thinks it necessary to libel and decry the doctrines of the philosophers; but a man must be blinded, indeed, by prejudice who can deny them a great degree of merit. I give them their just due, and yet maintain that the morality of Jesus as taught by himself, and freed from the corruptions of latter times, is far superior. Their philosophy went chiefly to the government of our passions, so far as respected ourselves, and the procuring our own tranquility. In our duties to others they were short and deficient. They extended their cares scarcely beyond our kindred and friends individually, and our country in the abstract. Jesus embraced with charity and philanthropy our neighbors, our countrymen, and the whole family of mankind. They confined themselves to actions; he pressed his sentiments into the region of our thoughts, and called for purity at the fountainhead.[39]

On July 5, 1814, Jefferson wrote to Adams that he had been reading through Plato's *Republic*, "the heaviest task-work I ever went through." Jefferson said:

His foggy mind is forever presenting the semblances of objects which, half seen thro' a mist, can be defined neither in form or dimension. Yet this which should have consigned him to early oblivion really procured him immortality of fame and reverence. The Christian priesthood, finding the doctrines of Christ levelled to every understanding, and too plain to need explanation, saw in the mysticisms of Plato, materials with which they might build up an artificial system which might, from it's indistinctness, admit everlasting controversy, give employment for their order, and introduce it to profit, power and pre-eminence. The doctrines which flowed from the lips of Jesus himself are within the comprehension of a child; but thousands of volumes have not yet explained the Platonisms engrafted on them: and for this obvious reason that nonsense can never be explained.[40]

Jefferson said, "Why have Christians been distinguished above all people who have ever lived for persecutions? Is it because it is the genius of their religion? No, its genius is the reverse. It is the refusing toleration to those of a different opinion which has produced all the bustles and wars on account of religion."[41]

In an 1825 letter to Alexander Smyth, Jefferson described the book of Revelation as "the ravings of a maniac, no more worthy nor capable of explanation than the incoherences of our own nightly dreams."[42]

Jefferson described himself as an Epicurean. In a letter to a friend, William Short, he said: "As you say of yourself, I too am an Epicurean. I consider the genuine (not the imputed) teachings of Epicurus as containing everything rational in moral philosophy, which Greece and Rome have left us."[43] According to presidential religion authors Fuller and Green, by the true doctrines of Epicurus Jefferson meant "that philosophy consisted in the wise conduct of life, to be attained by reliance on the evidence of the senses, and the elimination of superstition and of the belief in supernatural intervention."[44]

Jefferson was also strongly influenced by Joseph Priestley. In an August 22, 1813, letter to John Adams, he said of Priestley and his work:

> You are right in supposing, in one of yours, that I had not read much of Priestley's Predestination, his No-soul system, or his controversy with Horsley. But I have read his Corruptions of Christianity, and Early opinions of Jesus, over and over again; and I rest on them, and on Middleton's writings, especially his letters from Rome, and to Waterland, as the basis of my own faith. These writings have never been answered, nor can be answered, by quoting historical proofs, as they have done. For these facts therefore I cling to their learning, as so much superior to my own. . . .
>
> But he [Priestley, in *The Doctrines of Heathen Philosophy Compared with Those of Revelation*] has omitted the important branch, which in your letter of Aug. 9. you say you have never seen executed, a comparison of the morality of the old testament with that of the new. And yet no two things were ever more unlike. I ought not to have asked him to give it. He dared not. He would have been eaten alive by his intolerant brethren, the Cannibal priests. And yet this was really the most interesting branch of the work.[45]

What, specifically, of Jesus' doctrines did Jefferson believe? In an 1822 letter to Dr. Benjamin Waterhouse, he said:

The doctrines of Jesus are simple, and tend all to the happiness of man:
1. That there is one only God, and He all perfect.
2. That there is a future state of rewards and punishments.
3. That to love God with all thy heart, and thy neighbor as thyself, is the sum of religion. . . . But compare with these the demoralizing dogmas of Calvin. . . . The impious dogmatists, as Athanasius and Calvin . . . are the false shepherds foretold [in the New Testament] as to enter not by the door into the sheepfold, but to climb up some other way. They are mere usurpers of the Christian name, teaching a counter-religion made up of the deliria of crazy imaginations, as foreign from Christianity as is that of Mahomet. Their blasphemies have driven thinking men into infidelity, who have too hastily rejected the supposed Author himself with the horrors so falsely imputed to Him. Had the doctrines of Jesus been preached always as pure as they came from his lips, the whole civilized world would now have been Christian.[46]

Jefferson also believed that there was a God who started and superintended the universe:

The wishes expressed, in your last favor, that I may continue in life and health until I become a Calvinist, at least in his exclamation of 'mon Dieu! jusque á quand'! would make me immortal. I can never join Calvin in addressing his god. He was indeed an Atheist, which I can never be; or rather his religion was Dæmonism. If ever man worshipped a false god, he did. The being described in his 5. points is not the God whom you and I acknolege [sic] and adore, the Creator and benevolent governor of the world; but a dæmon of malignant spirit. It would be more pardonable to believe in no god at all, than to blaspheme him by the atrocious attributes of Calvin. Indeed I think that every Christian sect gives a great handle to Atheism by their general dogma that, without a revelation, there would not be sufficient proof of the being of a god. Now one sixth of mankind only are supposed to be Christians: the other five sixths then, who do not believe in the Jewish and Christian revelation, are without a knolege [sic] of the existence of a god! This gives compleatly a gain de cause to the disciples of Ocellus, Timacus, Spinosa, Diderot and D'Holbach. The argument which they rest on as triumphant and unanswerable is that, in every hypothesis of Cosmogony you must admit an eternal pre-existence of something; and according to the rule of sound philosophy, you are never to employ two principles to solve a difficulty when one will suffice. They say then that it is more simple to believe at once in the eternal pre-existence of the world, as it is now going on, and may for ever go on by the principle of reproduction which we see and witness, than to believe in the eternal pre-existence of an ulterior cause, or Creator of the world, a being whom we see not, and know not, of whose form substance and mode or place of existence, or of action no sense informs us, no power of the mind enables us to delineate or comprehend. On the contrary I hold (without appeal to revelation) that when we take a view of the Universe, in it's parts general or particular, it is impossible for the human mind not to perceive and feel a conviction of design, consummate skill, and indefinite power in every atom of it's composition. The movements of the heavenly bodies, so exactly held in their course by the balance of centrifugal and centripetal forces, the structure of our earth itself, with it's distribution of lands, waters and atmosphere, animal and vegetable bodies, examined in all their minutest particles, insects mere atoms of life, yet as perfectly organised as man or mammoth, the mineral substances, their generation and uses, it is impossible, I say, for the human mind not to believe that there is, in all this, design, cause and effect, up to an ultimate cause, a fabricator of all things from matter and motion, their preserver and regulator while permitted to exist in their present forms, and their regenerator into new and other forms. We see, too, evident proofs of the necessity of a superintending power to maintain the Universe in it's course and order. Stars, well known, have disappeared, new ones have come into view, comets, in their incalculable courses, may run foul of suns and planets and require renovation under other laws; certain races of animals are become extinct; and, were there no restoring power, all existences might extinguish successively, one by one, until all should be reduced to a shapeless chaos. So irresistible are these evidences of an intelligent and powerful Agent that, of the infinite numbers of men who have existed thro' all time, they have believed, in the proportion of a million at least to Unit, in the hypothesis of an eternal pre-existence of a creator, rather than in that of a self-existent Universe. Surely this unanimous sentiment renders this more probable than that of the few in the other hypothesis. Some early Christians indeed have believed in the coeternal preexistence of both the Creator and the world, without changing their relation of cause and effect.[47]

To Benjamin Rush, Jefferson wrote:

His [Jesus'] parentage was obscure; his condition poor; his education null; his natural endowments great; his life correct and innocent; he was meek, benevolent, patient, firm, disinterested, and of the sublimest eloquence....According to the ordinary fate of those who attempt to enlighten and reform mankind, he fell an early victim to the jealousy and combination of the altar and the throne, at about thirty-three years of age.

[His] system of morals,...if filled up in the style and spirit of the rich fragments he left us, would be the most perfect and sublime that has ever been taught by man. . . . 1. He corrected the deism of the Jews, confirming them in their belief of one only God, and giving them juster notions of His attributes and government. 2. His moral doctrines relating to kindred and friends were more pure and perfect than those of the most correct of the philosophers, and greatly more so than those of the Jews; and they went far beyond both in inculcating universal philanthropy, not only to kindred and friends, to neighbors and countrymen, but to all mankind, gathering all into one family under the bonds of love, charity, peace, common wants, and common aids. A development of this head will evince the peculiar superiority of the system of Jesus over all others. 3. The precepts of philosophy, and of the Hebrew code, laid hold of actions only. He pushed his scrutinies into the heart of man, erected his tribunal in the region of his thoughts, and purified the waters at the fountainhead. 4. He taught emphatically the doctrines of a future state, which was either doubted or disbelieved by the Jews, and wielded it with efficacy as an important incentive, supplementary to the other motives to moral conduct.[48]

What, specifically, of Jesus' doctrines did Jefferson *not* believe? He denied the Trinity. In an August 22, 1813, letter to John Adams, he said:

It is too late in the day for men of sincerity to pretend that they believe in the Platonic mysticisms that three are one, and one is three; and yet the one is not three, and the three are not one: to divide mankind by a single letter into sians and sians ["consubstantialists and like-substantialists"]. But this constitutes the craft, the power and the profit of the priests. Sweep away their gossamer fabrics then, like the quakers, live without an order of priests, moralise for ourselves, follow the oracle of conscience, and say nothing about what no man can understand, nor therefore believe; for I suppose belief to be the assent of the mind to an intelligible proposition.[49]

In an 1821 letter to Timothy Pickering, Jefferson wrote:

No one sees with greater pleasure than myself the progress of reason in its advances towards rational Christianity. When we shall have done away the incomprehensible jargon of the Trinitarian arithmetic, that three are one and one is three; when we shall have knocked down the artificial scaffolding reared to mask from view the simple structure of Jesus; when, in short, we shall have unlearned everything which has been taught since His day, and got back to the pure and simple doctrines He inculcated, we shall then be truly and worthily His disciples; and my opinion is that if nothing had ever been added to what flowed purely from His lips, the whole world would at this day have been Christian....The religion-builders have so distorted and deformed the doctrines of Jesus, so muffled them in mysticisms, fancies, and falsehoods, have caricatured them into forms so monstrous and inconceivable, as to shock reasonable thinkers, to revolt them against the whole, and drive them rashly to pronounce its Founder an impostor.[50]

He did not believe in a literal virgin birth:

And the day will come when the mystical generation of Jesus, by the supreme being as his father in the womb of a virgin will be classed with the fable of the generation of Minerva in the brain of Jupiter.[51]

He did not believe that Jesus was divine. In an 1803 letter to Dr. Benjamin Rush, he said:

My views of [the Christian religion]...are the result of a life of inquiry and reflection, and very different from that anti-Christian system imputed to me by those who know nothing of my opinions. To the corruptions of Christianity I am, indeed, opposed; but not to the genuine precepts of Jesus himself. I am a Christian, in the only sense in which he wished anyone to be-sincerely attached to his doctrines, in preference to all others; ascribing to himself every human excellence, and believing he never claimed any other.[52]

He also believed that Jesus was "good if ever man was."[53]

He believed (or at least hoped) that there were many paths to heaven. In an 1814 letter, he wrote:

I must ever believe that religion substantially good which produces an honest life, and we have been authorized, by One whom you and I equally respect, to judge of the tree by its fruit. Our particular principles of religion are a subject of accountability to our God alone. I inquire after no man's, and trouble none with mine; nor is it given to us in this life to know whether yours or mine, our friends or foes, are exactly the right. Nay, we have heard it said that there is not a Quaker or a Baptist, a Presbyterian or an Episcopalian, a Catholic or a Protestant in heaven; that, on entering that gate, we leave those badges of schism behind, and find ourselves united in those principles only in which God has united us all. Let us not be uneasy, then, about the different roads we may pursue, as believing them to be the shortest to that, our last abode; but, following the guidance of a good conscience, let us be happy in the hope that by these different paths we shall all meet in the end. And that you and I may there meet and embrace is my earnest prayer.[54]

He believed there was no existence that was not material. In an 1820 letter, he wrote to John Adams:

To talk of immaterial existences is to talk of nothings. To say that the human soul, angels, God, are immaterial is to say they are nothings, or that there is no God, no angels, no soul. I cannot reason

otherwise; but I believe I am supported in my creed of material-
ism by the Lockes, the Tracys, and the Stewarts. At what age of
the Christian church this heresy of immaterialism, or masked atheism, crept in, I do not exactly know. But a heresy it certainly is.
Jesus taught nothing of it.[55]

He denied that John 1:1 referred to Jesus and that Jesus had a role
in the Creation. He stated that the "Cosmogony of the world is very
clearly laid down in the 3 first verses of the 1st. chapter of John," which
he translated:

Which truly translated means "in the beginning God existed, and
reason (or mind) was with God, and that mind was God. This was
in the beginning with God. All things were created by it, and without it was made not one thing which was made." Yet this text, so
plainly declaring the doctrine of Jesus that the world was created
by the supreme, intelligent being, has been perverted by modern
Christians to build up a second person of their tritheism by a mis-
translation of the word λογόσ. One of it's legitimate meanings
indeed is 'word.' But, in that sense, it makes an unmeaning jargon: while the other meaning 'reason', equally legitimate, explains
rationally the eternal preexistence of God, and his creation of the
world. Knowing how incomprehensible it was that 'a word,' the
mere action or articulation of the voice and organs of speech could
create a world, they undertake to make of this articulation a second
preexisting being, and ascribe to him, and not to God, the creation
of the universe. The Atheist here plumes himself on the uselessness
of such a God, and the simpler hypothesis of a self-existent universe. The truth is that the greatest enemies to the doctrines of
Jesus are those calling themselves the expositors of them, who have
perverted them for the structure of a system of fancy absolutely
incomprehensible, and without any foundation in his genuine
words. And the day will come when the mystical generation of
Jesus, by the supreme being as his father in the womb of a virgin
will be classed with the fable of the generation of Minerva in the
brain of Jupiter. But we may hope that the dawn of reason and
freedom of thought in these United States will do away [with] all
this artificial scaffolding, and restore to us the primitive and genuine doctrines of this the most venerated reformer of human

errors. So much for your quotation of Calvin's 'mon dieu! jusqu'a quand' in which, when addressed to the God of Jesus, and our God, I join you cordially, and await his time and will with more readiness than reluctance. May we meet there again, in Congress, with our ancient Colleagues, and receive with them the seal of approbation 'Well done, good and faithful servants.'[56]

While he hoped there was life beyond death, he believed this was not because of anything that the Bible said. In an 1817 letter to Abigail Adams, he wrote:

Our next meeting must . . . be in the country to which [our past years] have flown—a country for us not now very distant. For this journey we shall need neither gold nor silver in our purse, nor scrip, nor coats, nor staves. Nor is the provision for it more easy than the preparation has been kind. Nothing proves more than this that the Being who presides over the world is essentially benevolent.[57]

In an 1823 letter to John Adams, Jefferson wrote: "An atheist . . . I can never be."[58] However, he knew and acknowledged that his beliefs were not orthodox. At least twice, he expressed his belief that his doctrine was unique: "I am of a sect by myself, as far as I know."[59]

Not surprisingly, some of Jefferson's least equivocal and most memorable religious statements were on the topic of religious freedom. In his book, *Notes on the State of Virginia*, he said: "Millions of innocent men, women, and children, since the introduction of Christianity, have been burnt, tortured, fined, imprisoned; yet we have not advanced one inch towards uniformity. What has been the effect of coercion? To make one half the world fools, and the other half hypocrites."[60]

In a September 23, 1800, letter to Benjamin Rush, Jefferson said that if he were elected president, he would not permit any church to become an established church, "for I have sworn upon the altar of God, eternal hostility against every form of tyranny over the mind of man."[61]

He died on July 4, 1826, in Charlottesville, Virginia.

CONCLUSION

Jefferson believed there was only one God and Jesus was a good teacher, a reforming rabbi, and a moral philosopher. He did not believe

Jesus was divine or that he was born of a virgin. While Jefferson cannot be termed a Christian under any biblical definition, he had a great respect for some of Jesus' moral teachings and encouraged that respect in others.

Perhaps the most accurate encapsulation of his religious beliefs was one he made himself: "I never had sense enough to comprehend the articles of faith of the Church."[62]

NOTES

1. Willard Sterne Randall, *Thomas Jefferson: A Life* (New York: Henry Holt, 1993), 11.

2. Fawn M. Brodie, *Thomas Jefferson: An Intimate History* (New York: Norton, 1974, 1998), 54.

3. Ibid., 55.

4. Thomas Jefferson, *The Papers of Thomas Jefferson*, ed. Julian P. Boyd, vol. 1 (Princeton, NJ: Princeton University Press, 1950, 1955), 3–4.

5. Ibid., 10.

6. Andrew M. Allison, *Thomas Jefferson: Champion of History*, 320–22, appendix: "An Intimate View of Jefferson by His Grandson." Allison notes: "The following undated letter was sent by Jefferson's oldest grandson, Thomas Jefferson Randolph, to the biographer Henry S. Randall. It was probably written in the 1850s, when Randall was preparing materials for his three-volume *Life of Thomas Jefferson* (New York: Derby & Jackson, 1858). The text of the letter is taken from the third volume of that work, pages 543–44 and 671–76. Punctuation and paragraphing have been altered somewhat for the sake of clarity, and topical subheadings have been inserted to facilitate reading."

7. Jefferson, *The Papers of Thomas Jefferson*, vol. 2, 6–7. The most significant change between Jefferson's draft and the draft adopted is that Jefferson referred to a desire to encourage and support the "Protestant Episcopal Church," to which Reverend Charles Clay belonged. Why, then, did this refer to Reverend Charles Clay of the "Calvinistical Reformed Church"? Julian Boyd, editor of Jefferson's papers, proposed the theory that Reverend Clay had abandoned the denominational identification with the Protestant Episcopal Church due to its association with the nation's enemy. Jefferson also subscribed thirty shillings per year for the support of a clerk to assist Reverend Clay (Jefferson, *The Papers of Thomas Jefferson*, vol. 2, 8–9).

8. Ibid., vol. 1, 116.

9. Ibid., vol. 1, 76–77.

10. Edmund Fuller and David E. Green, *God in the White House: The Faiths of American Presidents* (New York: Crown Publishers, 1968), 36.

11. Jefferson, *The Papers of Thomas Jefferson*, vol. 3, 177–79.

12. Thomas Jefferson, *The Writings of Thomas Jefferson*, eds. Albert Ellery, Thomas Lipscomb, and Andrew Bergh, vol. 6 (Washington, DC: The Thomas Jefferson Memorial Association, 1907), 258.

13. Paul F. Boller Jr., *Presidential Campaigns* (New York and Oxford: Oxford University Press, 1984), 12.

14. Jefferson, *Messages and Papers of the Presidents: Thomas Jefferson, 1801.* March 4, 1801. First inaugural address.

15. Ibid.

16. John McCollister, *So Help Me God: The Faith of America's Presidents* (Louisville: Westminster/John Knox Press, 1991), 27.

17. Claude Bowers, *Jefferson in Power: The Death Struggle of the Federalists* (Boston and New York: Houghton Mifflin, 1936, 1967), 22.

18. Brodie, *Thomas Jefferson*, 377. Found in Jefferson, *Writings of Thomas Jefferson*, eds. Ellery, Lipscomb, and Bergh, vol. 10, 299.

19. Bowers, *Jefferson in Power*, 261.

20. Jefferson, March 4, 1805. Second inaugural address.

21. Ibid.

22. Jefferson, *The Writings of Thomas Jefferson*, eds. Ellery, Lipscomb, and Bergh, vol. 13, 389. Fuller and Green quoted parts of the letter in *God in the White House*, 34–35; Benjamin Weiss, *God in American History: A Documentation of America's Religious Heritage* (Grand Rapids: Zondervan, 1966), 61.

23. John Adams and Thomas Jefferson, *The Complete Correspondence between Thomas Jefferson and Abigail and John Adams,* ed. Lester J. Cappon, vol. 2, (Chapel Hill: University of North Carolina Press, 1959, 1988), 421. From a January 24, 1814, letter that Jefferson wrote to Adams.

24. Randall, *Thomas Jefferson*, 555.

25. Fuller and Green, *God in the White House*, 35; Weiss, *God in American History*, 61.

26. Fuller and Green, *God in the White House*, 34.

27. Allison, *Thomas Jefferson*, 320–22.

28. Brodie, *Thomas Jefferson*, 371.

29. Jefferson, *The Writings of Thomas Jefferson*, eds. Ellery, Lipscomb, and Bergh, vol. 15, 60.

30. Allison, *Thomas Jefferson*, 300–303.

31. Jefferson, *The Writings of Thomas Jefferson*, eds. Ellery, Lipscomb, and Bergh, vol. 10, 375.

32. Ibid., vol. 14, 81.

33. Adams and Jefferson, *The Complete Correspondence,* vol. 2, 359.

34. Jefferson, *The Writings of Thomas Jefferson*, eds. Ellery, Lipscomb, and Bergh, vol. 14, 385.

35. Bergh, *The Writings of Thomas Jefferson*, vol. 14, pg. 385. From an 1816 letter that Jefferson wrote to Charles Thompson.

36. Allison, *Thomas Jefferson*, 300–303.

37. Jefferson, *The Writings of Thomas Jefferson,* eds. Ellery, Lipscomb, and Bergh, vol. 14, 288.

38. Ibid., vol. 15, 391.

39. Ibid., vol. 10, 376; Bowers, *Jefferson in Power,* 200.

40. Adams and Jefferson, *The Complete Correspondence,* vol. 1, 433.

41. Thomas Jefferson, *The Writings of Thomas Jefferson,* ed. Paul Leicester Ford, vol. 2 (New York: G. P. Putnam's Sons, 1892–1899), 103.

42. Brodie, *Thomas Jefferson,* 453; Jefferson, *The Writings of Thomas Jefferson,* eds. Ellery, Lipscomb, and Bergh, vol. 16, 101.

43. Fuller and Green, *God in the White House,* 33.

44. Ibid.

45. Adams and Jefferson, *The Complete Correspondence,* vol. 2, 368.

46. Jefferson, *The Writings of Thomas Jefferson,* eds. Ellery, Lipscomb, and Bergh, vol. 15, 383; Fuller and Green, *God in the White House,* 35.

47. Adams and Jefferson, *The Complete Correspondence,* vol. 2, 591–94.

48. Jefferson, *The Writings of Thomas Jefferson,* eds. Ellery, Lipscomb, and Bergh, vol. 10, 383–84.

49. Adams and Jefferson, *The Complete Correspondence,* vol. 2, 368.

50. Jefferson, *The Writings of Thomas Jefferson,* eds. Ellery, Lipscomb, and Bergh, vol. 15, 323.

51. Adams and Jefferson, *The Complete Correspondence,* vol. 2, 591–94.

52. Jefferson, *The Writings of Thomas Jefferson,* eds. Ellery, Lipscomb, and Bergh, vol. 10, 379.

53. Claude Bowers, *Jefferson and Hamilton: The Struggle for Democracy in America* (Boston and New York: Houghton & Mifflin, 1925, 1945), 104.

54. Jefferson, *The Writings of Thomas Jefferson,* eds. Ellery, Lipscomb, and Bergh, vol. 14, 198.

55. Ibid., vol. 15, 274.

56. Adams and Jefferson, *The Complete Correspondence,* vol. 2, 591–94.

57. Jefferson, *The Writings of Thomas Jefferson,* eds. Ellery, Lipscomb, and Bergh, vol. 15, 96.

58. Ibid., 425.

59. Jefferson, *The Writings of Thomas Jefferson,* eds. Ellery, Lipscomb, and Bergh, vol. 15, 203. From a June 25, 1819, letter to Ezra Stiles. Also expressed in a January 11, 1817, letter to John Adams found in Adams and Jefferson, *The Complete Correspondence,* 506.

60. Brodie, *Thomas Jefferson,* 157.

61. Ibid., 326.

62. Randall, *Thomas Jefferson,* 203. He made the statement when turning down an invitation to become a child's godfather. Randall quoted Merrill D. Petersen, *Thomas Jefferson and the New Nation* (New York and Oxford: Oxford University Press, 1970), 50.

JOHN ADAMS

JOHN ADAMS was born on October 30, 1735, in Braintree (now Quincy), Massachusetts. The First Church was central to town life, and his father was a deacon in the church.[1]

John Adams was raised a Calvinist; this was his heritage. While he remained religious and what he would have called a "Christian" all his life, he eventually abandoned the central doctrines of his Calvinist heritage. His first step was evidenced in a letter he wrote on September 1, 1755, to Nathan Webb. In this letter—his first extant—he referred to sacrificing Sundays to "the frigid John Calvin."[2]

In a letter written to Charles Cushing (a friend who had urged him to enter the ministry) on April 1, 1756, Adams described the life of a minister. He indicated he had intended to become a minister but was not going to do it "suddenly." He said:

> The Divine [pastor] has a Thousand Obstacles to encounter. He has his own and his Peoples Prejudices to Combat—the capricious Humours and Fancies of the Vulgar to submit to—Poverty to struggle with—the charge of Heresy to bear—systematical Divinity, alias systematical vexation of spirit to study and sift. But on the other hand He has more Leisure to inform his mind, to subdue his Passions—fewer Temptations to intemperance and injustice, tho' more to trimming and Hypocrisy—an opportunity of diffusing Truth and Virtue among his People. Upon the Whole I think if he relies on his own understanding more than the decrees

of Councils, or the sentiments of Fathers, if he resolutely discharges the Duties of his Station, according to the Dictates of his mind, if he spends his Time in the improvement of his Head in Knowledge and his heart in Virtue, instead of sauntering about the streets, he will be able to do more good to his fellow men and make better provision for his own future Happiness in this Profession, than in any other.

However I am as yet very contented in the place of a School Master. I shall not therefore very suddenly become a preacher. When I do I hope to live in the same neighbourhood with you.[3]

He added the postscript: "P.S.—There is a story about town that I am an *Ormenian* [Armenian]."[4] To be charged with Armenianism in eighteenth-century Calvinist New England was, in effect, to be charged with heresy: The Armenian emphases on free will and the possibility of universal salvation sharply contrasted with the Calvinist emphases on God's sovereignty and predestination.

On August 21, 1756, he contracted with a Mr. Putnam to "study law under his inspection for two years." Yet he struggled with the decision between law and the ministry. He wrote the next day in his diary:

Necessity drove me to this determination, but my inclination was, I think, to preach. However, that would not do. But I set out with firm resolutions, I think, never to commit any meanness or injustice in the practice of law. The study and practice of law, I am sure, does not dissolve the obligations of morality or of religion. And although the reason of my quitting divinity was my opinion concerning some disputed points, I hope I shall not give reason of offence to any in that profession by imprudent warmth.[5]

What were those disputed points? Adams hinted at them in several subsequent letters. In an August 29, 1756, letter to Richard Cranch, he said:

I have engagd [sic] with Mr. Putnam to study Law with him, 2 years, and to keep the school at the same time. It will be hard work, but the more difficult and dangerous the Enterprize, a brighter Crown of Lawrell [sic] is bestowed on the Conqueror.

However, I am not without apprehensions concerning the success of this resolution, but I am under much fewer Apprehensions than I was when I thought of preaching. The frightful Engines of Ecclesiastical concils [sic], of diabolical Malice and Calvinistical good-nature never failed to terrify me exceedingly whenever I thought of Preaching. But the Point is now determined, and I shall have Liberty to think for myself without molesting others or being molested myself.[6]

In a letter written that September to John Wentworth, he expressed his thoughts in similar language:

However the Anxiety of mind that has made me uneasy to myself and friends for this year past is at length in some Measure removed. I have begun the study of Law with Mr. Putnam a very sensible and agreeable Gentleman of the Profession in this Town. How I shall succeed in the Law, God only knows. I am not without Apprehensions, but I am much less troubled with them than I was before I was determind [sic] what Profession to follow. I never thought of the frightful Ecclesiastical Apparatus, of Councils, Creeds &c. without extream [sic] Horror.[7]

And so Adams stepped out on a course that led to the legal profession, a life involved in public affairs, and, eventually, to the presidency.

Despite his August 21, 1756, resolution "to not give reason of offence to any in that profession [preaching] by imprudent warmth,"[8] he vented his feelings about the profession in correspondence. In a letter written to Charles Cushing on October 19, 1756, he said: "As far as I can observe, people are not disposed to inquire for piety, integrity, good sense or learning in a young preacher, but for stupidity (for so I must call the pretended sanctity of some dunces), irresistible grace and original sin. I have not in one expression exceeded the limits of truth, tho' you think I am warm. Could you advise me, then, who you know have not the highest opinion of what is called Orthodoxy, to engage in a profession like this."[9]

In a 1763 essay entitled, "All Men Would Be Tyrants if They Could," Adams moved from a discussion of the tyranny of standing armies to a discussion of what he believed was the tyranny of the clergy. He said:

> Was there ever a Clergy, that have gained, by their Natural
> Ascendancy over private Consciences, any important Power in the
> State, that did not restlessly aspire by every Art, by Flattery and
> Intrigues, by Bribery and Corruption, by wresting from the People
> the Means of Knowledge, and by inspiring mysterious and awful
> apprehensions of themselves by Promises of Heaven and by
> Threats of D——mnation, to establish themselves in opulence,
> Indolence, and Magnificence, at the Expence of the Toil, and
> Industry, the Limbs, the Liberties and Lives of all the rest of
> Mankind.[10]

In other correspondence, Adams made it clear that he did not
believe in the doctrine of predestination. In a letter written to Samuel
Quincy on April 22, 1761, Adams said:

> The same vanity which gave rise to that strange religious Dogma,
> that God elected a precious few (of which however every Man
> who believes the doctrine is always One) to Life eternal without
> regard to any foreseen Virtue, and reprobated all the Rest, with-
> out regard to any foreseen Vice—A doctrine which, with serious
> gravity, represents the world, as under the government of Humour
> and Caprice, and which Hottentots and Mohawks would reject
> with horror.[11]

Over time, Adams became settled in his law practice; his correspondence from this period deals little with theological matters.

He married Abigail Smith on October 25, 1764.

While John Adams was attending the Continental Congress in
Philadelphia, he attended two or three services a day. He visited
Anglican, Methodist, Baptist, Presbyterian, Quaker, and Moravian
churches. He even visited a "Romish" church—once. He commented
on each service in his diary.[12]

During the Continental Congress, Jefferson opposed a proposal for
a fast day that Adams supported. Adams thought this opposition "cast
aspersions on Christianity," in the words of David McCullough.[13]

Benjamin Rush wrote Adams about Adams's own reaction later:

> You rose and defended the motion, and in reply to Mr. Jefferson's
> objections to Christianity you said you were sorry to hear such sen-

timents from a gentleman whom you so highly respected and with whom you agreed on so many subjects, and it was the only instance you had ever known of a man of sound sense and genius that was an enemy to Christianity. You suspected, you told me, that you had offended him, but that he soon convinced you to the contrary by crossing the room and taking a seat in the chair next to you.[14]

In a speech (c. 1776) in favor of the Declaration of Independence, Adams said:

Sir, before God, I believe that the hour is come. My judgment approves this measure, and my whole heart is in it. All that I have, and all that I am, and all that I hope, in this life, I am now ready here to stake upon it; and I leave off as I began, that live or die, survive or perish, I am for the Declaration. It is my living sentiment, and by the blessing of God it shall be my dying sentiment, Independence *now*, and INDEPENDENCE FOREVER.[15]

He was elected president in 1796 and served one term. In his inaugural address, he discussed the formation of the republic. He said: "Relying, however, on the purity of their intentions, the justice of their cause, and the integrity and intelligence of the people, under an overruling Providence which had so signally protected this country from the first, the representatives of this nation, then consisting of little more than half its present number, not only broke to pieces the chains which were forging and the rod of iron that was lifted up, but frankly cut asunder the ties which had bound them, and launched into an ocean of uncertainty."[16]

In the speech, he added: "[W]ith humble reverence, I feel it to be my duty to add, if a veneration for the religion of a people who profess and call themselves Christians, and a fixed resolution to consider a decent respect for Christianity among the best recommendations for the public service, can enable me in any degree to comply with your wishes, it shall be my strenuous endeavor that this sagacious injunction of the two Houses shall not be without effect."[17]

Adams concluded: "And may that Being who is supreme over all, the Patron of Order, the Fountain of Justice, and the Protector in all ages of the world of virtuous liberty, continue His blessing upon this nation and its Government and give it all possible success and duration consistent with the ends of His providence."[18]

On March 23, 1798, Adams issued this call for prayer:

As the safety and prosperity of nations ultimately and essentially depend on the protection and the blessing of Almighty God, and the national acknowledgment of this truth is not only an indispensable duty which the people owe to Him, but a duty whose natural influence is favorable to the promotion of that morality and piety without which social happiness can not exist nor the blessings of a free government be enjoyed; and as this duty, at all times incumbent, is so especially in seasons of difficulty or of danger, when existing or threatening calamities, the just judgments of God against prevalent iniquity, are a loud call to repentance and reformation; and as the United States of America are at present placed in a hazardous and afflictive situation by the unfriendly disposition, conduct, and demands of a foreign power, evinced by repeated refusals to receive our messengers of reconciliation and peace, by depredation on our commerce, and the infliction of injuries on very many of our fellow-citizens while engaged in their lawful business on the seas—under these considerations it has appeared to me that the duty of imploring the mercy and benediction of Heaven on our country demands at this time a special attention from its inhabitants.

I have therefore thought fit to recommend, and I do hereby recommend, that Wednesday, the 9th day of May next, be observed throughout the United States as a day of solemn humiliation, fasting, and prayer; that the citizens of these States, abstaining on that day from their customary worldly occupations, offer their devout addresses to the Father of Mercies agreeably to those forms or methods which they have severally adopted as the most suitable and becoming; that all religious congregations do, with the deepest humility, acknowledge before God the manifold sins and transgressions with which we are justly chargeable as individuals and as a nation, beseeching Him at the same time, of His infinite grace, through the Redeemer of the World, freely to remit all our offenses, and to incline us by His Holy Spirit to that sincere repentance and reformation which may afford us reason to hope for his inestimable favor and heavenly benediction; that it be made the subject of particular and earnest supplication that our country may be protected from all the dangers which threaten it; that our civil and religious privileges may be preserved inviolate and perpetuated to the latest generations; that our public councils and magistrates may be especially enlightened and directed at this critical period; that the American people may be united in those bonds of amity and mutual confidence and inspired with that vigor and fortitude by which they have in times past been so highly distinguished and by which they have obtained such invaluable advantages; that the health of the inhabitants of our land may be preserved, and their agriculture, commerce, fisheries, arts, and manufactures be blessed and prospered; that the principles of genuine piety and sound morality may influence the minds and govern the lives of every description of our citizens, and that the blessings of peace, freedom, and pure religion may be speedily extended to all the nations of the earth.

And finally, I recommend that on the said day the duties of humiliation and prayer be accompanied by fervent thanksgiving to the Bestower of Every Good Gift, not only for His having hitherto protected and preserved the people of these United States in the independent enjoyment of their religious and civil freedom, but also for having prospered them in a wonderful progress of population, and for conferring on them many and great favors conducive to the happiness and prosperity of a nation.[19]

Adams issued another call for prayer on March 6, 1799. He said:

As no truth is more clearly taught in the Volume of Inspiration, nor any more fully demonstrated by the experience of all ages, than that a deep sense and a due acknowledgment of the governing providence of a Supreme Being and of the accountableness of men to Him as the searcher of hearts and righteous distributer of rewards and punishments are conducive equally to the happiness and rectitude of individuals and to the well-being of communities; as it is also most reasonable in itself that men who are made capable of social acts and relations, who owe their improvements to the social state, and who derive their enjoyments from it, should, as a society, make their acknowledgments of dependence and obligation to Him who hath endowed them with these capacities and elevated them in the scale of existence by these distinctions; as it is likewise a plain dictate of duty and a strong sentiment of nature that in circumstances of great urgency and seasons of imminent danger earnest and particular supplications should be made to Him who is able to defend or to destroy; as, moreover, the most precious interests of the people of the United States are still held in jeopardy by the hostile designs and insidious acts of a foreign nation, as well as by the dissemination among them of those principles, subversive of the foundations of all religious, moral, and social obligations, that have produced incalculable mischief and misery in other countries; and as, in fine, the observance of special seasons for public religious solemnities is happily calculated to avert the evils which we ought to deprecate and to excite to the performance of the duties which we ought to discharge by calling and fixing the attention of the people at large to the momentous truths already recited, by affording opportunity to teach and inculcate them by animating devotion and giving to it the character of a national act:

For these reasons I have thought proper to recommend, and I do hereby recommend accordingly, that Thursday, the 25th day of April next, be observed throughout the United States of America as a day of solemn humiliation, fasting, and prayer; that the citizens on that day abstain as far as may be from their secular occupations, devote the time to the sacred duties of religion in public and in private; that they call to mind our numerous offenses against the Most High God, confess them before Him with the sincerest penitence, implore His pardoning mercy, through the Great Mediator and Redeemer, for our past transgressions, and that through the grace of His Holy Spirit we may be disposed and enabled to yield a more suitable obedience to His righteous requisitions in time to come; that He would interpose to arrest the progress of that impiety and licentiousness in principle and practice so offensive to Himself and so ruinous to mankind; that He would make us deeply sensible that "righteousness exalteth a nation, but sin is a reproach to any people"; that He would turn us from our transgressions and turn His displeasure from us; that He would withhold us from unreasonable discontent, from disunion, faction, sedition, and insurrection; that He would preserve our country from the desolating sword; that He would save our cities and towns from a repetition of those awful pestilential visitations under which they have lately suffered so severely, and that the health of our inhabitants generally may be precious in His sight; that He would favor us with fruitful seasons and so bless the labors of the husbandman as that there may be food in abundance for man and beast; that He would prosper our commerce, manufactures, and fisheries, and give success to the people in all their lawful industry and enterprise; that He would smile on our colleges, academies, schools, and seminaries of learning, and make them nurseries of sound science, morals, and religion; that He would bless all magistrates, from the highest to the lowest, give them the true spirit of their station, make them a terror to evil doers and a praise to them that do well; that He would preside over the councils of the nation at this critical period, enlighten them to a just discernment of the public interest, and save them from mistake, division, and discord; that He would make succeed our preparations for defense and bless our armaments by land and by sea; that He would put an end to the effusion of human blood and the accumulation of human misery among the contending nations of the earth by disposing them to justice, to equity, to benevolence, and to peace; and that he would extend the blessings of knowledge, of true liberty, and of pure and undefiled religion throughout the world.

And I do also recommend that with these acts of humiliation, penitence, and prayer fervent thanksgiving to the Author of All Good be united for the countless favors which He is still continuing to the people of the United States, and which render their condition as a nation eminently happy when compared with the lot of others.[20]

These calls for prayer are reprinted because they provide a useful balance to some of Adams' later privately expressed religious opinions. As will be seen, Adams eventually denied Jesus' divinity and other essential doctrines. These later statements, which do, I believe, accurately reflect Adams' opinions on those topics, must be viewed in light of the fact that he *did* believe in a divine God (the Father) who oversaw the course of nations and was guiding and directing the United States.

In the years following his presidency, Adams reexamined and modified his religious opinions. In letters to Christians, he still expressed a profound respect for the Christian religion. In a letter to Benjamin Rush, he said:

> The Christian religion, as I understand it, is the brightness of glory and the express portrait of the eternal, self-existent, independent, benevolent, all-powerful and all-merciful Creator, Preserver and Father of the Universe. . . . It will last as long as the world. Neither savage nor civilized man could ever have discovered or invented it. Ask me not then whether I am a Catholic or Protestant, Calvinist or Arminian. As far as they are Christians, I wish to be a fellow disciple of them all.[21]

At another time, he described the Christian religion in these words:

> The Christian religion is, above all the religions that ever prevailed or existed in ancient or modern times, the religion of virtue, equity, and humanity, let the blackguard Paine say what he will; it is resignation to God, it is goodness itself to man.[22]

Yet though his definition of the term "Christianity" had changed, Adams still retained respect for elements of the Christian religion—including a belief that Jesus was "more than mortal." A biography by his grandson quoted him as saying that he believed the "Sermon on the Mount as a perfect code presented to man by a more than mortal teacher."[23]

Adams viewed Jesus as more than mortal but less than divine. Perhaps his most dramatic—and most saddening—religious statement is when in a letter to Thomas Jefferson, he stated that even if God told him in person that there was a Trinity, he still would reject God's statement and believe in his Unitarian god. Adams said:

> Had you and I been forty days with Moses on Mount Sinai and admitted to behold the divine Shekinah, and there told that one was three and three, one: We might not have had courage to deny it, but We could not have believed it. The thunders and Lightenings and Earthqu[ak]es and the transcendent Splendors and Glories, might have overwhelmed Us with terror and Amazement: but We could not have believed the doctrine. We should be more likely to say in our hearts, whatever We might say

with our Lips, This is Chance. There is no God! No Truth. This is all delusion, fiction and a lie: or it is all Chance. But what is Chance? It is motion; it is Action; it is Event; it is Phenomenon, without Cause. Chance is no cause at all. It is nothing. And Nothing has produced all this Pomp and Splendor; and Nothing may produce Our eternal d——-ation in the flames of Hell fire and Brimstone for what We know, as well as this tremendous Exhibition of Terror and Falsehood.[24]

After stating the doctrine of orthodox Christian theologians (that God "created this Speck of Dirt and the human Species for his glory"), he questioned:

Now, my Friend, can Prophecies, or miracles convince You, or Me, that infinite Benevolence, Wisdom and Power, created and preserves, for a time, innumerable millions to make them miserable, forever; for his own Glory? Wretch! What is his Glory? Is he ambitious? does he want promotion? Is he vain? tickled with adulation? Exulting and tryumphing in his Power and the Sweetness of his Vengeance? Pardon me, my Maker, for these Aweful Questions. My answer to them is always ready: I believe no such Things. My Adoration of the Author of the Universe is too profound and too sincere. The Love of God and his Creation; delight, joy, Tryumph, Exultation in my own existence, 'tho but an Atom, a Molecule Organique, in the Universe, are my religion. Howl, snarl, bite, Ye Calvinistick! Ye Athanasian Divines, if you will. Ye will say, I am no Christian: I say Ye are no Christians: and there the Account is ballanced. Yet I believe all the honest men among you, are Christians in my Sense of the Word.[25]

Another doctrine Adams rejected was the doctrine of universal depravity (the doctrine that mankind fell from a perfect state and that we only do good with God's help). In an April 19, 1817, letter to Jefferson, he wrote that several times during his recent reading he had been on the point of exclaiming that "This would be the best of all possible worlds if there were no religion in it." But, he said, "Without Religion this World would be Something not fit to be mentioned in polite Company, I mean Hell. So far from believing in the total and universal depravity of human Nature; I believe there is no Individual totally depraved. The most abandoned Scoundrel that ever existed, never Yet Wholly extinguished his Conscience, and while Conscience remains there is some Religion."[26]

While Adams believed there was a future state after death, his hope was based on logic and not on the Bible. After Abigail Adams died, Thomas Jefferson sent John Adams a letter of consolation. Adams replied:

> I do not know how to prove physically, that we shall meet and know each other in a future state; nor does Revelation, as I can find, give us any positive assurance of such a felicity. My reasons for believing it, as I do most undoubtedly, are that I cannot conceive such a being could make such a species as the human, merely to live and die on this earth. If I did not believe in a future state, I should believe in no God. This Universe, this all would appear, with all of its swelling pomp, a boyish firework. And if there be a future state, why should the Almighty dissolve forever all the tender ties which unite us so delightfully in this world, and forbid us to see each other in the next?[27]

Adams also denied miracles. He believed that the fact that God had set up laws to govern the world excluded God from superseding those laws upon occasion. In a June 20, 1815, letter to Jefferson, Adams wrote: "The question before the human race is, Whether the God of nature shall govern the World by his own laws, or Whether Priests and Kings shall rule it by fictitious Miracles? Or, in other Words, whether Authority is originally in the People? or whether it has descended for 1800 Years in a succession of Popes and Bishops, or brought down from Heaven by the holy Ghost in the form of a Dove, in a Phyal of holy oil?"[28]

Adams closed the letter: "It has been long, very long a settled opinion in my Mind that there is not now, never will be, and never was but one being who can Understand the Universe. And that it is not only vain but wicked for insects to pretend to comprehend it."[29]

He wished to reduce the Bible to what he could understand. On November 14, 1813, Adams wrote Jefferson: "If I had Eyes and Nerves, I would go through both Testaments and mark all that I understand."[30]

Not surprisingly, Adams thought that men should be able to debate publicly whether the Bible was inspired. In a January 2, 1825, letter to

Jefferson, Adams said that throughout the whole Christian world it was deemed a crime to deny the divine inspiration of the Bible. He discussed the punishments meted out by various countries for blasphemy, and stated fine and imprisonment awaited any who would question that in the United States. He then asked:

> Now what free inquiry when a writer must surely encounter the risk of fine or imprisonment for adducing any argument for investigation into the divine authority of these books? Who would run the risk of translating Volney's Recherches Nouvelles? who would run the risk of translating Dupuis? but I cannot enlarge upon this subject, though I have it much at heart. I think such laws a great embarrassment, great obstructions to the improvement of the human mind. Books that cannot bear examination ought not to be established as divine inspiration by penal laws. It is true few persons appear desirous to put such laws in execution and it is also true that some few persons are hardy enough to venture to depart from them; but as long as they continue in force as laws the human mind must make an awkward and clumsy progress in its investigations. I wish they were repealed. The substance and essence of Christianity as I understand it is eternal and unchangeable and will bear examination forever but it has been mixed with extraneous ingredients, which I think will not bear examination and they ought to be separated.[31]

He wanted to see the writings of pagan religions made available so later Americans could decide for themselves which religion was true. Adams wrote: "Translations of the Bible into all languages and sent among the people, I hope will produce translations into English and French, Spanish and German and Italian of sacred books of the Persians, the Chinese, the Hindoos, etc., etc., etc. Then our grandchildren and my great-grandchildren may compare notes and hold fast all that is good."[32] (Yet the concept that "man determines truth" is the foundational principle not of Christianity but of humanism.)

Even with these unorthodox doctrines, Adams reckoned himself a Christian. He did this by redefining Christianity as he saw fit. He believed that the doctrinal teaching of orthodox Christians was a corrupted form of Christianity. In his correspondence, he frequently referred to Christianity as corrupted. In a November 24, 1816, letter to Jefferson concerning the establishment of the American Bible Society, he said:

> We have now, it seems a National Bible Society, to propagate King James's Bible, through all nations. Would it not be better, to apply these pious subscriptions, to purify Christendom from the Corruptions of Christianity; than to propagate those Corruptions in Europe, Asia, Africa and America!
>
> Suppose, We should project a Society to translate Dupuis into all Languages and offer a Reward in Medals and Diamonds to any Man or Body of Men who would produce the best answer to it.[33]

> I almost shudder at the thought of alluding to the most fatal Example of the Abuses of Grief, which the History of Man kind has preserved. The Cross. Consider what calamities that Engine of Grief has produced! With the rational respect that is due to it, knavish Priests have added Prostitutions of it, that fill or might fill the blackest and bloodiest pages of human history.[34]

He referred to priests as "knavish" in the quote above, and in an unfriendly way in the following quote from a July 6, 1813, letter to Jefferson:

> John Quincy Adams, has written for Years, to his two Sons, Boys of 10 and 12, a Series of Letters, in which he pursues a plan more extensive than yours, but agreeing in most of the essential points. I wish these Letters could be preserved in the Bosoms of his Boys: but Women and Priests will get them: and I expect, if he makes a peace he will be obliged to retire like a Jay to study Prophecies to the End of his life.[35]

Also in the same letter, he stated that the Christian philosophy was "the most sublime and benevolent," agreeing with Jefferson, but stating that he was not "sufficiently acquainted" with Confucius, Zoroaster, Mahomet of the Druids, the Hindus, and other religions, to "form a decisive Opinion" as to whether the effects on their Systems of history had perverted their religions.

What had happened to change this essentially Calvinistic thinker into an agnostic? Adams's fatal theological flaw was that he believed he could decide what was true for himself. Yet Christians are to accept what God has told us is true.

This decision made him open to accepting alternative theological views. In later life, Adams came under the influence of Reverend Joseph Priestley. Compare his statements about the Bible above to these statements about Priestley in a July 22, 1813, letter to Jefferson:

> If Priestley had lived, I should certainly have corresponded with him. His Friend Cooper, who unfortunately for him and me, and you, had as fatal an influence over him as Hamilton had over Washington; and whose rash hot head led Priestley into all his Misfortunes and most [of] his Errors in Conduct, could not have prevented explanations between Priestley and me.
>
> I should propose to him a thousand, a million Questions. And no M[an] was more capable or better disposed to answer them candidly than Dr. Priestley. Scarcely any thing that has happened to me, in my curious Life has made a deeper Impression upon me, than that such a learned ingenious scientific and talented Madcap as Cooper, could have had influence enough to make Priestley my enemy.[36]
>
> Oh! that Priestley could live again! and have leisure and means. An Enquirer after Truth, who had neither time nor means might request him to search and research for answers to a few Questions.
>
> 1. Have We more than two Witnesses of the Life of Jesus? Matthew and John?
> 2. Have We one Witness to the Existence of Matthews Gospell in the first century?
> 3. Have We one Witness to the Existence of Johns Gospell in the first century?
> 4. Have We one Witness to the Existence of Marks Gospell in the first century?
> 5. Have We one Witness to the Existence of Lukes Gospell in the first century?
> 6. Have We any Witness to the existence of St. Thomas's Gospell, that is the Gospell of the Infancy in the first Century?
> 7. Have We any Evidence of the Existence of the Acts of the Apostles in the first Century?

8. Have We any Evidence of the Existence of the Supplement to the Acts of the Apostles, Peter and Paul, or Paul and Tecle, in the first Century?[37]

Who was this Reverend Joseph Priestley who so interested Adams and Jefferson? He was an eighteenth-century Unitarian minister and author. His best-remembered theological work was *History of the Corruptions of Christianity* (London, 1782). In his four-volume *History of Early Opinions Concerning Jesus Christ* (London, 1786), he advanced the doctrine that Christ was fallible. His son, Joseph, edited *Memoirs of the Reverend Joseph Priestley to the Year 1795, Written by Himself with a Continuation, to the Time of His Decease, by His Son, Joseph Priestley* (London, 1809). Reverend Priestley also wrote *The Doctrines of Heathen Philosophy Compared with Those of Revelation* (Northumberland, PA, 1804) and *Socrates and Jesus Compared*. Priestley advanced his Unitarian views, challenging the doctrines of orthodox Christianity on the grounds that they were corruptions.

To the end of his life, Adams retained respect for a few Christian doctrines. In 1816, he wrote that "the Ten Commandments and The Sermon on the Mount contain my religion."[38] In another letter written in the same year, he added that his "moral or religious Creed" had "for 50 or 60 years been contained in four short Words '*Be just and good.*' "[39]

He retained respect for the Sabbath (referring to Sunday) and was reluctant to travel on that day.[40]

To the end of his life, he expressed belief in a God who oversaw the course of nations—a "Providence" who may or may not have been a personal God. And he believed that this Providence's guidelines, the "general Principles of Christianity," formed a basis for the founding of our nation. On June 28, 1813, he wrote: "The *general Principles*, on which the Fathers Atchieved [sic] Independence, were the only Principles in which that beautiful Assembly of Gentlemen could Unite, and these Principles only could be intended by them in their Address, or by me in my Answer. And what were these *general Principles*? I answer, the general Principles of Christianity, in which all those Sects were United: And the *general Principles* of English and American Liberty, in which all those young Men United, and which had United all Parties in America, in Majorities sufficient to assert and maintain her Independence.

"Now I will avow, as I then believed, and now believe, that those general Principles of Christianity, are as eternal and immutable, as the Existence and Attributes of God; and that those Principles of Liberty, are as unalterable as human Nature and our terrestrial, mundane System."[41]

Adams died on July 4, 1826. Perhaps the best summary of his religion was made by his grandson and biographer, Charles Francis Adams, who wrote:

> He devoted himself to a very elaborate examination of the religion of all ages and nations, the results of which he communicated to paper in a desultory manner. The issue of it was the formation of his theological opinions very much in the mould adopted by the Unitarians of New England. Rejecting with the independent spirit which had in early life driven him from the ministry, the prominent doctrines of Calvinism, the trinity, atonement, and election, he was content to settle down upon the Sermon on the Mount as a perfect code presented to man by a more than mortal teacher.[42]

CONCLUSION

Though John Adams was raised a Calvinist, he abandoned Calvinism in his youth and gradually moved away from the doctrines of orthodox Christianity. If asked whether he was a Christian, he would have responded affirmatively—but only because he had redefined the term "Christian." By old age, he was not a Christian in the orthodox sense of the term.

The fact that he denied Christ's divinity, however, must be viewed in light of the fact that he did maintain a belief in basic Christian theism. Christian theists view an Almighty God as the ruler of the universe, whether or not their other doctrinal beliefs fall within the boundaries of orthodox Christianity.

NOTES

1. David McCullough, *John Adams* (New York: Simon and Schuster, 2001), 29–30; John Adams, *Papers of John Adams,* ed. Robert J. Taylor, vol. 1 (Cambridge, MA: Harvard University Press/Belknap Press, 1977), 33. In Deacon John Adams's will, he said: "Calling to mind the Mortality of my Body

and knowing that it is appointed for man once to dye, Do make and ordain this my last Will and Testam[ent], That is to Say, Principally and first of all I Give and Recommend my soul into the Hands of God that gave it, hopeing thro' the Merits, death and Passion of my saviour Jesus Christ, to have full and free pardon and forgiveness of all my Sins and to Enherit Eternal life. My Body I commit to the Earth to be decently buried at the discretion of my Executors hereafter named Believing that at the General Resurrection I shall Receive the same again by the Mighty power of God." (Printed with comments noted on the cover of the will by President John Adams.)

2. John Quincy Adams and Charles Frances Adams, *The Life of John Adams,* vol. 1, (1870), 35; John Adams, *Papers of John Adams*, vol. 1, 1. The letter cannot be quoted in greater detail because part of the page was torn off and lost.

3. John Adams, *Papers of John Adams,* vol. 1, 13.

4. Ibid.

5. Adams and Adams, *The Life of John Adams,* 43.

6. John Adams, *Papers of John Adams,* vol. 1, 17; Adams and Adams, *The Life of John Adams,* 46–47.

7. John Adams, *Papers of John Adams,* vol. 1, 19.

8. Adams and Adams, *The Life of John Adams,* 43.

9. John Adams, *Papers of John Adams,* vol. 1, 21–22.

10. Ibid., 83.

11. Ibid., 49.

12. McCullough, *John Adams,* 83–84.

13. Ibid., 113.

14. Ibid., 113–114.

15. Benjamin Weiss, *God in American History: A Documentation of America's Religious Heritage* (Grand Rapids: Zondervan, 1966), 57.

16. Adams, March 4, 1797. Inaugural address.

17. Ibid.

18. Ibid.

19. Adams, *Messages and Papers of the Presidents: John Adams, 1798.* March 23, 1798; Charles Francis Adams, *The Works of John Adams: Second President of the United States,* vol. 9 (repr., Easton, PA: Easton Press, 1992), 170.

20. Adams, *Messages and Papers of the Presidents: John Adams, 1799.* March 6, 1799.

21. Edmund Fuller and David E. Green, *God in the White House: The Faiths of American Presidents* (New York: Crown Publishers, 1968), 25.

22. Ibid.

23. Adams and Adams, *The Life of John Adams,* vol. 2, 384.

24. John Adams and Thomas Jefferson, *The Complete Correspondence between Thomas Jefferson and Abigail and John Adams,* ed. Lester. J. Cappon, vol. 2 (Chapel Hill, NC: University of North Carolina Press, 1959), 373–74.

25. Ibid.

26. Adams and Jefferson, *The Complete Correspondence*, vol. 2, 509.

27. Fuller and Green, *God in the White House*, 27.

28. Adams and Jefferson, *The Complete Correspondence*, vol. 2, 445.

29. Ibid., 375.

30. Ibid., 397.

31. Ibid., 607–08.

32. Fuller and Green, *God in the White House*, 26.

33. Adams and Jefferson, *The Complete Correspondence*, vol. 2, 493–94.

34. Ibid., 488.

35. Ibid., 360.

36. Ibid., 363. Thomas Cooper was a scientist, a Unitarian, and president of the University of South Carolina.

37. Ibid., 405.

38. Ibid., 494.

39. Ibid., 499.

40. McCullough, *John Adams*, 20.

41. Adams and Jefferson, *The Complete Correspondence*, vol. 2, 340.

42. Adams and Adams, *The Life of John Adams*, vol. 2, 384.

CHAPTER 42

GEORGE WASHINGTON

G EORGE WASHINGTON was born on February 22, 1732, in
Pope's Creek, Westmoreland County, Virginia. He was baptized
on April 5, 1732.[1]

While Washington was an officer during the French and Indian
War, he served under the government of Virginia. He successfully persuaded Virginia's government to appoint chaplains for its troops[2]

In the Battle of Monongahela, General Edward Braddock, the
British officer under whom Washington served, was killed. However,
since the chaplain had been severely wounded, no clergyman was available to conduct the funeral service. George Washington had a copy of
the Anglican prayer book in one of his pockets, so he read the funeral
service for General Braddock before Braddock's body was buried.[3]

He married Martha Dandridge Custis on January 6, 1759. (We do
not know whether the wedding took place at Martha's White House
plantation or at an Episcopal church.[4])

Washington began a c. 1769 letter to Burwell Bassett, his cousin,
by saying:

Dear Sir,

I was favored with your epistle wrote on a certain 25th of July
when you ought to have been at church, praying as becomes every
good Christian man who has as much to answer for as you have.
Strange it is that you will be so blind to truth that the enlightening
sounds of the Gospel cannot reach your ear, nor examples awaken

you to a sense of goodness. Could you but behold with what religious zeal I hie me to church on every Lord's day, it would do
your heart good, and fill it, I hope, with equal fluency.[5]

While some historians have attempted to dismiss the letter as sarcastic, Washington could well have been in earnest.

He was active in his local Episcopalian (Protestant Episcopalian)
church in the Truro Parish. On October 25, 1762, Washington was
elected a vestryman in the church. Biographer Douglas Southall
Freeman said that this followed four years in which Washington struggled to make Mount Vernon a profitable tobacco plantation; during
these years, Freeman said Washington "had been drawn closer to the
church."[6]

One book on the faith of America's presidents states that George
Washington was "nominally a vestryman of the Episcopal Church."[7]
This is far from the truth, for Washington's services were far from nom-
inal. Freeman noted some of Washington's many duties:

> Another continuing, perhaps increasing, interest was in the affairs
> of Truro Parish. Now that he was a vestryman, he had duties
> which he acknowledged with diligence. Dr. Charles Green having
> died in 1765, the Reverend Lee Massey became minister and pro-
> ceeded to appeal for the erection of a new church. Washington was
> one of five named to "view and examine" the structure at inter-
> vals. The master of Mount Vernon was designated also to handle
> the parish collection and, with George William Fairfax, to sell the
> parish tobacco for the payment of the minister and the erection of
> the new place of prayer. In signing these accounts, Washington was
> authorized to write "Warden" after his name.[8]

Another author stated that Washington's duties as a vestryman "had
no special significance religiously," and that he became a vestryman to
be eligible to "become a member of the House of Burgesses."[9] Though
eligibility for a seat in the House of Burgesses might have had an influence in his decision to become a vestryman, Washington would not
have done so unless he desired the honor and the duties of the job
itself—duties that were by no means light or nominal.

Agnostic authors have made much of the fact that Washington did
not attend church every Sunday. However, as the nearest church was

seven miles from his house, bad roads and weather (or both factors) at times prevented him from attending church.

Eleanor ("Nelly") Custis, granddaughter of Martha Washington and adopted daughter of George Washington, wrote an account of Washington's religious principles and practices regarding observing the Sabbath for Washington biographer Jared Sparks. She wrote:

> General Washington had a pew in Pohick Church, and one in Christ Church at Alexandria. He was very instrumental in establishing Pohick Church, and I believe subscribed largely. His pew was near the pulpit. I have a perfect recollection of being there, before his election to the Presidency, with him and my grandmother. It was a beautiful church, and had a large, respectable, and wealthy congregation, who were regular attendants.
>
> He attended the church at Alexandria, when the weather and roads permitted a ride of 10 miles. In New York and Philadelphia he never omitted attendance at church in the morning, unless detained by indisposition. The afternoon was spent in his own room at home; the evening with his family, and without company. Sometimes an old and intimate friend called for an hour or two; but visitors and visiting were prohibited for the day. No one in church attended to the services with more reverential respect.
>
> My grandmother, who was eminently pious, never deviated from her early habits. She always knelt. The General, as was then the custom, stood during the devotional service. On communion Sundays, he left the church with me, after the blessing [before communion] and returned home and we sent the carriage back for my grandmother.
>
> It was his custom to retire to his library at nine or 10 o'clock where he remained an hour before he went to his chamber. He always rose before the sun, and remained in his library until called to breakfast. I never witnessed his private devotions. I never inquired about them. I should have thought it the greatest heresy to doubt his belief in Christianity. His life, his writings, prove that he was a Christian. He was not one of those who act or pray, 'that they be seen of men.' He communed with his God in secret.[10]

Much of what has been written about Washington's faith has come from sources who never knew him. Custis's account is one of the few remaining firsthand accounts. In that light, it is worth mentioning that her account concludes with this description of Washington's death: "After 40 years of uninterrupted affection and uninterrupted happiness, she [Martha Washington] resigned him without a murmur into the arms of his Saviour and his God, with the assured hope of eternal felicity. Is it necessary that any one should ever certify, 'General Washington avowed himself to me a believer in Christianity?' As well may we question his patriotism, his heroic, disinterested devotion to his country."[11]

Biographer Sparks also found a witness of Washington's daily devotions. Robert Lewis, Washington's nephew, was his private secretary during part of his presidency. Lewis stated that "he had accidentally witnessed his [Washington's] private devotions in his library both morning and evening; that on those occasions he had seen him in a kneeling posture with a Bible open before him, and that he believed such to have been his daily practice."[12]

Washington commanded the American forces during the American War for Independence.

In 1775 general orders, Washington said: "The General most earnestly requires and expects . . . of all officers and soldiers, not engaged on actual duty, a punctual attendance on divine service, to implore the blessings of heaven upon the means used for our safety and defense."[13]

In 1776 general orders, Washington said: "The Continental Congress having ordered Friday to be observed as a day of 'fasting, humiliation and prayer, humbly to supplicate the mercy of Almighty God, that it would please him to pardon all our manifold sins and transgressions, and to prosper the arms of the united colonies, and finally, establish the peace and freedom of America upon a solid and lasting foundation'—the General commands all officers and soldiers to pay strict obedience to the orders of the Continental Congress, and by their unfeigned and pious observance of their religious duties, incline the Lord, and Giver of Victory, to prosper our arms."[14]

Washington added:

> The honorable Continental Congress having been pleased to allow a chaplain to each regiment . . . the colonels or commanding officers of each regiment are directed to procure chaplains accordingly, persons of good characters and exemplary lives, [and] to see that all inferior officers and soldiers pay them a suitable respect and

attend carefully upon religious exercises. The blessing and protection of Heaven are at all times necessary, but especially so in times of public distress and danger. The General hopes and trusts that every officer and man will endeavor so to live and act as becomes a Christian soldier defending the dearest rights and liberties of his country.[15]

By some accounts current in Washington's day, he could be found praying on his knees at Valley Forge.[16]

In 1775, George Washington wrote a letter of instructions to Benedict Arnold. He said: "Avoid all disrespect to or contempt of the religion of the country and its ceremonies. Prudence, policy, and a true Christian spirit will lead us to look with compassion upon their errors without insulting them. While we are contending for our own liberty, we should be very cautious of violating the rights of conscience in others, ever considering that God alone is the judge of the hearts of men, and to him only in this case they are answerable."[17]

When Arnold proved to be a traitor, Washington wrote that "in no instance since the commencement of the war has the interposition of Providence appeared more conspicuous than in the rescue of the post and garrison of West Point from Arnold's villianous perfidy."[18]

In 1776, Washington wrote (or spoke) to the officers and soldiers of the Pennsylvania Associators, saying: "The honor and safety of our bleeding country, and every other motive that can influence the brave and heroic patriot, call loudly upon us to acquit ourselves with spirit. In short, we must now determine to be enslaved or free. If we make freedom our choice, we must obtain it by the blessings of Heaven on our united and vigorous efforts."[19]

He also said to them: "Liberty, honor, and safety are all at stake, and I trust Providence will smile upon our efforts and establish us once more the inhabitants of a free and happy country."[20]

On May 2, 1778, Washington issued this general order to the soldiers and American people:

> The commander-in-chief directs that divine service be performed every Sunday at eleven o'clock in those brigades [in] which there are chaplains; those which have none [are] to attend the places of worship nearest to them. It is expected that officers of all ranks will by their attendance set an example to their men. While we

are zealously performing the duties of good citizens and soldiers, we certainly ought not to be inattentive to the higher duties of religion. To the distinguished character of patriot, it should be our highest glory to laud the more distinguished character of Christian. The signal instances of Providential Goodness which we have experienced and which have now almost crowned our labors with complete success demand from us in a peculiar manner the warmest returns of Gratitude and Piety to the Supreme Author of all Good.[21]

In 1778, when his army was outside New York while the British were fortifying inside, Washington wrote a letter to Thomas Nelson, in which he said:

It is not a little pleasing, nor less wonderful, to contemplate that after two years' maneuvering and undergoing the strangest vicissitudes that perhaps ever attended any one contest since the creation, both armies are brought back to the very point they set out from, and that that which was the offending party in the beginning is now reduced to the use of the spade and pick-axe for defense. The hand of Providence has been so conspicuous in all this that he must be worse than an infidel that lacks faith, and more than wicked that has not gratitude enough to acknowledge his obligations—but it will be time enough for me to turn preacher when my present appointment ceases, and therefore I shall add no more on the Doctrine of Providence.[22]

In his 1783 farewell orders to the Armies of the United States, Washington wrote: "The disadvantageous circumstances on our part, under which the war was undertaken, can never be forgotten. The singular interpositions of Providence in our feeble condition were such as could scarcely escape the attention of the most unobserving; while the unparalleled perseverance of the armies of the United States, through almost every possible suffering and discouragement for the space of eight long years, was little short of a standing miracle."[23]

Washington believed that the result of the American Revolution was due to God's intervention. "To the great Ruler of events, not to any exertions of mine," he wrote, "is to be ascribed the favorable termination of our late contest for liberty. I never considered the fortunate issue of any measure in any other light than as the ordering of a kind Providence."[24]

On a trip returning to the United States' seat of government at Philadelphia after a visit to Mount Vernon, Washington attended a Dutch Reformed church service in York, Pennsylvania. He commented on the service: "There being no Episcopal minister present in the place, I went to hear morning service performed in the Dutch Reformed Church—which, being in that language (not a word of which I understood), I was in no danger of becoming a proselyte to its religion by the eloquence of the preacher."[25]

Washington had a little-known interest in evangelizing the Indians. In a 1788 letter to the Reverend John Ettwein, Washington wrote: "If an event so long and so earnestly desired as that of converting the Indians to Christianity, and consequently to civilization, can be effected, the Society of Bethlehem bids fair to bear a very considerable part in it."[26]

In a 1789 letter to the Society of United Brethren for Propagating the Gospel Among the Heathen, he wrote: "In proportion as the general government of the United States shall acquire strength by duration, it is probable they may have it in their power to extend a salutary influence to the aborigines in the extremities of their territory. In the meantime, it will be a desirable thing for the protection of the Union to cooperate, as far as circumstances may conveniently admit, with the disinterested endeavors of your society to civilize and Christianize the savages of the wilderness."[27]

He was elected president in 1788 and served two terms.

In his first inaugural address, Washington asked for God's help in consecrating the government of the United States. He said that "it would be peculiarly improper to omit in this first official act my fervent supplications to that Almighty Being who rules over the universe, who presides in the councils of nations, and whose providential aids can supply every human defect, that His benediction may consecrate to the liberties and happiness of the people of the United States a Government instituted by themselves for these essential purposes, and may enable every instrument employed in its administration to execute with success the functions allotted to his charge. In tendering this homage to the Great Author of every public and private good, I assure myself that it expresses your sentiments not less than my own, nor those of my fellow-citizens at large less than either. No people can be bound to acknowledge and adore the Invisible Hand which conducts the affairs of men more than those of the United States."[28]

He said that he trusted that "the foundation of our national policy will be laid in the pure and immutable principles of private morality, and the preeminence of free government be exemplified by all the attributes which can win the affections of its citizens and command the respect of the world." He continued:

> I dwell on this prospect with every satisfaction which an ardent love for my country can inspire, since there is no truth more thoroughly established than that there exists in the economy and course of nature an indissoluble union between virtue and happiness; between duty and advantage; between the genuine maxims of an honest and magnanimous policy and the solid rewards of public prosperity and felicity; since we ought to be no less persuaded that the propitious smiles of Heaven can never be expected on a nation that disregards the eternal rules of order and right which Heaven itself has ordained; and since the preservation of the sacred fire of liberty and the destiny of the republican model of government are justly considered, perhaps, as deeply, as finally, staked on the experiment entrusted to the hands of the American people.[29]

He concluded:

> Having thus imparted to you my sentiments as they have been awakened by the occasion which brings us together, I shall take my present leave; but not without resorting once more to the benign Parent of the Human Race in humble supplication that, since He has been pleased to favor the American people with opportunities for deliberating in perfect tranquillity, and dispositions for deciding with unparalleled unanimity on a form of government for the security of their union and the advancement of their happiness, so His divine blessing may be equally conspicuous in the enlarged views, the temperate consultations, and the wise measures on which the success of this Government must depend.[30]

On December 16, 1795, the House of Representatives sent Washington a message concerning the state of the country. His reply, dated the next day, began:

GENTLEMEN: Coming as you do from all parts of the United States, I receive great satisfaction from the concurrence of your testimony in the justness of the interesting summary of our national happiness which, as the result of my inquiries, I presented to your view. The sentiments we have mutually expressed of profound gratitude to the source of those numerous blessings, the Author of all Good, are pledges of our obligations to unite our sincere and zealous endeavors, as the instruments of Divine Providence, to preserve and perpetuate them.[31]

George Washington believed that it was the "duty of all nations to acknowledge the providence of Almighty God." On October 3, 1789, he issued a Thanksgiving proclamation, which said:

A National Thanksgiving. Whereas it is the duty of all nations to acknowledge the providence of Almighty God, to obey his will, to be grateful for His benefits, and humbly implore His protection and favor; and

Whereas both Houses of Congress have, by their joint committee, requested me to recommend to the people of the United States a day of public thanksgiving and prayer, to be observed by acknowledging with grateful hearts the many signal favors of Almighty God, especially by affording them an opportunity peaceably to establish a form of government for their safety and happiness:

Now therefore I do recommend and assign Thursday, the 26th day of November next, to be devoted by the People of these States to the service of that great and glorious Being, who is the beneficent Author of all the good that was, that is, or that will be. That we may then all unite in rendering unto him our sincere and humble thanks, for his kind care and protection of the People of this country previous to their becoming a Nation, for the signal and manifold mercies, and the favorable interpositions of his providence, which we experienced in the course and conclusion of the late war, for the great degree of tranquillity, union, and plenty, which we have since enjoyed, for the peaceable and rational manner in which we have been enabled to establish constitutions of government for our safety and happiness, and particularly the national One now lately instituted, for the civil and religious liberty with which we are blessed, and the means we have of acquiring and diffusing useful knowledge and in general for all the great and various favors which he hath been pleased to confer upon us.

And also that we may then unite in most humbly offering our prayers and supplications to the great Lord and Ruler of Nations and beseech him to pardon our national and other transgressions, to enable us all, whether in public or private stations, to perform our several and relative duties properly and punctually, to render our national government a blessing to all the People, by constantly being a government of wise, just and constitutional laws, discreetly and faithfully executed and obeyed, to protect and guide all Sovereigns and Nations (especially such as have shown kindness unto us) and to bless them with good government, peace, and concord. To promote the knowledge and practice of true religion and virtue, and the encrease of science among them and Us, and generally to grant unto all Mankind such a degree of temporal prosperity as he alone knows to be best.

Given under my hand, at the city of New York, the 3d day of October, A.D. 1789.

GO. WASHINGTON.[32]

In 1789, he prepared a proposed address to Congress, which he never delivered. A sentence of the proposed message read: "The blessed religion revealed in the word of God will remain an eternal and awful monument to prove that the best institutions may be abused by human depravity, and that they may even, in some instances, be made subservient to the vilest of purposes."[33]

Washington once said, "It is impossible to rightly govern the world without God and the Bible."[34]

Washington's presidential writings contain several references to his belief in religious freedom. In 1789, he wrote: "While all men within our territories are protected in worshipping the Deity according to the dictates of their consciences, it is rationally to be expected from them in return that they will all be emulous of evincing the sanctity of their professions by the innocence of their lives and the beneficence of their actions; for no man who is profligate in his morals, or a bad member of the civil community, can possibly be a true Christian or a credit to his own religious society."[35]

In a 1789 letter to the general committee of the United Baptist Churches in Virginia, Washington wrote: "If I could conceive that the general government might ever be so administered as to render the liberty of conscience insecure, I beg you will be persuaded that no one would be more zealous than myself to establish effectual barriers against the horrors of spiritual tyranny, and every species of religious persecution."[36]

He also said: "I have often expressed my sentiments that every man, conducting himself as a good citizen, and being accountable to God alone for his religious opinions, ought to be protected in worshipping the Deity according to the dictates of his own conscience."[37]

In a 1789 letter to the Quakers, he said: "The liberty enjoyed by the people of these states of worshipping Almighty God agreeably to their consciences is not only among the choicest of their blessings, but also of their rights. While men perform their social duties faithfully, they do all that society or the state can with propriety demand or expect, and remain responsible only to their Maker for the religion or modes of faith which they may prefer or profess."[38]

In a 1793 letter to the members of the New Church in Baltimore, he wrote: "We have abundant reason to rejoice that in this land the light of truth and reason has triumphed over the power of bigotry and superstition, and that every person may here worship God according to the dictates of his own heart. In this enlightened age and in this land of equal liberty, it is our boast that a man's religious tenets will not forfeit the protection of the laws, nor deprive him of the fight of attaining and holding the highest offices that are known in the United States."[39]

Washington died on December 14, 1799. At his funeral four days later, he was given both Episcopalian order of burial and full Masonic rites.[40] The Reverend Mr. Davis administered the order of burial from the Episcopal prayer book; the full Masonic rites were conducted by Dr. Elisha Cullen Dick, Grand Master of the Alexandria Lodge, with the assistance of their chaplain, the Reverend Mr. Muir.[41]

"I am the Resurrection and the Life," a phrase from John 11:25, is inscribed on the tombstones of George and Martha Washington.[42]

In a letter Washington sent to Lafayette, he said: "Being no bigot myself to any mode of worship, I am disposed to indulge the professors of Christianity in the church, that road to heaven which to them shall seem the most direct, plainest, easiest, and least liable to exception."[43]

HISTORICAL CONTROVERSIES

Was George Washington a communicant in the Episcopal Church?

Before the American Revolution, according to his adopted daughter Nelly Custis, George Washington received Communion.[44] During and after the American Revolution, he did not regularly receive communion. He never stated the reason for changing his practices.

Washington biographer Jared Sparks said:

> It is probable that, after he took command of the army, finding his thoughts and attention necessarily engrossed by business that devolved upon him, in which frequently little distinction could be observed between Sunday and other days, he may have believed it improper to partake of an ordinance, which, according to the ideas he entertained of it, imposed severe restrictions on his outward conduct, and a sacred pledge to perform duties impractical in his situation. Such an impression would be natural to a serious mind; and though it might be founded on erroneous views of the nature of the ordinance, it would have had the less weight with a man of delicate conscience and habitual reverence for religion.[45]

However, George Washington's ministers after the American Revolution were under the impression that he was never a communicant. One, the Reverend Dr. James Abercrombie, pastor of St. Peter's Episcopal Church in Philadelphia, expressed his recollections in a letter. He said:

> With respect to the inquiry you make, I can only state the following facts: that as pastor of the Episcopal Church, observing that, on sacramental Sundays George Washington, immediately after the desk and pulpit services, went out with the greater part of the congregation—always leaving Mrs. Washington with the other communicants—I considered it my duty, in a sermon on public worship, to state the unhappy tendency of example, particularly of those in elevated stations, who uniformly turned their backs on the Lord's Supper. I acknowledge the remark was intended for the President; and as such he received it. A few days after, in conversation, I believe, with a Senator of the United States,

he told me he had dined the day before with the President, who, in the course of conversation at the table, said that, on the previous Sunday, he had received a very just rebuke from the pulpit for always leaving the church before the administration of the sacrament; that he honored the preacher for his integrity and candor; that he had never sufficiently considered the influence of his example, and that he would not again give cause for repetition of the reproof; and that, as he had never been a communicant, were he to become one then, it would be imputed to an ostentatious display of religious zeal, arising altogether from his elevated station. Accordingly, he never afterwards came on sacrament Sunday, though at other times he was a constant attendant in the morning.[46]

Decades after Washington's death, the following question was sent to the Right Reverend William White (Bishop White), minister of Christ Church in Philadelphia: "I have a desire, dear sir, to know whether General Washington was a member of the Protestant Episcopal Church, or whether he occasionally went to the communion only, or if he ever did so at all. No authority can be so authentic and complete as yours on this point."[47]

Bishop White responded: "In regard to the subject of your inquiry, truth requires me to say that General Washington never received the communion in the churches of which I am the parochial minister. Mrs. Washington was an habitual communicant."[48]

In a different letter, Bishop White said that Washington's "behavior in church was always serious and attentive," though he "never heard anything from him which could manifest his opinions on the subject of religion."[49]

Did George Washington regularly attend church?

George Washington attended two churches: Pohick Church (Truro Parish) and Christ Church (Fairfax Parish).

The Reverend Lee Massey, who was the rector of the former church when Washington attended, said this:

I never knew so constant an attendant in church as Washington. And his behavior in the house of God was ever so deeply reverential that it produced the happiest effect on my congregation, and greatly assisted me in my pulpit labors. No company ever withheld him from church. I have often been at Mt. Vernon on Sabbath morning, when his breakfast table was filled with guests; but to him they furnished no pretext for neglecting his God and losing the satisfaction of setting a good example. For instead of staying at home, out of false complaisance to them, he used constantly to invite them to accompany him.[50]

His step-granddaughter and adopted daughter Nelly Custis said:

He attended the church at Alexandria, when the weather and roads permitted a ride of 10 miles. In New York and Philadelphia he never omitted attendance at church in the morning, unless detained by indisposition. The afternoon was spent in his own room at home; the evening with his family, and without company. Sometimes an old and intimate friend called for an hour or two; but visitors and visiting were prohibited for the day. No one in church attended to the services with more reverential respect.[51]

In an incomplete diary, Washington noted some of the times he went to church. In his diary, he made specific mention of fifteen visits in 1768, ten in 1769, nine in 1770, six in 1771, five in 1772, eighteen in 1774, one in 1785, one in 1786, three in 1787, and one in 1788. This evidence was collected by atheist/agnostic Franklin Steiner, whose anti-Christian bias shows in the fact that while he admitted that Washington attended church regularly during his presidency, Steiner omitted those years in this count.

During his presidency, Washington lived in a city. He was thus able to and did attend church regularly. He attended Trinity or St. Paul's Chapel while in New York and Christ Church or St. Peter's while in Philadelphia.[52]

In a letter, Reverend Dr. James Abercrombie testified to Washington's regularity of attendance while he was in Philadelphia. He said that though Washington never "never came on sacrament Sunday . . . at other times he was a constant attendant in the morning."[53]

In the last three years of his life (1797, 1798, and 1799), once Washington had moved home to Mt. Vernon, he mentioned attending church less frequently in his diary. He mentioned attending four times in 1797, once in 1798, and twice in 1799.[54] It must be emphasized that he could have attended and not made mention of the fact. The fact that he does not mention attendance is not proof that he did not attend.

Is George Washington's prayer book genuine?

This prayer book was discovered in about 1900 in an old trunk.[55] The book was said to have been composed or copied in Washington's youth. Dr. W. A. Croffutt traced some of the prayers to a prayer book printed between 1583 and 1625, during the reign of James I of England.

In his book *Faith of Our Founding Fathers*, Tim LaHaye quotes from this book. Some of the sentences read:

> "I beseech Thee, my sins, remove them from Thy presence, as far as the east is from the west, and accept of me for the merits of Thy Son, Jesus Christ, that when I come into Thy temple, and compass Thine altar, my prayers may come before Thee as incense; and as Thou wouldst hear me calling upon Thee in my prayers, so give me grace to hear Thee calling on me in Thy word, that it may be wisdom, righteousness, reconciliation and peace to the saving of my soul in the day of the Lord Jesus."[56]
>
> "I have sinned and done very wickedly, be merciful to me, O God, and pardon me for Jesus Christ sake."[57]
>
> "That I may know my sins are forgiven by His death and Passion."[58]

If this was genuine, Washington was a Christian.

However, Washington experts, such as Worthington C. Ford and those at the Smithsonian Institution, have stated that the handwriting was not Washington's.[59] As of 1936, the Smithsonian Institution did not accept it as genuine.[60]

Due to the testimony of the experts, we cannot say with certainty that the prayer book was not a forgery. There is a possibility which has, to the best of my knowledge, been overlooked—that Washington may have written and spelled better[61] in his childhood, when he had more time to concentrate on learning the skills and fewer activities forcing him to write quickly.

There is also a chance that Washington may have been assigned the prayers as a copying assignment. He would then have been required to write neatly and spell correctly.

The case is not closed on this dispute. Further research and new evidence may provide the information necessary to change conclusions.

Was Parson Mason Weems Washington's pastor?

Parson Weems is remembered for his 1800 volume *The Life of Washington*, one of the most widely read books in the first half-century of the United States' history. On the title page of the original edition, Weems stated that he had been "Rector of Mt. Vernon Parish."

Parson Weems is mentioned once in Washington's diaries. However, he was not Washington's regular minister, and there was no "Mt. Vernon Parish."

This is pertinent because Weems' book is our sole secondary source (source derived from primary sources) for several incidents of Washington's life, including the famous cherry tree incident. Weems' accuracy has been questioned. In response, Weems' defenders have stated that he was Washington's pastor and thus might have heard stories that nobody else heard. However, this response loses its impact when it is discovered that though Weems met Washington and was mentioned once in his diary, he was not Washington's regular pastor.

Was George Washington a deist?

Many writers have stated that George Washington was a deist. One writer, Robert Dale Owen, said in 1831 that he spoke to a man[62] who spoke to one of Washington's ministers, Reverend Abercrombie. The man said that Reverend Abercrombie said, "Sir, Washington was a Deist."[63]

Reverend Abercrombie did not have access to Washington's private correspondence. If he said what he is reputed to have said, he was mistaken. It can be irrefutably proven from Washington's correspondence that he was not a deist.

It would be useful to review the basic beliefs of a deist. A deist believes that a Supreme Being created the world but has maintained no contact with it since. Deists hold that the laws of nature cannot be superseded, so no miracle is possible. They believe all history was determined at the creation of the world, and humans are merely part of the universe clockwork. Therefore, they believe God plays no role in the course of events.[64]

George Washington's letters show a firm belief in a Supreme Being who remains in contact with the world, who has miraculous power to direct human events. In a 1755 letter to John Augustine Washington, Washington wrote: "As I have heard . . . a circumstantial account of my death and dying speech, I take this early opportunity of contradicting both, and of assuring you that I now exist and appear in the land of the living by the miraculous care of Providence, that protected me beyond all human expectation; I had four bullets through my coat, and two horses shot under me, and yet escaped unhurt."[65]

George Washington also believed that God directs the events of history. He expressed this belief several times in his correspondence. In a 1788 letter to the Marquis de Lafayette, he said:

Maryland has ratified the federal Constitution by a majority of 63 to 11 voices. That makes the seventh state which has adopted it. Next Monday the convention in Virginia will assemble; we have still good hopes of its adoption here, though by no great plurality of votes. South Carolina has probably decided favorably before this time. The plot thickens fast. A few short weeks will determine the political fate of America for the present generation and probably produce no small influence on the happiness of society through a long succession of ages to come. Should everything proceed with harmony and consent according to our actual wishes and expectations, I will confess to you sincerely, my dear Marquis, it will be so much beyond anything we had a right to imagine or expect eighteen months ago that it will demonstrate as visibly the finger of Providence as any possible event in the course of human affairs can ever designate it. It is impracticable for you or anyone who has not been on the spot to realize the change in men's minds and the progress towards rectitude in thinking and acting which will then have been made.[66]

In a 1781 letter to John Armstrong, he wrote:

Our affairs are brought to an awful crisis, that the hand of Providence, I trust, may be more conspicuous in our deliverance. The many remarkable interpositions of the divine government in the hours of our deepest distress and darkness have been too luminous to suffer me to doubt the happy issue of the present contest.[67]

He wrote to the Reverend Israel Evans in 1778, saying:

It will ever be the first wish of my heart to aid your pious endeavors to inculcate a due sense of the dependence we ought to place in that all-wise and powerful Being on whom alone our success depends.[68]

In 1781, he wrote to Thomas McKean and said:

The interposing Hand of Heaven in the various instances of our extensive preparations for this operation has been most conspicuous and remarkable.[69]

In a 1781 letter to the synod of the Reformed Dutch Church in North America, he said:

If such talents as I possess have been called into action by great events, and those events have terminated happily for our country, the glory should be ascribed to the manifest interposition of an overruling Providence.[70]

In a 1792 letter to the attorney general, he said:

As the All-wise Disposer of events has hitherto watched over my steps, I trust that in the important one I may soon be called upon to take [i.e., commencing a second term as President], he will mark the course so plainly as that I cannot mistake the way.[71]

Washington not only believed that God interposed in the course of history, but he also believed that God influenced the course of history on behalf of the United States. In a 1781 letter, he said: "We have . . . abundant reason to thank Providence for its many favorable interpositions in our behalf. It has at times been my only dependence, for all other resources seemed to have failed us."[72]

In a 1789 letter to the Connecticut legislature, he said: "I was but the humble agent of favoring Heaven, whose benign interference was so often manifested in our behalf, and to whom the praise of victory alone is due."[73]

He wrote Benjamin Harrison in 1778, saying, "Providence has heretofore taken us up when all other means and hope seemed to be departing from us; in this I will confide."[74]

In a 1788 letter to Benjamin Lincoln, he said, "I trust in that Providence which has saved us in six troubles, yea, in seven, to rescue us again from any imminent, though unseen, dangers. Nothing, however, on our part ought to be left undone."[75]

To Landon Carter in 1777, he wrote, "A superintending Providence is ordering everything for the best, and . . . in due time all will end well."[76]

In a 1778 letter to Gov. Jonathan Trumbull, he said, "A wise Providence . . . no doubt directs [events] for the best of purposes, and to bring round the greatest degree of happiness to the greatest number of his people."[77]

He wrote to Trumbull again in 1788, saying, "We may, with a kind of pious and grateful exultation, trace the fingers of Providence through those dark and mysterious events which first induced the states to appoint a general convention, and then led them one after another . . . into an adoption of the system recommended by that general convention, thereby, in all human probability, laying a lasting foundation for tranquility and happiness, when we had but too much reason to fear that confusion and misery were coming rapidly upon us. That the same good Providence may still continue to protect us, and prevent us from dashing the cup of national felicity just as it has been lifted to our lips, is [my] earnest prayer."[78]

He wrote to the mayor, aldermen, and common council of Philadelphia in 1789, "When I contemplate the interposition of Providence, as it was manifested in guiding us through the revolution, in preparing us for the reception of a general government, and in conciliating the good will of the people of America towards one another after its adoption, I feel myself...almost overwhelmed with a sense of the divine munificence."[79]

Washington's thoughts on the topic could be summed up when he said, "I am sure there never was a people who had more reason to acknowledge a divine interposition in their affairs than those of the United States; and I should be pained to believe that they have forgotten that agency which was so often manifested during our revolution, or that they failed to consider the omnipotence of that God who is alone able to protect them."[80]

He believed that the United States would not have been able to form without God's help. In fact, he told the executive of New Hampshire in 1789, "The success which has hitherto attended our united efforts we owe to the gracious interposition of Heaven, and to that interposition let us gratefully ascribe the praise of victory and the blessings of peace."[81]

To the general assembly of Rhode Island in 1797, he said, "Without the beneficent interposition of the Supreme Ruler of the universe, we could not have reached the distinguished situation which we have attained with such unprecedented rapidity. To him, therefore, should we bow with gratitude and reverence, and endeavor to merit a continuance of his special favors."[82]

Washington believed that he needed God's aid to perform his arduous duties. To the Reverend William Gorden he wrote in 1776, "No man has a more perfect reliance on the all-wise and powerful dispensations of the Supreme Being than I have, nor thinks His aid more necessary."[83]

In a 1789 letter to the citizens of Baltimore, he said: "I know the delicate nature of the duties incident to the part which I am called to perform; and I feel my incompetence, without the singular assistance of Providence, to discharge them in a satisfactory manner."[84]

For these favorable interpositions of Providence, Washington expressed "humble and grateful thanks." He wrote Landon Carter in 1778, saying, " Providence has a...claim to my humble and grateful thanks for its protection and direction of me through the many difficult and intricate scenes which this contest has produced, and for the constant interposition in our behalf when the clouds were heaviest and seemed ready to burst upon us."[85]

In a 1797 letter, he said, "I am...grateful to that Providence which has directed my steps, and shielded me through the various changes and chances through which I have passed, from my youth to the present moment."[86]

He did not take God's guidance of the country for granted, but he prayed that it would continue. In a 1783 letter to the governors of the states, he wrote:

> I now make it my earnest prayer that God would have you, and the state over which you preside, in his holy protection; that he would incline the hearts of the citizens to cultivate a spirit of

subordination and obedience to government, to entertain a brotherly affection and love for one another, for their fellow citizens of the United States at large, and particularly for their brethren who have served in the field; and finally, that he would most graciously be pleased to dispose us all to do justice, to love mercy, and to demean ourselves with that charity, humility, and pacific temper of mind which were the characteristics of the Divine Author of our blessed religion, and without an humble imitation of whose example in these things we can never hope to be a happy nation.[87]

In a speech when Washington resigned his commission in 1783, he said: "I consider it an indispensable duty to close this last solemn act of my official life by commending the interests of our dearest country to the protection of Almighty God, and those who have the superintendence of them to his holy keeping."[88]

To the secretary of war, he said in 1788, "I earnestly pray that the Omnipotent Being who has not deserted the cause of America in the hour of its extremest hazard will never yield so fair a heritage of freedom a prey to anarchy or despotism."[89]

In his message to the Congress in 1794, he said: "Let us unite . . . in imploring the Supreme Ruler of nations to spread his holy protection over these United States, to turn the machinations of the wicked to the confirming of our Constitution, to enable us at all times to root out internal sedition and put invasion to flight, to perpetuate to our country that prosperity which his goodness has already conferred, and to verify the anticipation of this government being a safeguard to human rights."[90]

When he spoke to the Congress in 1796, he said:

The situation in which I now stand, for the last time, in the midst of the representatives of the people of the United States, naturally recalls the period when the administration of the present form of government commenced; and I cannot omit the occasion to congratulate you and my country on the success of the experiment, nor to repeat my fervent supplications to the Supreme Ruler of the Universe and Sovereign Arbiter of Nations that his Providential care may still be extended to the United States, that the virtue and happiness of the people may be preserved, and that the government which they have instituted for the protection of their liberties may be perpetual.[91]

Washington also believed that God directed the courses of individual lives. When his niece died, Washington wrote to her father, Burwell Bassett, in 1773 and said: "The ways of Providence being inscrutable, and the justice of it not to be scanned by the shallow eye of humanity, nor to be counteracted by the utmost efforts of human power and wisdom, resignation, and, as far as the strength of our reason and religion can carry us, a cheerful acquiescence to the Divine Will is what we are to aim."[92]

In a 1773 letter to Reverend Bryan Fairfax, he said: "The determinations of Providence are always wise, often inscrutable, and, though its decrees appear to bear hard upon us at times, nevertheless meant for gracious purposes."[93]

He wrote to Lund Washington in 1779 and said, "I look upon every dispensation of Providence as designed to answer some valuable purpose, and I hope I shall always possess a sufficient degree of fortitude to bear without murmuring any stroke which may happen either to my person or estate from that quarter."[94]

To William Pearce he wrote in 1794, "At disappointments and losses which are the effects of Providential acts I never repine, because I am sure the divine disposer of events knows better than we do what is best for us, or what we deserve."[95]

In a 1793 letter to Reverend Bryan Fairfax, he said, "I thank you for your kind condolence on the death of my nephew. It is a loss I sincerely regret, but as it is the will of Heaven, whose decrees are always just and wise, I submit to it without a murmur."[96]

In a 1797 letter to Henry Knox he said that it "is not for man to scan the wisdom of Providence. The best he can do is to submit to its decrees. Reason, religion, and philosophy teach us to do this; but it is time alone that can ameliorate the pangs of humanity, and soften its woes."[97]

In 1793, he wrote, "[How things will] terminate is known only to the great ruler of events; and confiding in his wisdom and goodness, we may safely trust the issue to him, without perplexing ourselves to seek for that which is beyond human ken, only taking care to perform the parts assigned to us in a way that reason and our own consciences approve of."[98]

To Thaddeus Kosciuszko, he wrote in 1797, "The ways of Providence are inscrutable, and mortals must submit."[99]

He wrote to George Augustine Washington in 1793, "The will of Heaven is not to be controverted or scrutinized by the children of this world. It therefore becomes the creatures of it to submit with patience and resignation to the will of the Creator, whether it be to prolong or to shorten the number of our days, to bless them with health or afflict them with pain."[100]

CONCLUSION

Deists believe that a Supreme Being created the world but has maintained no contact with it since. They believe that the Supreme Being does not direct the course of nations, and the clockwork of the universe does not permit any miraculous suspensions of nature's laws. George Washington rejected all the fundamental doctrines of deism.

George Washington believed in a God who directed the destinies of nations and of individuals. While we know little of Washington's doctrinal views, we can at least be confident of the fact that Washington was a theist who held that God directs the destinies of nations and individuals.

NOTES

1. Benjamin Weiss, *God in American History: A Documentation of America's Religious Heritage* (Grand Rapids: Zondervan, 1966), 49.

2. Franklin Steiner, *The Religious Beliefs of Our Presidents* (Girard, KS: Haldeman-Julius, 1936; repr., Amherst, NY: Prometheus Books, 1995), 165. Quoted George Washington, *The Writings of George Washington with a Life of the Author*, ed. Jared Sparks, 12 vols. (Boston: American Stationers, 1834–37), 518–25.

3. Bliss Isley, *The Presidents: Men of Faith* (Boston: W. A. Wilde, 1953), 3. Isley noted that the service included the words, "I am the resurrection and the life," the same phrase that appeared on Washington's tombstone.

4. James Thomas Flexner, *George Washington: The Forge of Experience, 1732–1775* (Boston and Toronto: Little, Brown, 1965–72), 227.

5. Ibid., 237.

6. Douglas Southall Freeman, abridged by Richard Harwell, *Washington: An Abridgment in One Volume by Richard Harwell of the Seven-Volume George Washington by Douglas Southall Freeman* (New York: Scribner, 1968), 150.

7. John Sutherland Bonnell, *Presidential Profiles: Religion in the Life of American Presidents* (Philadelphia: Westminster Press, 1971), 19. Referring to Hall, *The Religious Background of American Culture.*

8. Freeman and Harwell, *Washington,* 167.

9. Steiner, *Religious Beliefs of Our Presidents,* 18.

10. Ibid., 166–67. Cited Washington, *The Writings of George Washington,* ed. Sparks, 518–25.

11. Ibid.

12. Tim LaHaye, *Faith of Our Founding Fathers* (Brentwood, TN: Wolgemuth & Hyatt, 1987), 103. Cited White, *Washington's Writings.*

13. George Washington, *The Writings of George Washington from the Original Manuscript Sources, 1745–1799,* ed. John C. Fitzpatrick, vol. 3, (Washington, DC: Government Printing Office, 1940), 309.

14. Ibid., 43.

15. Ibid., vol. 5, 244; Andrew M. Allison, *The Real George Washington* (Washington, DC: The National Center for Constitutional Studies, 1991), 171–72.

16. Allison, *The Real George Washington,* 172.

17. Washington, *The Writings of George Washington,* ed. Fitzpatrick, vol. 3, 492.

18. James Thomas Flexner, *George Washington: In the American Revolution, 1775–1783* (Boston and Toronto: Little, Brown, 1968), 395; Washington, *The Writings of George Washington,* ed. Fitzpatrick, vol. 20, 173.

19. Washington, *The Writings of George Washington,* ed. Fitzpatrick, vol. 5, 398.

20. Ibid.

21. Ibid., vol. 11, 342; Bonnell, *Presidential Profiles,* 22.

22. Washington, *The Writings of George Washington,* ed. Fitzpatrick, vol. 12, 343; Flexner, *George Washington: In the American Revolution,* 319.

23. Washington, *The Writings of George Washington,* ed. Fitzpatrick, vol. 27, 223.

24. Ibid., vol. 34, 130. From a 1795 letter to Jonathan Williams.

25. Allison, *The Real George Washington,* 547.

26. Washington, *The Writings of George Washington,* ed. Fitzpatrick, vol. 29, 489.

27. Ibid., vol. 30, 355.

28. Washington, March 4, 1789. First inaugural address.

29. Ibid.

30. Ibid.

31. Washington, *Messages and Papers of the Presidents: George Washington, 1795.* December 17, 1795. Reply of the president.

32. Washington, *The Writings of George Washington,* ed. Sparks, vol. 12, 119; Washington, *Messages and Papers of the Presidents,* October 3, 1798. A national Thanksgiving; Weiss, *God in American History,* 54.

33. Washington, *The Writings of George Washington,* ed. Fitzpatrick, vol. 30, 301.

34. Olga Anna Jones, *Churches of the Presidents in Washington: Visits to Fifteen National Shrines* (New York: Exposition Press, 1954), 52.

35. Washington, *The Writings of George Washington,* ed. Sparks, vol. 12, 152.

36. Washington, *The Writings of George Washington,* ed. Fitzpatrick, vol. 30, 321n.

37. Ibid.

38. Washington, *The Writings of George Washington,* ed. Sparks, vol.12, 168.

39. Washington, *The Writings of George Washington,* ed. Fitzpatrick, vol. 32, 315.

40. Freeman and Harwell, *Washington,* 754.

41. Ibid., 751, 754.

42. Isley, *The Presidents,* 8.

43. Washington, *The Writings of George Washington,* ed. Fitzpatrick, vol. 29, 259; Flexner, *George Washington: The Forge of Experience,* 243.

44. In an 1833 letter, Washington's step-granddaughter and adopted daughter Nelly Custis stated that her mother said "that General Washington always received the sacrament with my grandmother before the Revolution."

45. Steiner, *Religious Beliefs of Our Presidents,* 168. Quoted Washington, *The Writings of George Washington,* ed. Sparks, 518–25.

46. Steiner, *Religious Beliefs of Our Presidents,* 26. Quoted William Buell Sprague, *Annals of the American Pulpit,* vol. 5, 1873, 394. Note that Washington took the rebuke in a humble way, willing to accept correction from a man of God. Unfortunately, several presidents who believed in the essentials of the Christian faith followed Washington's pattern in delaying to make public statements of faith due to the importance and impartiality of their office. In two cases, those of William Henry Harrison and Abraham Lincoln, the delays cost them their only opportunities of joining churches. Others, such as Andrew Jackson and James Buchanan, were able to follow through on their intentions after their tenures as president of the United States.

47. From a letter by Colonel Mercer of Fredericksburg, Virginia, dated August 13, 1835, and quoted in Steiner's *The Religious Beliefs of Our Presidents,* 27.

48. From a letter by Bishop White quoted in Steiner's *The Religious Beliefs of Our Presidents,* 27. Found in *Memoirs of Bishop White,* 196–97.

49. Steiner, *The Religious Beliefs of Our Presidents,* 27. Also found in *Memoirs of Bishop White,* 189–91. The letter was dated November 28, 1832, and was sent to the Reverend B. C. C. Parker.

50. Steiner, *Religious Beliefs of Our Presidents*, 17. Quoted Paul Leicester Ford, *The True George Washington*, 77–78. Ford said of the quote: "This seems to have been written more with an eye to the effect upon others than to its strict accuracy." This is perhaps accurate, unless due to the rural setting and the bad roads, Washington was one of the most frequent attendees.

51. Steiner, *Religious Beliefs of Our Presidents*, 166–67. Quoted Washington, *The Writings of George Washington*, ed. Sparks, 518–25. Sparks quoted from a letter from Eleanor "Nelly" Custis, dated "Woodlawn, 26 February 1833."

52. Steiner, *Religious Beliefs of Our Presidents*, 18.

53. Ibid., 26.

54. Ibid.

55. Ibid., 20.

56. Tim LaHaye, *Faith of Our Founding Fathers* (Brentwood, TN: Wolgemuth & Hyatt, 1987), 111. Quoted from Washington's *Personal Prayer Book*.

57. Ibid., 112.

58. Ibid., 113.

59. Steiner, *Religious Beliefs of Our Presidents*, 21.

60. Ibid.

61. Ibid. According to Steiner, "All of the words [in the prayer book] are spelled correctly." In Washington's other compositions, this was not always the case.

62. Reverend Dr. Wilson, biographer of Bishop White, who had preached an 1831 sermon on the religion of the presidents. The Albany *Daily Advertiser* published this in 1831.

63. Steiner, *Religious Beliefs of Our Presidents*, 26–27.

64. For additional information on deism, consult James Sire's book *The Universe Next Door: A Basic Worldview Catalog* (Downers Grove, IL: InterVarsity Press, 1997).

65. Washington, *The Writings of George Washington*, ed. Fitzpatrick, vol. 1, 152.

66. Ibid., vol. 29, 507.

67. Ibid., vol. 21, 378.

68. Ibid., vol. 11, 78.

69. Ibid., vol. 23, 343.

70. Washington, *The Writings of George Washington*, ed. Sparks, vol. 12, 167.

71. Washington, *The Writings of George Washington*, ed. Fitzpatrick, vol. 32, 136.

72. Ibid., vol. 21, 332.

73. Washington, *The Writings of George Washington*, ed. Sparks, vol. 12, 169.

74. Washington, *The Writings of George Washington,* ed. Fitzpatrick, vol. 13, 468.

75. Ibid., vol. 30, 63.

76. Ibid., vol. 9, 454.

77. Ibid., vol. 12, 406.

78. Ibid., vol. 30, 22.

79. Washington, *The Writings of George Washington*, ed. Sparks, vol. 12, 145.

80. Washington, *The Writings of George Washington*, ed. Fitzpatrick, vol. 32, 2.

81. Ibid., vol. 30, 453.

82. Ibid., vol. 35, 341.

83. Ibid., vol. 37, 526.

84. Ibid., vol. 30, 288.

85. Ibid., vol. 11, 492.

86. Ibid., vol. 36, 49.

87. Ibid., vol. 26, 496.

88. Ibid., vol. 27, 285.

89. Ibid., vol. 30, 30.

90. Ibid., vol. 34, 37.

91. Ibid., vol. 35, 319.

92. Flexner, *George Washington: The Forge of Experience,* 244.

93. Washington, *The Writings of George Washington*, ed. Fitzpatrick, vol. 11, 3.

94. Ibid., vol. 15, 180.

95. Ibid., vol. 33, 375.

96. Ibid., vol. 32, 376.

97. Ibid., vol. 35, 409.

98. Flexner, *George Washington: The Forge of Experience,* 244–45.

99. Washington, *The Writings of George Washington,* ed. Fitzpatrick, vol. 36, 22.

100. Ibid., vol. 32, 315.

CHARACTER

WHY WOULD an appendix such as this be included in a book on the presidents' religious beliefs? I include it for two reasons:

First, I cannot in good conscience paint a president as a holy, righteous man when the facts suggest otherwise. I have no desire to deliberately misrepresent a president's character.

Second, we know a tree by its fruits. One measure of how deeply a president held his religious convictions is whether his actions lined up with his words.

INAPPROPRIATE RELATIONSHIPS

The purpose of this book is not to investigate or give details about any president's inappropriate relationships. I will summarize the pertinent information as briefly as possible.

It is reasonably certain that James Garfield,[1] Grover Cleveland,[2] Woodrow Wilson,[3] Warren Harding,[4] Franklin D. Roosevelt,[5] John F. Kennedy,[6] and William Clinton had extramarital affairs. Correspondence survived from Garfield, Wilson, Harding, and Roosevelt documenting their affairs; Cleveland and Clinton admitted theirs publicly. (Cleveland's affair was before his marriage.) Garfield reconciled with his wife and attempted to make things right with the other woman involved. Wilson's affair might have been merely one of inappropriate emotions.

Credible but unproved statements have been made that Thomas Jefferson[7] and Dwight D. Eisenhower[8] had affairs. (Jefferson's supposed affair was after his wife died, so it was not strictly extramarital.)

While allegations have been made about other presidents, there is no need to mention mere rumors.

OCCULT PRACTICES

Due to the fact that occult practices involve participation with spiritual forces in opposition to Christianity, I have here listed both what involvement presidents had in the occult and what they permitted their wives and families to have.

John Tyler. According to first ladies historian Carl Anthony, Tyler's wife Julia "hosted a party to contact 'the other side,' but only managed to levitate a table."[9] She also said she had an ability to foresee the future through her dreams.[10]

Franklin Pierce. Pierce's wife was so crushed by their son Benjamin's death that she consulted mediums like the Fox sisters in a White House séance in an attempt to communicate with him.[11]

Abraham Lincoln. A *Boston Gazette* writer described a White House "spiritual soirée,"[12] which "Abraham Lincoln, president of the United States, was induced to give . . . in the crimson room at the White House."[13] Since the account was printed in a major newspaper during Lincoln's lifetime and could easily have been denied if false, there is every reason to believe that Lincoln permitted the event. His wife Mary Lincoln, after their son Willie's death, also consulted mediums and held a White House séance.[14]

Ulysses S. Grant. Grant's wife, Julia, claimed to have extrasensory perception with "complete visualization of Grant's upcoming military battles."[15] Historian Carl Anthony stated that her predictions "often came true."[16]

Theodore Roosevelt. Theodore Roosevelt wanted William Taft to succeed him in the presidency. At a dinner with the Tafts, Roosevelt pretended he was a swami and said: "I am the seventh son of a seventh daughter and I have clairvoyant powers. I see a man weighing 350 pounds. There is something hanging over his head. I cannot make out what it is. . . . At one point it looks like the presidency, then again it looks like the chief justiceship."[17]

Though Roosevelt likely intended this to be taken lightly, his daughter Alice took such things seriously. (She had rejected her faith at a young age when she read Darwin's *Evolution of the Species*.)[18] Alice did not like Nellie Taft (William Taft's wife); and since Alice was involved in witchcraft, she decided to lay a curse on the Tafts. Before she left the White House, she buried a voodoo doll in the White House lawn and, in the words of Margaret Truman, "called on the gods to visit woe on the new occupants."[19] Nellie Taft suffered a paralyzing stroke two months into her husband's presidency.

Alice Roosevelt also laid a curse on President Woodrow Wilson, who had fallen sick while on a trip. When he returned home, Alice was in the crowd. She "crossed her fingers, made the sign of the evil eye, and called down an ancient curse."[20] When Wilson was paralyzed by a stroke, Alice "reportedly took full credit."[21]

Although some biographers have made light of the curses,[22] Alice took them seriously. Of course, Alice Roosevelt's witchcraft does not necessarily mean that Theodore Roosevelt was also into it. However, what he likely meant as a joke, his daughter took seriously.

Woodrow Wilson. In 1917, the Ouija board was a fad, "frequently brought into use when someone died."[23] On March 11, shortly after Edith Wilson's sister Annie Lee died, a Ouija board was used at the White House. Wilson's friend, Colonel House, wrote about the game in his diary, "This is an innovation the President has inaugurated since I was last here. He says he finds that it diverts him more than reading."[24] I do not know if Wilson had any reason to believe this was wrong.

Warren Harding. Harding's wife, Florence, was rather superstitious. She scheduled her marriage ceremony so it would take place after a half-hour, so the hands of the clock would be going up and not down when the ceremony took place. She believed that a marriage performed when the minute and hour hands of the clock were moving downwards would not be successful.

Some accounts have claimed that Florence Harding consulted a soothsayer. One account, mentioned in a letter by Chief Justice William Howard Taft, claimed that one soothsayer she consulted first predicted that her husband would be nominated and elected president of the United States, and later predicted that Harding would not survive his term.[25]

Dwight Eisenhower. On at least one occasion before World War II, Mamie Eisenhower invited a Gypsy fortuneteller to a party to read cards, and the fortuneteller predicted that Eisenhower would become president.[26]

Ronald Reagan. During the years Reagan lived in Hollywood, he knew astrologer Carroll Righter and read his newspaper horoscopes.[27] In Reagan's first autobiography, *Where's the Rest of Me?*, he openly admitted to this involvement with astrology: "One of our good friends is Carroll Righter, who has a syndicated column on astrology. Every morning Nancy and I turn to see what he has to say about people of our respective birth signs. On the morning of the meeting I looked, and almost suspected an MCA plot: my word for the day read, 'This is a day to listen to the advice of experts.' "[28] This involvement with astrology continued through his Hollywood years and while he was governor of California.

However, by the time Reagan became president, he realized that astrology could be a political liability. Though Reagan never directly denied his involvement in astrology, his family and friends downplayed its influence on his life. Michael Reagan said it was "no big deal" to his father, and that "He would laugh and say to us, 'Hey listen to this today. . . .' "[29] Ed Meese stated that Reagan read horoscopes for "entertainment" and "amusement."

During Reagan's term, it became public knowledge that Nancy Reagan consulted an astrologer. Though the accounts were true, former staff member Donald Regan's irresponsible claim that "virtually every major move and decision the Reagans made" was affected by astrology has been refuted by the testimony of many other people.

Ronald Reagan stated: "No policy or decision in my mind has ever been influenced by astrology."[30] He also said: "[N]o decision was ever made by me on the basis of astrology."[31] Another time, a reporter asked him if he would continue to "allow astrology to play a part in the makeup of your daily schedule." To this Reagan responded, "I can't, because I never did."[32]

However, Reagan aide Michael Deaver stated that he would at times avoid scheduling events (without Reagan's knowledge) on certain days, "simply for Nancy's peace of mind."[33]

Any influence that astrology had on Ronald Reagan's schedule was through his wife's requests to his staffers, and through his staffers acting behind his back. Ronald Reagan himself did not use astrology to make decisions during his presidency.

William Clinton. George Stephanopoulos, a Clinton political adviser, said that at one point during his presidency, Mr. and Mrs. Clinton invited "New age self-help gurus Tony Robbins and Marianne Williamson to a secret session up at Camp David."[34]

NOTES

1. Allan Peskin, *Garfield* (Kent, OH: Kent State University Press, 1978), 160, 279–80; Carl Sferazza Anthony, *First Ladies: The Saga of the Presidents' Wives and Their Power, 1789–1961* (New York: Morrow, 1990), 236. Reference is made to correspondence between Garfield and his wife, July 7, July 8, and December 7, 1867.

2. Account from several sources, among them Anthony, *First Ladies,* 262.

3. Sources include ibid., 301.

4. Robert K. Murray, *The Harding Era: Warren G. Harding and His Administration* (Minneapolis: University of Minnesota Press, 1969), 528; Margaret Truman, *First Ladies: An Intimate Group Portrait of White House Wives* (New York: Random House, 1995), 237; Doug Wead, *All the Presidents' Children* (New York: Atria Books, 2003), 355.

5. Russell Freedman, *Eleanor Roosevelt: A Life of Discovery* (New York: Clarion Books, 1993, 1997), 61–63.

6. Robert Dallek, *John F. Kennedy: An Unfinished Life, 1917–1963* (New York: Little, Brown, 2003), 195. Dozens (if not hundreds) of sources document this. A telling comment concerning Kennedy's attitude was one he is reported to have made at his brother Ted's wedding. The tape of the wedding purportedly caught him whispering to Ted that "being married didn't really mean that you had to be faithful to your wife." Dallek quoted from Adam Clymer's *Edward M. Kennedy: A Biography,* 24.

7. Joseph J. Ellis, *Founding Brothers* (New York: Knopf, 2001), 198–209; Fawn M. Brodie, *Thomas Jefferson: An Intimate History* (New York: Norton, 1974). While DNA evidence has purportedly proven the Hemings' family claim that they are descended from Thomas Jefferson (a claim originally made by Madison Hemings, who stated that Jefferson was his father), some scholars dispute the validity of the DNA research.

8. Merle Miller, *Plain Speaking: An Oral Biography of Harry S. Truman* (New York: Berkeley Publishing/G. P. Putnam's Sons, 1973, 1974), 339–40. The primary witness against Eisenhower is President Truman, who said he destroyed evidence that would have incriminated Eisenhower. When

Eisenhower's wife heard about the relationship and wrote her husband a letter asking about it, he responded that Mamie was his "only girl" and that "you will know that I've no emotional involvements and will have none." (He did not, incidentally, deny physical involvements.)

9. Anthony, *First Ladies*, 157.

10. Ibid. One example was foretelling her husband's death six days before it happened (ibid., 182).

11. Ibid.

12. A "soirée" means an evening party or reception, but this might more properly be described as a séance.

13. Carl Sandburg, *Abraham Lincoln: The War Years*, vol. 3 (New York: Harcourt, Brace, & World, 1939), 343.

14. Anthony, *First Ladies*, 182.

15. Ibid., 184.

16. Ibid.

17. Truman, *First Ladies*, 104.

18. Wead, *All the Presidents' Children*, 50.

19. Truman, *First Ladies*, 105.

20. Wead, *All the Presidents' Children*, 50.

21. Ibid.

22. Ishbel Ross, *Power with Grace: The Life Story of Mrs. Woodrow Wilson* (New York: G. P. Putnam's Sons, 1975), 195–96.

23. Ibid., 91.

24. Ibid.

25. William Allen White, *A Puritan in Babylon: The Story of Calvin Coolidge* (New York: Macmillan, 1938; repr., Simon Publications, 2001), 229. The 1921 letter drew on the (as of 1938) unpublished correspondence of William H. Taft.

26. Anthony, *First Ladies*, 456–57.

27. Paul Kengor, *God and Ronald Reagan: A Spiritual Life* (New York: ReganBooks/HarperCollins, 2004), 193.

28. Ronald Reagan with Richard G. Hubler, *Where's the Rest of Me?* (New York: Duell, Sloan & Pearce, 1965), 169.

29. Kengor, *God and Ronald Reagan*, 193.

30. Ibid.

31. Ibid., 192.

32. Ibid.

33. Ibid., 191.

34. George Stephanopoulos, *All Too Human* (Boston: Little, Brown and Company, 1999), 324.

OUR PRESIDENTS WHO WERE MASONS

FOURTEEN PRESIDENTS of the United States—George Washington, James Monroe, Andrew Jackson, James Polk, James Buchanan, Andrew Johnson, James Garfield, William McKinley, Theodore Roosevelt, William Taft, Warren Harding, Franklin Roosevelt, Harry Truman, Lyndon Johnson, and Gerald Ford—were Masons. Though some lists of presidents who were Masons include James Madison and Herbert Hoover, most lists do not. If they were Masons, then we have had sixteen Masonic presidents.

A seventeenth president, Zachary Taylor, purportedly stated as president that he would have become a Mason if time and circumstances had permitted him to do so. An eighteenth, Ronald Reagan, was made an honorary Mason.

Some presidents, most notably Truman and Andrew Johnson, rose high in the Masonic ranks and became members of the Order of the Scottish Rite. Washington and Andrew Johnson had full Masonic rites at their funerals.

Some presidents, such as Jackson, Polk, and Buchanan, became Masons while young but became Christians later in life. It is not known how active they remained as Masons or if they remained Masons at all after their conversions to Christianity.

On the other hand, Garfield, McKinley, and Harding were converted to Christianity early in their lives but became Masons later on.

How can a president's Masonic membership influence his religious beliefs? Its primary influence would be if the Masons teach doctrines incompatible with Christianity and if the president believed those doctrines.

Do Masons maintain doctrines antithetical to orthodox Christianity? To answer the question, the Masonic structure and procedure must be briefly outlined.

All who wish to take part in Masonic activities must have received the first three degrees of Freemasonry, the Entered Apprentice (first degree), Fellow Craft or Fellowcraft (second degree), and Master Mason (third degree) levels.

After the first three degrees are received, competing rites offer higher levels of Masonic mysteries. The two most common in the United States are the Scottish Rite and the Knights Templar (York Rite). No president is known to have received higher degrees in any other form of higher Masonry.

Each of the presidents who belonged to the Masons is believed to have gone through at least the first three degrees of Masonry, with the exception of Lyndon Johnson, who did not go beyond the First Degree.

FIRST DEGREE: GRADE OF ENTERED APPRENTICE

In the first degree, the candidate is blindfolded. The senior deacon escorts him around the lodge room. The junior warden asks, "Who comes here?"

The response is: "Mr._____, who has long been in darkness and now seeks to be brought to Light and to receive the rights and benefits of this Worshipful Lodge, erected to God and dedicated to the holy Sts. John, as all brothers have done before." (Note the implication that anyone who is not a Mason, whether Christian or not, is in darkness.) The candidate then swears he will not reveal any of the mysteries of Freemasonry.

SECOND DEGREE: DEGREE OF FELLOW CRAFT

In the second degree, the candidate is again blindfolded, or, as the ritual states, "hoodwinked." (The ritual might predate the derogatory use of the term.) The Mason swears an oath to not reveal the secrets of Fellow Craft Masons to anyone except other Fellow Craft Masons.

The Fellow Craft Mason is then led to a staircase (sometimes symbolic, sometimes real) leading "to the Middle Chamber of the Temple of Solomon" and flanked by columns Joachin and Boaz. He is then told that the first three steps of the staircase represent youth, manhood, and old age, "equated to the initiation as Entered Apprentice in his youth, maturation into knowledge and good works as a Fellow Craft, and living out his days as a Master Mason in confidence of immortal life, as he reflects on his honorable life as a Freemason."[1]

THIRD DEGREE: DEGREE OF MASTER MASON

Before receiving the third degree, the Master Mason swears another oath to keep the secrets of the degree. Then the candidate enters into the central part of the third degree. The purpose of degree is for the Mason to "relive the passion of Hiram, the murdered architect" of Solomon's Temple.[2] According to Masonic legend, Hiram Abiff designed Solomon's temple and was then murdered. The purpose of the Third Degree is for the Freemason to live "through the passion of Hiram."[3] The Hebrew name Hiram Abiff means "the teacher from the father,"[4] and Masons admit "how obvious the correspondence is between this story and the story of the death of the Christian Master related in the Gospels."[5] Hiram Abiff is the center of all Masonic ceremony.

The Mason, representing Hiram Abiff, is conducted to three "ruffians," who attempt to force him to reveal the secrets of a Master Mason. When the Mason refuses all three requests, Masons pull the candidate to the floor, symbolizing his death. The ruffians decide to bury him under a pile of rubble. They do so. The candidate remains there until "King Solomon" orders twelve Fellow Craft Masons to find the candidate. They capture the ruffians, who confess their crime to King Solomon. The candidate is then found; his body is pulled from the rubble and brought to King Solomon. King Solomon then whispers the word of the Master Mason to the Candidate, warning him that it is never to be revealed to any person except to Master Masons under the conditions provided in the oath. This secret word is "Mah-hah-bone."

The candidate is then told what the preceding drama symbolizes. According to older Masonic writers, the drama symbolizes death and resurrection. Arthur Waite, a Mason and Masonic expert, states that the Mason "hears of direct relations between man and his Creator, with suggestions of judgment to come. He is also brought face to face with the mystery of death and of that which follows thereafter, being the great mystery of Raising."[6]

How is the Mason brought "face to face with the mystery of death?" In the third degree, the candidate undergoes a "mystical death." According to the *Encyclopedia of Freemasonry*, "The time of his interned condition is marked by three episodes, which are so many attempts to restore him, of which the last alone is successful."[7]

This is viewed as a candidate's "resurrection and rebirth." Albert G. Mackey, a prominent Masonic author, wrote about the ritual in *Mackey's Encyclopedia of Freemasonry*. He said: "The Master Mason represents man, when youth, manhood, old age, and life itself, have passed away as fleeting shadows, yet raised from the grave of iniquity, and quickened into another and better existence. By its legend and all its ritual it is implied that we have been redeemed from the death of sin and the sepulcher of pollution."[8]

Recent revisionist Masonic writers have contested the claim, stating that the ceremony does not really symbolize resurrection. In all likelihood, what the ceremony symbolizes is interpreted differently by various people; it can be accurately stated that, at the very least, many or most Masons perceive the ceremony as symbolizing resurrection. In addition, the more recent statements that it does not symbolize resurrection have been made since the most recent Masonic presidents joined their lodges: The common perception when they joined was that this level symbolizes resurrection.

Any Mason who wishes to partake in Masonic activities must take all three degrees. In what way could the teachings of basic Masonry—Blue Lodge Masonry—have affected their religious beliefs?

In this section, I draw upon the oaths and ceremonies discussed in the preceding section, as well as other material pertinent to Blue Lodge Masonry.

1. Masonry excludes Jesus Christ.

All Masonic ceremonies are composed so as to exclude the mention of Jesus Christ in rites or prayers. Doctrinal discussion—specifically including the mention of Jesus Christ—is forbidden in Masonic lodges. These provisions are made so that Jews, Muslims, and members of other religions are not offended by the mention of Jesus or of Christianity. This leads to the second point.

2. "Christian" Masons become brothers with members of other religions.

In the Entered Apprentice degree, candidates are told: "By the exercise of brotherly love we are taught to regard the whole human species as one family; the high and the low, the rich and the poor; who, as created by one Almighty Parent and inhabitants of the same planet, are to aid, support and protect each other. On this principle, Masonry unites men of every country, sect and opinion, and conciliates true friendship among those who might otherwise have remained at a perpetual distance."[9]

Masonic lodges have frequent prayers. These prayers are either addressed to "God" or to the generic Masonic term for their god, "The Great Architect of the Universe." These prayers are never addressed to Jesus Christ. Christians who have asked their Masonic leadership if they can pray to Jesus Christ are informed that they must pray to "God" and that they can believe that the term "Great Architect of the Universe" refers to Jesus Christ if they so desire. Likewise, Muslims can believe that the term "Great Architect of the Universe" refers to Allah.

Every time a new member joins, a work called *The Constitutions of the Freemasons*, written by James Anderson and published in 1723, is read aloud. The first article states: "But though in ancient Times Masons were charg'd in every Country to be of the Religion of that Country or Nation, whatever it was, yet 'tis now thought more expedient only to oblige them to that Religion in which all Men agree, leaving their particular Opinions to themselves; that is, to be *good men and true*, or Men of Honour and Honesty, by whatever Denominations or Persuasions they may be distinguish'd; whereby Masonry becomes the *Center of Union*, and the Means of conciliating true Friendship among Persons that must have remain'd at a perpetual Distance."[10]

Members of any other religion that recognizes a god can become Masons, and they interpret corporate prayers to refer to their god. (Pantheists have been admitted to the Masons on the grounds that their many gods represent the Great Architect of the Universe in spirit.) This leads to the third point.

3. Masonry offers eternal life to members of any religion.

In the Fellow Craft (second) degree, the Mason is led to a staircase and informed that the first three steps represent the first three levels of Masonry. As the author of one book endorsed by several Masonic organizations and publications puts it, the third step represents a man "living out his days as a Master Mason in confidence of immortal life, as he reflects on his honorable life as a Freemason."[11]

Thus, all Master Masons—whether Jews, Christians, Muslims, Hindus, or members of any other religion—are told that they have "confidence of immortal life."

My case does not rest upon this one quote. Masonic newsletters will introduce obituaries of Masons in words like these: "Whereas it pleased Almighty God in his infinite wisdom to call from the sacred lodge below to that Grand Lodge of the New Jerusalem above the soul of our believed friend and brother . . ."[12]

Additionally, during the third degree, a hymn known as *Pleyel's Hymn* is sung in some lodges before the Masons attempt to resurrect the "dead" body of the "murdered" initiate, representing Hiram Abiff. In the last verse, the hymn states, "Lord of all! below, above, fill our hearts with truth and love; When dissolves our earthly tie, take us to Thy Lodge on high."[13] This dirge is also sung in some Masonic burial rituals.[14]

Other references could be cited; these references were cited because they are all from the lower levels of Masonry. Masonry teaches that Master Masons will have eternal life.

Masons are often permitted to believe that they have received redemption through their own church's proceedings. However, they are taught in Masonry that members of other religions receive redemption through those other religions and through the teachings of the Masons. This is why comments about the "religious tolerance" of Masonic presidents, such as William McKinley, sound alarm bells in the minds of those familiar with Masonic ritual.

This objection, along with the objection of Christian Masons being brothers with non-Christians, are probably the two doctrines in Blue Lodge Masonry that would have most strongly affected the religious beliefs of the presidents who attained these levels. While it might not have caused them to deny their faith in Jesus Christ (for those presidents who came into the Masons with that faith), it would have at least inclined them to believe that other ways to God are also legitimate.

Yet Jesus said in John 14:6, "I am the way, the truth, and the life: no man cometh unto the Father, but by me." Jesus' claim is exclusive. It's hard to believe that a true Christian can accept Jesus' words and also accept the Masonic doctrine.

4. **Masonry teaches that candidates, including Christians, are "in darkness" until they become Masons.**

Candidates about to receive the First Degree are blindfolded, symbolizing a condition of darkness. When they are brought into the room, they are asked, "Who comes here?"

Whether the prospective Mason is a Christian or not, the following response is given: "Mr. _____, who has long been in darkness and now seeks to be brought to Light and to receive the rights and benefits of this Worshipful Lodge, erected to God and dedicated to the holy Sts. John, as all brothers have done before."

Masonry makes the claim that non-Masons are in darkness until they become Masons. (Since women and children are excluded, they must remain in darkness.)

Christianity also makes a similar claim. Non-Christians are in darkness until they accept Jesus, the Light of the World, as their Lord and Savior (see John 1).

These claims are mutually exclusive. If it is true that a person is in darkness until he becomes a Mason, he can become a Christian before becoming a Mason and still be in darkness. If, on the other hand, a person is in darkness until he becomes a Christian, he can become a Mason and still remain in darkness.

This brief examination of the teachings of the Masons in the first three degrees shows that even in the lower degrees some tenets of Freemasonry contradict Christianity.

Can a president who was a Mason still be a Christian? Yes, but he would have had to deny certain Masonic teachings.

Some presidents have undoubtedly been social Masons, who go through the motions but do not accept Masonic doctrine, just as some presidents have been social Christians, who read the creeds aloud with their churches yet deny them in their hearts.

Since much of this information on the Masons has been recently uncovered, some widely held conclusions about the religion of the presidents may need to be reassessed. My information has been compiled from authoritative sources; however, due to the fact that many of the assertions (whether originally made by Masons or by apostate Masons) contained in this appendix would be contested by Masons interested in preserving Masonic secrets, I have not examined the religion and the Masonic membership together for each president in detail. Perhaps, as more information becomes available, these conclusions can be reexamined.

For further information on the teachings of the Masons, consult the books mentioned in the bibliography. The best one written from a Christian perspective is probably Steven Tsoukalas's *Masonic Rites and Wrongs: An Examination of Freemasonry*, while the most informative book, written from a Masonic perspective, is John Robinson's *Born in Blood: The Lost Secrets of Freemasonry*.

Notes

1. John J. Robinson, *Born in Blood: The Lost Secrets of Freemasonry* (New York: M. Evans, 1990), 213–14.

2. Daniel Béresniak and Laziz Hamani, *Symbols of Freemansonry* (New York: Assouline Books, 2000), 11.

3. Ibid., 102.

4. W. L. Wilmshurst, *The Meaning of Masonry* (New York: Gramercy Books, 1927, 1980.), 45.

5. Ibid., 44.

6. Arthur Edward Waite, *New Encyclopedia of Freemasonry*, vol. 1 (Avenel, NJ: Wings Books, 1970), 156.

7. Ibid., 109–110.

8. Albert G. MacKey and H. L. Haywood, *Encyclopedia of Freemasonry* (Kila, MT: Kessinger Publishing, 2003), 474–75, as quoted in Pat Hardeman, *Can a Christian Be a Mason?* (Tampa, FL: Temple Publishers, 1953), 27.

9. Found in the 1983 *Masonic Ritual of the Grand Lodge of Georgia*, 27, as quoted in Steven Tsoukalas, *Masonic Rites and Wrongs: An Examination of Freemasonry* (Phillipsburg, NJ: P & R Publishing, 1995), 70.

10. Béresniak, *Symbols of Freemasonry*, 12. All emphases are in the original.

11. Robinson, *Born in Blood*, 213–14; Tsoukalas, *Masonic Rites and Wrongs*, 34, quoting Massachusetts' *Official Cipher*, 169.

12. One such notice was quoted in Hardeman, *Can a Christian Be a Mason?*, 10.

13. Tsoukalas, *Masonic Rites and Wrongs*, 81. He quoted the *Maine Masonic Text Book*, 56, and stated that the words are found in a majority of Masonic rituals in the United States. He also noted that the *Colorado Craftsman* stated that Masonic lecturer David Vinton wrote the dirge during the early 1800s. (Thus, George Washington and James Monroe would not have sung it, and Jackson might not have. Yet Vinton expressed already-established concepts when he wrote the hymn.)

14. Ibid., 115, quoting the Michigan Masonic burial service.

★ BIBLIOGRAPHICAL ESSAY

IF YOU HAVE never heard of another book on the faith of America's presidents, you are not alone. When I began this book, I had no idea that such a book existed. (That is why I decided to write one.) As I began research in this fascinating field, I found a few books about the topic. I will discuss each of them here.

PREVIOUS BOOKS ON THE FAITH OF AMERICA'S PRESIDENTS

Year	President	Author	Title	Viewpoint
1932	Hoover	E. Stacy Matheny	*American Patriotic Devotions*	Ecumenical
1936	Roosevelt, F.	Franklin Steiner	*Religious Beliefs of Our Presidents*	Atheist, Agnostic
1953	Eisenhower	Bliss Isley	*The Presidents: Men of Faith*	Methodist
1966	Johnson	Benjamin Weiss	*God in American History*	Unknown
1968	Johnson	Fuller and Green	*God in the White House*	Presbyterian, Episcopalian
1971	Nixon	John S. Bonnell	*Presidential Profiles*	Presbyterian
1991	Bush (#40)	John McCollister	*So Help Me God*	Presbyterian (?)

The best of these books was Edmund Fuller and David E. Green's *God in the White House: The Faiths of American Presidents*. The authors are affiliated with the Presbyterian and the Episcopalian churches and wrote from their backgrounds. This 1968 volume covers from George Washington through Lyndon Baines Johnson and is 246 pages long.

John Sutherland Bonnell's *Presidential Profiles: Religion in the Life of America's Presidents* is a much smaller volume that could almost be termed an abridgement of *God in the White House*. *Presidential Profiles*, while interesting, does not go into depth on most presidents. An average of about four pages is devoted to the religion of each president. The exceedingly complex issue of Abraham Lincoln's Christianity is dealt with in six pages. Dr. Bonnell was a Presbyterian and wrote from that viewpoint. This 1971 volume covers from George Washington through Richard Nixon.

John McCollister's more recent *So Help Me God* is about the same size as *Presidential Profiles*. While McCollister used new research that came to light since previous works, the 205-page book is a brief treatment of the topic. It include forty-three full-page illustrations, several near-full-page illustrations, and eight blank pages in between chapters. *So Help Me God* is well-written; but is too short to treat the topic adequately. (A caution: In case you consider purchasing this book, please note that it includes several vulgar words in the chapter on Harry Truman.) As the book was published by Westminster/John Knox Press, it is either from a Presbyterian viewpoint or compatible with that viewpoint. This 1991 book deals with presidents from George Washington through George H. W. Bush.

Is my work standing on the shoulders of these previous works? While these books provide a good starting point for study, the most honest answer is no. In-depth biographies have been written on each president; nearly every president has a biography that goes into more depth on his religion than the previous books on the Christianity of the presidents. There are several treatments of the religion of individual presidents (e.g, Washington, Lincoln, and G.W. Bush) that are quite useful. The most useful source for each president is their own writings; I have consulted their published papers where possible.

My book stands on the shoulders of the presidents' writings. Without them, I would have been unable to write a work as definitive as this one. They provide the best information available and are all we have on what they believed until eternity arrives.

Now I move to the books on or having a section on the Christianity of presidents. Benjamin Weiss's *God in American History: A Documentation of America's Religious Heritage* had a section on United States presidents (through 1966). He mostly limited himself to a few quotes from presidents' inaugural addresses.

E. Stacy Matheny's *American Patriotic Devotions* covers the presidents through Herbert Hoover. Matheny's brief comments typically focus on a president's denomination and church attendance record, though he does record a Harding conversion experience found nowhere else.

For selected presidents, it would be worthwhile to point out a few biographies that were particularly helpful.

THOMAS JEFFERSON

As I started my research, I was influenced by accounts such as Catherine Millard's *Great American Statesmen and Heroes*. These accounts portrayed Jefferson as quite religious and possibly an evangelical Christian himself. As I found more of Jefferson's own religious statements, I was forced to abandon this position. I eventually came to agree with William Lee Miller's insightful observation on the topic. He said that "eventually popular American attitudes did to Thomas Jefferson something like what Jefferson did to Jesus: they granted him very high honor indeed, but at the same time were highly selective in what was to be taken from his teaching, and in what he was to be interpreted as having stood for."

ANDREW JACKSON

The best place to start research is James Parton's three-volume *Life of Andrew Jackson*. The first volume was published in 1859, and the last two volumes were published in 1860. The book is full of anecdotes and stories. Jackson was a figure in recent memory at the time of the writing; he died less than fifteen years before the first volume was printed. Parton interviewed and corresponded with many people who knew Andrew Jackson well; some accounts, such as the account of Jackson's joining the Presbyterian church after his wife's death (written by the pastor who preached the sermon that led Jackson to that decision), are not available anywhere else, except when other books quote this one.

JOHN TYLER

In researching John Tyler's Christianity, *John Tyler: Champion of the Old South* is a good place to start. It includes two pages about Tyler's religion and its footnotes point toward other sources.

JAMES POLK

Paul Bergeron's *The Presidency of James K. Polk* lays the groundwork for the understanding of Polk's religion. Eugene McCormac's Polk biography, the first scholarly biography, adds useful information, as does Charles Sellers's definitive two-volume Polk biography. However, none of these biographers treated his religion as an important aspect of his life. In each of the biographies, his religious training merited references, as did his 1833 camp-meeting experience. Yet in these biographies, Polk's religion remained a side issue, disposed of in a sentence here or paragraph there.

FRANKLIN PIERCE

Roy Nichols's *Franklin Pierce: Young Hickory of the Granite Hills* (1931) is a valuable starting point in the study of Pierce's religion. On the whole, Nichols was supportive of Pierce's religious opinions and presented them in a reliable way. However, he did not like the effects of the Pierces' "rigorous Calvinistic self-questioning" after their son Benjamin died. Nichols included an account of Pierce's 1865 public confession of faith and baptism. The account was supplied him by Reverend Arthur P. Phinney of Concord, New Hampshire.

JAMES BUCHANAN

If you can find a copy of George Ticknor Curtis's two-volume *Life of James Buchanan*, published in 1883, start there. Chapter 30 is entitled "1868: Death of Mr. Buchanan—His Character as a Statesman, a Man and a Christian." This chapter includes several testimonies by ministers and family members that Curtis collected for the biography.

Abraham Lincoln

Among the multivolume biographies, I found Carl Sandburg's *Abraham Lincoln: The War Years* interesting and useful. Among the one-volume biographies, Benjamin Thomas's *Abraham Lincoln: A Biography* is a basic but useful starting place.

Rutherford B. Hayes

Hayes' *Diary and Letters* was a valuable primary source.

Franklin D. Roosevelt

A useful source for Roosevelt's public proclamations was the *Public Papers of Franklin D. Roosevelt* collection. Personal details were provided by Elliott Roosevelt's *F.D.R.: His Personal Letters*, Eleanor Roosevelt's *This I Remember*, and Otis Graham Jr. and Meghan Wander's *Franklin D. Roosevelt: His Life and Times: An Encyclopedic View*.

Kenneth Davis's magnum opus, a five-volume biography on Roosevelt, provided a few useful details. However, Roosevelt's religion was not a major concern to Davis (who cared about the precise details of Roosevelt's religion about as much as Roosevelt himself did.) Joseph Lash's *Eleanor and Franklin: The Story of Their Relationship Based on Eleanor Roosevelt's Private Papers* provided a few useful details, as did Geoffrey C. Ward's book, *A First-Class Temperament: The Emergence of Franklin Roosevelt: An Intimate Portrait of the Private World, Personal Ordeal, and Public Triumph of the Man Who Became FDR*, a book that actually *is* bigger than its title would suggest, also provided some useful details.

Ronald Reagan

Ronald Reagan's autobiographies, *An American Life* and *Where's the Rest of Me?*, were both useful primary sources, as were the autobiographies of several of Reagan's associates.

Reagan's papers are being published, albeit in editions of selected writings. I have found several books coedited by Kiron K. Skinner, Annelise Anderson, and Martin Anderson to be particularly helpful—*Reagan: A Life in Letters* and *Reagan's Path to Victory*.

Paul Kengor's book, *God and Ronald Reagan: A Spiritual Life*, was quite helpful. One afternoon shortly after the book was published, I called the local library to see if they had the book and ask for it to be sent to my local branch. They had it, and said they would send it. Shortly afterwards, probably less than an hour after I called, I turned on the radio and heard the news that Reagan had died that afternoon. Because I called just before the news came out, I avoided the otherwise inevitable months of waiting for a reserved book, as the event of his death sparked interest in his religion.

GEORGE H. W. BUSH

In a 1988 campaign biography written by Doug Wead, *Man of Integrity*, George Bush shared his thoughts on religion extensively. He expressed his thoughts and feelings on religion in terms that the conservative Christian audience used and understood. The book was written to increase Bush's support in the conservative Christian community.

GEORGE W. BUSH

George W. Bush is one of only a handful of presidents who have had a book written on their religion. I consulted both Steven Mansfield's *The Faith of George W. Bush* and David Aikman's *A Man of Faith: The Spiritual Journey of George W. Bush*. Both volumes have their merits, but Aikman's book is better researched and more comprehensive.

✭ BIBLIOGRAPHY

This is not an exhaustive list of the books I've consulted, but these books have information regarding the religions of the presidents. In researching, I consulted the most readily available biographies of each president.

PART 1
BOOKS ABOUT PRESIDENTIAL CHRISTIANITY

Bonnell, John Sutherland. *Presidential Profiles: Religion in the Life of America's Presidents*. Philadelphia: Westminster Press, 1971.

Fuller, Edmund, and David E. Green. *God in the White House: The Faiths of American Presidents*. New York: Crown Publishers, 1968.

Isley, Bliss. *The Presidents: Men of Faith*. Boston: W. A. Wilde, 1953.

Jones, Olga Anna. *Churches of the Presidents in Washington: Visits to Fifteen National Shrines*. New York: Exposition Press, 1954.

Matheny, E. Stacy. *American Patriotic Devotions*. New York: Association Press, 1932.

McCollister, John. *So Help Me God: The Faith of America's Presidents*. Louisville: Westminster/John Knox Press, 1991.

Steiner, Franklin. *The Religious Beliefs of Our Presidents*. Girard, KS: Haldeman-Julius, 1936. Reprint, Amherst, NY: Prometheus Books, 1995.

Weiss, Benjamin. *God in American History: A Documentation of America's Religious Heritage*. Grand Rapids: Zondervan, 1966.

PART 2
SOURCES ON EACH PRESIDENT
GEORGE WASHINGTON

Allison, Andrew M. *The Real George Washington*. Washington, DC: National Center for Constitutional Studies, 1991.

Bonnell, John Sutherland. *Presidential Profiles: Religion in the Life of American Presidents*. Philadelphia: Westminster Press, 1971.

Ellis, Joseph J. *Founding Brothers*. New York: Knopf, 2001.

Flexner, James Thomas. *George Washington*. Vol. 1, *The Forge of Experience (1732–1775)*. Vol. 2, *In the American Revolution (1775–1783)*. Vol. 3, *Anguish and Farewell (1793–1799)*. Boston and Toronto: Little, Brown, 1965–72.

Freeman, Douglas Southall. Abridged by Richard Harwell. *Washington: An Abridgment in One Volume by Richard Harwell of the Seven-volume George Washington by Douglas Southall Freeman*. New York: Scribner, 1968.

Isley, Bliss. *The Presidents: Men of Faith*. Boston: W. A. Wilde, 1953.

LaHaye, Tim. *Faith of Our Founding Fathers*. Brentwood, TN: Wolgemuth & Hyatt, 1987.

Sparks, Jared. *Life of George Washington*. Kila, MT: Kessinger Publishing, 2006.

Steiner, Franklin. *The Religious Beliefs of Our Presidents*. Girard, KS: Haldeman-Julius, 1936. Reprint, Amherst, NY: Prometheus Books, 1995.

Washington, George. *The Writings of George Washington from the Original Manuscript Sources, 1745–1799*. Edited by John C. Fitzpatrick. 39 vols. Washington, DC: Government Printing Office, 1931–44.

Washington, George. *The Writings of George Washington with a Life of the Author.* Edited by Jared Sparks. 12 vols. Boston: American Stationers, 1834–37.

JOHN ADAMS

Adams, Charles Francis. *The Works of John Adams: Second President of the United States*. Library of the Presidents. Norwalk, CT: Easton Press, 1992.

Adams, John. *Papers of John Adams*. In *The Adams Papers*. Series 3. *General Correspondence and Other Papers of the Adams Statesmen*. Edited by Robert J. Taylor. Cambridge, MA: Harvard University Press/Belknap Press, 1977.

Adams, John Quincy, and Charles Francis Adams. *The Life of John Adams*. 2 vols. 1870.

Adams, John, and Thomas Jefferson, *The Complete Correspondence between Thomas Jefferson and Abigail and John Adams*. Edited by Lester J. Cappon. 2 vols. Chapel Hill: University of North Carolina Press, 1959.

Fuller, Edmund, and David E. Green. *God in the White House: The Faiths of American Presidents.* New York: Crown Publishers, 1968.

Matheny, E. Stacy. *American Patriotic Devotions.* New York: Association Press, 1932.

McCullough, David. *John Adams.* New York: Simon & Schuster, 2001.

Weiss, Benjamin. *God in American History: A Documentation of America's Religious Heritage.* Grand Rapids: Zondervan, 1966.

THOMAS JEFFERSON

Adams, John, and Thomas Jefferson. *The Complete Correspondence between Thomas Jefferson and Abigail and John Adams.* Edited by Lester J. Cappon. 2 vols. Chapel Hill: University of North Carolina Press, 1959, 1988.

Allison, Andrew M. *Thomas Jefferson: Champion of History.*

Boller, Paul F. Jr. *Presidential Campaigns.* New York and Oxford: Oxford University Press, 1984.

Bowers, Claude. *Jefferson and Hamilton: The Struggle for Democracy in America.* Boston and New York: Houghton Mifflin, 1925, 1945.

_____. *Jefferson in Power: The Death Struggle of the Federalists.* Boston and New York: Houghton Mifflin, 1936, 1967.

Brodie, Fawn M. *Thomas Jefferson: An Intimate History.* New York: Norton, 1974, 1998.

Jefferson, Thomas. *The Papers of Thomas Jefferson.* Edited by Julian P. Boyd. 3 vols. Princeton, NJ: Princeton University Press, 1950–51.

Jefferson, Thomas. *The Writings of Thomas Jefferson.* Edited by Albert Ellery, Thomas Lipscomb, and Andrew Bergh. 20 vols. Washington, DC: The Thomas Jefferson Memorial Association, 1907.

Jefferson, Thomas. *The Writings of Thomas Jefferson.* Edited by Paul Leicester Ford. 10 vols. New York: G. P. Putnam's Sons, 1892–99.

McCollister, John. *So Help Me God: The Faith of America's Presidents.* Louisville: Westminster/John Knox Press, 1991.

Randall, Willard Sterne. *Thomas Jefferson: A Life.* New York: Henry Holt, 1993.

Weiss, Benjamin. *God in American History: A Documentation of America's Religious Heritage.* Grand Rapids: Zondervan, 1966.

JAMES MADISON

Anthony, Carl Sferazza. *First Ladies: The Saga of the Presidents' Wives and Their Power, 1789–1961.* New York: Morrow, 1990.

Brant, Irving. *James Madison: The Virginia Revolutionist, 1751–1780*. Indianapolis: Bobbs-Merrill, 1941.

Eidsmoe, John, and D. James Kennedy. *Christianity and the Constitution: The Faith of Our Founding Fathers*. Grand Rapids: Baker Book House, 1987.

Hunt, Gaillard, *The Life of James Madison*. Library Reprints, 2002.

Isley, Bliss. *The Presidents: Men of Faith*. Boston: W. A. Wilde, 1953.

Ketcham, Ralph. *James Madison: A Biography*. Charlottesville and London: University Press of Virginia, 1971, 1990, 1998.

LaHaye, Tim. *Faith of Our Founding Fathers*. Brentwood, TN: Wolgemuth & Hyatt, 1987.

Meade, William. *Old Churches, Ministers, and Families of Virginia*. Baltimore: Genealogical Publishing, 1857, 1910, 1995.

Rives, William. *History of the Life and Times of James Madison*. 1859. Kila, MT: Kessinger Publishing, 2006.

JAMES MONROE

Jones, Olga Anna. *Churches of the Presidents in Washington: Visits to Fifteen National Shrines*. New York: Exposition Press, 1954.

Kane, Joseph Nathan. *Facts abut the Presidents: A Compilation of Biographical and Historical Data*. 1st ed. New York: H. W. Wilson, 1959.

Matheny, E. Stacy. *American Patriotic Devotions*. New York: Association Press, 1932.

JOHN QUINCY ADAMS

Adams, John Quincy. *The Diary of John Quincy Adams, 1794–1845*. Edited by Allan Nevins. New York: Longmans, Green, 1929; abridged, Charles Scribners, 1951.

Adams, John Quincy. *Memoirs of John Quincy Adams, Comprising Portions of His Diary from 1795 to 1848*. Edited by Charles Francis Adams. 12 vols. Philadelphia, 1874–77.

Bemis, Samuel Flagg. *John Quincy Adams and the Foundations of American Foreign Policy*. New York: Knopf, 1949.

_____. *John Quincy Adams and the Union*. New York: Knopf, 1956.

Falkner, Leonard, *The President Who Wouldn't Retire: John Quincy Adams, Congressman from Massachusetts*. New York: Coward-McCann, 1967.

Fuller, Edmund, and David E. Green. *God in the White House: The Faiths of American Presidents*. New York: Crown Publishers, 1968.

Hargreaves, Mary W. M. *The Presidency of John Quincy Adams*. Lawrence: University Press of Kansas, 1985.

Kennedy, John Fitzgerald. *Profiles in Courage*. New York: Harper & Brothers, 1955.

Morse, John Torrey. *John Quincy Adams.* American Statesmen Series. Boston and New York: Houghton Mifflin, 1882, 1898, 1910, 1912.

Nagel, Paul C. *John Quincy Adams: A Public Life, A Private Life.* New York: Knopf, 1997.

Truman, Margaret. *First Ladies: An Intimate Group Portrait of White House Wives.* New York: Random House, 1995.

ANDREW JACKSON

Boller, Paul F. Jr. *Presidential Campaigns.* New York and Oxford: Oxford University Press, 1984.

Booraem, Hendrik. *Young Hickory: The Making of Andrew Jackson.* Dallas: Taylor Trade Publishing, 2001.

Jones, Olga Anna. *Churches of the Presidents in Washington: Visits to Fifteen National Shrines.* New York: Exposition Press, 1954.

Parton, James. *The Life of Andrew Jackson.* 3 vols. Boston and New York: Houghton Mifflin, 1859, 1860.

Remini, Robert V. *Andrew Jackson and the Course of American Democracy, 1833–1845.* New York: Harper & Row, 1984.

_____. *Andrew Jackson and the Course of the American Empire, 1767–1821.* New York: Harper & Row, 1977.

MARTIN VAN BUREN

Federer, William J., ed. *America's God and Country: Encyclopedia of Quotations.* 8th ed. Coppel, TX: Fame Publishing, 1994.

Fuller, Edmund, and David E. Green. *God in the White House: The Faiths of American Presidents.* New York: Crown Publishers, 1968.

Isley, Bliss. *The Presidents: Men of Faith.* Boston: W. A. Wilde, 1953.

Jones, Olga Anna. *Churches of the Presidents in Washington: Visits to Fifteen National Shrines.* New York: Exposition Press, 1954.

Lynch, Dennis Tilden. *An Epoch and a Man: Martin Van Buren and His Times.* New York: Horace Liveright, 1929.

Steiner, Franklin. *The Religious Beliefs of Our Presidents.* Girard, KS: Haldeman-Julius, 1936. Reprint, Amherst, NY: Prometheus Books, 1995.

Wead, Doug. *All the Presidents' Children.* New York: Atria Books, 2003.

WILLIAM HENRY HARRISON

Anthony, Carl Sferazza. *First Ladies: The Saga of the Presidents' Wives and Their Power, 1789–1961.* New York: Morrow, 1990.

Cash, James. *Unsung Heroes.* Wilmington, OH: Orange Frazer Press, 1998.

Cleaves, Freeman. *Old Tippecanoe: William Henry Harrison and His Time.* New York: Charles Scribner's Sons, 1939. Reprint, Port Washington, NY: Kennikat Press, 1965.

Fuller, Edmund, and David E. Green. *God in the White House: The Faiths of American Presidents.* New York: Crown Publishers, 1968.

Isley, Bliss. *The Presidents: Men of Faith.* Boston: W. A. Wilde, 1953.

Jones, Olga Anna. *Churches of the Presidents in Washington: Visits to Fifteen National Shrines.* New York: Exposition Press, 1954.

Sievers, Harry J. and Katherine Speirs, *Benjamin Harrison.* 2nd ed., rev. Vol. 1, *Hoosier Warrior: Through the Civil War Years, 1833–1865.* Vol. 2, *Hoosier Statesman: From the Civil War to the White House, 1865–88.* Vol. 3, *Hoosier President: The White House and After.* New York: University Publishers, 1960–68.

Steiner, Franklin. *The Religious Beliefs of Our Presidents.* Girard, KS: Haldeman-Julius, 1936. Reprint, Amherst, NY: Prometheus Books, 1995.

JOHN TYLER

Chitwood, Oliver Perry. *John Tyler: Champion of the Old South.* New York: Russell & Russell, 1939, 1964.

McCollister, John. *So Help Me God: The Faith of America's Presidents.* Louisville: Westminster/John Knox Press, 1991.

Seager, Robert II. *And Tyler Too: A Biography of John and Julia Gardiner Tyler.* New York: McGraw-Hill, 1963.

Steiner, Franklin. *The Religious Beliefs of Our Presidents.* Girard, KS: Haldeman-Julius, 1936. Reprint, Amherst, NY: Prometheus Books, 1995.

JAMES POLK

Anthony, Carl Sferazza. *First Ladies: The Saga of the Presidents' Wives and Their Power, 1789–1961.* New York: Morrow, 1990.

Isley, Bliss. *The Presidents: Men of Faith.* Boston: W. A. Wilde, 1953.

McCormac, Eugene Irving. *James K. Polk: A Political Biography to the End of a Career, 1845–1849.* New York: Russell & Russell, 1965.

Nevins, Allan. *Polk: The Diary of a President, 1845–1849.* London, New York, and Toronto: Longmans, Green, 1929, 1952.

Sellers, Charles. *James K. Polk: Jacksonian, 1795–1843.* Princeton, NJ: Princeton University Press, 1957.

_____. *James K. Polk: Continentalist, 1843–1846.* Princeton, NJ: Princeton University Press, 1966.

Weiss, Benjamin. *God in American History: A Documentation of America's Religious Heritage.* Grand Rapids: Zondervan, 1966.

ZACHARY TAYLOR

Fuller, Edmund, and David E. Green. *God in the White House: The Faiths of American Presidents*. New York: Crown Publishers, 1968.

Isley, Bliss. *The Presidents: Men of Faith*. Boston: W. A. Wilde, 1953.

Steiner, Franklin. *The Religious Beliefs of Our Presidents*. Girard, KS: Haldeman-Julius, 1936. Reprint, Amherst, NY: Prometheus Books, 1995.

MILLARD FILLMORE

Fuller, Edmund, and David E. Green. *God in the White House: The Faiths of American Presidents*. New York: Crown Publishers, 1968.

Isley, Bliss. *The Presidents: Men of Faith*. Boston: W. A. Wilde, 1953.

Rayback, Robert J. *Millard Fillmore: Biography of a President*. Buffalo: Buffalo Historical Society/Henry Stewart, 1959.

FRANKLIN PIERCE

Bartlett, D. W. *The Life of General Franklin Pierce of New Hampshire*. Auburn, ME: Derby & Miller, 1852.

Fuller, Edmund, and David E. Green. *God in the White House: The Faiths of American Presidents*. New York; Crown Publishers, 1968.

Nichols, Roy Franklin. *Franklin Pierce: Young Hickory of the Granite Hills*. Philadelphia: University of Philadelphia Press, 1931.

Steiner, Franklin. *The Religious Beliefs of Our Presidents*. Girard, KS: Haldeman-Julius, 1936. Reprint, Amherst, NY: Prometheus Books, 1995.

JAMES BUCHANAN

Curtis, George Ticknor. *The Life of James Buchanan: Fifteenth President of the United States*. 2 vols. New York: Harper & Brothers, 1883.

Fuller, Edmund, and David E. Green. *God in the White House: The Faiths of American Presidents*. New York: Crown Publishers, 1968.

Klein, Philip S. *President James Buchanan: A Biography*. University Park: Pennsylvania State University Press, 1962. Reprint, Newton, CT: American Political Biography Press, 1995.

ABRAHAM LINCOLN

Bancroft, George, Bishop Simpson, and R. S. Storrs Jr. *Our Martyr President, Abraham Lincoln: Lincoln Memorial Addresses*. New York: Tibbals & Whiting, 1865. Reprint, Nashville: Abingdon Press, 1915.

Bishop, Jim. *The Day Lincoln Was Shot*. New York: Random House/Gramercy, 1984.

Boller, Paul F. Jr. *Presidential Wives: An Anecdotal History*. New York and Oxford: Oxford University Press, 1998.

Hill, John Wesley. *Abraham Lincoln: Man of God*. New York: G. P. Putnam's Sons, 1926.

Isley, Bliss. *The Presidents: Men of Faith*. Boston: W. A. Wilde, 1953.

Jones, Olga Anna. *Churches of the Presidents in Washington: Visits to Fifteen National Shrines*. New York: Exposition Press, 1954.

McCollister, John. *So Help Me God: The Faith of America's Presidents*. Louisville: Westminster/John Knox Press, 1991.

Nicholay, Helen. *A Boy's Life of Abraham Lincoln*. First World Library, 2006, http://1stworldlibrary.com.

Sandburg, Carl. *Abraham Lincoln: The War Years*. 4 vols. New York: Harcourt, Brace & World, 1939. Reprint, New York: Dell, 1974.

Steiner, Franklin. *The Religious Beliefs of Our Presidents*. Girard, KS: Haldeman-Julius, 1936. Reprint, Amherst, NY: Prometheus Books, 1995.

Thomas, Benjamin P. *Abraham Lincoln: A Biography*. New York: Knopf, 1952. Reprint, New York: Barnes and Noble Books, 1994.

Wilson, Douglas L., and Rodney O. Davis. *Herndon's Informants: Letters, Interviews, and Statements about Abraham Lincoln*. Urbana and Chicago: University of Illinois Press, 1998.

Winik, Jay. *April 1865*. New York: HarperCollins/Perennial, 2001.

ANDREW JOHNSON

Fuller, Edmund, and David E. Green. *God in the White House: The Faiths of American Presidents*. New York: Crown Publishing, 1968.

Johnson, Andrew. *The Papers of Andrew Johnson*. Edited by Leroy P. Graff and Ralph W. Haskins. 7 vols. Edited by Paul H. Bergeron, et al. 9 vols. Knoxville: University of Tennessee Press, 1967–2000.

McCollister, John. *So Help Me God: The Faith of America's Presidents*. Louisville: Westminster/John Knox Press, 1991.

Savage, John. *The Life and Public Services of Andrew Johnson: Seventeenth President of the United States*. Auburn, ME: Derby & Miller, 1866.

Thomas, Lately. *The First President Johnson: The Three Lives of the Seventeenth President of the United States of America*. New York: Morrow, 1968.

Trefousse, Hans L. *Andrew Johnson: A Biography*. New York and London: Norton, 1989.

ULYSSES S. GRANT

Boyd, James Penny. *Military and Civil Life of General Ulysses S. Grant*. Garretson, 1885.

Cash, James. *Unsung Heroes.* Wilmington, OH: Orange Frazer Press, 1998.

Fuller, Edmund, and David E. Green. *God in the White House: The Faiths of American Presidents.* New York: Crown Publishers, 1968.

Grant, Ulysses S. *The Papers of Ulysses S. Grant, 1837–1875.* Edited by John Y. Simon. 26 vols. Carbondale and Edwardsville, IL: Southern Illinois University Press, 1967–2003.

Isley, Bliss. *The Presidents: Men of Faith.* W. A. Wilde, 1953.

Jones, Olga Anna. *Churches of the Presidents in Washington; Visits to Fifteen National Shrines.* New York: Exposition Press, 1954.

Thayer, William M. *From Tannery to the White House: The Life of Ulysses S. Grant: His Boyhood, Youth, Manhood, Public and Private Life and Services.* Chicago: Albert Whitman, 1927.

Young, John Russell, and Michael Fellman, eds. *Around the World with General Grant.* 2 vols. New York, 1879. Reprint, Baltimore: Johns Hopkins University Press, abridged ed., 2002.

RUTHERFORD BIRCHARD HAYES

Cash, James. *Unsung Heroes.* Wilmington, OH: Orange Frazer Press, 1998.

Fuller, Edmund, and David E. Green. *God in the White House: The Faiths of American Presidents.* New York: Crown Publishers, 1968.

Hayes, Rutherford B., *Diary and Letters of Rutherford B. Hayes.* Edited by Charles Richard Williams. 5 vols. Columbus: The Ohio State Archaeological and Historical Society, 1922–26.

Kane, Joseph Nathan. *Facts about the Presidents: From George Washington to Bill Clinton*, 6th ed. New York: H. W. Wilson, 1993.

Reid, Daniel G., et al., *Concise Dictionary of Christianity in America.* Downers Grove, IL: InterVarsity Press, 1995.

Tugwell, Rexford G. *How They Became President: Thirty-Five Ways to the White House.* New York: Simon & Schuster, 1964.

Williams, Charles Richard. *The Life of Rutherford Birchard Hayes: Nineteenth President of the United States.* 2 vols. Boston and New York: Houghton Mifflin, 1914.

JAMES GARFIELD

Ackerman, Kenneth D. *Dark Horse: The Surprise Election and Political Murder of President James A. Garfield.* New York: Carroll & Graf, 2003.

Booraem, Hendrik V. *The Road to Respectability: James A. Garfield and His World, 1844–1852.* Western Reserve Historical Society. Lewisburg: Bucknell University Press/London: Associated University Presses, 1988.

Caldwell, Robert Granville. *James A. Garfield: Party Chieftain.* New York: Dodd, Mead, 1931.

Fuller, Edmund, and David E. Green. *God in the White House: The Faiths of American Presidents*. New York: Crown Publishing, 1968.

Garfield, James and Lucretia. *Crete and James: Personal Letters of James and Lucretia Garfield*. Edited by John Shaw. East Lansing: Michigan State University Press, 1994.

Jones, Olga Anna. *Churches of the Presidents in Washington: Visits to Fifteen National Shrines*. New York: Exposition Press, 1954.

Peskin, Allan. *Garfield: A Biography*. Kent, OH: Kent State University Press, 1978. Reprint, Library of the Presidents, Easton, PA: Easton Press, 2004.

Reid, Daniel G., et al. *Concise Dictionary of Christianity in America*. Downers Grove, IL: InterVarsity Press, 1995.

Smith, Theodore C. *The Life and Letters of James Abram Garfield*. Hamden, CT: Archon Books, 1968.

Steiner, Franklin. *The Religious Beliefs of Our Presidents*. Girard, KS: Haldeman-Julius, 1936. Reprint, Amherst, NY: Prometheus Books, 1995.

Taylor, John M. *Garfield of Ohio: The Available Man*. New York: Norton, 1970.

CHESTER ARTHUR

Fuller, Edmund, and David E. Green. *God in the White House: The Faiths of American Presidents*. New York: Crown Publishing, 1968.

Howe, George Frederick. *Chester A. Arthur: A Quarter-Century of Machine Politics*. New York: Dodd, Mead, 1935. Reprint, New York: Frederick Unger, 1957.

Reeves, Thomas C. *Gentleman Boss: The Life of Chester Alan Arthur*. New York: Knopf, 1975.

GROVER CLEVELAND

Hutcheson, Richard G. Jr. *God in the White House: How Religion Has Changed the Modern Presidency*. New York: Macmillan, 1988.

McElroy, Robert M. *Grover Cleveland: The Man and the Statesman: An Authorized Biography*. 2 vols. New York: Harper & Brothers, 1923.

Nevins, Allan. *Grover Cleveland: A Study in Courage to the End of a Career*. New York: Dodd, Mead, 1932.

Steiner, Franklin. *The Religious Beliefs of Our Presidents*. Girard, KS: Haldeman-Julius, 1936. Reprint, Amherst, NY: Prometheus Books, 1995.

Welch, Richard E. Jr. *The Presidencies of Grover Cleveland*. Lawrence: University Press of Kansas, 1988.

BENJAMIN HARRISON

Boller, Paul F. Jr. *Presidential Campaigns*. New York and Oxford: Oxford University Press, 1984.

Fuller, Edmund, and David E. Green. *God in the White House: The Faiths of American Presidents.* New York: Crown Publishers, 1968.

Jones, Olga Anna. *Churches of the Presidents in Washington: Visits to Fifteen National Shrines.* New York: Exposition Press, 1954.

Sievers, Harry J. and Katherine Speirs. *Benjamin Harrison.* Vol. 1, *Hoosier Warrior: Through the Civil War Years, 1833–1865.* Vol. 2, *Hoosier Statesman: From the Civil War to the White House, 1865–1888.* Vol. 3, *Hoosier President: The White House and After, 1889–.* New York: University Publishers, 1968.

Socolofsky, Homer E., and Allan B. Spetter. *The Presidency of Benjamin Harrison.* Lawrence: University Press of Kansas, 1987.

WILLIAM MCKINLEY

Daniels, Josephus. *The Wilson Era: Years of Peace, 1910–1917.* Chapel Hill: University of North Carolina Press, 1944.

Fuller, Edmund, and David E. Green. *God in the White House: The Faiths of American Presidents.* New York: Crown Publishers, 1968.

Gould, Lewis L. *The Presidency of William McKinley.* Lawrence: Regents Press of Kansas, 1980.

Jones, Cranston. *Homes of the American Presidents.* New York: Bonanza Books, 1962.

Leech, Margaret. *In the Days of McKinley.* New York: Harper & Brothers, 1959.

Olcott, Charles Sumner. *The Life of William McKinley.* 2 vols. Boston and New York: Houghton Mifflin, 1916. Reprint, American Statesmen Series.

Reid, Daniel G., et al. *Concise Dictionary of Christianity in America.* Downers Grove, IL: InterVarsity Press, 1995.

Weiss, Benjamin. *God in American History: A Documentation of America's Religious Heritage.* Grand Rapids: Zondervan, 1966.

THEODORE ROOSEVELT

Brands, H. W. *Theodore Roosevelt: The Last Romantic.* New York: Perseus Books/Basic Books, 1997.

Fuller, Edmund, and David E. Green. *God in the White House: The Faiths of American Presidents.* New York: Crown Publishing, 1968.

Harbaugh, William Henry. *Power and Responsibility: The Life and Times of Theodore Roosevelt.* New York: Farrar, Straus, 1961.

Jones, Olga Anna. *Churches of the Presidents in Washington: Visits to Fifteen National Shrines.* New York: Exposition Press, 1954.

Matheny, E. Stacy. *American Patriotic Devotions.* New York: Association Press, 1932.

Morris, Edmund. *Theodore Rex.* New York: Random House, 2001.

Pringle, Henry Fowles. *Theodore Roosevelt: A Biography.* New York: Harcourt, Brace, 1931, 1958.

Roosevelt, Theodore. *Fear God and Take Your Own Part.* New York: George H. Doran, 1914, 1915, 1916.

WILLIAM TAFT

Cash, James. *Unsung Heroes.* Wilmington, OH: Orange Frazer Press, 1998.

Fuller, Edmund, and David E. Green. *God in the White House: The Faiths of American Presidents.* New York: Crown Publishing, 1968.

Pringle, Henry Fowles. *The Life and Times of William Howard Taft: A Biography.* 2 vols. New York: Holt, Rinehart, & Winston, 1939.

WOODROW WILSON

Baker, Ray Stannard. *Woodrow Wilson: Life and Letters.* Vol. 1, *Youth, 1856–1890.* Vol. 2, *Princeton, 1890–1910.* Vol. 3, *Governor, 1910–1913.* Vol. 4, *President, 1913–1914.* Vol. 5, *Neutrality, 1914–1915.* Vol. 6, *Facing War, 1915–1917.* Vol. 7, *War Leader, 1917–1918.* Vol. 8, *Armistice.* Garden City, NY: Doubleday, Page, 1917–39.

Daniels, Josephus. *The Life of Woodrow Wilson, 1856–1924.* Philadelphia: Winston, 1924.

_____. *The Wilson Era: Years of Peace, 1910–1917.* Chapel Hill: University of North Carolina Press, 1944, 1974.

Fuller, Edmund, and David E. Green. *God in the White House: The Faiths of American Presidents.* New York: Crown Publishing, 1968.

Heckscher, August. *Woodrow Wilson: A Biography.* New York: Scribner, 1991.

Jones, Olga Anna. *Churches of the Presidents in Washington: Visits to Fifteen National Shrines.* New York: Exposition Press, 1954.

McAdoo, Eleanor Wilson, in collaboration with Margaret Y. Gaffey. *The Woodrow Wilsons.* New York: Macmillan, 1937.

Mulder, John M. *Woodrow Wilson: The Years of Preparation.* Princeton, NJ: Princeton University Press, 1978.

Ross, Ishbel. *Power with Grace: The Life Story of Mrs. Woodrow Wilson.* New York: G. P. Putnam's Sons, 1975. (Re. the second Mrs. Wilson, Edith Bolling Galt)

Walworth, Arthur. *Woodrow Wilson.* Boston and New York: Houghton Mifflin, 1965, 1978.

Wilson, Woodrow. *The Papers of Woodrow Wilson, 1856–1907.* Edited by Arthur Stanley Link. 16 vols. Princeton, NJ: Princeton University Press, 1966–73.

WARREN HARDING

Downes, Ralph Chandler. *The Rise of Warren Gamaliel Harding, 1865–1920*. Columbus: Ohio State University Press, 1970.

Jones, Olga Anna. *Churches of the Presidents in Washington: Visits to Fifteen National Shrines*. New York: Exposition Press, 1954.

Matheny, E. Stacy. *American Patriotic Devotions*. New York: Association Press, 1932.

McCollister, John. *So Help Me God: The Faith of America's Presidents*. Louisville: Westminster/John Knox Press, 1991.

Murray, Robert K. *The Harding Era: Warren G. Harding and His Administration*. Minneapolis: University of Minnesota Press, 1969.

Sinclair, Andrew. *The Available Man: The Life behind the Masks of Warren Gamaliel Harding*. New York: Morrow, 1965.

White, William Allen. *A Puritan in Babylon: The Story of Calvin Coolidge*. New York: Macmillan, 1938.

CALVIN COOLIDGE

Coolidge, Calvin. *The Autobiography of Calvin Coolidge*. New York: Cosmopolitan Book Corp., 1929.

Ferrell, Robert H. *The Presidency of Calvin Coolidge*. Lawrence: University Press of Kansas, 1998.

Fuess, Claude M. *Calvin Coolidge: The Man from Vermont*. New York: Little, Brown, 1939. Reprint, Hamden, CT: Archon Books, 1965.

Isley, Bliss. *The Presidents: Men of Faith*. Boston: W. A. Wilde, 1953.

Jones, Olga Anna. *Churches of the Presidents in Washington: Visits to Fifteen National Shrines*. New York: Exposition Press, 1954.

McCollister, John. *So Help Me God: The Faith of America's Presidents*. Louisville: Westminster/John Knox Press, 1991.

McCoy, Donald R. *Calvin Coolidge: The Quiet President*. New York: Macmillan, 1967.

White, William Allen. *A Puritan in Babylon: The Story of Calvin Coolidge*. New York: Macmillan, 1938.

HERBERT HOOVER

Federer, William J., ed. *America's God and Country: Encyclopedia of Quotations*. 8th ed. Coppel, TX: Fame Publishing, 1994.

Hoover, Herbert. *Memoirs of Herbert Hoover*. Vol. 1, *Years of Adventure, 1874–1920*. Vol. 2, *The Cabinet and the Presidency, 1920–1933*. Vol. 3, *The Great Depression, 1929–1941*. New York: Macmillan, 1951–52.

Hoover, Herbert. *Public Papers of the Presidents of the United States: Herbert Hoover, 1929–1933.* 4 vols. Washington, DC: Government Printing Office, 1974–77.

Jones, Cranston. *Homes of the American Presidents.* New York: Bonanza Books, 1962.

Lyons, Eugene. *Herbert Hoover: A Biography.* Garden City, NY: Doubleday, 1964.

Mayer, Dale C. *Lou Henry Hoover: A Prototype for First Ladies.* New York: Nova History Publications, 2004.

FRANKLIN DELANO ROOSEVELT

Davis, Kenneth S. *Franklin Delano Roosevelt.* Vol. 1, *The Beckoning of Destiny, 1882–1928.* Vol. 2, *The New York Years, 1928–1933.* Vol. 3, *The New Deal Years, 1933–1937.* Vol. 4, *Into the Storm, 1937–1940.* Vol. 5, *The War President, 1940–1943.* Westminster, MD: Random House, 1972–2000.

Freidel, Frank. *Franklin D. Roosevelt: A Rendezvous with Destiny.* Boston: Little, Brown, 1990.

Fuller, Edmund, and David E. Green. *God in the White House: The Faiths of American Presidents.* New York: Crown Publishers, 1968.

Graham, Otis L. Jr. and Meghan Robinson Wander. *Franklin D. Roosevelt: His Life and Times: An Encyclopedic View.* Boston: G. K. Hall, 1985.

Isley, Bliss. *The Presidents: Men of Faith.* Boston: W. A. Wilde, 1953.

Jones, Olga Anna. *Churches of the Presidents in Washington: Visits to Fifteen National Shrines.* New York: Exposition Press, 1954.

Lash, Joseph P. *Eleanor and Franklin: The Story of Their Relationship Based on Eleanor Roosevelt's Private Papers.* New York: Norton, 1971.

Roosevelt, Eleanor. *This I Remember.* New York: Harper & Brothers, 1949.

Roosevelt, Franklin D. *F.D.R.: His Personal Letters.* Edited by Elliott Roosevelt. 3 vols. New York: Duell, Sloan & Pearce, 1947–50.

Roosevelt, Franklin Delano. *Public Papers of the Presidents of the United States: Franklin D. Roosevelt, 1933–1945.* 13 vols. Washington, DC: Government Printing Office.

Ward, Geoffrey C. *A First-Class Temperament: The Emergence of Franklin Roosevelt: An Intimate Portrait of the Private World, Personal Ordeal, and Public Triumph of the Man Who Became FDR.* New York: Harper & Row, 1989.

HARRY S TRUMAN

Clotworthy, William G. *Presidential Sites: A Directory of Places Associated with Presidents of the United States.* Blacksburg, VA: McDonald & Woodward, 1998.

Fuller, Edmund, and David E. Green. *God in the White House: The Faiths of American Presidents.* New York: Crown Publishers, 1968.

Hamby, Alonzo L. *Man of the People: A Life of Harry S Truman.* New York and Oxford: Oxford University Press, 1995.

Isley, Bliss. *The Presidents: Men of Faith.* Boston: W. A. Wilde, 1953.

McCullough, David. *Truman.* New York: Simon & Schuster, 1992.

Miller, Merle. *Plain Speaking: An Oral Biography of Harry S Truman.* New York: Berkeley Publishing/G. P. Putnam's Sons, 1973, 1974.

Truman, Harry S. *Off the Record: The Private Papers of Harry S Truman.* Edited by Robert H. Ferrell. New York: Harper & Row, 1980.

Truman, Harry S. *Public Papers of Presidents of the United States: Harry S Truman, 1945–1953.* 8 vols. Washington, DC: Government Printing Office.

DWIGHT DAVID EISENHOWER

Ambrose, Stephen E. *Eisenhower.* Vol. 1, *Soldier, General of the Army, President-Elect, 1890–1952.* New York: Simon & Schuster, 1983.

Eisenhower, Dwight D. *Public Papers of the Presidents of the United States: Dwight D. Eisenhower, 1953–1961.* 10 vols. Washington, DC: Government Printing Office.

_____. *The White House Years.* Vol. 1, *Mandate for Change, 1953–1956.* Vol. 2, *Waging Peace, 1956–1961.* Garden City, NY: Doubleday, 1963–65.

Ferrell, Robert H. *The Eisenhower Diaries.* New York and London: Norton, 1981.

Fuller, Edmund, and David E. Green. *God in the White House: The Faiths of American Presidents.* New York: Crown Publishing, 1968.

Graham, Billy. *Just As I Am: The Autobiography of Billy Graham.* New York: HarperSanFrancisco/Zondervan, 1997.

Hutcheson, Richard G. Jr. *God in the White House: How Religion Has Changed the Modern Presidency.* New York: Macmillan, 1988.

Johnson, Lyndon B. *The Vantage Point: Perspectives of the Presidency, 1963–1969.* New York, Chicago, and San Francisco: Holt, Rinehart & Winston, 1971.

Jones, Cranston. *Homes of the American Presidents.* New York: Bonanza Books, 1962.

Jones, Olga Anna. *Churches of the Presidents in Washington: Visits to Fifteen National Shrines.* New York: Exposition Press, 1954.

Truman, Margaret. *First Ladies: An Intimate Group Portrait of White House Wives.* New York: Random House, 1995.

JOHN FITZGERALD KENNEDY

Anthony, Carl Sferazza. *As We Remember Her: Jacqueline Kennedy Onassis in the Words of Her Friends and Family.* New York: HarperCollins, 1997.

_____. *The Kennedy White House: Family Life and Pictures, 1961–1963.* Reprint, London: Touchstone, 2002.

Dallek, Robert. *John F. Kennedy: An Unfinished Life, 1917–1963.* New York: Little, Brown, 2003.

Graham, Billy. *Just As I Am: The Autobiography of Billy Graham.* New York: HarperSanFrancisco/Zondervan, 1997.

Kennedy, John Fitzgerald. *Public Papers of the Presidents of the United States: John F. Kennedy, 1961–1963.* Washington, DC: Government Printing Office.

Kennedy, Rose Fitzgerald. *Times to Remember.* Garden City, NY: Doubleday, 1974.

Manchester, William. *The Death of a President.* New York: Harper & Row, 1967.

Sorensen, Theodore C. *Kennedy.* New York: Bantam Books, 1966.

Wead, Doug. *All the Presidents' Children.* New York: Atria Books, 2003.

Lyndon Baines Johnson

Anderson, Jack. *Peace, War, and Politics.* New York: Tom Doherty Associates, 1999.

Barzman, Sol. *Madmen and Geniuses: The Vice Presidents of the United States.* Chicago: Follett Publishing, 1974.

Califano, Joseph A. Jr. *The Triumph and Tragedy of Lyndon Johnson: The White House Years.* New York: Simon & Schuster, 1991.

Dallek, Robert. *John F. Kennedy: An Unfinished Life, 1917–1963.* New York: Little, Brown, 2003.

_____. *Lyndon Johnson and His Times.* Vol. 1, *Lone Star Rising, 1908–1960.* Vol. 2, *Flawed Giant, 1961–1973.* New York and Oxford: Oxford University Press, 1991, 1998.

Graham, Billy. *Just As I Am: The Autobiography of Billy Graham.* New York: HarperSanFrancisco/Zondervan, 1997.

Johnson, Lyndon B. *Public Papers of the Presidents of the United States: Lyndon B. Johnson, 1963–1969.* 5 vols. Washington, DC: Government Printing Office.

_____. *The Vantage Point: Perspectives of the Presidency, 1963–1969.* New York, Chicago, and San Francisco: Holt, Rinehart, & Winston, 1971.

Manchester, William. *The Death of a President.* New York, Evanston, IL, and London: Harper & Row, 1967.

Richard Milhous Nixon

Aitken, Jonathan. *Nixon: A Life.* Washington, DC: Regnery, 1993.

Crowley, Monica. *Nixon Off the Record: His Candid Commentary on People and Politics.* New York: Random House, 1996.

Graham, Billy. *Just As I Am: The Autobiography of Billy Graham.* New York: HarperSanFrancisco/Zondervan, 1997.

Haldeman, Harry R. *The Haldeman Diaries: Inside the Nixon White House.* New York: G. P. Putnam's Sons, 1994.

Morris, Roger. *Richard Milhous Nixon: The Rise of an American Politician.* New York: Henry Holt, 1990.

Nixon, Richard. *In the Arena: A Memoir of Victory, Defeat, and Renewal.* New York: Simon & Schuster, 1990.

_____. *Public Papers of the Presidents of the United States: Richard M. Nixon, 1969–1974.* 6 vols. Washington, DC: Government Printing Office.

Summers, Anthony. *The Arrogance of Power.* London: Weidenfeld & Nicholson, 2001.

GERALD FORD

Boller, Paul F. Jr. *Presidential Campaigns.* New York and Oxford: Oxford University Press, 1984.

Cannon, James. *Time and Chance: Gerald Ford's Appointment with History.* New York: HarperCollins, 1994.

Ford, Gerald R. *Public Papers of the Presidents of the United States: Gerald R. Ford, 1974–1977.* 3 vols. Washington, DC: Government Printing Office.

_____. "Commencement Address to Gordon-Conwell Theological Seminary Graduates," May 28, 1977.

Graham, Billy. *Just As I Am: The Autobiography of Billy Graham.* New York: HarperSanFrancisco/Zondervan, 1997.

Hutcheson, Richard G. Jr. *God in the White House: How Religion Has Changed the Modern Presidency.* New York: Macmillan, 1988.

JAMES EARL CARTER

Bourne, Peter G. *Jimmy Carter: A Comprehensive Biography from Plains to Postpresidency.* New York: Scribner, 1997.

Carter, Jimmy. *Keeping Faith: Memoirs of a President.* New York: Bantam Books, 1982.

_____. *Living Faith.* New York: Random House/Times Books, 1996.

_____. *The Personal Beliefs of Jimmy Carter: Winner of the 2002 Nobel Peace Prize.* Includes the complete texts of the *New York Times* bestsellers *Sources of Strength* and *Living Faith.* New York: Random House/Three Rivers Press, 2002.

_____. *Public Papers of the Presidents of the United States: James Earl Carter, 1977–1981.* Washington, DC: Government Printing Office.

_____. *Sources of Strength.* New York: Random House/Times Books, 1997.

Carter, Jimmy and Rosalynn Carter. *Everything to Gain: Making the Most of the Rest of Your Life*. New York: Random House, 1987.

RONALD REAGAN

Barletta, John R., with Rochelle Schweizer. *Riding with Reagan: From the White House to the Ranch*. New York: Kensington Publishing/Citadel Press, 2005.

Brown, Mary Beth. *Hand of Providence: The Strong and Quiet Faith of Ronald Reagan*. Nashville: Thomas Nelson/WND Books, 2004.

Edwards, Anne. *Early Reagan: The Rise to Power*. New York: Morrow, 1987, 1990.

Hutcheson, Richard G. Jr. *God in the White House: How Religion Has Changed the Modern Presidency*. New York: Macmillan, 1988.

Kengor, Paul. *God and Ronald Reagan: A Spiritual Life*. New York: HarperCollins/ReganBooks, 2004.

Noonan, Peggy. *What I Saw at the Revolution: A Political Life in the Reagan Era*. New York: Random House, 1990.

_____. *When Character Was King: A Story of Ronald Reagan*. New York: Viking, 2001.

Pemberton, William E. *Exit with Honor: The Life and Presidency of Ronald Reagan*. Armonk, NY, and London: M. E. Sharpe, 1997.

Reagan, Michael, with Jim Denney. *Twice Adopted*. Nashville: Broadman & Holman, 2004.

Reagan, Ronald. *Public Papers of the Presidents of the United States: Ronald Reagan, 1981–1989*. 8 vols. Washington, DC: Government Printing Office.

Reed, Ralph. *Active Faith: How Christians Are Changing the Soul of American Politics*. New York: Simon & Schuster/The Free Press, 1996.

Skinner, Kiron K., Annelise Anderson, and Martin Anderson. *Reagan: A Life in Letters*. New York: Simon & Schuster/The Free Press, 2004.

_____. *Reagan's Path to Victory*. New York: Simon & Schuster/The Free Press, 2004.

Truman, Margaret. *First Ladies: An Intimate Group Portrait of White House Wives*. New York: Random House, 1995.

GEORGE HERBERT WALKER BUSH

Aikman, David. *A Man of Faith: The Spiritual Journey of George W. Bush*. Nashville: Thomas Nelson/W Publishing, 2004.

Bush, Barbara. *Reflections: Life After the White House*. New York: Scribner, 2003.

Bush, George Herbert Walker. *Public Papers of the Presidents of the United States: George H. W. Bush, 1989–1993*. Washington, DC: Government Printing Office.

_____. and Barbara Bush. *Heartbeat: George Bush in His Own Words*. Compiled by Jim McGrath. New York: Scribner, 2001, 2003.

Bush, George Walker, with Doug Wead. *George Bush: Man of Integrity*. Eugene, OR: Harvest House, 1988.

Fleischer, Ari. *Taking Heat: The President, the Press, and My Years in the White House*. New York: HarperCollins/William Morrow, 2005.

Mansfield, Stephen. *The Faith of George W. Bush*. Lake Mary, FL: Charisma House, 2003.

Minutaglio, Bill. *First Son: George W. Bush and the Bush Family Dynasty*. New York: Random House/Times Books, 1999.

Parmet, Herbert. *George Bush: The Life of a Lone Star Yankee*. Piscataway, NJ: Transaction Publishers, 2000.

Reed, Ralph. *Politically Incorrect: The Emerging Faith Factor in American Politics*. Dallas: Word Publishing, 1994.

Schwizer, Peter, and Rochelle Schweizer. *The Bushes: Portrait of a Dynasty*. New York: Doubleday, 2004.

WILLIAM JEFFERSON CLINTON

Clinton, William Jefferson. *My Life*. New York: Random House, 2004.

_____. *Public Papers of the Presidents of the United States: William J. Clinton, 1993–2001*. Washington, DC: Government Printing Office.

Marriss, David. *First in His Class: A Biography of Bill Clinton*. New York: Simon & Schuster, 1995.

Morris, Richard. *Behind the Oval Office: Winning the Presidency in the Nineties*. New York: Random House, 1997.

Stephanopolous, George. *All Too Human: A Political Education*. New York: Little, Brown, 1999.

GEORGE WALKER BUSH

Aikman, David. *A Man of Faith: The Spiritual Journey of George W. Bush*. Nashville: Thomas Nelson/W Publishing, 2004.

Bush, Barbara. *Reflections: Life After the White House*. New York: Scribner, 2003.

Bush, George Walker, and Karen Hughes. *A Charge to Keep*. New York: Morrow, 1999.

Mansfield, Stephen. *The Faith of George W. Bush*. Lake Mary, FL: Charisma House, 2003.

Minutaglio, Bill. *First Son: George W. Bush and the Bush Family Dynasty*. New York: Random House/Time Books, 1999.

Schweizer, Peter, and Rochelle Schweizer. *The Bushes: Portrait of a Dynasty*. New York: Doubleday, 2004.

Singer, Peter. *The President of Good and Evil: Questioning the Ethics of George W. Bush.* New York: Dutton, 2004.

PART 3
AN ALPHABETICAL LISTING
OF MAJOR SOURCES

Ackerman, Kenneth D. *Dark Horse: The Surprise Election and Political Murder of President James A. Garfield.* New York: Carroll & Graf, 2003.

Adams, Charles Francis. *The Works of John Adams: Second President of the United States.* Library of the Presidents. Easton, PA: Easton Press, 1992.

Adams, John Quincy. *The Diary of John Quincy Adams, 1794–1845.* Edited by Allan Nevins. New York: Longmans, Green, 1929; abridged, New York: Charles Scribners, 1951.

Adams, John Quincy. *Memoirs of John Quincy Adams, Comprising Portions of His Diary from 1795 to 1848.* Edited by Charles Francis Adams. 12 vols. Philadelphia, 1874–77.

Adams, John. *Papers of John Adams.* In *The Adams Papers.* Series 3. *General Correspondence and Other Papers of the Adams Statesmen.* Edited by Robert J. Taylor. Cambridge, MA: Harvard University Press/Belknap Press, 1977.

Adams, John Quincy, and Charles Francis Adams. *The Life of John Adams.* 2 vols. 1870.

Adams, John, and Thomas Jefferson, *The Complete Correspondence between Thomas Jefferson and Abigail and John Adams.* Edited by Lester J. Cappon. 2 vols. Chapel Hill: University of North Carolina Press, 1959, 1988.

Aikman, David. *A Man of Faith: The Spiritual Journey of George W. Bush.* Nashville: Thomas Nelson/W Publishing, 2004.

Aitken, Jonathan. *Nixon: A Life.* Washington, DC: Regnery, 1993.

Allison, Andrew M. *The Real George Washington.* Washington, DC: National Center for Constitutional Studies, 1991.

———. *Thomas Jefferson: Champion of History.*

Ambrose, Stephen E. *Eisenhower.* Vol. 1, *Soldier, General of the Army, President-Elect, 1890–1952.* New York: Simon & Schuster, 1983.

Anderson, Jack. *Peace, War, and Politics.* New York: Tom Doherty Associates, 1999.

Anthony, Carl Sferazza. *As We Remember Her: Jacqueline Kennedy Onassis in the Words of Her Friends and Family.* New York: HarperCollins, 1997.

———. *First Ladies: The Saga of the Presidents' Wives and Their Power, 1789–1961.* New York: Morrow, 1990.

_____. *The Kennedy White House: Family Life and Pictures, 1961–1963.* Reprint, London: Touchstone, 2002.

Baker, Ray Stannard. *Woodrow Wilson: Life and Letters.* Vol. 1, *Youth, 1856–1890.* Vol. 2, *Princeton, 1890–1910.* Vol. 3, *Governor, 1910–1913.* Vol. 4, *President, 1913–1914.* Vol. 5, *Neutrality, 1914–1915.* Vol. 6, *Facing War, 1915–1917.* Vol. 7, *War Leader, 1917–1918.* Vol. 8, *Armistice.* Garden City, NY: Doubleday, Page, 1917–39.

Bancroft, George, Bishop Simpson, and R. S. Storrs Jr. *Our Martyr President, Abraham Lincoln: Lincoln Memorial Addresses.* New York: Tibbals & Whiting, 1865.

Barletta, John R., with Rochelle Schweizer. *Riding with Reagan: From the White House to the Ranch.* New York: Kensington Publishing/Citadel Press, 2005.

Bartlett, D. W. *The Life of General Franklin Pierce of New Hampshire.* Auburn, ME: Derby & Miller, 1852.

Barzman, Sol. *Madmen and Geniuses: The Vice Presidents of the United States.* Chicago: Follett, 1974.

Bemis, Samuel Flagg. *John Quincy Adams and the Foundations of American Foreign Policy.* New York: Knopf, 1949.

_____. *John Quincy Adams and the Union.* New York: Knopf, 1956.

Bergeron, Paul H. *The Presidency of James K. Polk.* Lawrence: University Press of Kansas, 1987.

Bishop, Jim. *The Day Lincoln Was Shot.* New York: Random House/Gramercy, 1984.

Boller, Paul F. Jr. *Presidential Campaigns.* New York and Oxford: Oxford University Press, 1984.

_____. *Presidential Wives: An Anecdotal History.* New York and Oxford: Oxford University Press, 1998.

Bonnell, John Sutherland. *Presidential Profiles: Religion in the Life of America's Presidents.* Philadelphia: Westminster Press, 1971.

Booraem, Hendrik V. *The Road to Respectability: James A. Garfield and His World, 1844–1852.* Western Reserve Historical Society. Lewisburg, PA: Bucknell University Press/London: Associated University Presses, 1988.

_____. *Young Hickory: The Making of Andrew Jackson.* Dallas: Taylor Trade Publishing, 2001.

Bourne, Peter G. *Jimmy Carter: A Comprehensive Biography from Plains to Postpresidency.* New York: Scribner, 1997.

Bowers, Claude. *Jefferson and Hamilton: The Struggle for Democracy in America.* Boston and New York: Houghton Mifflin, 1925, 1945.

_____. *Jefferson in Power: The Death Struggle of the Federalists.* Boston and New York: Houghton Mifflin, 1936, 1967.

Boyd, James Penny. *Military and Civil Life of General Ulysses S. Grant.* Garretson, 1885.

Brands, H. W. *Theodore Roosevelt: The Last Romantic.* New York: Perseus Books/Basic Books, 1997.

Brant, Irving. *James Madison: The Virginia Revolutionist, 1751–1780.* Indianapolis: Bobbs-Merrill, 1941.

Brodie, Fawn M. *Thomas Jefferson: An Intimate History.* New York: Norton, 1974, 1998.

Brown, Mary Beth. *Hand of Providence: The Strong and Quiet Faith of Ronald Reagan.* Nashville: Thomas Nelson/WND Books, 2004.

Bush, Barbara. *Reflections: Life After the White House.* New York: Scribner, 2003.

Bush, George Herbert Walker. *Public Papers of the Presidents of the United States: George H. W. Bush, 1989–1993.* Washington, DC: Government Printing Office.

_____. and Barbara Bush. *Heartbeat: George Bush in His Own Words.* Compiled by Jim McGrath. New York: Scribner, 2001, 2003.

Bush, George Walker, and Karen Hughes. *A Charge to Keep.* New York: Morrow, 1999.

Bush, George Walker, with Doug Wead. *George Bush: Man of Integrity.* Eugene, OR: Harvest House, 1988.

Caldwell, Robert Granville. *James A. Garfield: Party Chieftain.* New York: Dodd, Mead, 1931. Reprint, Hamden, CT: Archon Books, 1965.

Califano, Joseph A. Jr. *The Triumph and Tragedy of Lyndon Johnson: The White House Years.* New York: Simon & Schuster, 1991.

Cannon, James. *Time and Chance: Gerald Ford's Appointment with History.* New York: HarperCollins, 1994.

Carter, Jimmy. *Keeping Faith: Memoirs of a President.* New York: Bantam Books, 1982.

_____. *Living Faith.* New York: Random House/Times Books, 1996.

_____. *The Personal Beliefs of Jimmy Carter: Winner of the 2002 Nobel Peace Prize.* Includes the complete texts of the *New York Times* bestsellers *Sources of Strength* and *Living Faith.* New York: Random House/Three Rivers Press, 2002.

_____. *Public Papers of the Presidents of the United States: James Earl Carter, 1977–1981.* Washington, DC: Government Printing Office.

_____. *Sources of Strength.* New York: Random House/Times Books, 1997.

Carter, Jimmy and Rosalynn Carter. *Everything to Gain: Making the Most of the Rest of Your Life.* New York: Random House, 1987.

Cash, James. *Unsung Heroes.* Wilmington, OH: Orange Frazer Press, 1998.

Chitwood, Oliver Perry. *John Tyler: Champion of the Old South.* New York: Russell & Russell, 1939, 1964.

Cleaves, Freeman. *Old Tippecanoe: William Henry Harrison and His Time.* New York: Charles Scribner's Sons, 1939. Reprint, Port Washington, NY: Kennikat Press, 1965.

Clinton, William Jefferson. *My Life.* New York: Random House, 2004.

_____. *Public Papers of the Presidents of the United States: William J. Clinton, 1993–2001.* Washington, DC: Government Printing Office.

Clotworthy, William G. *Presidential Sites: A Directory of Places Associated with Presidents of the United States.* Blacksburg, VA: McDonald & Woodward, 1998.

Coolidge, Calvin. *The Autobiography of Calvin Coolidge.* New York: Cosmopolitan Book Corp., 1929.

Crowley, Monica. *Nixon Off the Record: His Candid Commentary on People and Politics.* New York: Random House, 1996.

Curtis, George Ticknor. *The Life of James Buchanan: Fifteenth President of the United States.* 2 vols. New York: Harper & Brothers, 1883.

Dallek, Robert. *John F. Kennedy: An Unfinished Life, 1917–1963.* New York: Little, Brown, 2003.

_____. *Lyndon Johnson and His Times.* Vol.1, *Lone Star Rising, 1908–1960.* Vol. 2, *Flawed Giant, 1961–1973.* New York and Oxford: Oxford University Press, 1991, 1998.

Daniels, Josephus. *The Life of Woodrow Wilson, 1856–1924.* Philadelphia: Winston, 1924.

_____. *The Wilson Era: Years of Peace, 1910–1917.* Chapel Hill: University of North Carolina Press, 1944, 1974.

Davis, Kenneth S. *Franklin Delano Roosevelt.* Vol. 1, *The Beckoning of Destiny, 1882–1928.* Vol. 2, *The New York Years, 1928–1933.* Vol. 3, *The New Deal Years, 1933–1937.* Vol. 4, *Into the Storm, 1937–1940.* Vol. 5, *The War President, 1940–1943.* Westminster, MD: Random House, 1972–2000.

Downes, Ralph Chandler. *The Rise of Warren Gamaliel Harding, 1865–1920.* Columbus: Ohio State University Press, 1970.

Edwards, Anne. *Early Reagan: The Rise to Power.* New York: Morrow, 1987, 1990.

Eidsmoe, John, and D. James Kennedy. *Christianity and the Constitution: The Faith of Our Founding Fathers.* Grand Rapids: Baker Book House, 1987.

Eisenhower, Dwight D. *Public Papers of the Presidents of the United States: Dwight D. Eisenhower, 1953–1961.* 10 vols. Washington, DC: Government Printing Office.

_____. *The White House Years.* Vol. 1, *Mandate for Change, 1953–1956.* Vol. 2, *Waging Peace, 1956–1961.* Garden City, NY: Doubleday, 1963–65.

Ellis, Joseph J. *Founding Brothers.* New York: Knopf, 2001.

Falkner, Leonard. *The President Who Wouldn't Retire: John Quincy Adams, Congressman from Massachusetts.* New York: Coward-McCann, 1967.

Federer, William J., ed. *America's God and Country: Encyclopedia of Quotations.* 8th ed. Coppel, TX: Fame Publishing, 1994.

Ferrell, Robert H. *The Eisenhower Diaries.* New York and London: Norton, 1981.

_____. *The Presidency of Calvin Coolidge*. Lawrence: University Press of Kansas, 1998.

Fleischer, Ari. *Taking Heat: The President, the Press, and My Years in the White House*. New York: HarperCollins/William Morrow, 2005.

Flexner, James Thomas. *George Washington*. Vol. 1, *The Forge of Experience (1732–1775)*. Vol. 2, *In the American Revolution (1775–1783)*. Vol. 3, *Anguish and Farewell (1793–1799)*. Boston and Toronto: Little, Brown, 1965–72.

Ford, Gerald R. *Public Papers of the Presidents of the United States: Gerald R. Ford, 1974–1977*. 3 vols. Washington, DC: Government Printing Office.

Freeman, Douglas Southall. Abridged by Richard Harwell. *Washington: An Abridgment in One Volume by Richard Harwell of the Seven-volume* George Washington *by Douglas Southall Freeman*. New York: Scribner, 1968.

Freidel, Frank. *Franklin D. Roosevelt: A Rendezvous with Destiny*. Boston: Little, Brown, 1954, 1990.

Fuess, Claude M. *Calvin Coolidge: The Man from Vermont*. New York: Little, Brown, 1939.

Fuller, Edmund, and David E. Green. *God in the White House: The Faiths of American Presidents*. New York: Crown Publishers, 1968.

Garfield, James and Lucretia. *Crete and James: Personal Letters of James and Lucretia Garfield*. Edited by John Shaw. East Lansing: Michigan State University Press, 1994.

Gould, Lewis L. *The Presidency of William McKinley*. Lawrence: Regents Press of Kansas, 1980.

Graham, Billy. *Just As I Am: The Autobiography of Billy Graham*. New York: HarperSanFrancisco/Zondervan, 1997.

Graham, Otis L. Jr. and Meghan Robinson Wander. *Franklin D. Roosevelt: His Life and Times: An Encyclopedic View*. Boston: G. K. Hall, 1985.

Grant, Ulysses S. *The Papers of Ulysses S. Grant, 1837–1875*. Edited by John Y. Simon. 26 vols. Carbondale and Edwardsville, IL: Southern Illinois University Press, 1967–2003.

Haldeman, Harry R. *The Haldeman Diaries: Inside the Nixon White House*. New York: G. P. Putnam's Sons, 1994.

Hamby, Alonzo L. *Man of the People: A Life of Harry S Truman*. New York and Oxford: Oxford University Press, 1995.

Harbaugh, William Henry. *Power and Responsibility: The Life and Times of Theodore Roosevelt*. New York: Farrar, Straus, 1961.

Hargreaves, Mary W. M. *The Presidency of John Quincy Adams*. Lawrence: University Press of Kansas, 1985.

Hayes, Rutherford B. *Diary and Letters of Rutherford B. Hayes*. Edited by Charles Richard Williams. 5 vols. Columbus: The Ohio State Archaeological and Historical Society, 1922–26.

Heckscher, August. *Woodrow Wilson: A Biography.* New York: Scribner, 1991.

Hill, John Wesley. *Abraham Lincoln: Man of God.* New York: G. P. Putnam's Sons, 1926.

Hoover, Herbert. *Memoirs of Herbert Hoover.* Vol. 1, *Years of Adventure, 1874–1920.* Vol. 2, *The Cabinet and the Presidency, 1920–1933.* Vol. 3, *The Great Depression, 1929–1941.* New York: Macmillan, 1951–52.

_____. *Public Papers of the Presidents of the United States: Herbert Hoover, 1929–1933.* 4 vols. Washington DC: Government Printing Office, 1974–77.

Howe, George Frederick. *Chester A. Arthur: A Quarter-Century of Machine Politics.* New York: Dodd, Mead, 1935. Reprint, New York: Frederick Unger, 1957.

Hunt, Gaillard. *The Life of James Madison.* Library Reprints, 2002.

Hutcheson, Richard G. Jr. *God in the White House: How Religion Has Changed the Modern Presidency.* New York: Macmillan, 1988.

Isley, Bliss. *The Presidents: Men of Faith.* Boston: W. A. Wilde, 1953.

Jefferson, Thomas. *The Papers of Thomas Jefferson.* Edited by Julian P. Boyd. 3 vols. Princeton, NJ: Princeton University Press, 1950–51.

Jefferson, Thomas. *The Writings of Thomas Jefferson.* Edited by Albert Ellery, Thomas Lipscomb, and Andrew Bergh. 20 vols. Washington, DC: The Thomas Jefferson Memorial Association, 1907.

Jefferson, Thomas. *The Writings of Thomas Jefferson.* Edited by Paul Leicester Ford. 10 vols. New York: G. P. Putnam's Sons, 1892–99.

Johnson, Andrew. *The Papers of Andrew Johnson.* Edited by Leroy P. Graff and Ralph W. Haskins. 7 vols. Edited by Paul H. Bergeron, et al. 9 vols. Knoxville: University of Tennessee Press, 1967–2000.

Johnson, Lyndon B. *Public Papers of the Presidents of the United States: Lyndon B. Johnson, 1963–1969.* 5 vols. Washington, DC: Government Printing Office.

_____. *The Vantage Point: Perspectives of the Presidency, 1963–1969.* New York, Chicago, and San Francisco: Holt, Rinehart, & Winston, 1971.

Jones, Cranston. *Homes of the American Presidents.* New York: Bonanza Books, 1962.

Jones, Olga Anna. *Churches of the Presidents in Washington: Visits to Fifteen National Shrines.* New York: Exposition Press, 1954.

Kane, Joseph Nathan. *Facts about the Presidents: A Compilation of Biographical and Historical Data.* 1st ed. New York: H. W. Wilson, 1959.

_____. *Facts about the Presidents: From George Washington to Bill Clinton.* 7th ed. New York: H. W. Wilson, 1993, 2001.

Kengor, Paul. *God and Ronald Reagan: A Spiritual Life.* New York: HarperCollins/ReganBooks, 2004.

Kennedy, John Fitzgerald. *Profiles in Courage.* Harper Perennial Modern Classics. New York: Harper & Brothers, 1955; HarperCollins, 2006.

_____. *Public Papers of the Presidents of the United States: John F. Kennedy, 1961–1963.* Washington, DC: Government Printing Office.

Kennedy, Rose Fitzgerald. *Times to Remember.* Garden City, NY: Doubleday, 1974.

Ketcham, Ralph. *James Madison: A Biography.* Charlottesville and London: University Press of Virginia, 1971, 1990, 1998.

Klein, Philip S. *President James Buchanan: A Biography.* University Park: Pennsylvania State University Press, 1962. Reprint, Newton, CT: American Political Biography Press, 1995.

LaHaye, Tim. *Faith of Our Founding Fathers.* Brentwood, TN: Wolgemuth & Hyatt, 1987.

Lash, Joseph P. *Eleanor and Franklin: The Story of Their Relationship Based on Eleanor Roosevelt's Private Papers.* New York: Norton, 1971.

Leech, Margaret. *In the Days of McKinley.* New York: Harper & Brothers, 1959. Reprint, Newton, CT: American Political Biography Press, 1999.

Lott, Davis Newton. *The Inaugural Addresses of the American Presidents.* New York: Holt, Rinehart & Winston, 1961.

Lynch, Dennis Tilden. *An Epoch and a Man: Martin Van Buren and His Times.* New York: Horace Liveright, 1929.

Lyons, Eugene. *Herbert Hoover: A Biography.* Garden City, NY: Doubleday, 1964.

Manchester, William. *The Death of a President.* New York: Harper & Row, 1967.

Mansfield, Stephen. *The Faith of George W. Bush.* Lake Mary, FL: Charisma House, 2003.

Marriss, David. *First in His Class: A Biography of Bill Clinton.* New York: Simon & Schuster, 1995.

Matheny, E. Stacy. *American Patriotic Devotions.* New York: Association Press, 1932.

McAdoo, Eleanor Wilson, in collaboration with Margaret Y. Gaffey. *The Woodrow Wilsons.* New York: Macmillan, 1937.

McCollister, John. *So Help Me God: The Faith of America's Presidents.* Louisville: Westminster/John Knox Press, 1991.

McCormac, Eugene Irving. *James K. Polk: A Political Biography to the End of a Career, 1845–1849.* New York: Russell & Russell, 1965.

McCoy, Donald R. *Calvin Coolidge: The Quiet President.* New York: Macmillan, 1967.

McCullough, David. *John Adams.* New York: Simon & Schuster, 2001.

_____. *Truman.* New York: Simon & Schuster, 1992.

McElroy, Robert M. *Grover Cleveland: The Man and the Statesman, An Authorized Biography.* 2 vols. New York: Harper & Brothers, 1923.

Meade, William. *Old Churches, Ministers, and Families of Virginia.* Baltimore: Genealogical Publishing, 1995.

Miller, Merle. *Plain Speaking: An Oral Biography of Harry S Truman*. New York: Berkeley Publishing/G. P. Putnam's Sons, 1973, 1974.

Minutaglio, Bill. *First Son: George W. Bush and the Bush Family Dynasty*. New York: Random House/Times Books, 1999.

Montgomery, H. *The Life of Major General Zachary Taylor*. Auburn, ME: Derby & Miller, 1850.

Morris, Edmund. *Theodore Rex*. New York: Random House, 2001.

Morris, Richard. *Behind the Oval Office: Winning the Presidency in the Nineties*. New York: Random House, 1997.

Morris, Roger. *Richard Milhous Nixon: The Rise of an American Politician*. New York: Henry Holt, 1990.

Morse, John Torrey. *John Quincy Adams*. American Statesmen Series. Boston and New York: Houghton Mifflin, 1882, 1898, 1910, 1912.

Mulder, John M. *Woodrow Wilson: The Years of Preparation*. Princeton, NJ: Princeton University Press, 1978.

Murray, Robert K. *The Harding Era: Warren G. Harding and His Administration*. Minneapolis: University of Minnesota Press, 1969.

Nagel, Paul C. *John Quincy Adams: A Public Life, A Private Life*. New York: Knopf, 1997.

Nevins, Allan. *Grover Cleveland: A Study in Courage to the End of a Career*. New York: Dodd, Mead, 1932.

_____. *Polk: The Diary of a President, 1845–1849*. London, New York, and Toronto: Longmans, Green, 1929, 1952.

Nicholay, Helen. *A Boy's Life of Abraham Lincoln*. First World Library, 2006.

Nichols, Roy Franklin. *Franklin Pierce: Young Hickory of the Granite Hills*. Philadelphia: University of Philadelphia Press, 1931.

Nixon, Richard. *In the Arena: A Memoir of Victory, Defeat, and Renewal*. New York: Simon & Schuster, 1990.

_____. *Public Papers of the Presidents of the United States: Richard M. Nixon, 1969–1974*. 6 vols. Washington, DC: Government Printing Office.

Noonan, Peggy. *What I Saw at the Revolution: A Political Life in the Reagan Era*. New York: Random House, 1990.

_____. *When Character Was King: A Story of Ronald Reagan*. New York: Viking, 2001.

Olcott, Charles Sumner. *The Life of William McKinley*. 2 vols. Boston and New York: Houghton Mifflin, 1916.

Parmet, Herbert. *George Bush: The Life of a Lone Star Yankee*. Piscataway, NJ: Transaction Publishers, 2000.

Parton, James. *The Life of Andrew Jackson*. 3 vols. Boston and New York: Houghton Mifflin, 1859, 1860.

Pemberton, William E. *Exit with Honor: The Life and Presidency of Ronald Reagan*. Armonk, NY, and London: M. E. Sharpe, 1997.

Peskin, Allan. *Garfield: A Biography*. Kent, OH: Kent State University Press, 1978. Reprint, Library of the Presidents, Easton, PA: Easton Press, 2004.

Pringle, Henry Fowles. *The Life and Times of William Howard Taft: A Biography*. 2 vols. New York: Holt, Rinehart & Winston, 1939.

_____. *Theodore Roosevelt: A Biography*. New York: Harcourt, Brace, 1931, 1958.

Randall, Willard Sterne. *Thomas Jefferson: A Life*. New York: Henry Holt, 1993.

Rayback, Robert J. *Millard Fillmore: Biography of a President*. Buffalo: Buffalo Historical Society/Henry Stewart, 1959.

Reagan, Michael, with Jim Denney. *Twice Adopted*. Nashville: Broadman & Holman, 2004.

Reagan, Ronald. *Public Papers of the Presidents of the United States: Ronald Reagan, 1981–1989*. 8 vols. Washington, DC: Government Printing Office.

Reed, Ralph. *Active Faith: How Christians Are Changing the Soul of American Politics*. New York: Simon & Schuster/The Free Press, 1996.

_____. *Politically Incorrect: The Emerging Faith Factor in American Politics*. Dallas: Word Publishing, 1994.

Reeves, Thomas C. *Gentleman Boss: The Life of Chester Alan Arthur*. New York: Knopf, 1975.

Reid, Daniel G., et al. *Concise Dictionary of Christianity in America*. Downers Grove, IL: InterVarsity Press, 1995.

Remini, Robert V. *Andrew Jackson and the Course of American Democracy, 1833–1845*. New York: Harper & Row, 1984.

_____. *Andrew Jackson and the Course of the American Empire, 1767–1821*. New York: Harper & Row, 1977.

Rives, William. *History of the Life and Times of James Madison*. Reprint, Kila, MT: Kessinger Publishing, 2006.

Roosevelt, Eleanor. *This I Remember*. New York: Harper & Brothers, 1949.

Roosevelt, Franklin D. *F.D.R.: His Personal Letters*. Edited by Elliott Roosevelt. 3 vols. New York: Duell, Sloan & Pearce, 1947–50.

Roosevelt, Franklin Delano. *Public Papers of the Presidents of the United States: Franklin D. Roosevelt, 1933–1945*. 13 vols. Washington, DC: Government Printing Office.

Roosevelt, Theodore. *Fear God and Take Your Own Part*. New York: George H. Doran, 1914, 1915, 1916.

Ross, Ishbel. *Power with Grace: The Life Story of Mrs. Woodrow Wilson*. New York: G. P. Putnam's Sons, 1975. Regarding the second Mrs. Wilson, Edith Bolling Galt.

Sandburg, Carl. *Abraham Lincoln: The War Years*. 4 vols. New York: Harcourt, Brace & World, 1939. Reprint, New York: Dell, 1974.

Savage, John. *The Life and Public Services of Andrew Johnson: Seventeenth President of the United States.* Auburn, ME: Derby & Miller, 1866.

Schweizer, Peter, and Rochelle Schweizer. *The Bushes: Portrait of a Dynasty.* New York: Doubleday, 2004.

Seager, Robert II. *And Tyler Too: A Biography of John and Julia Gardiner Tyler.* New York: McGraw-Hill, 1963.

Sellers, Charles. *James K. Polk: Jacksonian, 1795–1843.* Princeton, NJ: Princeton University Press, 1957.

_____. *James K. Polk: Continentalist, 1843–1846.* Princeton, NJ: Princeton University Press, 1966.

Sievers, Harry J. and Katherine Speirs, *Benjamin Harrison.* 2nd ed., rev. Vol. 1, *Hoosier Warrior: Through the Civil War Years, 1833–1865.* Vol. 2, *Hoosier Statesman: From the Civil War to the White House, 1865–88.* Vol. 3, *Hoosier President: The White House and After.* New York: University Publishers, 1960–1968. Reprint, Newton, CT: American Political Biography Press, 1997.

Sinclair, Andrew. *The Available Man: The Life behind the Masks of Warren Gamaliel Harding.* New York: Morrow, 1965.

Singer, Peter. *The President of Good and Evil: Questioning the Ethics of George W. Bush.* New York: Dutton, 2004.

Skinner, Kiron K., Annelise Anderson, and Martin Anderson. *Reagan: A Life in Letters.* New York: Simon & Schuster/The Free Press, 2004.

_____. *Reagan's Path to Victory.* New York: Simon & Schuster/The Free Press, 2004.

Smith, Theodore. *The Life and Letters of James Abram Garfield.* Hamden, CT: Archon Books, 1968.

Socolofsky, Homer E., and Allan B. Spetter. *The Presidency of Benjamin Harrison.* Lawrence: University Press of Kansas, 1987.

Sorensen, Theodore C. *Kennedy.* New York: Bantam Books, 1966.

Sparks, Jared. *Life of George Washington.* Kila, MT: Kessinger Publishing, 2006.

Steiner, Franklin. *The Religious Beliefs of Our Presidents.* Girard, KS: Haldeman-Julius, 1936. Reprint, Amherst, NY: Prometheus Books, 1995.

Stephanopolous, George. *All Too Human: A Political Education.* New York: Little, Brown, 1999.

Summers, Anthony. *The Arrogance of Power.* London: Weidenfeld & Nicholson, 2001.

Taylor, John M. *Garfield of Ohio: The Available Man.* New York: Norton, 1970.

Thayer, William M. *From Tannery to the White House: The Life of Ulysses S. Grant: His Boyhood, Youth, Manhood, Public and Private Life and Services.* Chicago: Albert Whitman, 1927.

Thomas, Benjamin P. *Abraham Lincoln: A Biography.* New York: Knopf, 1952. Reprint, New York: Barnes and Noble Books, 1994.

Thomas, Lately. *The First President Johnson: The Three Lives of the Seventeenth President of the United States of America.* New York: Morrow, 1968.

Trefousse, Hans L. *Andrew Johnson: A Biography.* New York and London: Norton, 1989.

Truman, Harry S. *Off the Record: The Private Papers of Harry S Truman.* Edited by Robert H. Ferrell. New York: Harper & Row, 1980.

_____. *Public Papers of Presidents of the United States: Harry S Truman, 1945–1953.* 8 vols. Washington, DC: Government Printing Office.

Truman, Margaret. *First Ladies: An Intimate Group Portrait of White House Wives.* New York: Random House, 1995.

Tugwell, Rexford G. *How They Became President: Thirty-Five Ways to the White House.* New York: Simon & Schuster, 1964.

Vos, Howard Frederic. *Exploring Church History.* Nashville: Thomas Nelson, 1994, 1997.

Walworth, Arthur. *Woodrow Wilson.* Boston and New York: Houghton Mifflin, 1965, 1978.

Ward, Geoffrey C. *A First-Class Temperament: The Emergence of Franklin Roosevelt: An Intimate Portrait of the Private World, Personal Ordeal, and Public Triumph of the Man Who Became FDR.* New York: Harper & Row, 1989.

Washington, George. *The Writings of George Washington from the Original Manuscript Sources, 1745–1799.* Edited by John C. Fitzpatrick. 39 vols. Washington, DC: Government Printing Office, 1931–44.

Washington, George. *The Writings of George Washington with a Life of the Author.* Edited by Jared Sparks. 12 vols. Boston: American Stationers, 1834–37.

Wead, Doug. *All the Presidents' Children.* New York: Atria Books, 2003.

_____. *The Raising of a President: The Mothers and Fathers of Our Nation's Leaders.* New York: Atria Books, 2005, 2006.

Weiss, Benjamin. *God in American History: A Documentation of America's Religious Heritage.* Grand Rapids: Zondervan, 1966.

Welch, Richard E. Jr. *The Presidencies of Grover Cleveland.* Lawrence: University Press of Kansas, 1988.

White, William Allen. *A Puritan in Babylon: The Story of Calvin Coolidge.* New York: Macmillan, 1938. Reprint, Rochester, NY: Simon Publications, 2001.

Williams, Charles Richard. *The Life of Rutherford Birchard Hayes: Nineteenth President of the United States.* 2 vols. Boston and New York: Houghton Mifflin, 1914.

Wilson, Douglas L., and Rodney O. Davis. *Herndon's Informants: Letters, Interviews, and Statements about Abraham Lincoln.* Urbana and Chicago: University of Illinois Press, 1998.

Wilson, Woodrow. *The Papers of Woodrow Wilson, 1856–1907.* Edited by Arthur Stanley Link. 16 vols. Princeton, NJ: Princeton University Press, 1966–73.

Winik, Jay. *April 1865.* New York: HarperCollins/Perennial, 2001.

Young, John Russell, and Michael Fellman, eds. *Around the World with General Grant.* 2 vols. New York, 1879. Reprint, Baltimore: Johns Hopkins University Press, abridged ed., 2002.